FASHION
PHOTOGRAPHY
THE STORY
IN 180 PICTURES

**EUGÉNIE
SHINKLE**

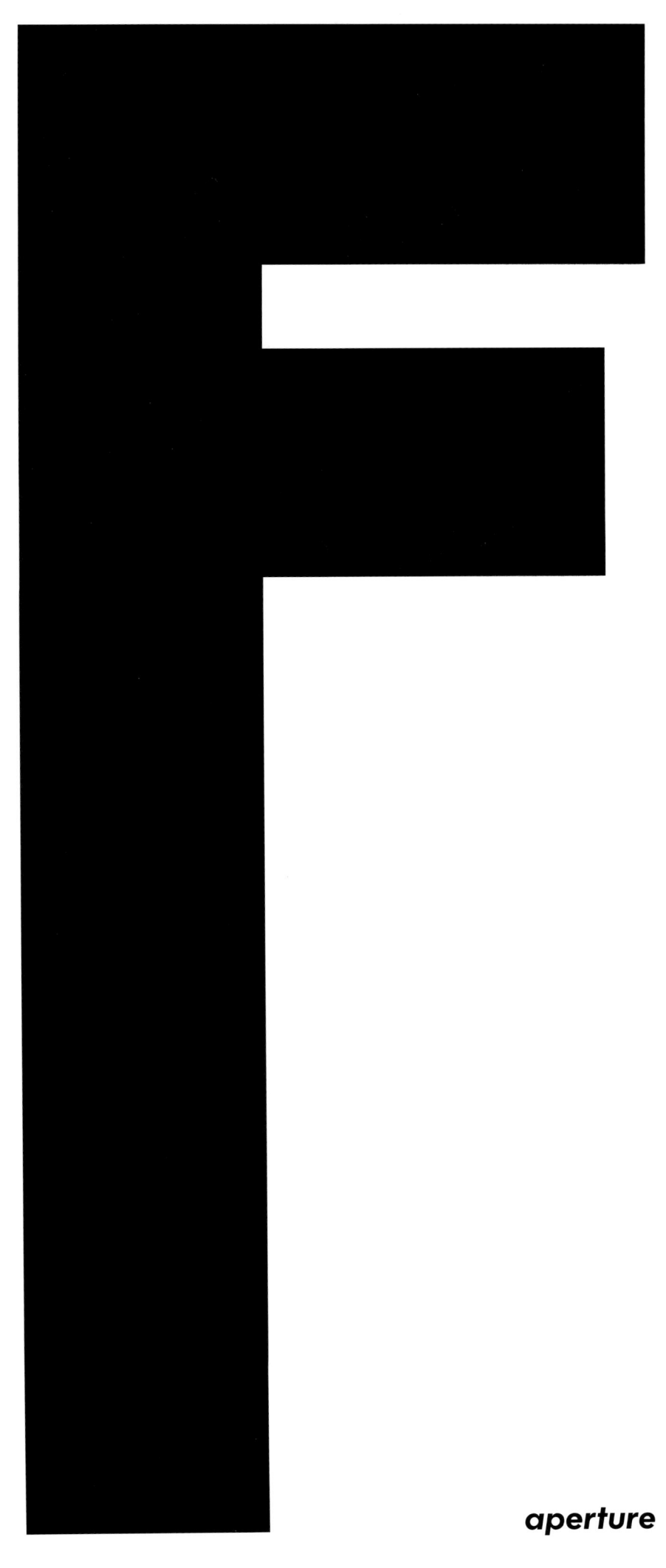

aperture

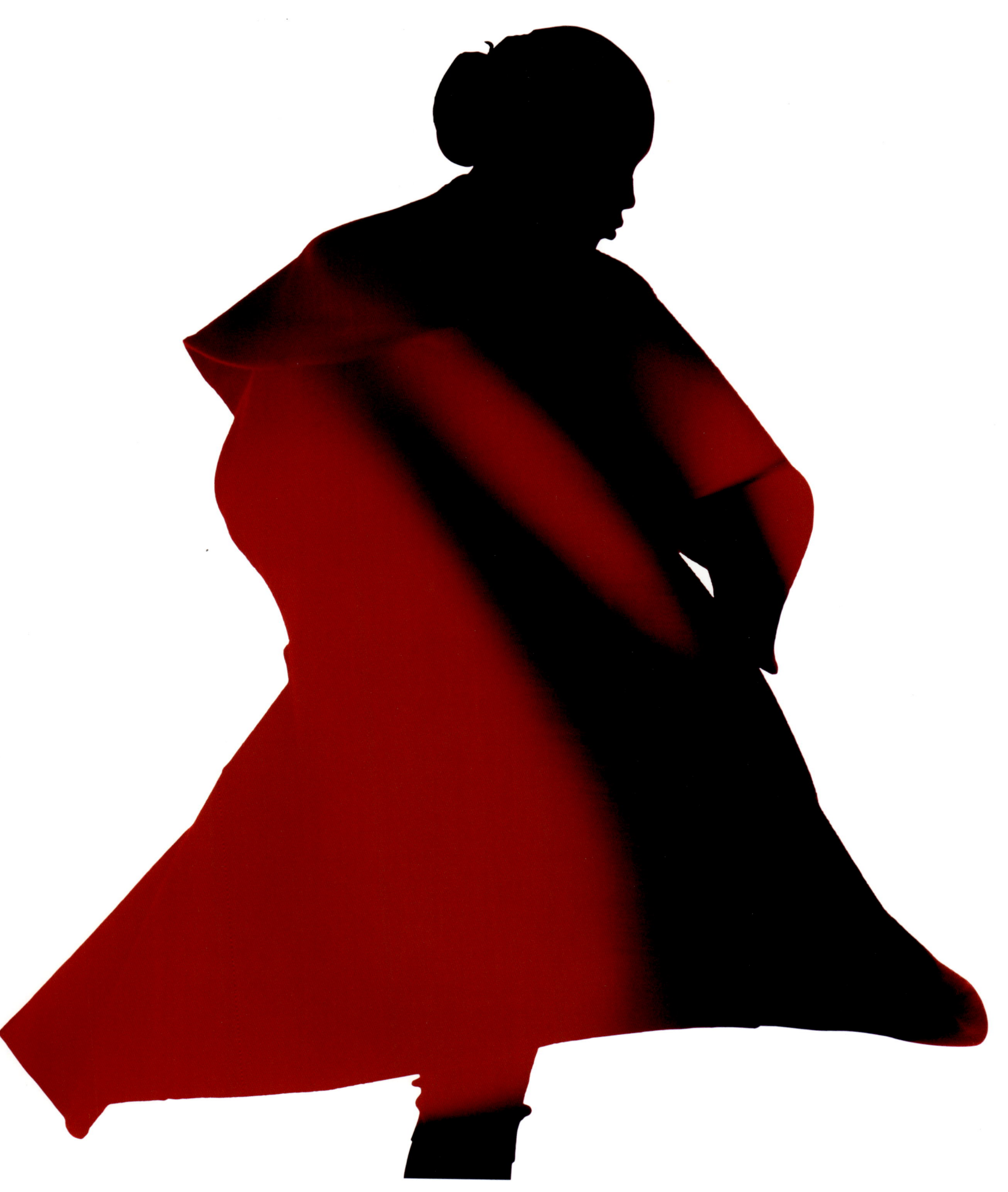

A Flower to Be Looked At
By Eugénie Shinkle, 4

1 1860S TO THE 1920S

2 1930S & '40S

3 1950S & '60S

4 1970S & '80S

5 1990S

6 2000S & '10S

Nick Knight,
Red Coat, Naomi Campbell for Yohji Yamamoto, 1987

A FLOWER TO BE LOOKED AT

THE STORY OF FASHION AND PHOTOGRAPHY
BY EUGÉNIE SHINKLE

The story of fashion photography begins in Western Europe in the late fourteenth century, long before the invention of the camera. During this period, clothing began to take on more complex social meanings, and traditional costumes were replaced by rapidly changing styles. Dress became an important means of self-expression, especially in larger urban centers. As fashion democratized aesthetic choice, however, it also embraced hierarchy and aspiration, with trendsetters constantly seeking new ways to set themselves apart from mere followers.

Printed images were the perfect vehicle for expressing fashion's heady combination of novelty, desire, fantasy, and visual seduction. Magazines first began to report on fashion in Paris in the seventeenth century; by the late nineteenth century, illustrated fashion magazines and pattern books were widespread in Europe and North America. Many of these new publications were aimed specifically at middle-class women, a growing market with increasing social visibility and spending power.

Liz Collins,
Call, London, 1999

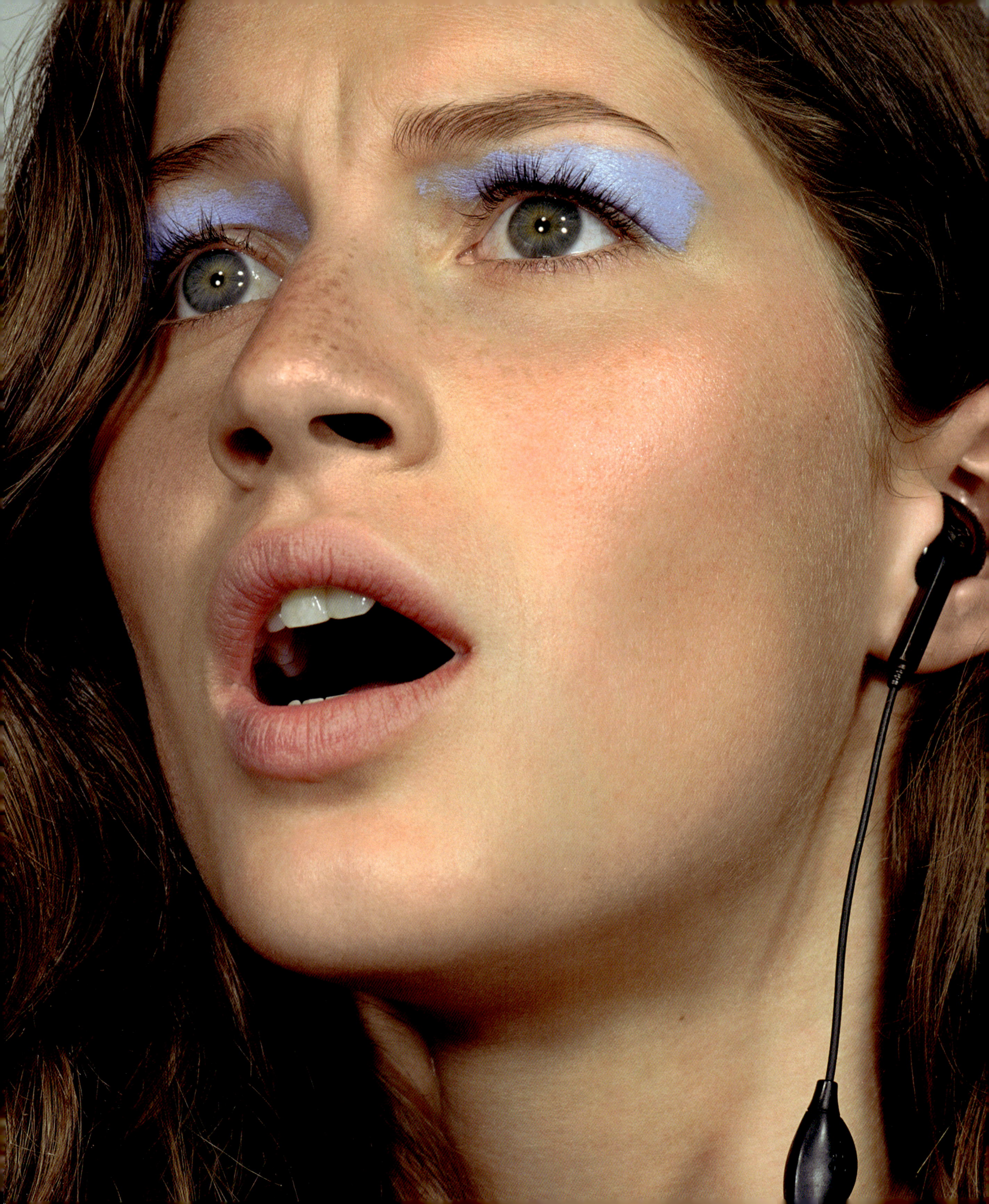

Photography arrived relatively late to the party, but it was well suited to the representation of rapidly changing styles. Fashion photographs began to circulate within a few years of the invention of the medium in 1839. Initially, such photographs were produced for private clients, such as designers and fashion houses, or as guides for hand-drawn illustrations, so they reached a fairly limited audience. With the late-nineteenth-century development of the halftone printing process, however, photographs could be inexpensively reproduced in large numbers, and within a few years, they began to appear regularly in the fashion press. By the middle of the 1930s, photos outnumbered hand-drawn illustrations in fashion publications.

A distinction emerged early on between images created specifically to advertise the products of commercial fashion companies and those commissioned by magazines for fashion stories or editorials—themed groups of photographs curated by fashion editors, often stretching across several pages. Eager to position their publications on the leading edge of culture, the fashion press reached out to the art world for inspiration, hiring high-profile photographers who had established reputations in the artistic avant-garde. Fashion advertisers were quick to catch on, and, by the 1920s, magazine editorials and high-end ad images shared similar artistic aspirations.

It's often argued that all fashion photography is advertising in disguise—that it's created to promote designers and fashion companies and, ultimately, to sell clothes. This may be true, but to become part of our collective memory, a fashion image must capture ideas, attitudes, and aspirations that go beyond advertising. Fashion photography is the ultimate cultural assimilator, absorbing and reimagining history and the present, high art and mass culture, the aesthetic and the political. It is the outcome of synergistic relationships between photographers and magazine editors, art directors, fashion designers, stylists, hairdressers, makeup artists, and models. Ephemeral by nature, fashion photography is quick to respond to changing tastes and technologies, aligning itself with the movements, shifts, and transformations that define the wider history of photography—and at times even driving these shifts. It shapes perceptions and encourages us to see ourselves not as we are, but as we could be. And if fashion photography registers our most fleeting obsessions, it also engages with more serious and enduring values, coming up against questions of race, class, and gender and capturing the spirit of the times with an immediacy that few other genres can match.

THE EARLY YEARS: 1860S TO THE 1920S

The first fashion photographs began to appear in women's magazines around the 1880s, but photographers had been engaging with clothing and fashion from the medium's earliest years. Taken by English photographer and publisher Michael Burr sometime around 1860, *The Old and New Styles* (p. 9) is a stereographic image: two photographs taken from slightly different viewpoints and mounted side by side on a card, so they would appear three-dimensional when seen through a special viewer called a stereoscope. Stereographic images were produced in the thousands in Europe, the United Kingdom, and the United States from the early 1850s until the 1930s, featuring subjects ranging from landscapes and architecture to current events and society figures. Humorous subjects were particularly popular, and fashion (especially its more excessive displays) was a frequent target.

In Burr's image, the woman on the left—conservatively dressed in a poke bonnet and demurely padded skirt—gazes in astonishment at her stylish counterpart, whose spectacular outfit, with its enormous hoopskirt, takes up more than half of the frame. Images such as these were not intended as documents of fashionable dress, but as social satire, offering scathing commentary on the female obsession with personal appearance (a relatively new phenomenon among the middle classes at the time), and on extreme fashions such as the "cage crinoline" featured here, which could reach six to eight feet in diameter and weigh up to fifty pounds. Despite its comic intent, the image is also a succinct embodiment of fashion's key mechanisms: constant novelty, aspiration, and the creation of desire.

Early fashion photographs followed different—and quite specific—social and aesthetic conventions than the satirical stereograph. Elaborate and often restrictive costumes limited models' movement, as did long exposure times and confined studio settings. High fashion was a privilege of the well-off middle and upper classes, and models displayed the dignified composure expected of well-bred young women. Their poses were statuesque, their expressions placid. The models were also, without exception, white.

Numerous fashion-focused magazines emerged in the first two decades of the twentieth century, including *Elegante Welt* and *Die Dame* in Germany and *L'Illustration des Modes* and *L'Officiel de la couture et de la mode de Paris* (later renamed *L'Officiel*) in France, as well as English-language titles such as *Ladies' Home Journal* and *Vanity Fair*. Until the middle of the twentieth century, however, two American publications dominated the landscape of fashion photography: in 1909, publisher Condé Nast purchased *Vogue*, which had until then been a rather staid fashion-and-society weekly; in 1913, *Vogue*'s rival *Harper's Bazaar*—which had launched as a fashion and literary journal in 1867—became part of William Randolph Hearst's publishing empire. For the next four decades, these two magazines would remain the ultimate destination for ambitious fashion photographers.

INVENTION AND EXPERIMENTATION: 1930S AND 1940S

By the mid-1930s, economies in North America and Europe began to recover from the shock of the Great Depression. More and more women took their places in the professional and public domains, and clothing began to signify more than social class. New, less-restrictive fashions not only allowed women to move more freely, they also represented new lifestyles, new definitions of femininity, and more relaxed social expectations. Faced with a changing market, fashion magazines sought new identities that appealed to their traditional, leisure-class clientele as well as the growing numbers of emancipated women with interests beyond the domestic sphere.

Carmel Snow took over the editorship of *Harper's Bazaar* in 1932. Along with art director Alexey Brodovitch, she transformed the magazine into a fashion-and-lifestyle bible, noted for its avant-garde design and photography. Though it never reached *Vogue*'s circulation numbers, *Harper's Bazaar* was seen as the more daring and innovative of the two, and star photographers moved back and forth between the publications.

The 1930s were watershed years for fashion magazines. With the introduction of Kodachrome color film in 1935, color photographs—which had featured sporadically in these publications since the turn of the century—began to appear more regularly. The first commercially available light meters appeared in the 1930s, along with new compact cameras (such as the Rolleiflex twin-lens reflex in 1929, the Leica rangefinder in 1932, and the Hasselblad HK7 in 1941) and higher-speed film. And although studio photography would remain the standard until after World War II, groundbreaking, documentary-style images by photographers such as Toni Frissell and Martin Munkácsi featured models actively engaged in outdoor pursuits.

World War II had a profound effect on the fashion and publishing industries. Paris had long been the undisputed hub of couture, producing high-fashion garments in limited numbers for an elite clientele. French fashion and publishing both suffered under German occupation, however, and by the end of the war, it was American publications and New York ready-to-wear—inexpensive, practical, and widely available—that defined the image of the modern, fashionable woman. Paris reclaimed its title briefly with the launch of Dior's "New Look" in 1947, an extravagantly feminine response to the austere fashions of the war years. Once established, however, America's reputation as a center of fashion continued to grow, and from this point on the two sides of the Atlantic were on equal terms. The tide was also turning for American photographers, as homegrown talents such as Irving Penn and Richard Avedon began to take over from European émigrés as the lead photographers at major magazines.

YEARS OF CHANGE: 1950S AND 1960S

The postwar years brought rapid transformations. Having proved their capabilities on the home front, many women were reluctant to return to the role of full-time homemaker. The ladylike, hat-and-white-gloves elegance that had defined fashionable women since the 1930s began to give way to a younger, more high-spirited image of femininity. In the 1960s, feminist writers including Betty Friedan encouraged women to look beyond the traditional roles of wife and mother, and civil-rights campaigners challenged long-standing policies of racial exclusion, particularly in the United States.

Editors, ever vigilant, recognized this new energy and sought to express it in their publications. In 1959, *Harper's Bazaar* became the first magazine to employ a nonwhite model, when the Portuguese-Chinese beauty China Machado appeared in an editorial by Richard Avedon; black model Donyale Luna was also featured on that magazine's cover in 1965, and the cover of British *Vogue* in 1966. Although documentary imagery had shaped the look of fashion photographs since the 1930s, the "new realism" introduced in the 1950s by vanguard image-makers such as William Klein and Frank Horvat was followed up by numerous others in the 1960s, as growing numbers of photographers moved back and forth between reportage and fashion. The increased ease of international travel also enabled photographers to move freely between Europe and North America, and to shoot in exotic locations throughout Africa and Asia—an opportunity that was also seized by more traditional image-makers, including Louise Dahl-Wolfe and John French. The pin-sharp studio aesthetic that had defined fashion photography since the 1920s was making room for other forms.

Released from both the studio and the restrictive rules of social decorum, younger photographers took the opportunity to interact with models in a more immediate, physical, and often shockingly intimate manner. In the late 1960s, French fashion magazine *Elle* took on a flock of new-realist photographers (including Mike Reinhardt, Gilles Bensimon, Patrick Demarchelier, Pierre Houlès, Alex Chatelain, and Arthur Elgort) who were collectively known as the "Paris Mob." Along with young English photographers such as Terence Donovan, David Bailey, John Cowan, and Brian Duffy, they brought a rock-and-roll sensibility to the tightly laced world of fashion photography, with sexual liaisons between models and photographers becoming the norm rather than the exception.

A host of new magazines appeared on the scene, challenging the dominance of *Vogue* and *Harper's Bazaar*. Under the artistic director Jacques Moutin, the innovative French title *Le Jardin des Modes* launched the careers of numerous photographers, including Helmut Newton, Frank Horvat, and Jeanloup Sieff. In Germany, art director Willy Fleckhaus brought a modernist aesthetic to the pages of *Twen* magazine. Other publications such as British *Elle*, *Queen*, *Nova*, and *Man About Town* targeted increasingly diverse audiences, including independent young women and a growing number of fashion-conscious men. The readers of these titles were not interested in the aspirational, elitist attitude of the mainstream glossies, which had been growing increasingly conservative since the 1950s, when advertising revenue began to play a more important role in their income streams. Editors and art directors who had enjoyed almost complete creative control over the look of their magazines found themselves deferring to advertisers, who demanded more and more editorial space in return for their cash. The distinction between advertising and editorial photography began to blur.

MONEY, POWER, AND SEX: 1970S AND 1980S

By the 1970s, the freedom and sexual choice that had been explored so exuberantly by fashion photographers during the 1960s started to give way to more disquieting motifs. Economic stagnation and growing social tensions in major cities such as London, New York, and Paris were offset by increasingly excessive lifestyles, and this was reflected in fashion photographs that hinted (often strongly) at sexual deviance, violence, and death. The gamine images of 1960s models like Twiggy and Jean Shrimpton were supplanted by a more aggressively sexual, even predatory mode of femininity—an effect that was particularly pronounced in the European fashion press, as *Vogue Paris* editor Francine Crescent gave photographers such as Helmut Newton and Guy Bourdin unprecedented freedom to explore erotic themes.

But as Western economies began to recover, fashion's mood became more optimistic. By the early 1980s, the decadence of the '70s was being replaced by a cleaner, less mannered photographic style and a crop of young models with a fresher look. *Vogue Paris*, now under the editorship of Irene Silvagni, provided a platform for the work of a new wave of photographers, including Peter Lindbergh, Herb Ritts, Paolo Roversi, Bruce Weber, Ellen von Unwerth, and Steven Meisel, as well as models who brought a wholesome, athletic sensibility to fashion imagery. These women—including Linda Evangelista, Cindy Crawford, Naomi Campbell, and Christy Turlington, among others—would become ubiquitous in the fashion press by the beginning of the 1990s, as would the highly paid, blue-chip photographers who worked with them. At their height, these new "supermodels" had massive selling power, although their initial appeal as representatives of a more authentic, natural kind of beauty dropped away as their celebrity status took over.

Throughout the late 1970s and into the early '80s, music magazines such as the UK's *NME*, *Sounds*, and *Melody Maker* had served as unofficial style bibles for a generation of British youth who felt alienated by the aspirational world of high fashion. The year 1980 marked the emergence of three zeitgeist-defining British magazines: *i-D*, *The Face*, and *BLITZ*. Along with American titles such as *Punk* and *Interview*—both of which had launched a few years earlier—they took their cues (as well as the odd journalist) from the music press, providing a creative outlet for a crop of younger photographers whose stripped-down aesthetic provided a rebellious alternative to the world of money and power represented by the blue-chip photographers. Style, as it was personified in the alternative press, didn't necessarily mean haute couture, or even clothes; these magazines were directed at an audience who were hungry for words, images, and ideas that reflected their own lifestyle and values. Social and political critique—which had been implicit in much fashion photography since the 1960s—began to make its way explicitly into the vocabulary of fashion photographers. The alternative press also brought a new focus to men's fashion, as stylists such as Judy Blame and Ray Petri played an increasingly important role in reshaping definitions of masculinity, alongside those of class and race.

Art and fashion—whose cozy relationship from the early part of the twentieth century had been disrupted during the 1950s—began to rediscover each other around the same time. Issey Miyake's wicker corset on the cover of *Artforum* in February 1982 was a watershed moment. Photographers such as Nan Goldin and Cindy Sherman, commissioned to shoot for alternative titles such as *Vue* and *Interview*, began to rekindle the affinity between art and fashion photography.

THE GRUNGE YEARS: 1990S

Peter Lindbergh's January 1990 British *Vogue* cover, featuring a roll call of the decade's most famous faces, is said to have marked the "official" beginning of the supermodel era. A few months before Lindbergh's cover appeared, however, British photographer Corinne Day found a Polaroid of a young, untested model named Kate Moss in the files of a London modeling agency. Her collaboration with Moss for the July 1990 issue of *The Face* ushered in a new era of nonconformist models and renegade photographers who took up the challenge launched by the alternative press in the 1980s, transforming it into the so-called "grunge" movement. Embracing lo-fi production values alongside political and cultural influences such as rave and drug culture, gender politics, and anticapitalism, grunge, as photographer Jason Evans wrote in 1998, was about "secondhand clothes; borrowing from documentary photography; models 'found' in the street; customization; snapshot aesthetics and 'poor' technique; no 'hair and makeup'; DIY attitudes; unexotic locations; nudity; ugly-beautiful; etc."

Many of the photographers who would define the grunge movement got their start working for the alternative press: Day, Juergen Teller, David Sims, and Glen Luchford at *The Face*; and Evans, Nick Knight, and Nigel Shafran at *i-D*. And, just as quickly, many went mainstream: in the early 1990s, Fabien Baron at *Harper's Bazaar* gave contracts to Sims, Mario Sorrenti, and Craig McDean, all of whom went on to land lucrative advertising work. Numerous stylists—those responsible for selecting clothes and accessories, and planning the overall style of a shoot—who worked alongside the grunge photographers would follow a similar path; Melanie Ward, Olivier Rizzo, Simon Foxton, Katie England, and Edward Enninful have all gone on to become key players in the fashion industry. (In 2017, Enninful became the first black *Vogue* editor-in-chief, taking the reins at the British edition of the magazine.) The revolution in menswear that had begun in the 1980s also gathered strength, with the emergence of a new wave of Belgian designers, including Martin Margiela and Raf Simons, as well as photographers such as Mark Borthwick and Willy Vanderperre, who brought their radical designs to life in clever, minimal images. By the mid-1990s, grunge had made its way into commercial fashion photography, and the first wave of alternative magazines had joined the ranks of the mainstream press.

Alongside grunge's stripped-down approach, photographers such as Nick Knight, Inez and Vinoodh, and Andrea Giacobbe were exploring the growing range of possibilities offered by digital postproduction, creating images with a hyperreal aesthetic. The digital revolution also brought with it a second wave of independent fashion and lifestyle magazines, facilitated by the ease of desktop publishing and—at least for their first few issues—relatively independent of advertisers. These so-called "niche" publications, such as *Purple*, *Self Service*, *Dutch*, *Big*, and *Visionaire*, began to appear in the early 1990s. Though most of these titles share a broadly similar format, drawing together art, culture, and fashion, they vary widely in their approach, with some celebrating luxury and frivolity while others follow a more intellectual or political path. Niche magazines also provided a platform for photographic artists such as Roe Ethridge, Collier Schorr, and Philip-Lorca diCorcia, among others, to cross over into fashion editorial and advertising.

THE NEW MILLENNIUM AND BEYOND

If the 1990s were the decade of the stylist, the early 2000s were the era of the "look book," as fashion advertisers once again flexed their muscles and began to dictate exactly which items would be featured in editorials. The fresh, anything-goes attitude that had carried the previous decade was replaced by a more market-driven approach and a resurgence in the extravagance of the supermodel era. Photographers such as Tim Walker, Steven Meisel, and Mert and Marcus now work regularly with large production teams, on shoots that resemble movie sets.

Print publications are now only one option amid a growing range of fashion media, including video, live-streams, Instagram, online magazines, and street-style and fashion blogs such as *The Sartorialist*. As well as providing a nonstop flow of images, from the street to the catwalk, many of these platforms increasingly blur the lines between personal style statements and commercial advertising campaigns, with popular bloggers generating substantial incomes from endorsements and promotional collaborations with major fashion and beauty brands. These brands will now pay increasingly astronomical sums—up to half

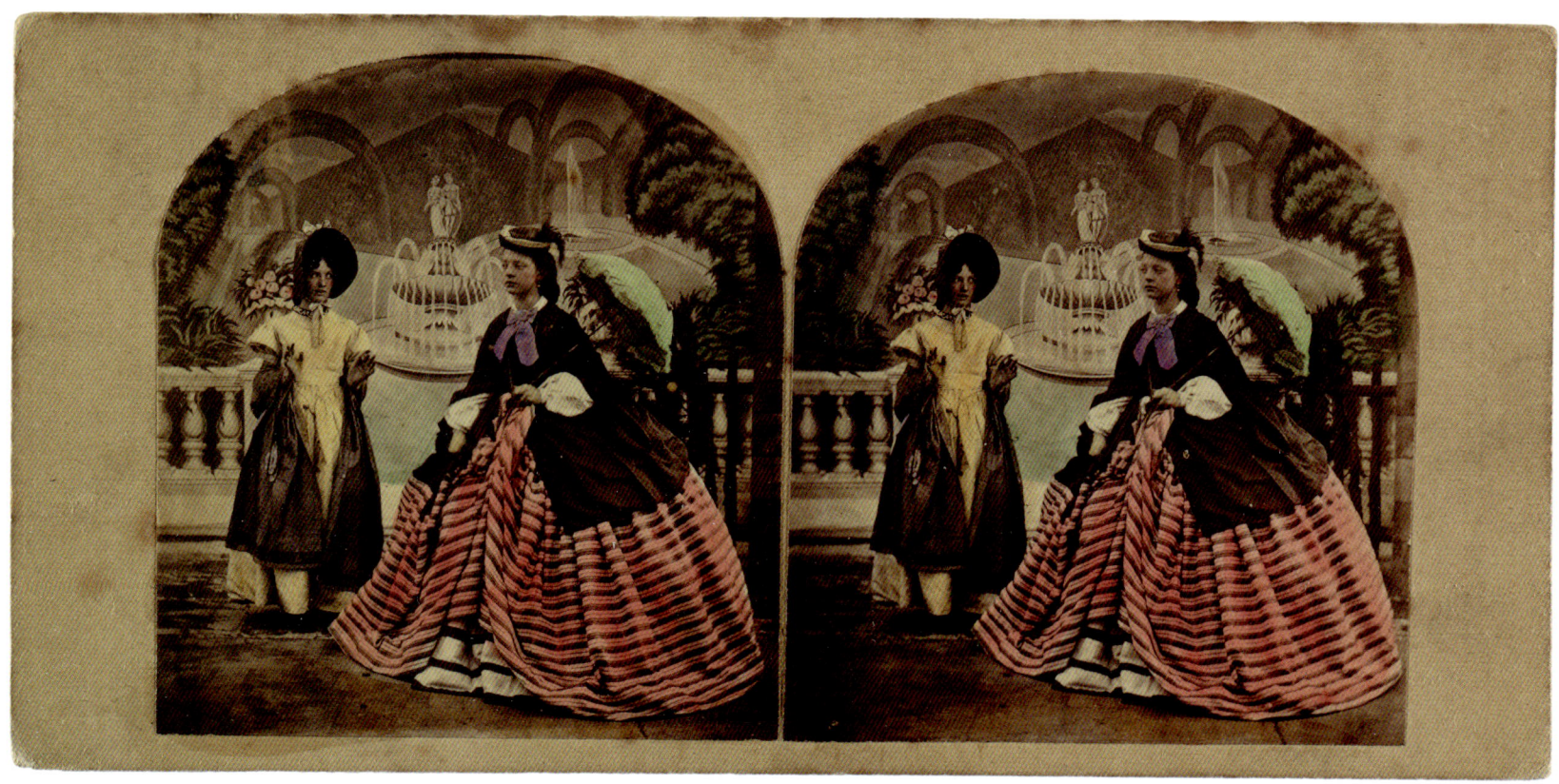

a million dollars, at last count—for a single sponsored blog entry or Instagram post by a celebrity blogger, whose millions-strong following may outstrip the circulation of printed magazines.

Even as print declines, however, fashion publishing continues to thrive; the language of still photography reinvents itself over and over, constantly evolving into new and fanciful forms. Fashion photographers can choose to work exclusively with analog cameras and film (Jamie Hawkesworth and Zoë Ghertner, for example), while others, such as Daniel Sannwald, embrace a high-tech, digital aesthetic. The field of niche and independent magazines has expanded enormously in the past two decades; titles such as *Garage*, *Re-Edition*, *The Gentlewoman*, *Fantastic Man*, *Dansk*, *Honore*, *Novembre*, *King Kong*, *Pylot*, and numerous others fuse distinctive aesthetic approaches with a focus on specific political and lifestyle choices. Many provide sophisticated platforms for the ongoing critique of race, gender, beauty, and sexuality, by photographers such

as Collier Schorr, Mark Borthwick, and Charlie Engman. And although Western titles such as *Vogue* and *Harper's Bazaar* remain influential —American *Vogue* editor Anna Wintour and creative-director-at-large Grace Coddington are household names—the beginning of the twenty-first century has seen a rush of innovation in Japan, Russia, China, and South Korea, too. The distinction between art and fashion photography is no longer as clear or as important as it once was; photographers such as Viviane Sassen and Blommers and Schumm produce images that resist easy categorization, and a growing number of young artists, such as Rita Lino, Devin N. Morris, and Namsa Leuba, create exciting crossover imagery that effortlessly brings a fashion sensibility into the realm of photographic art.

This book stops just short of the present moment; it is only in retrospect that histories show themselves clearly. *Fashion Photography: The Story in 180 Pictures* brings together a selection of images from fashion photography's past, charting its turning points, signal moments, and era-defining images. Like all epic tales told in condensed form, it necessarily leaves out many wonderful photographers and iconic pictures; it also glosses

distinctions—such as that between fashion and beauty photography—that some might consider important. As well as classic fashion photographs, it includes pictures by lesser-known photographers who touched the world of fashion from outside the field, sometimes briefly, and left behind lasting changes, and influential images that were never intended as fashion photographs. Last but not least, this book celebrates fashion photography's endless capacity for reinvention—its ability to extend beyond the fashion industry and reach out into the world around us; to get under our skin and show us our desires; to question and confront, to tempt and seduce, to surprise and delight.

Michael Burr,
The Old and New Styles, ca. 1860s

Camille Silvy,
*Marie of Baden, Princess
of Leiningen*, 1860

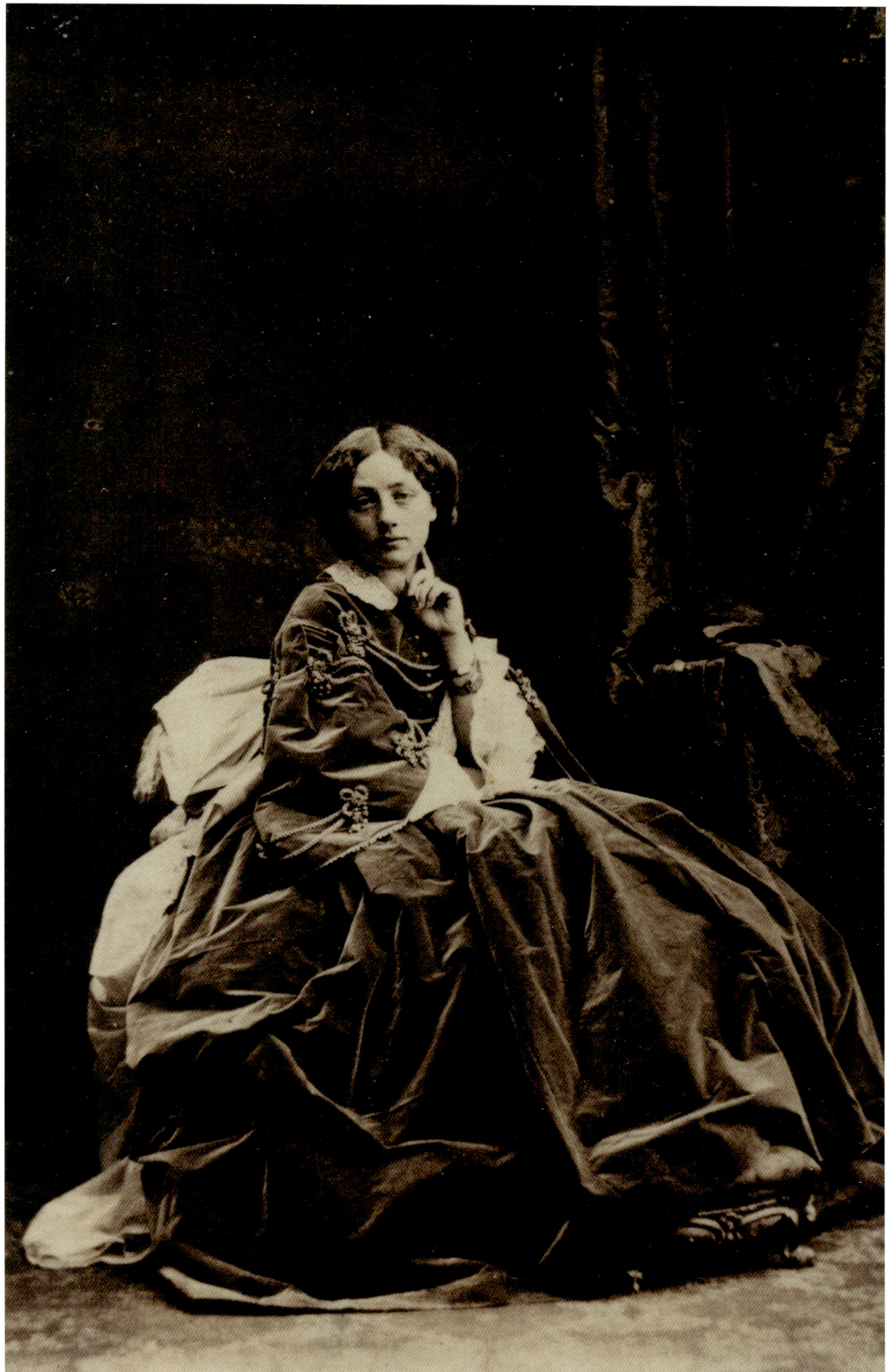

CAMILLE SILVY

Born in Nogent-le-Rotrou,
France, 1834;
died in Saint-Maurice,
France, 1910

Trained as a lawyer, Camille Silvy took up a diplomatic post in the French foreign office and was posted to London in 1854, where he was introduced to photography by an acquaintance. In 1859, he left the diplomatic corps and moved to London to pursue a career in photography. Charming and talented, Silvy took over a photographic studio in Bayswater and soon established a flourishing portraiture business. The society women who flocked to his studio were required by their social position to look elegant and fashionable, and his photographs were carefully posed and lit to show off his sitters' outfits to best advantage. Skilled at lighting fabric to show its weight and texture, Silvy also had an expert eye for detail, often using mirrors to show both the sitter's face and features of her costume and hair. Although his photographs were not produced to sell garments, Silvy's skillful use of the camera—which flattered both the subject and her outfit—anticipated the sensibility that later photographers would bring to the pages of the fashion press.

Camille Silvy,
untitled, ca. early 1860s

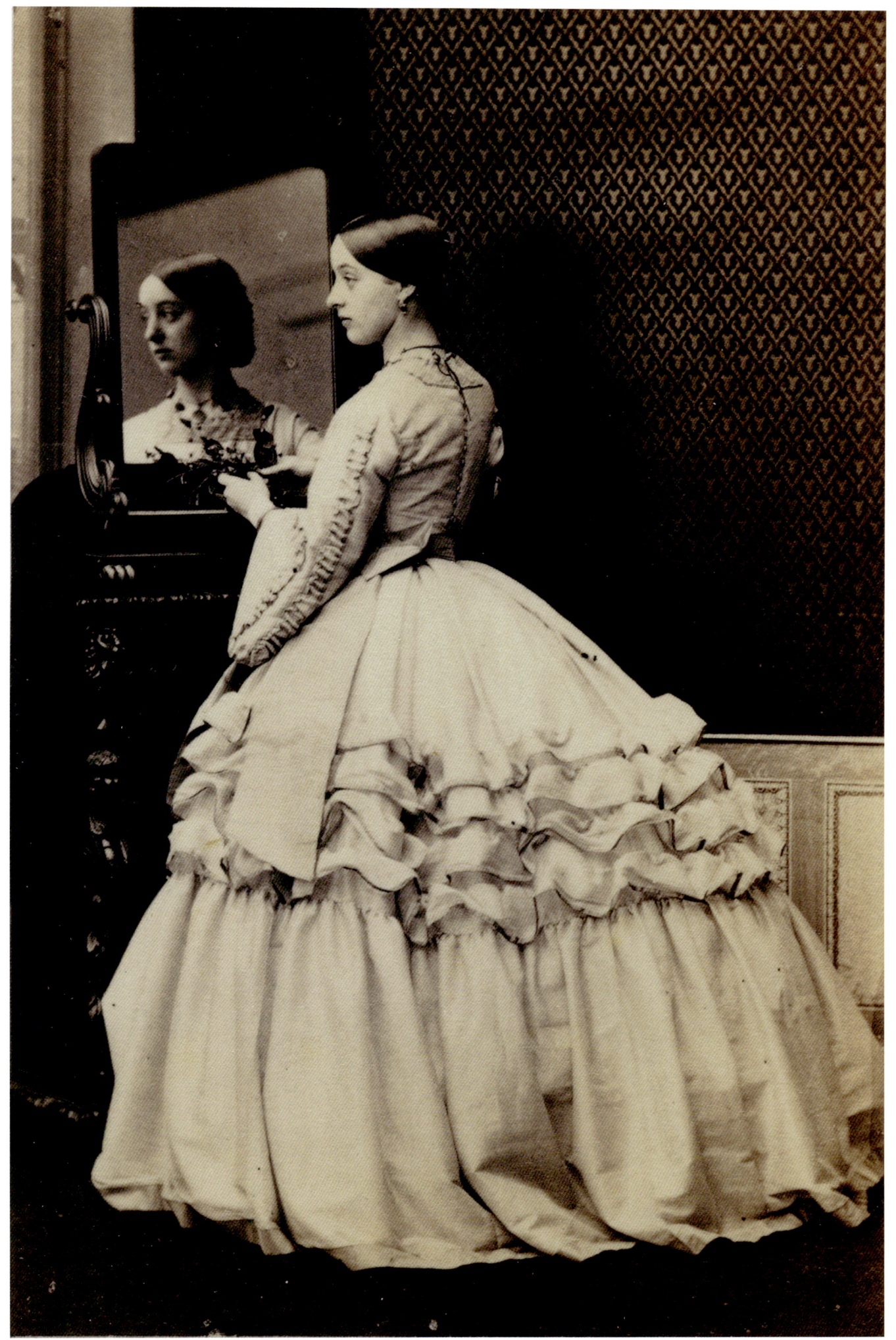

EARLY PHOTO STUDIOS

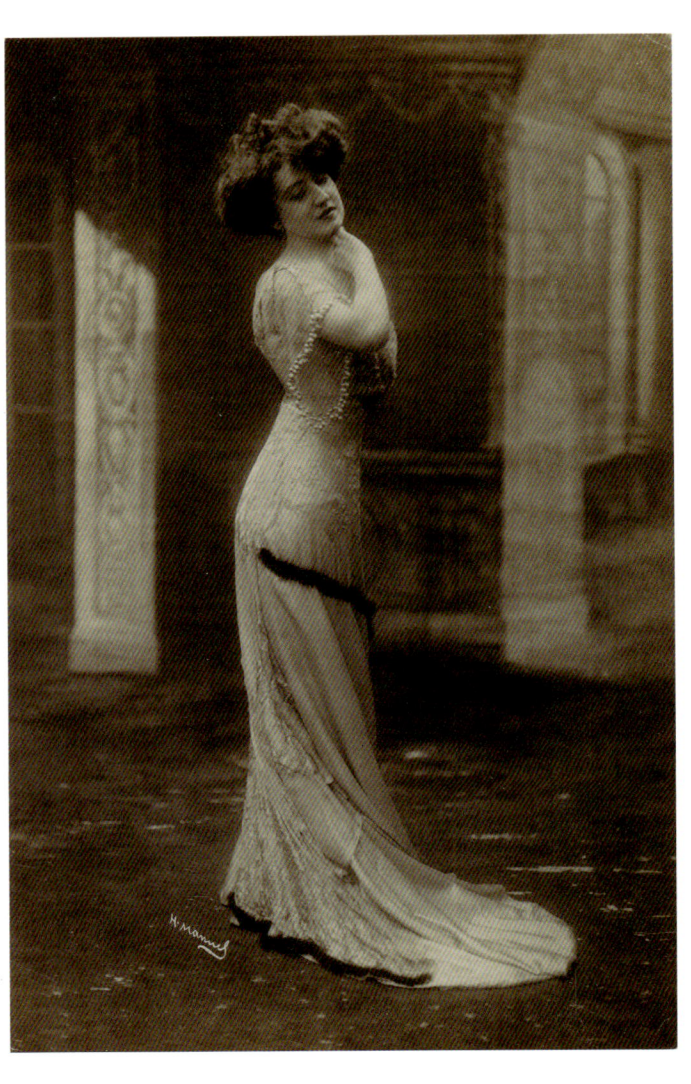

Henri Manuel, untitled, ca. 1908–10
Right: Talbot studio, untitled, ca. 1912–13

Photographic records of fashionable dress began
to appear within a few years of the medium's
invention. During the 1850s and '60s, portrait
studios such as Atelier Reutlinger, Talbot,
and Félix—all based in Paris—did a brisk trade
in formally posed photographs of society
women, actresses, and models wearing the latest
couture creations. Initially, such photographs
would have been produced for private clients,
or used as references for the engravers who
supplied fashion illustrations for the press.
With the development of the halftone printing
process—which converts the various tones in
a photograph into differently sized dots—in the
1880s, large numbers of photographs could be
mechanically reproduced, quickly and at a low
cost. Images of the latest fashions could now
circulate widely, as illustrations in newspapers,
magazines, and pattern books, as well as in
the form of advertisements. It has been said that
this new association with commerce marked
the emergence of "true" fashion photography.

Most of the early photographs shown here
were taken sometime between 1906 and 1910,
and the poses appear stiff and unnatural to
modern eyes—due, in part, to the elaborate
costumes that they depict: voluminous skirts and
closely fitted bodices adorned with yards of trim
and given their elegant "S-curve" shape through
padding and tightly laced corsets. But the images'
distinctive style can also be attributed to the
influence of hand-drawn fashion plates and
studio portraiture, with its ornate painted
backdrops—both of which continued to shape
the look of fashion photography into the early
years of the twentieth century.

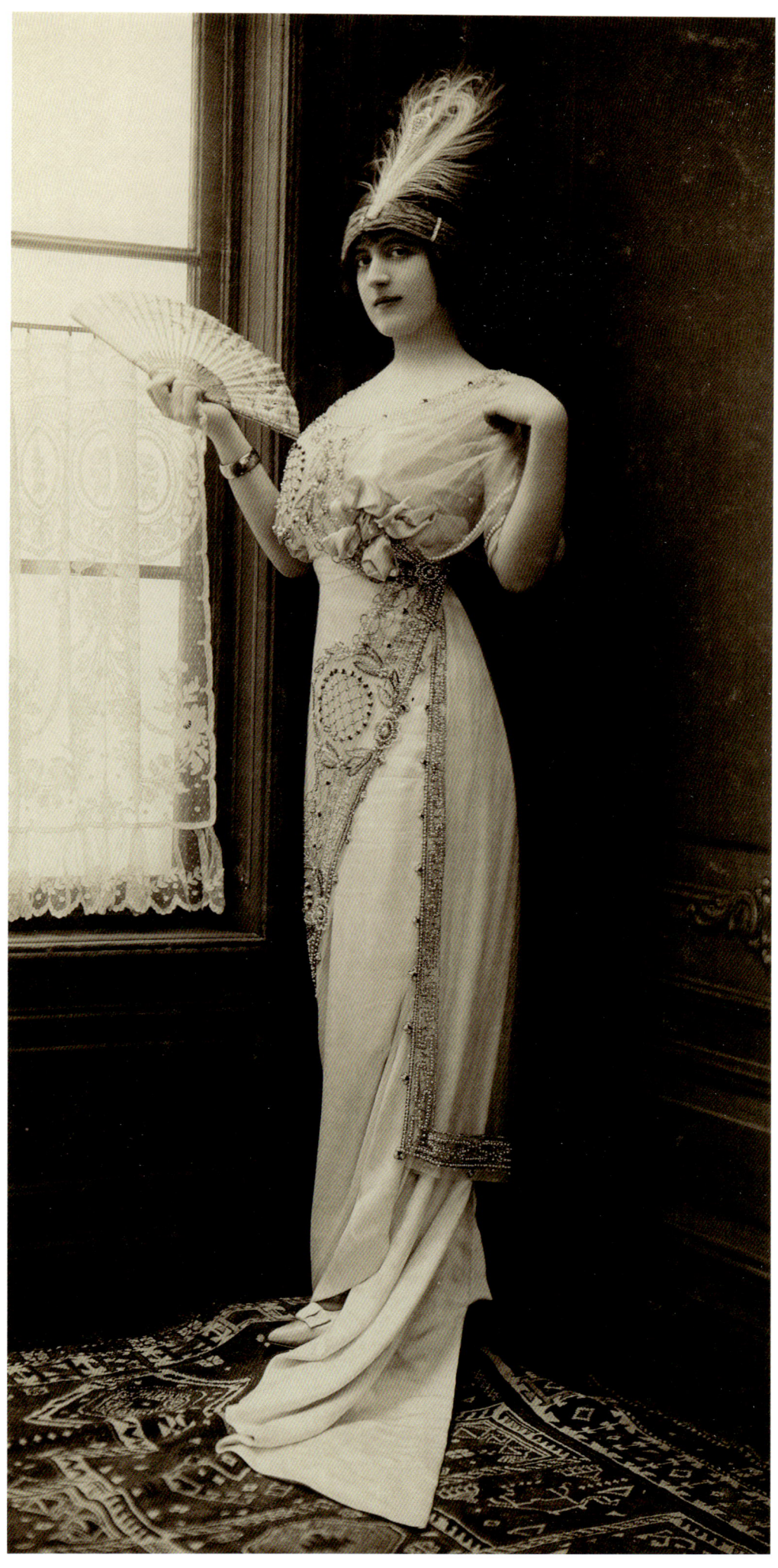

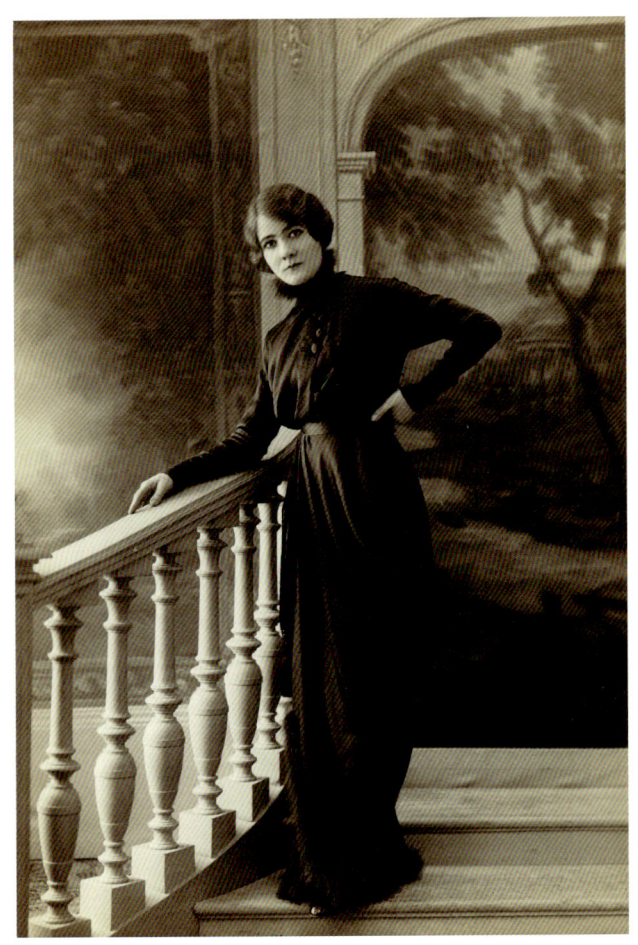

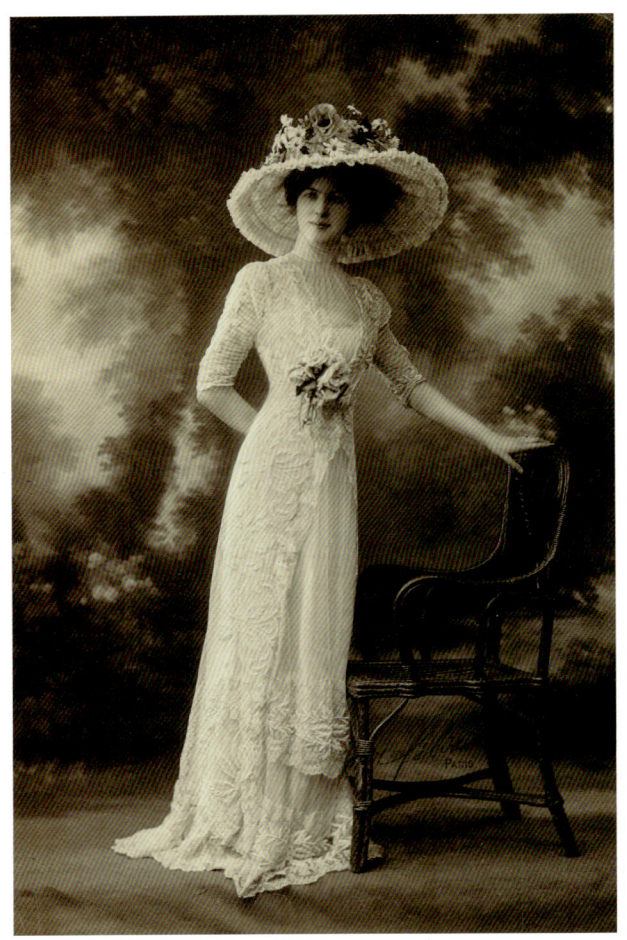

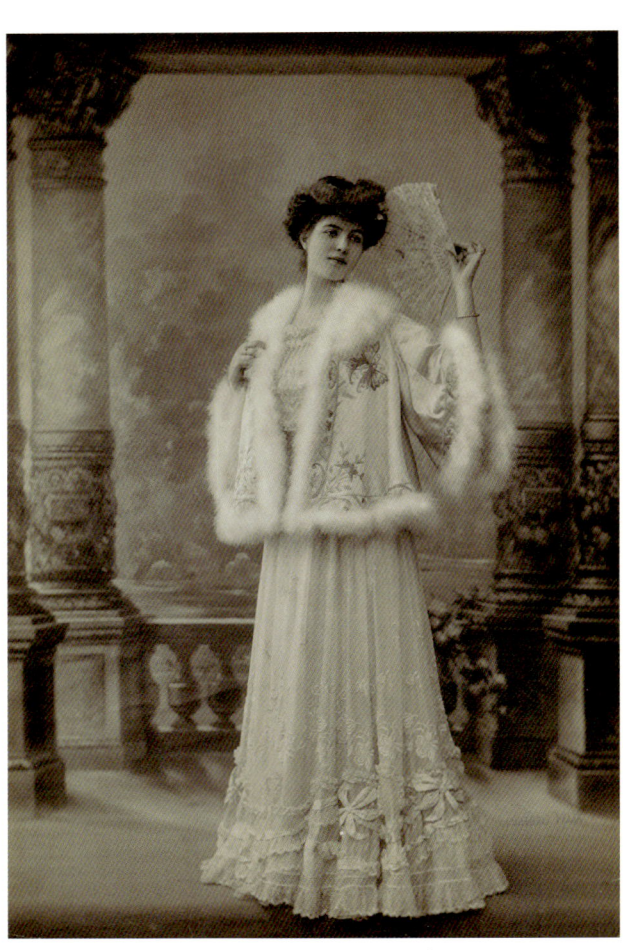

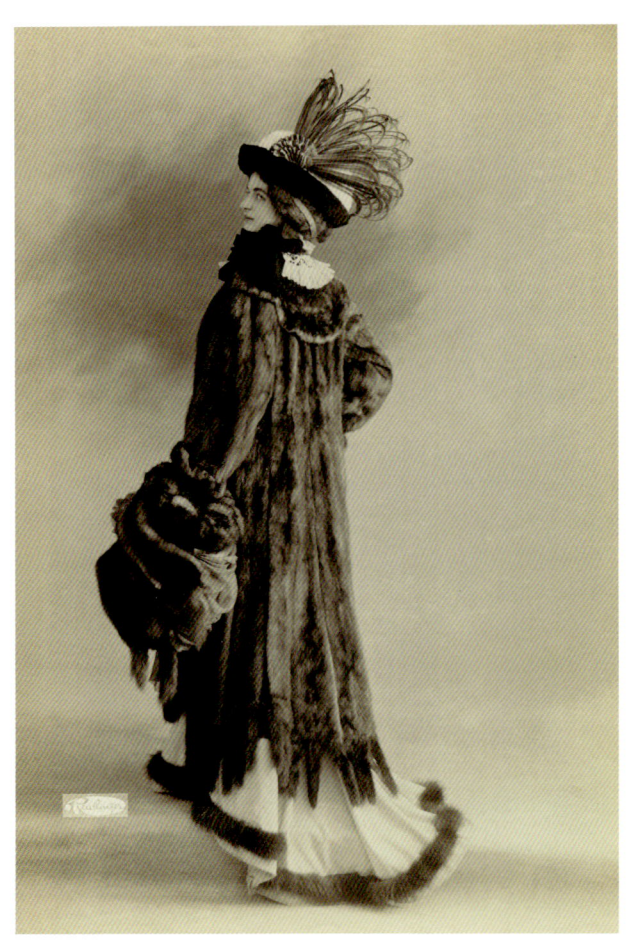

Clockwise from top left: Félix studio, untitled, ca. 1913;
Félix studio, *Robe Drecoll*, ca. 1910; Reutlinger studio,
untitled, ca. 1910; Félix studio, *Mantelet forme japonisante
satin vert pâle brodé*, ca. 1908

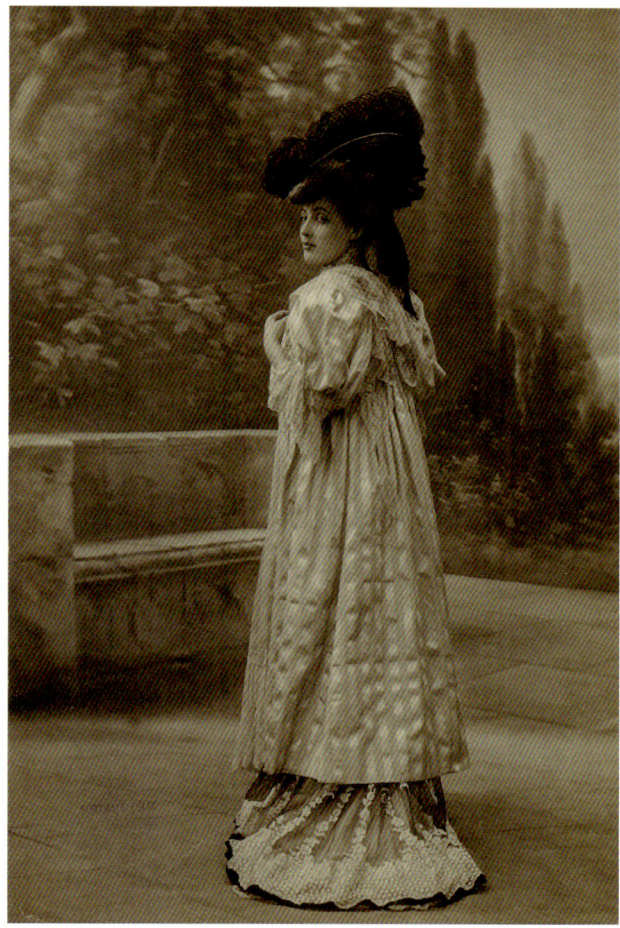

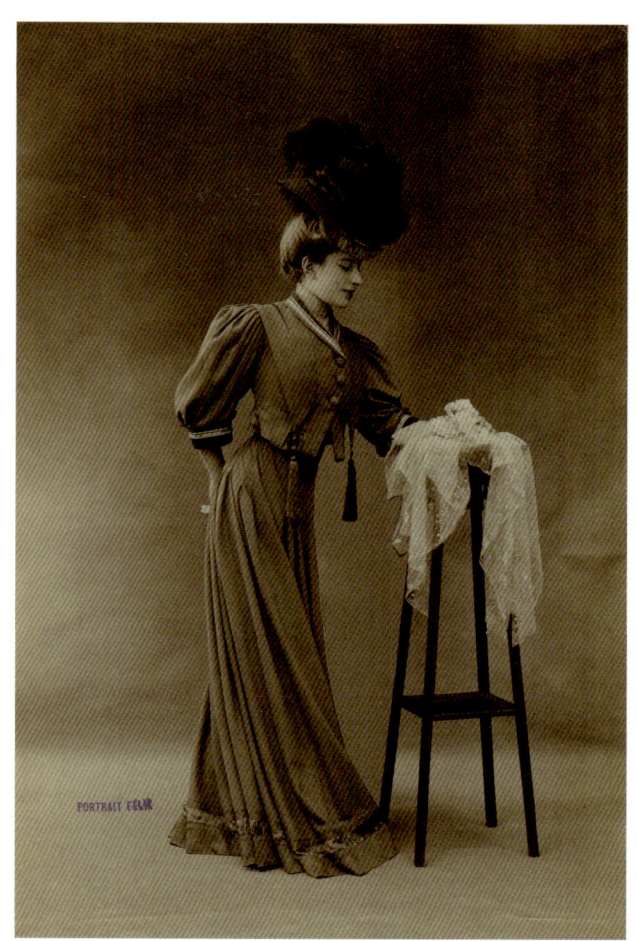

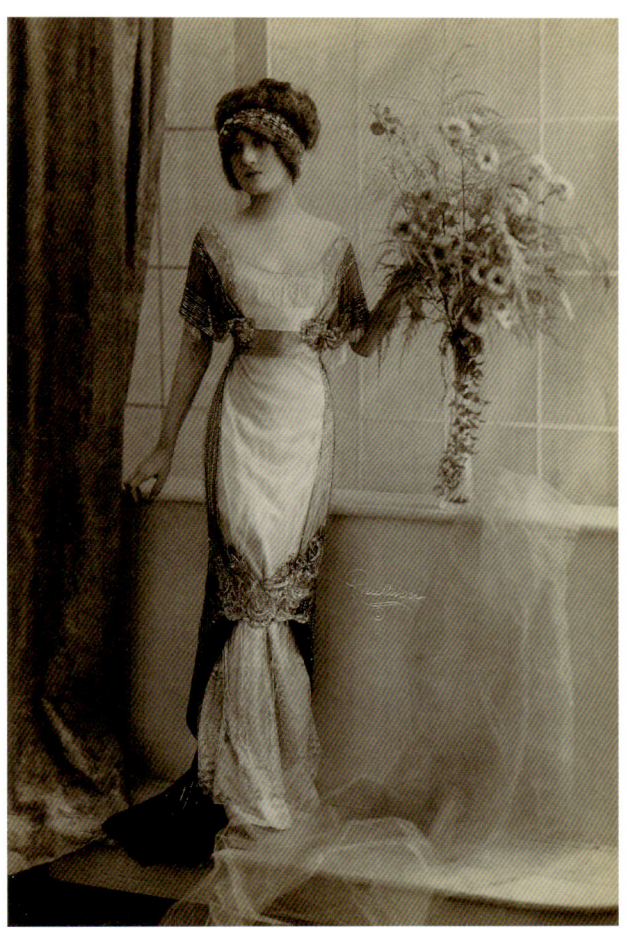

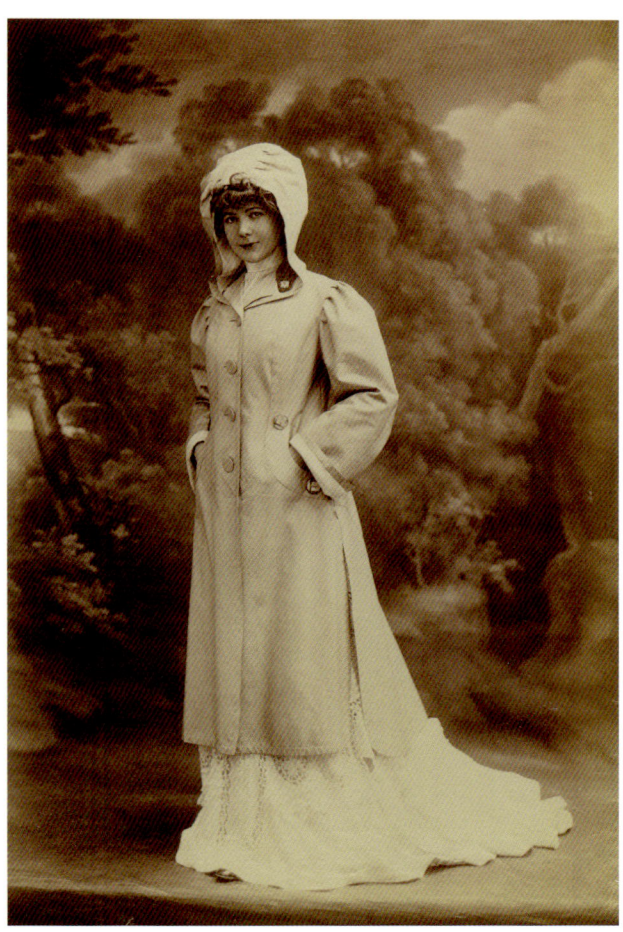

Clockwise from top left: Félix studio, untitled, ca. 1910;
Félix studio, untitled, ca. 1910; Reutlinger studio,
untitled, ca. 1906–8; Reutlinger studio, untitled, ca. 1909

PIERRE-LOUIS PIERSON

Virginia Oldoini,
Countess of Castiglione:
born in Florence, 1837;
died in Paris, 1899

Pierre-Louis Pierson:
born in Hinckange,
France, 1822; died in 1913

The Countess of Castiglione was a French noblewoman in the court of Napoleon III and the wife of the Austrian ambassador. A renowned beauty, the countess was also known to be obsessed with her appearance. As one of her contemporaries wrote, "She seemed so imbued with her triumphant beauty, so totally occupied with it, that after only a few minutes she got on your nerves. Not a movement, not a gesture, nothing that wasn't rehearsed." Photography provided an ideal outlet for the countess's vanity. In July 1856, she had her first sitting at the studio of Mayer and Pierson, a highly regarded firm of Parisian photographers. The studio enjoyed the patronage of the emperor, and its clientele included the social, political, and artistic elite of the era. From early on, the countess showed an astute awareness of the way that the camera could transform and enhance her appearance. Soon after her first sitting, she became Pierson's private client, and the two would go on to collaborate extensively until 1895. Their most productive years were those between 1861 and 1867, when the countess, temporarily isolated from court life, turned to portraiture as an outlet for her narcissism.

Their work from this period was inventive and spontaneous, with the countess rejecting the stock vocabulary of portrait poses and adopting a more graceful visual language drawn from contemporary fashion plates. The pair worked closely together to style the images, carefully planning the countess's coiffures and outfits to maximize their visual impact. Some of the photographs were shockingly intimate for the era, displaying the countess in various states of undress.

It was during this period that *Scherzo di Follia*, one of their most celebrated images, was shot. Using a black velvet photo frame as a mask, the countess regards the viewer with a knowing look—an acknowledgment, perhaps, of the photograph's ability to immortalize her beauty.

Pierre-Louis Pierson,
Scherzo di Follia, 1863–66

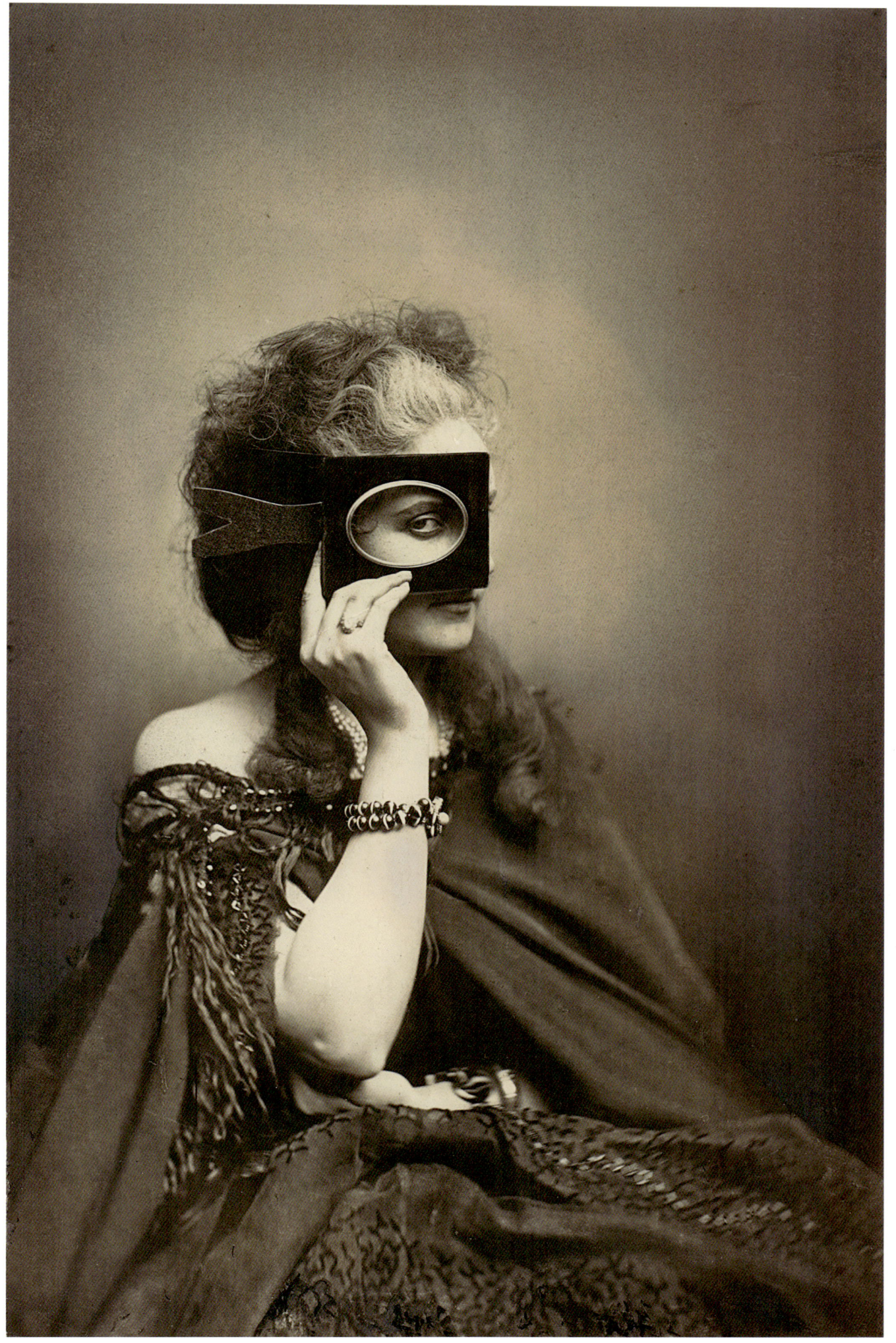

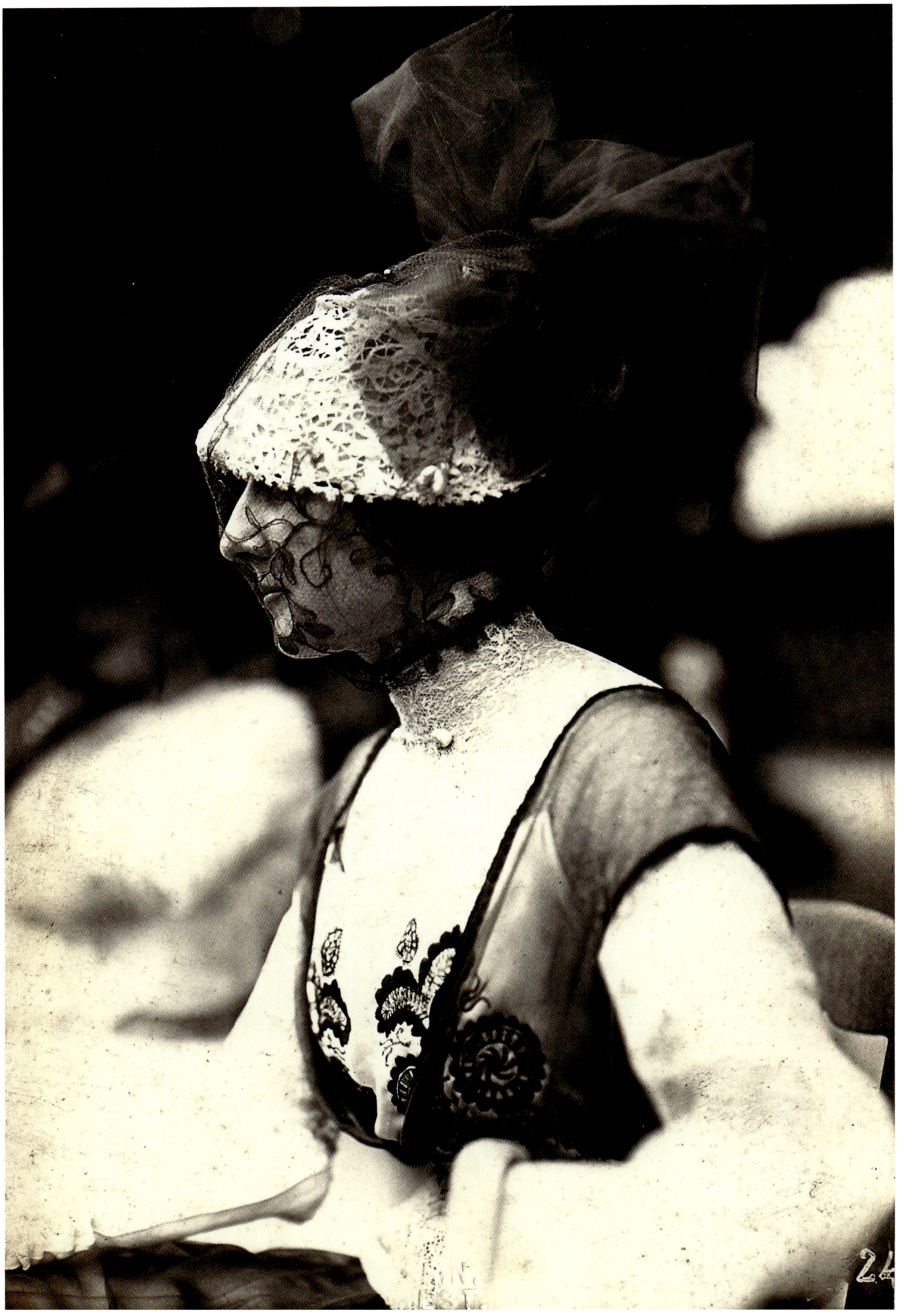

SÉEBERGER FRÈRES

Jules Séeberger,
(1872–1932)

Louis Séeberger,
(1874–1946)

Henri Séeberger,
(1876–1956),

Jean Séeberger,
(1910–1979)

Albert Séeberger
(1914–1999)

The Séeberger Frères are often credited with inventing fashion photography. However, these two generations of brothers initially worked as photojournalists, photographing fashionable subjects on the streets of Paris, at society events such as horse races, and at seaside resorts. The business was established in 1909 by Jules, Louis, and Henri Séeberger, amid a growing demand for images of fashionable society. Numerous such studios were active around the same time, photographing models and society women in haute-couture finery for the society pages of magazines such as *Vogue*, *Harper's Bazaar*, *Le Jardin des Modes*, and *Femina*. What set the Séebergers apart from their competitors was their knowledge of the subject. Their studio was located in Paris's tenth arrondissement, then the heart of the fashion district, and the brothers had insiders' insight into the small but significant details of cut, color, and trimming that marked the latest fashions from more run-of-the-mill offerings. The studio's first business stationery was headed: "High-Fashion Snapshots. Photographic Accounts of Parisian Style."

Until the late 1930s, the Séebergers worked exclusively outdoors. Before publication, a print would be sent to a photograph's subject for approval, just in case inappropriate behavior or an illicit meeting had been recorded. Many of the brothers' photographs—shot quickly, with little time to direct the subjects—mirror the formal refinement of studio photographs of the era. Other images include more relaxed attitudes and spontaneous gestures, which would later be incorporated into the vocabulary of modern fashion photography.

Though their output is usually associated with the fashions of France's Belle Époque (the period from 1871 to 1914, when World War I broke out), the Séebergers were active as fashion photojournalists until 1939. It was not until 1945 that the studio—under the ownership of the second generation of brothers, Jean and Albert—moved toward more conventional fashion photography, shooting models in the studio in outfits sent by the designers. When the business finally closed in 1975, its archives included a collection of some sixty thousand negatives and prints (now in the collection of the Bibliothèque Nationale de France).

Séeberger Frères,
Chapeau, Deauville, France, 1912

21

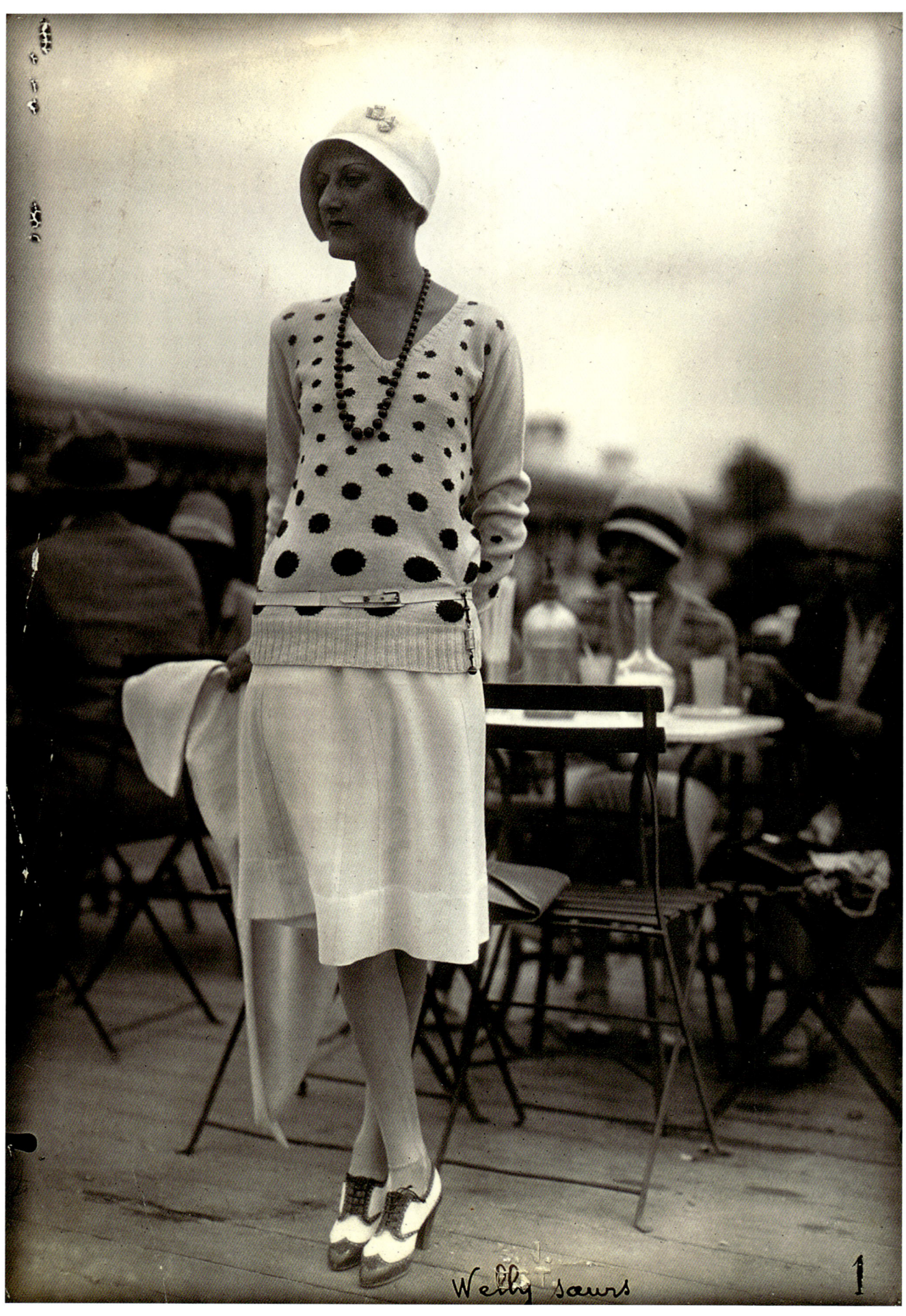

Séeberger Frères,
Ensemble Welly Soeurs, Deauville, France, August 9, 1928

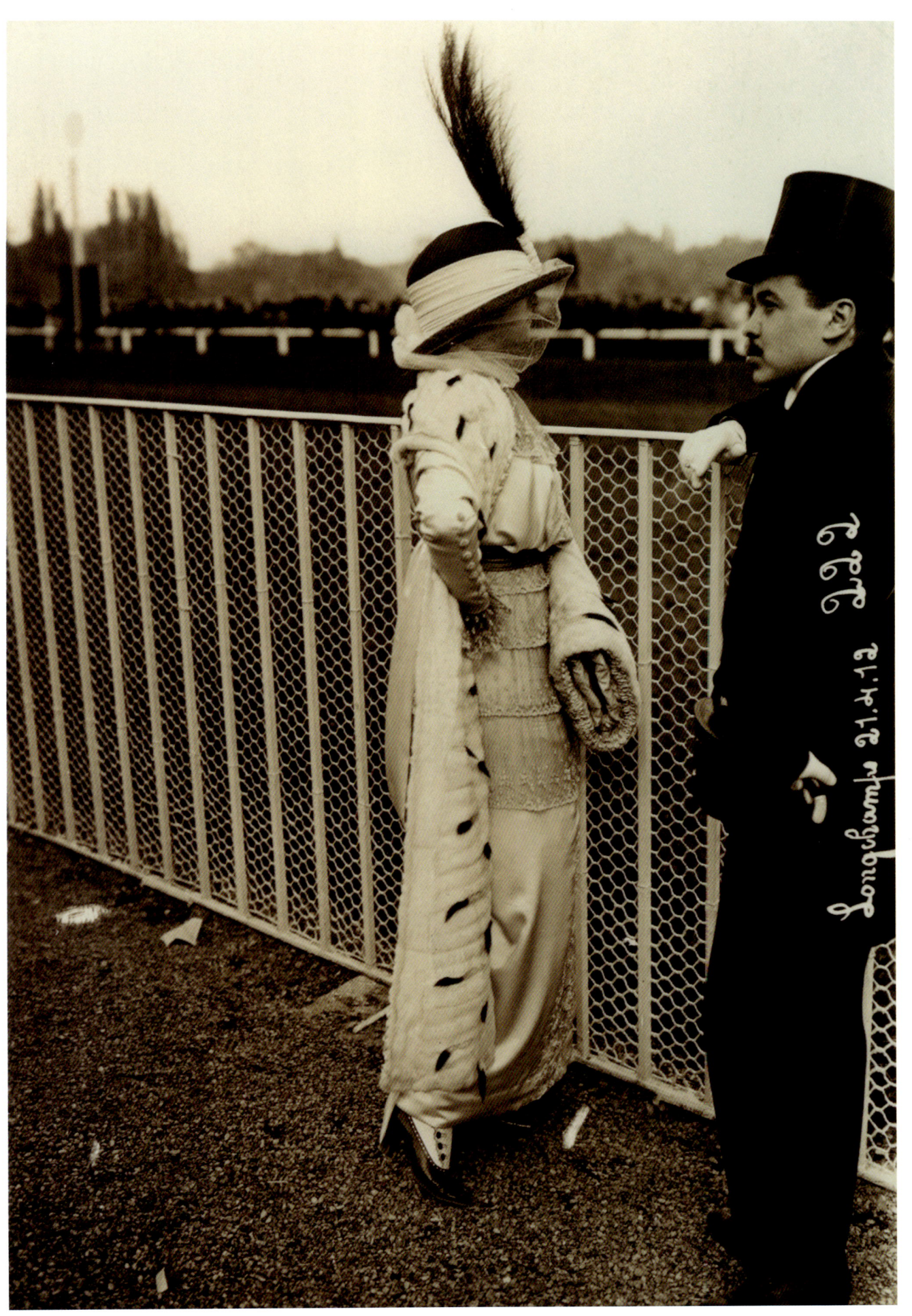

Photographer unknown,
for the Société des Nouveautés Textiles at the
Longchamp Racecourse, Paris, April 21, 1912

23

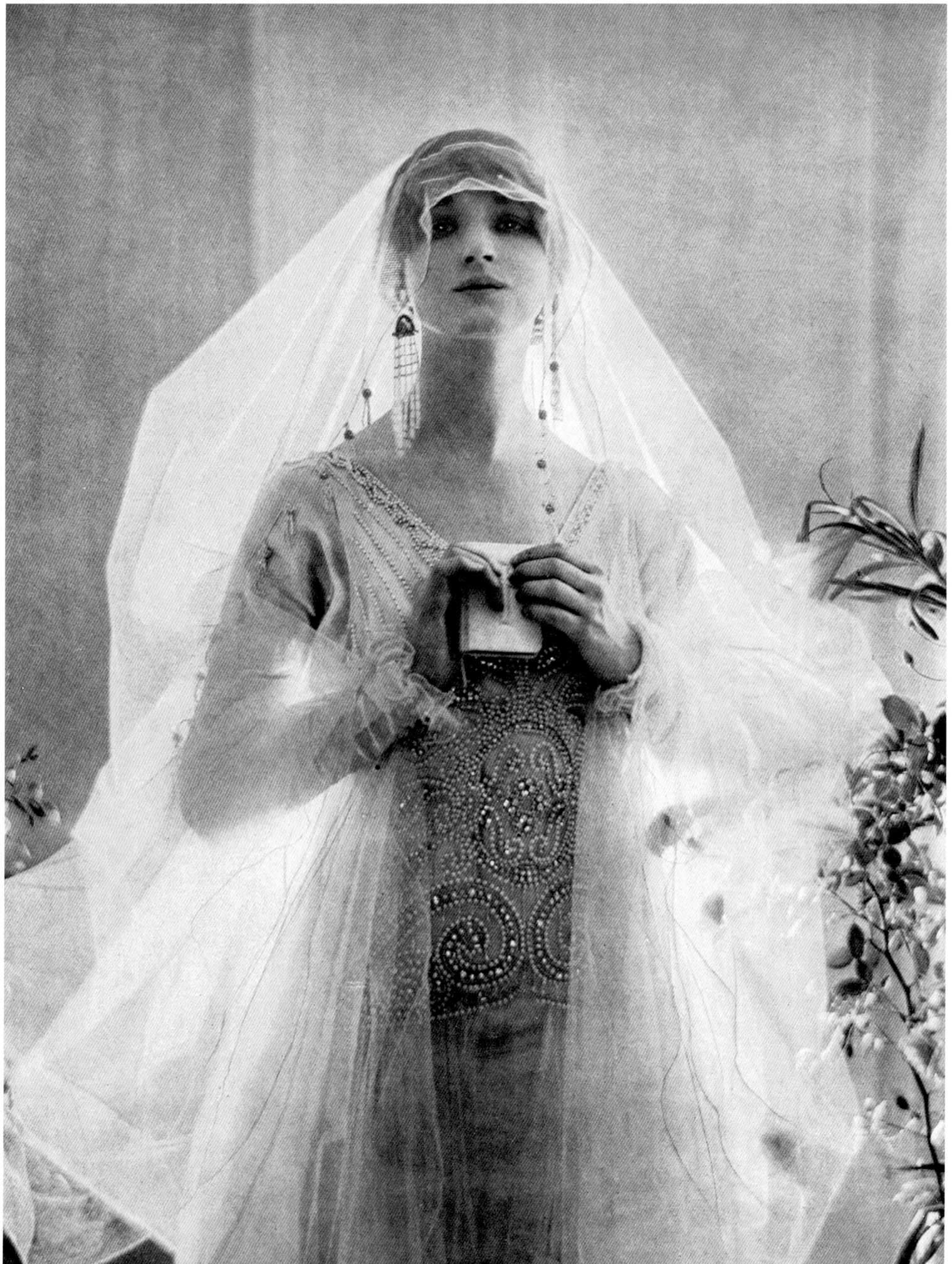

Born in Dresden,
Germany, 1968;
died in Los Angeles,
1946

In the early twentieth century, fashion magazines
—eager to share in the growing prestige
of photography as an art form—began to hire
high-profile photographers to shoot fashion
editorials. Before turning his hand to fashion
photography, Adolph de Meyer was already
a respected photographer in avant-garde circles.
He moved to London in the mid-1890s, where
he joined the Brotherhood of the Linked Ring,
a photographic society dedicated to the
advancement of photographic art. The group's
Pictorialist style, which emulated the look
and feel of paintings or charcoal drawings, was
vital to the formation of de Meyer's aesthetic,
as was the influence of American photographer
Alfred Stieglitz, whom he regarded as a mentor.

In 1913, following a move to New York, de
Meyer—by this time an established society-
portrait photographer—was offered a job as a staff
photographer at *Vogue*. His style went on to
dominate fashion photography for the next two
decades. Among his innovations was the use of
soft focus, which he achieved by using a Pinkerton-
Smith lens (sharply focused at the center,
softening gradually toward the edges) or stretching
gauze over the lens. The diffused lines gave his
images an atmospheric feeling that was radically
different from the documentary style of earlier
studio photography, and his poses, though hardly
dynamic by modern standards, were more
relaxed and natural. De Meyer's most important
innovation, however, was his backlighting
technique, which highlighted the profiles of his
subjects and allowed him to create dramatic effects.

By 1916, *Vogue* was using more and more
of de Meyer's images, grouping them together
in sets. He would later develop these into "fashion
essays"—precursors of the modern fashion
editorial—following a move to rival publication
Harper's Bazaar in 1922.

ADOLPH DE MEYER

Adolph de Meyer,
"The Bride's Yearbook," *Vogue*, May 1, 1918

JAMES VAN DER ZEE

Born in Lenox,
Massachusetts, 1886;
died in Washington,
DC, 1983

James Van Der Zee was one of the earliest and most significant photographic chroniclers of African American life. He acquired his first camera as a fourteen-year-old, and soon established a modest reputation as a portrait photographer in his hometown. However, his first professional photography work did not come until 1915, when he was hired as a darkroom assistant at Getz's Department Store in Newark, New Jersey. Van Der Zee's technical expertise grew along with his renown, and he opened his own photographic studio in Harlem, New York City, in 1916.

At the time of Van Der Zee's arrival, Harlem was on the cusp of a major cultural revival known as the Harlem Renaissance. From about 1919 until the mid-1930s, Harlem was a gathering place for African American talent: writers, artists, musicians, actors, sportsmen and women, and political leaders such as Marcus Garvey all gravitated there, drawn by a growing sense of community and pride in their African heritage. Van Der Zee was the unofficial photographer of the Harlem Renaissance, documenting local organizations and sports teams, street life, politics and celebrities, family groups, and the fashionable elite. The sophistication of his subjects—and the dignity with which he portrayed them—stood in sharp contrast to the racial stereotypes that were still prevalent in the mainstream press.

Although Van Der Zee's photographs appeared frequently in local papers and magazines, his African American subjects meant that the photos would have been considered "unsuitable" for publication in mass-market fashion titles. In 1939, several of Van Der Zee's group and wedding portraits appeared, uncredited, in *Cecil Beaton's New York*, along with Beaton's scornful summation of the work as "sentimental." Five years later, Gordon Parks (p. 90) became the first African American photographer at *Vogue*, but it would be at least another decade before the fashion press in America would begin to feature more photographers and models of color, and not until the late 1960s that Van Der Zee's work came to be known beyond his immediate circle of friends and clients.

James Van Der Zee,
Stepping Out, 1930

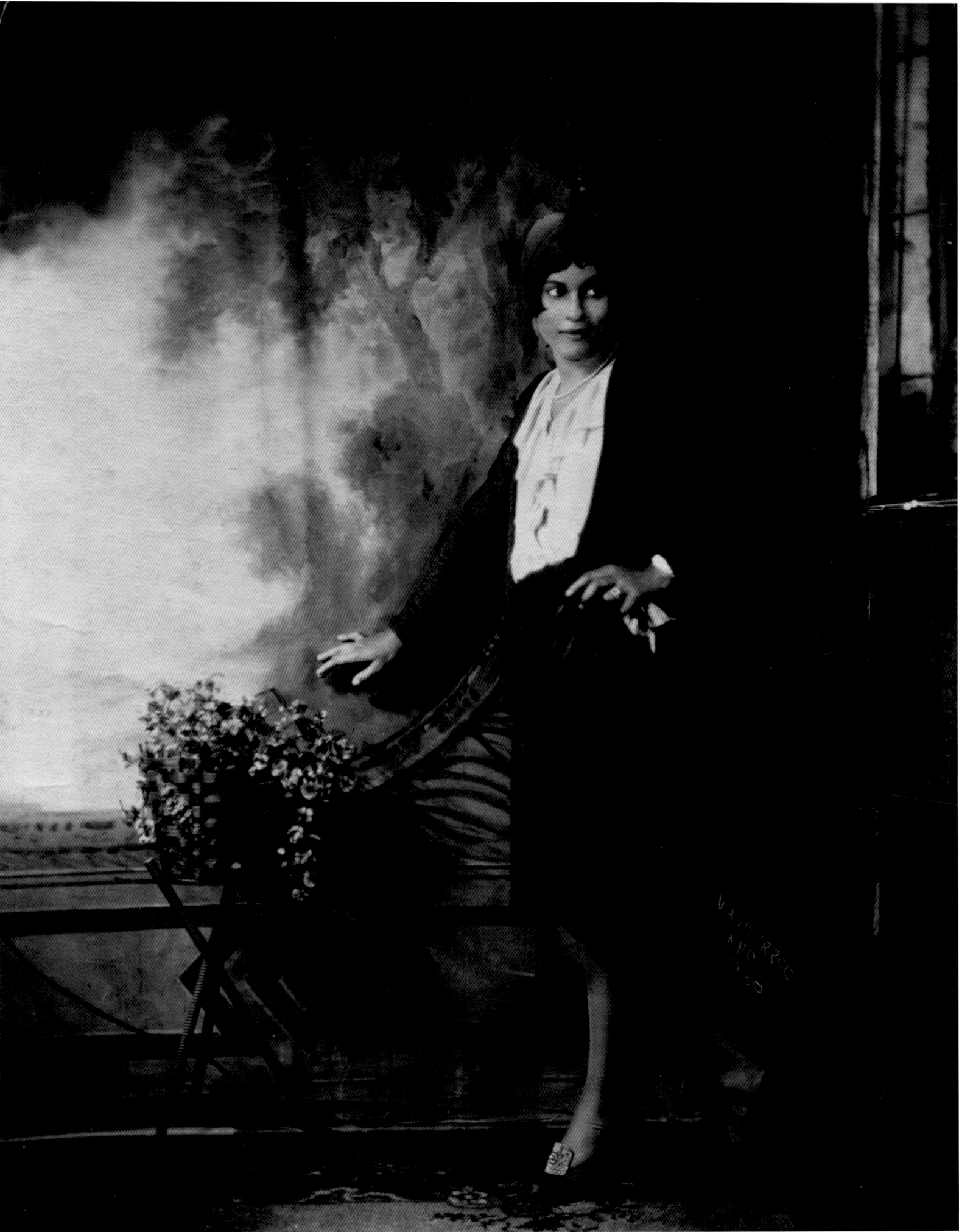

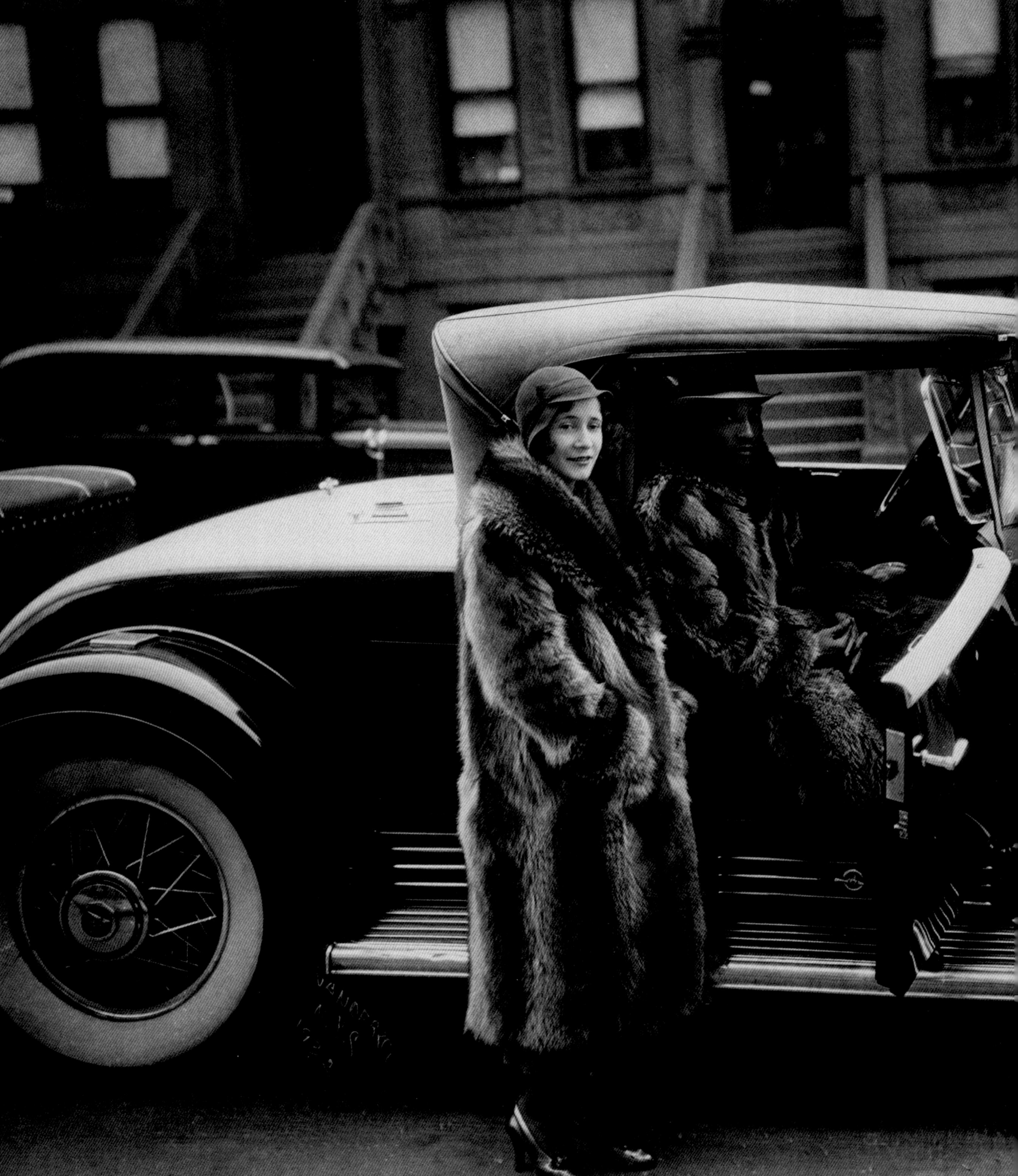

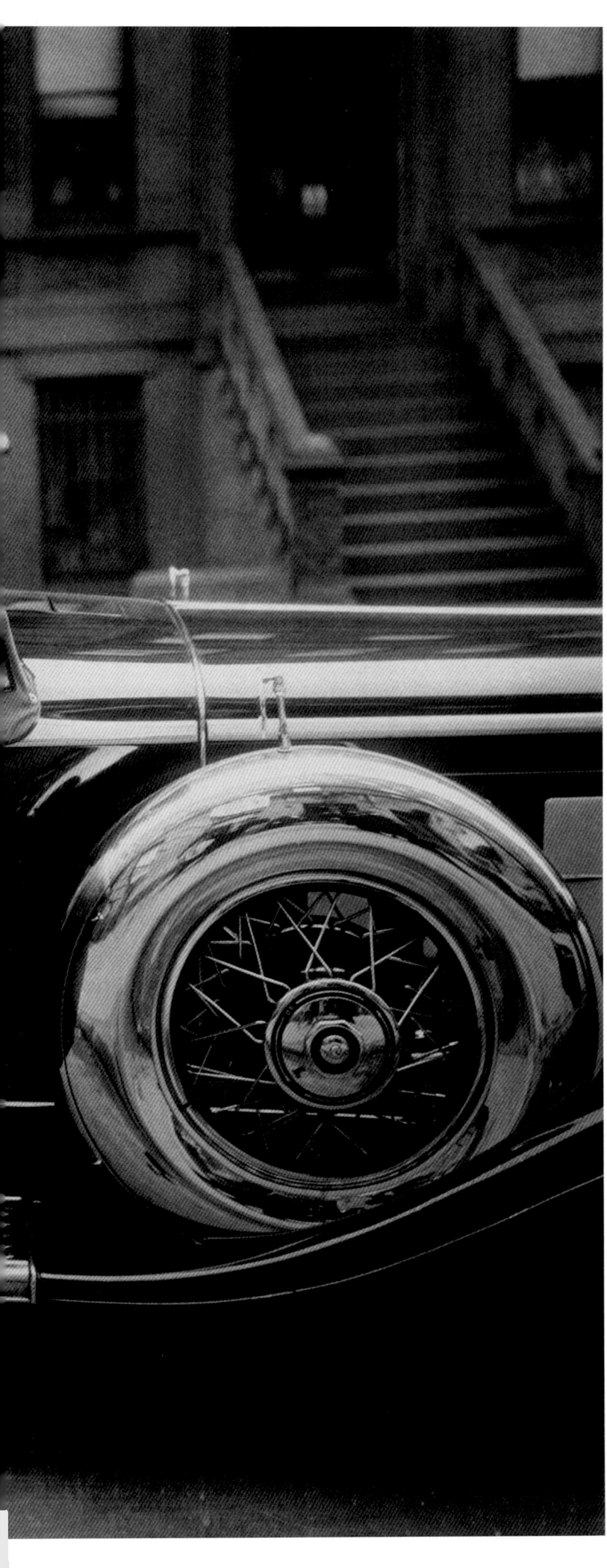

James Van Der Zee,
Couple in Raccoon Coats, 1932

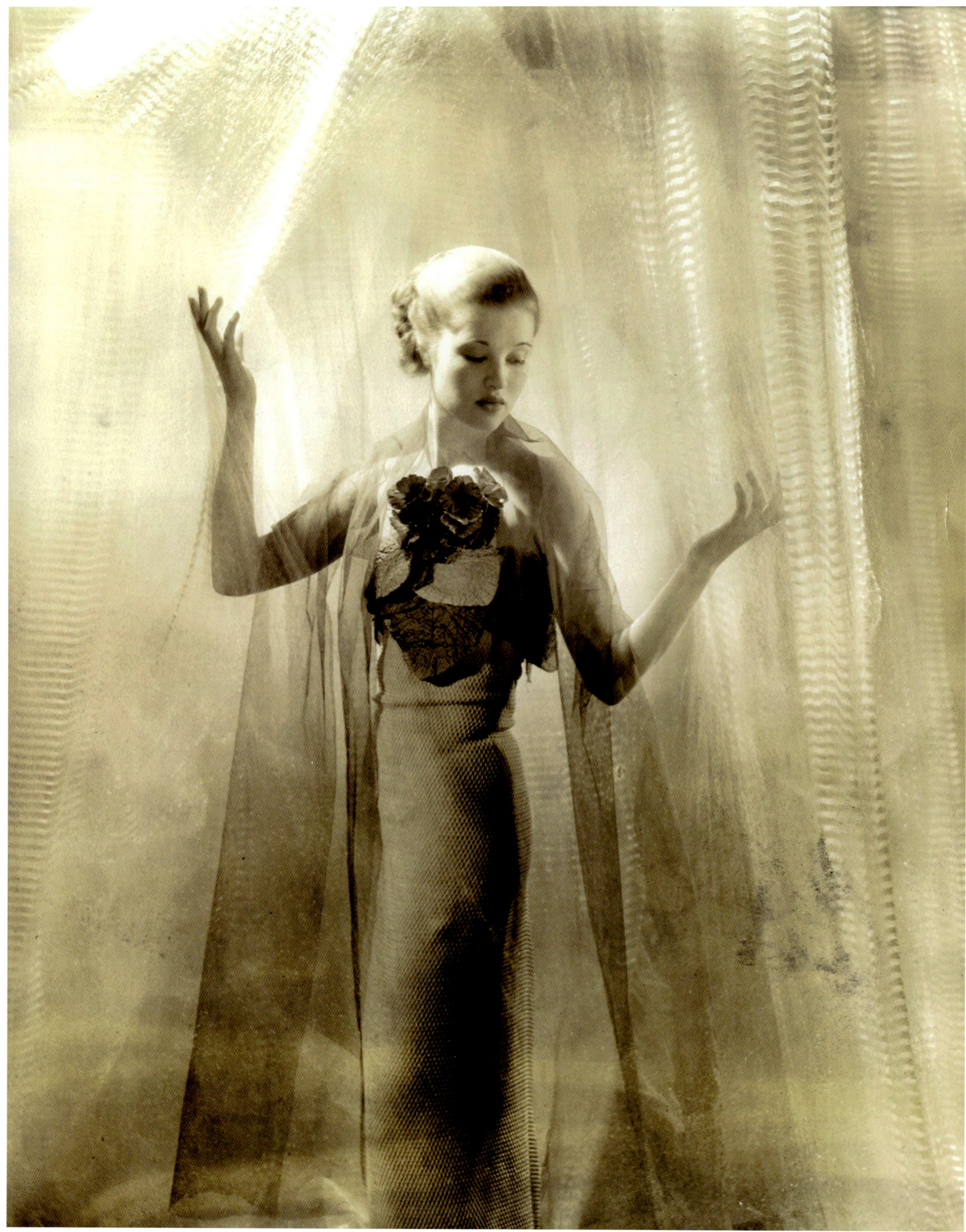

Cecil Beaton's career at *Vogue* lasted over fifty years. His roles included social columnist, fashion illustrator, travel writer, and war correspondent, but his most lasting and significant contribution was to fashion photography. His mature work was extraordinarily versatile and inventive, ranging from stark, modernist imagery to understated formalism, incorporating Surrealist influences alongside a more romantic, theatrical sensibility.

Beaton acquired his first camera in 1915 at the age of eleven, and learned the craft of photography in a darkroom set up at the family home. By the mid-1920s, Beaton was working as a staff photographer for *Vanity Fair* and British *Vogue* and had a growing reputation as a society portraitist. In 1929, he traveled to New York on the invitation of *Vogue* editor Edna Woolman Chase to shoot some photographs for the magazine.

Beaton's early style was closely modeled on the Pictorialist photography of his hero, Adolph de Meyer (p. 24), whose work he described in vivid prose: "He invented a new universe; a high-key world of water sparkling with sunshine, or moonlight and candlelight . . . of tissues and gauzes, of pearly luster and dazzling sundrops." Beaton's 1928 portrait of his sister Nancy as a shooting star—an extravaganza of shiny foil and crinkled, backlit cellophane—pays homage to this glittering world.

At the outbreak of World War II, Beaton put fashion photography aside to focus on his work as a war correspondent. Although he produced some memorable images in his later career—such as his iconic 1948 ensemble shot of Charles James evening dresses (p. 34)—the best of his work was behind him. Rising stars such as Irving Penn (p. 70) and Richard Avedon (p. 94) were bringing a fresh, modern look to the pages of *Vogue* and *Harper's Bazaar*, while the work of upstarts such as William Klein (p. 102) and Frank Horvat (p. 106) took fashion onto the streets and into the sights of the documentary photographer. Beaton's theatrical style began to look passé, and his contract with *Vogue* was terminated in 1955.

Beaton continued to photograph fashion for *Vogue* on a freelance basis for the next two decades, but from this point onward, most of his creative energy was focused on costume and set design for film and theater productions. During the 1960s, he worked with a new generation of models, such as Twiggy and Jean Shrimpton, but admitted to feeling out of touch with the younger generation: "They are like creatures from another planet," he remarked. Beaton's last fashion shoot was in 1979, covering the Paris fall collections for *Vogue Paris*.

Born in London, 1904; died in Broad Chalke, England, 1980

Cecil Beaton, *Vogue*, July 1, 1935
Following pages: Cecil Beaton, (left) *Vogue*, July 1, 1933; (right) *Nancy Beaton as a Shooting Star*, 1928

CECIL BEATON

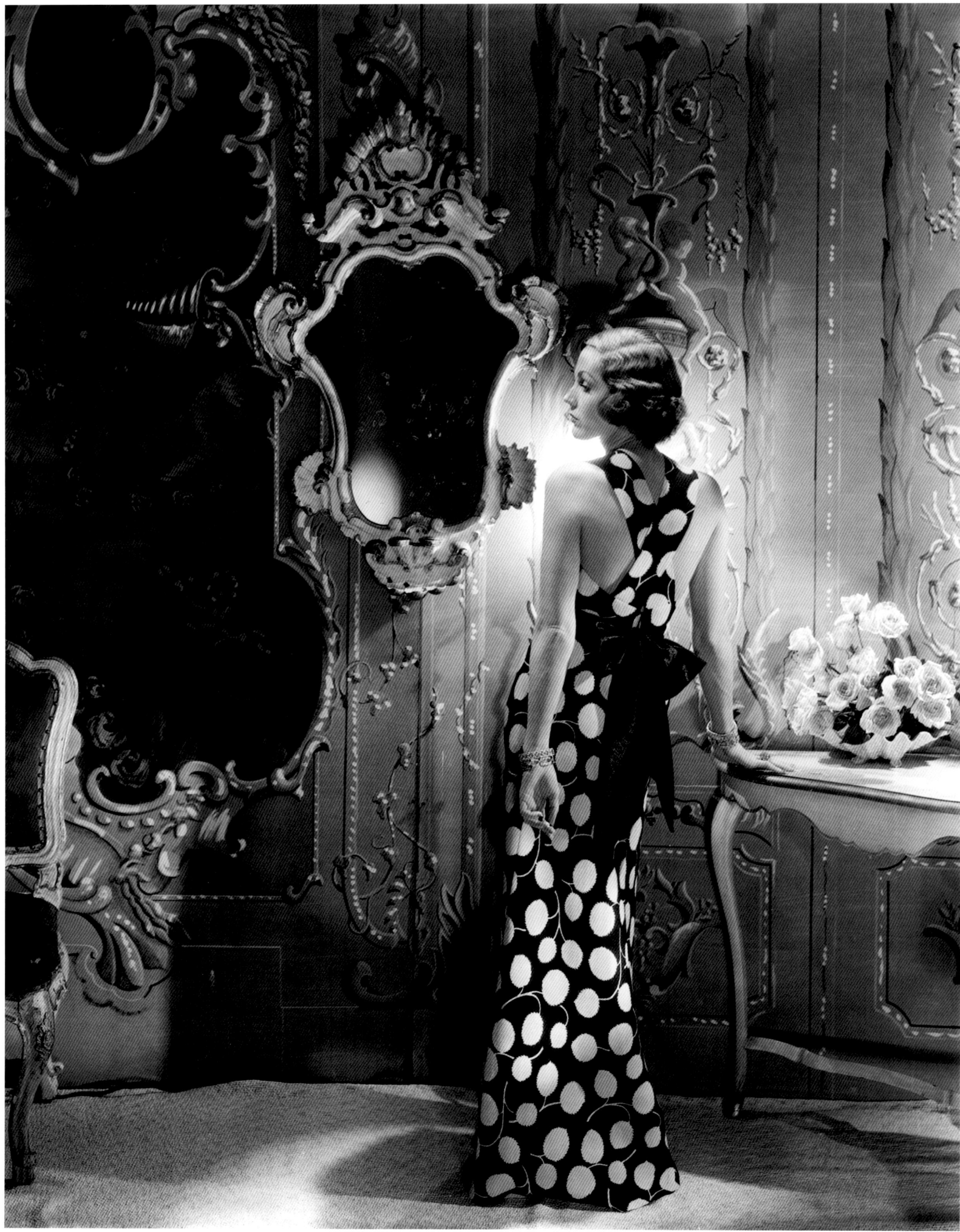

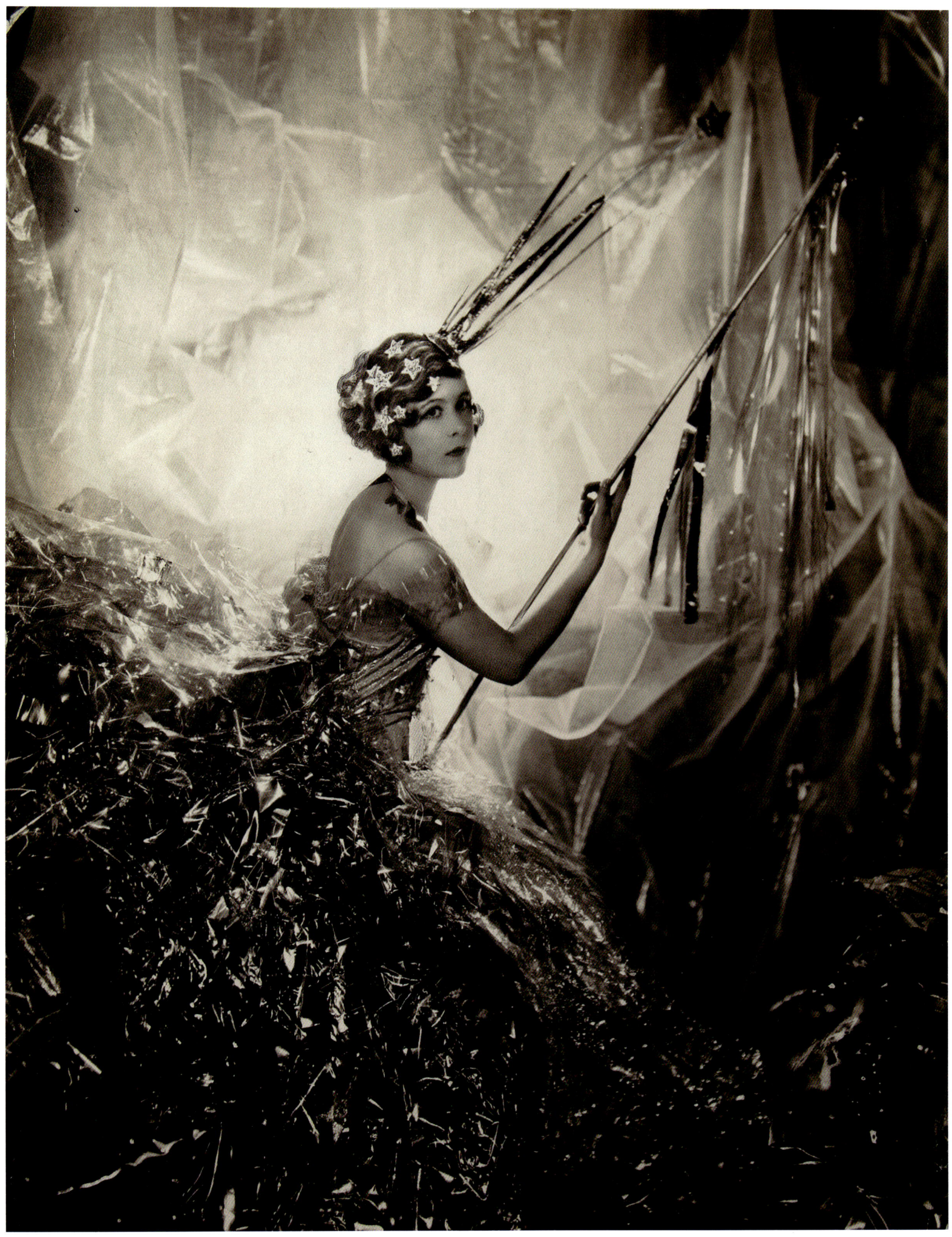

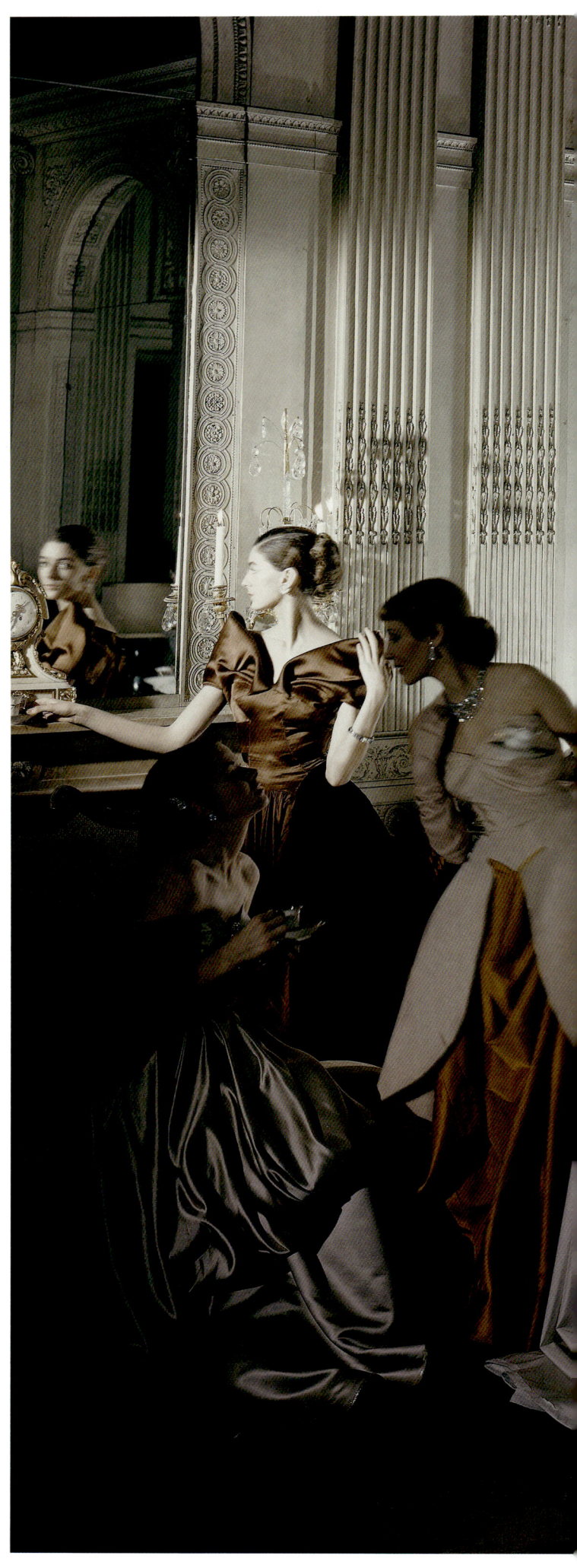

Cecil Beaton,
Vogue, June 1, 1948

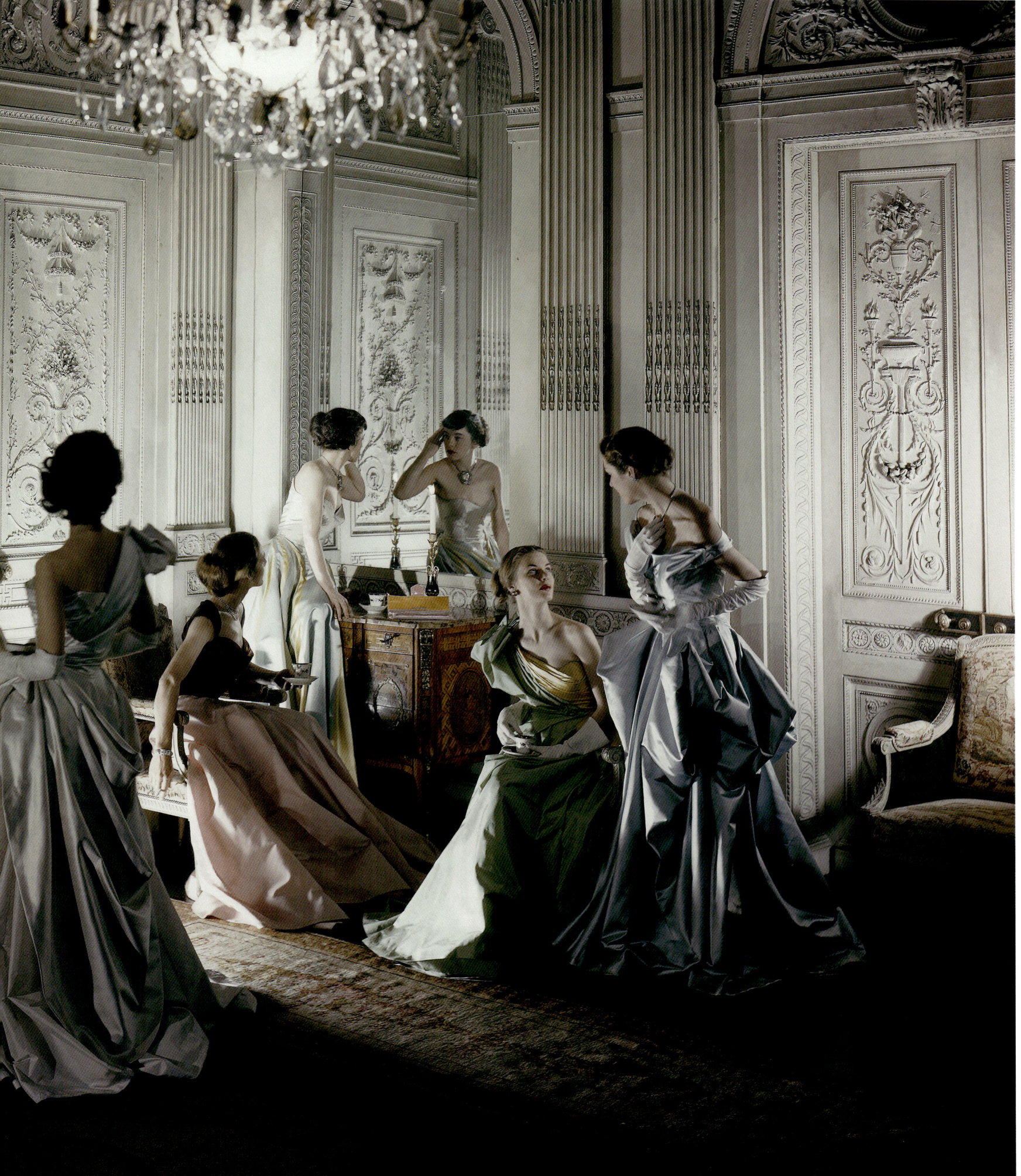

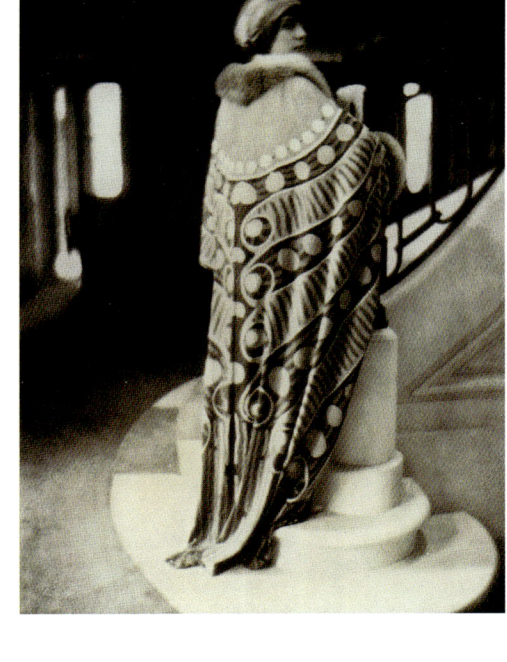

EDWARD STEICHEN

Born in Bivange,
Luxembourg, 1879;
died in Redding,
Connecticut, 1973

Following Adolph de Meyer's (p. 24) move from *Vogue* to *Harper's Bazaar* in 1922, Edward Steichen —his reputation as an art photographer already well established—decided to accept the position of chief photographer at *Vanity Fair* and *Vogue*. Steichen's first fashion photographs, however, had been taken for the French magazine *Art et Décoration* some years earlier, in 1911. Commissioned to photograph dresses by the couturier Paul Poiret, Steichen produced eleven plates shot in the Pictorialist style. Though not a fashion editorial in the sense that we understand the term today, Steichen's departure from the mannered, statuesque poses of earlier fashion images, and his consistent treatment of narrative, mood, and atmosphere over several pages, anticipated the photographic spreads that would begin to appear regularly in the fashion press by the mid-1930s.

Steichen's early work for *Vogue* was also shot in the Pictorialist style, but he gradually abandoned this aesthetic in favor of a more modern look. "Straight photography" did away with attempts to emulate painting, instead adopting the clean lines, tonal clarity, and sharp focus that were claimed, at the time, to be the defining characteristics of the medium. The new aesthetic had been popular among the photographic avant-garde for some years, and Steichen adapted it seamlessly to his fashion work, replacing theatrical settings with geometric backdrops, and labored poses with more relaxed attitudes that highlighted models' characters and personalities. Ultimately, however, the world of fashion would not prove sufficiently stimulating for Steichen. He left Condé Nast in 1937 and went on to become the director of the Naval Photographic Institute and, later, director of photography at New York's Museum of Modern Art.

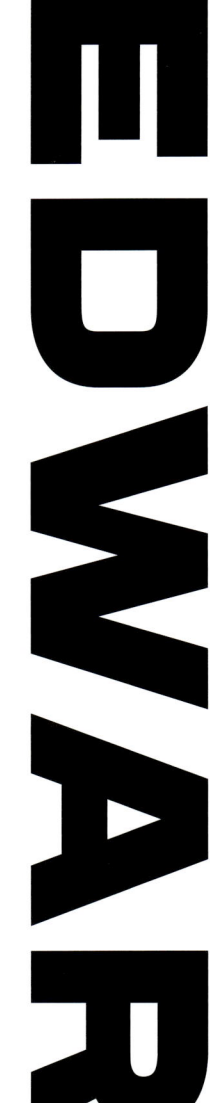

Edward Steichen, "Battick," *Art et Décoration*, April 1911
Right: Edward Steichen, *The White Evening Wrap*, *Vogue*, July 15, 1928

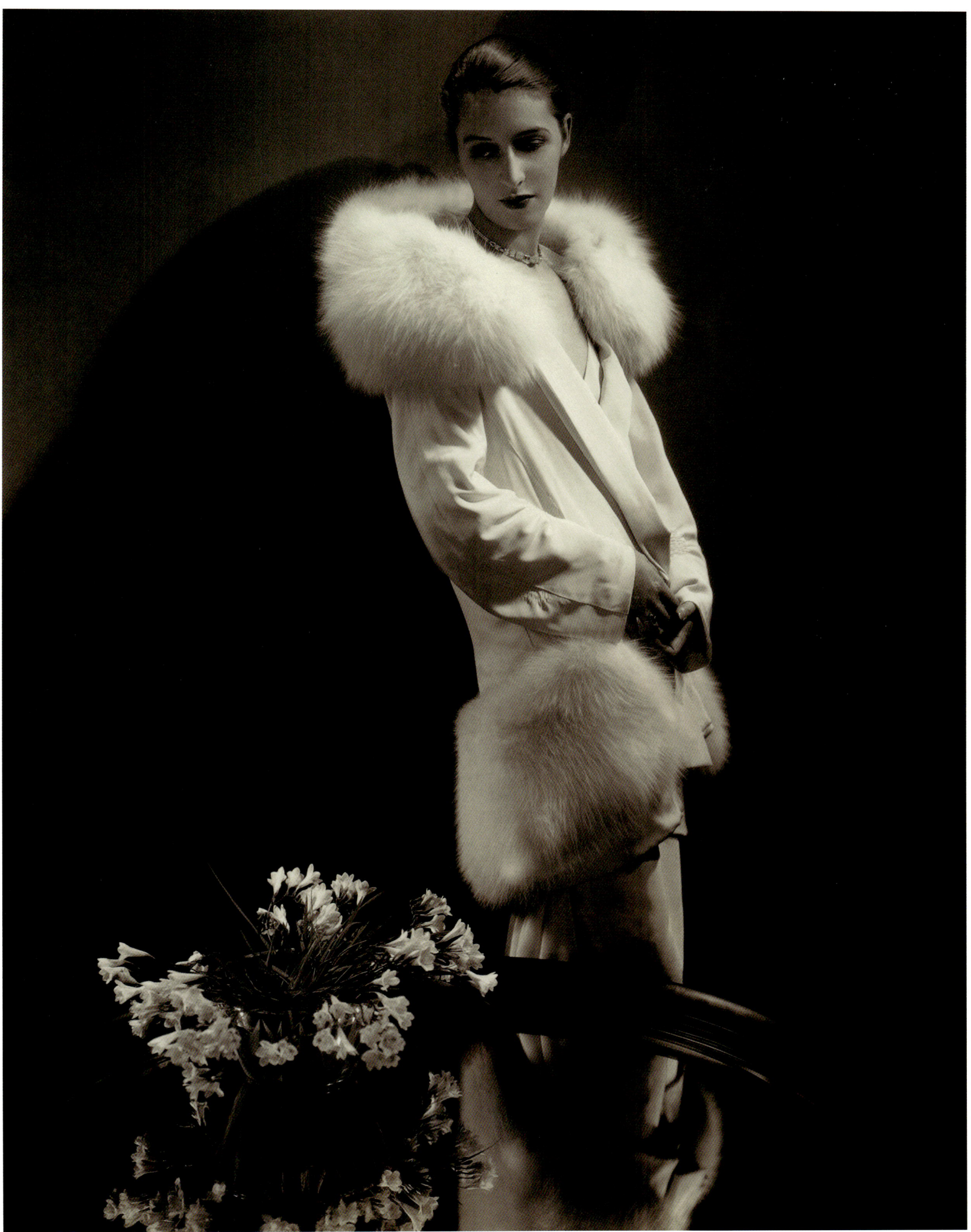

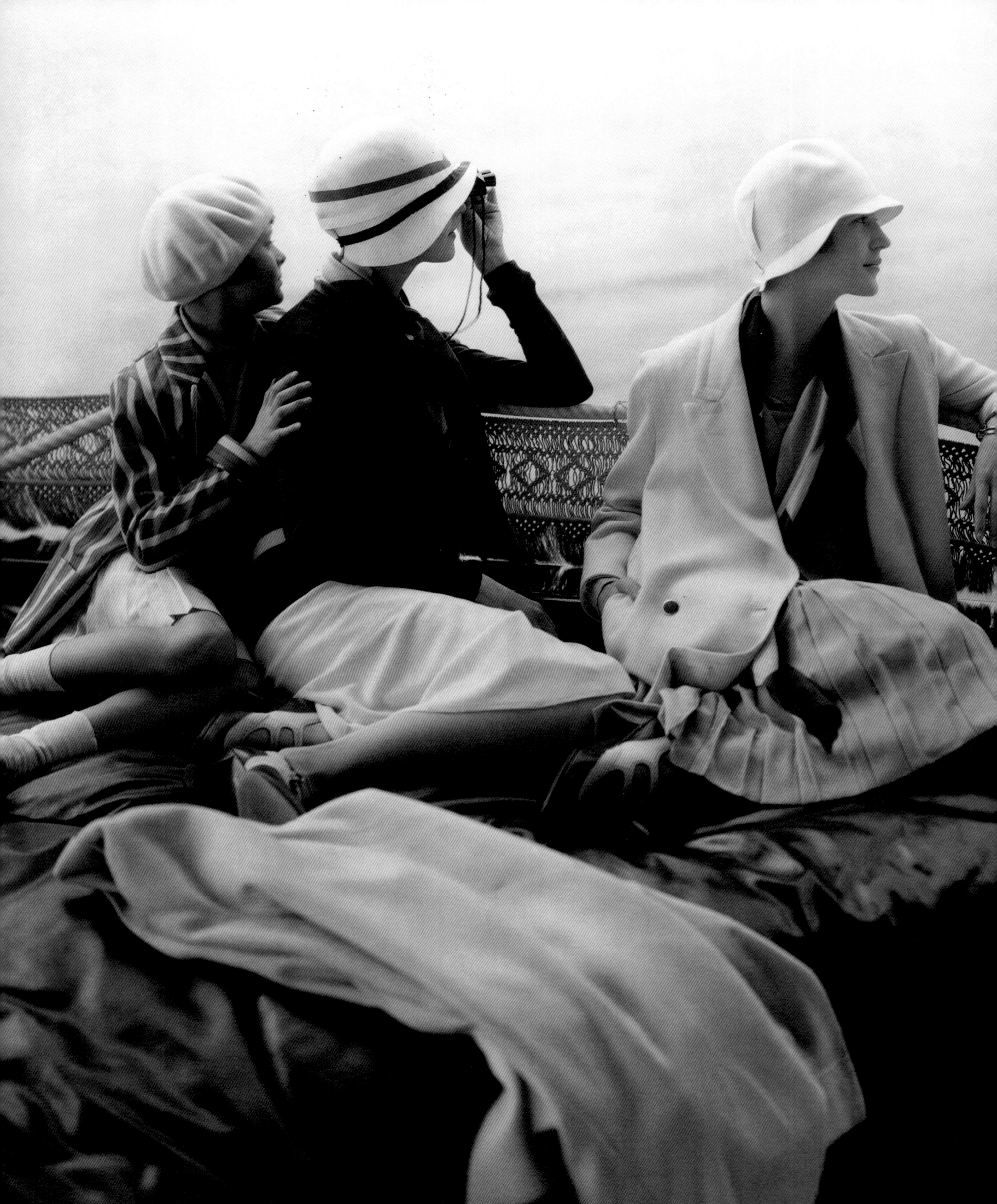

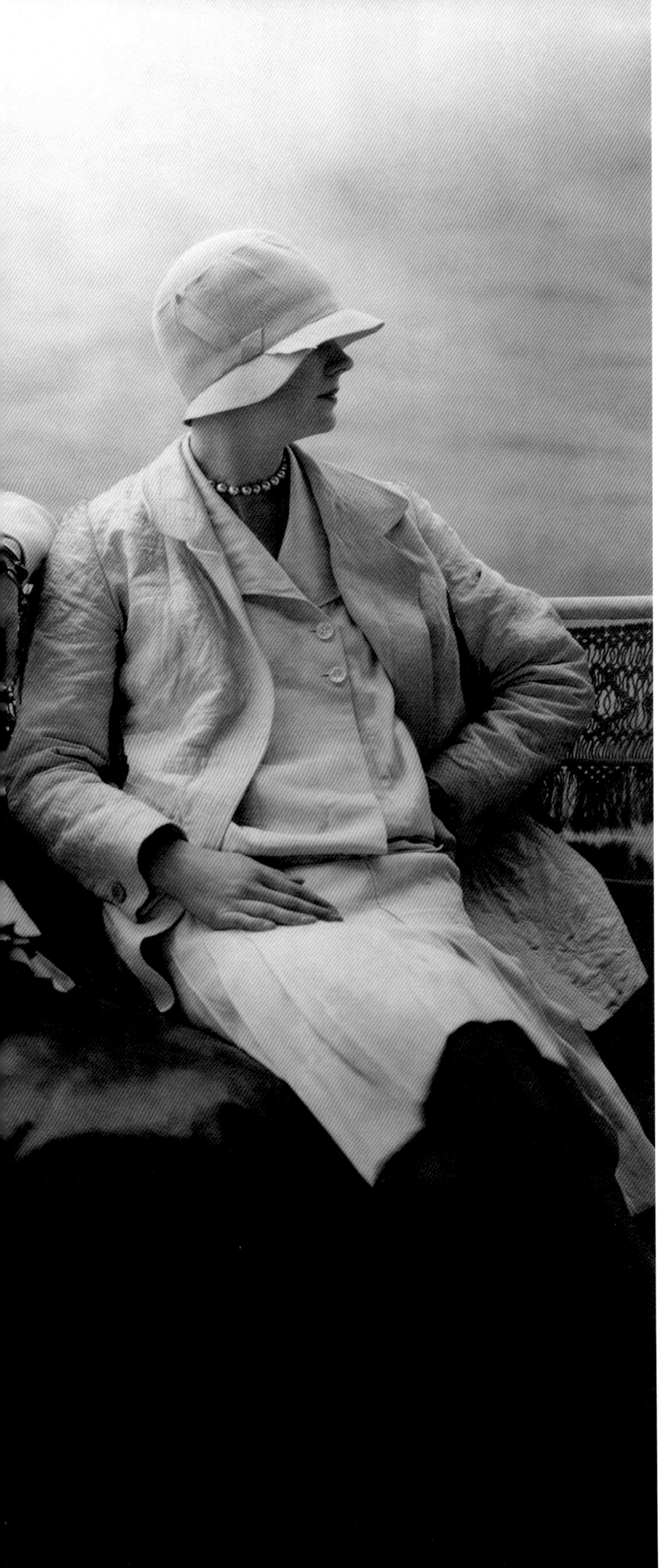

Edward Steichen,
On George Baher's Yacht, 1928, *Vogue*, April 27, 1929

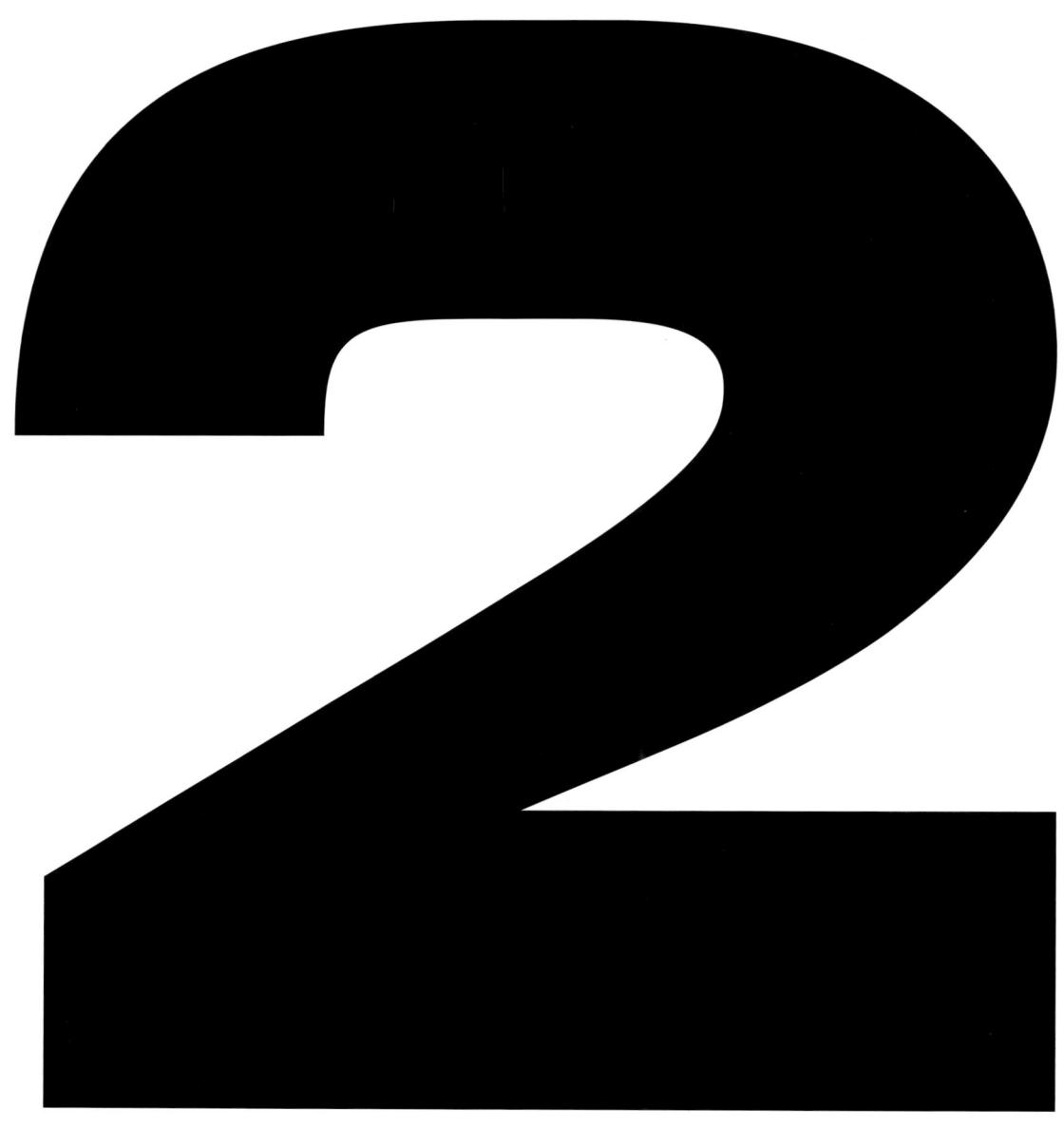

George Hoyningen-Huene,
Swimwear, Paris, 1929;
Horst P. Horst with models

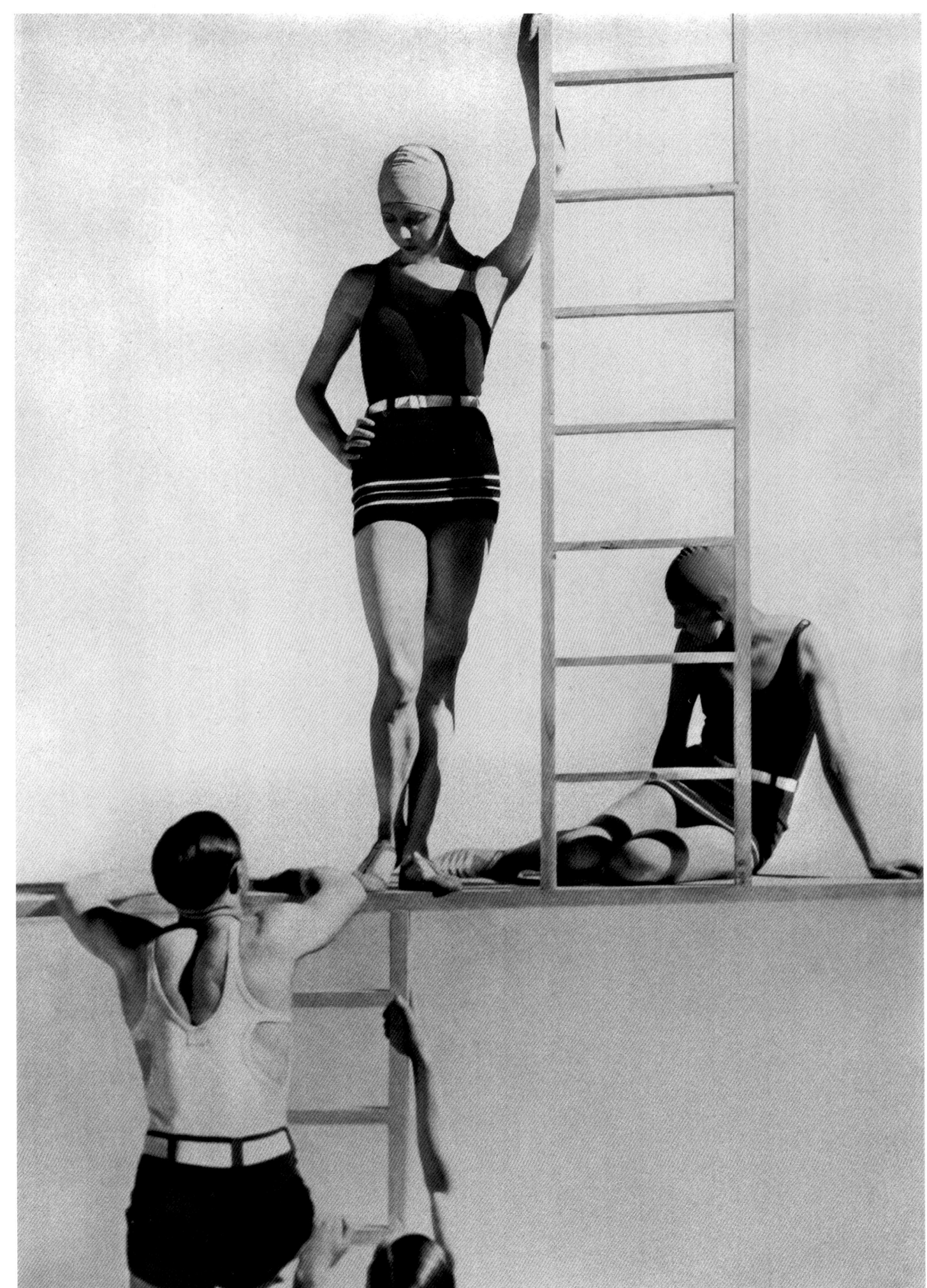

GEORGE HOYNINGEN-HUENE

Born in St. Petersburg,
Russia, 1900; died
in Los Angeles, 1968

George Hoyningen-Huene was born to aristocratic parents and enjoyed a privileged childhood. After moving to England and serving in the British Expeditionary Forces in World War I, Hoyningen-Huene found himself in Paris, where his sister had opened a dressmaking establishment. A naturally talented artist, Hoyningen-Huene began producing sketches for his sister's catalogues and attending drawing classes with the French Cubist painter André Lhote. By 1925, Hoyningen-Huene was selling his fashion illustrations to *Harper's Bazaar* and, shortly after, was offered an exclusive contract as an illustrator with *Vogue*.

His first published fashion photographs came about by accident, when a *Vogue* photographer failed to turn up for an assignment. Hoyningen-Huene was asked to fill in, and a new career was launched. Initially, his work closely imitated that of *Vogue*'s chief photographer, Edward Steichen (p. 36). However, within a short time, Hoyningen-Huene was drawing on influences from his diverse circle of friends—including writers and artists involved with Cubism, Surrealism, and other avant-garde movements—and his fascination with classical Greece, to develop his own signature style.

Using a combination of precise composition, dramatic lighting, and selective focus, Hoyningen-Huene transformed his sitters into heroic forms, as timeless and monumental as the sculptures that inspired him. His 1930 photograph of a young couple sitting on what appears to be a diving board, looking out to sea, was in fact shot on the roof of a building, with the balustrade, just out of focus, suggesting the horizon. (The male model in the photograph is Horst P. Horst, p. 58.) Hoyningen-Huene left *Vogue* for *Harper's Bazaar* in 1935, where he remained for the next decade, eventually leaving to pursue a career in Hollywood as a "color coordinator." By that time, his austere, neoclassical aesthetic was considered outdated; within months of his departure from *Harper's Bazaar*, newcomer Richard Avedon (p. 94) would take fashion photography into a new era.

George Hoyningen-Huene,
The Divers, Paris, 1930; Horst P. Horst with model

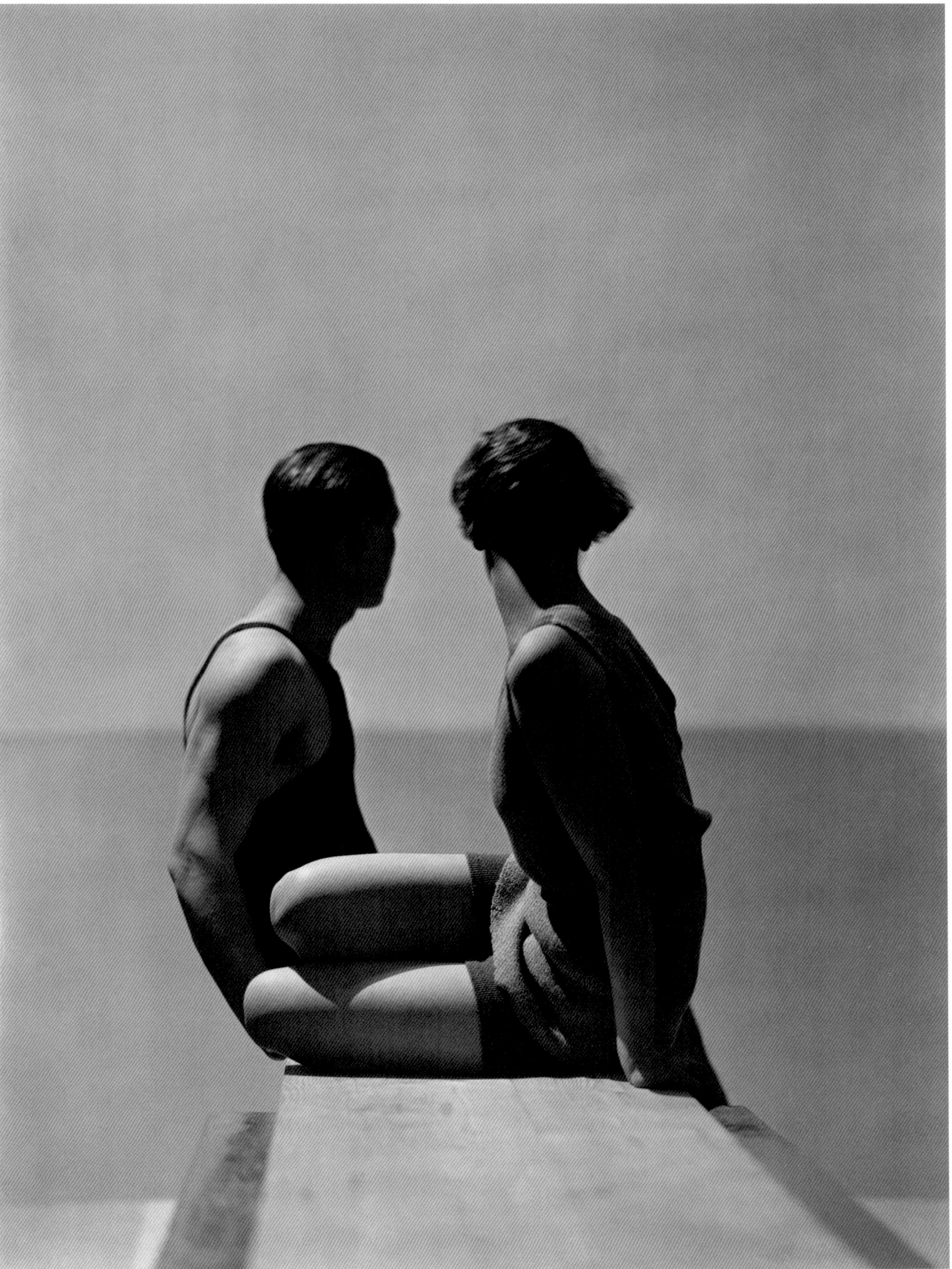

Born in Vienna, 1881;
died in Frohnleiten,
Austria, 1963

MADAME D'ORA

In the first decades of the twentieth century, photography was not considered a suitable profession for a well-bred young woman, so Dora Kallmus's decision to open her own portrait studio was a brave one. Born to a distinguished Jewish family, Kallmus was the first woman to attend lectures on photographic theory at the Graphische Lehr-und Versuchsanstalt in Vienna. She later completed a five-month apprenticeship in Berlin, where she learned the basics of camera work and retouching. Studio d'Ora opened in Vienna in 1907, with Arthur Benda acting as Kallmus's studio manager and eventual business partner.

Kallmus set out to establish the studio's artistic credentials early on, drawing initially on the Pictorialist idiom and later moving to a more formal, modernist style. The studio enjoyed rapid success, and within a few years Madame d'Ora—as Kallmus now called herself—was the photographer of choice for the Austro-Hungarian aristocracy. Kallmus herself never operated the camera, but her innate sense of staging, lighting, and composition meant that she was very much the auteur behind the studio's images. She was interested in fashion early on (her atmospheric 1910 photographs of hats designed by Viennese painter and designer Rudolf Krieser were advanced for their time), but it wasn't until the 1920s—when style magazines began publishing photographs regularly—that the d'Ora studio moved seriously into fashion photography.

In 1925, Kallmus moved the studio to Paris and quickly rose to prominence, winning contracts with magazines such as *L'Officiel de la couture et de la mode de Paris* and *Die Dame*. Alongside her work in fashion photography, she was one of the first photographers to focus on modern dance—an emerging avant-garde art form at the time. Modern dance had a new, expressive visual language that Kallmus was quick to adapt to her fashion and portrait work.

Madame d'Ora,
*Jane Blanchot, L'Officiel de la couture
et de la mode de Paris* 144, 1933

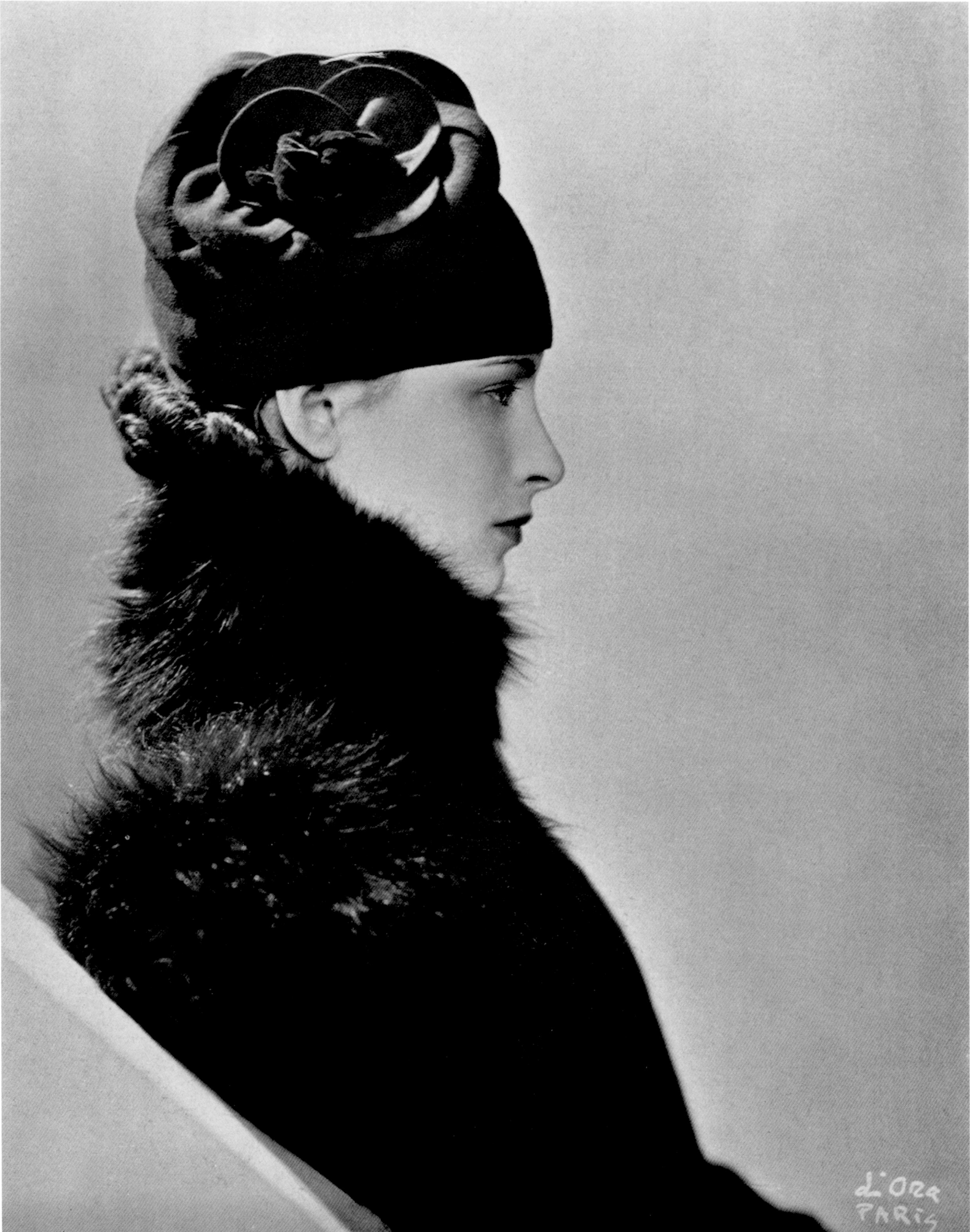

MAN RAY

Born in Philadelphia,
1880; died in Paris, 1976

The artistic avant-garde enjoyed a fruitful relationship with mass-circulation magazines throughout the 1920s and '30s. Man Ray and contemporaries such as Jean Cocteau, Salvador Dalí, and Brassaï all produced commissioned work throughout this period, as fashion magazines sought to increase their cachet by associating themselves with the popular Surrealist movement.

Within months of his arrival in Paris from New York in 1921, Man Ray—already a celebrated artist—had established a successful portrait studio, photographing artists, writers, and socialites. The following year, he was introduced to the couturier Paul Poiret, who hired him to photograph his collections. Poiret, an avid collector of modern art, encouraged Man Ray to bring his Surrealist aesthetic to fashion photography, and by 1925, Man Ray's fashion work was appearing in the newly launched *Vogue Paris*.

In 1934, Man Ray was offered work by *Harper's Bazaar*. Nearly all his most innovative fashion photography was produced during his years at the magazine, then under the art directorship of Alexey Brodovitch. An early editorial—"Fashions by Radio," shot to illustrate the season's new fashion silhouette—featured a series of Rayographs, produced by placing objects directly onto photographic paper (a technique that Man Ray claimed to have invented). The resulting pictures, which hinted at a female outline without depicting it explicitly, were characteristic of the Surrealists' penchant for subconscious suggestion and dreamlike imagery. As Richard Avedon (p. 94) later remarked, Man Ray "broke the stranglehold of reality on fashion photography."

The creative interaction between the worlds of art and commercial publishing was short-lived, however, coming to an end with the onset of World War II. After his return to New York in 1940, with his reputation as a fashion photographer eclipsing his work as an artist, Man Ray gave up magazine work to focus on his career as a painter.

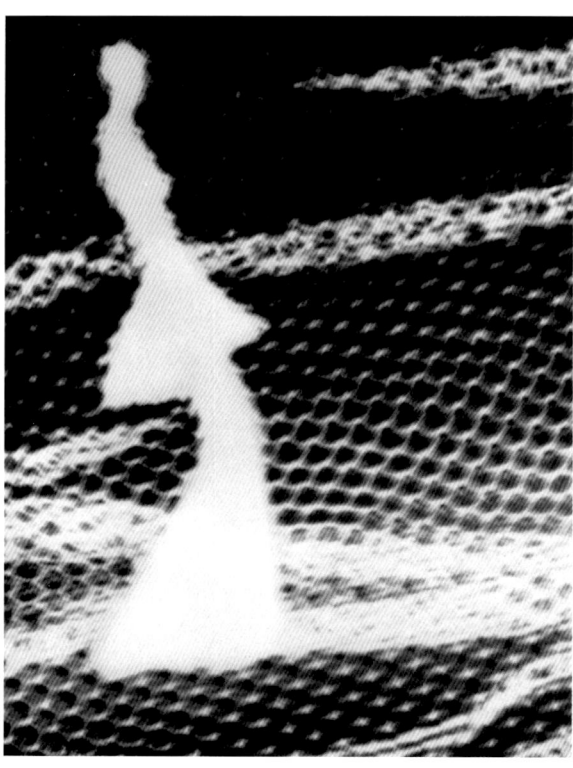

Man Ray, *Fashion by Radio*, 1934
Right: Man Ray, *The Best Madness of the Moment,
Paquin's Feather Boa in All the Colors of Harlem*, 1937

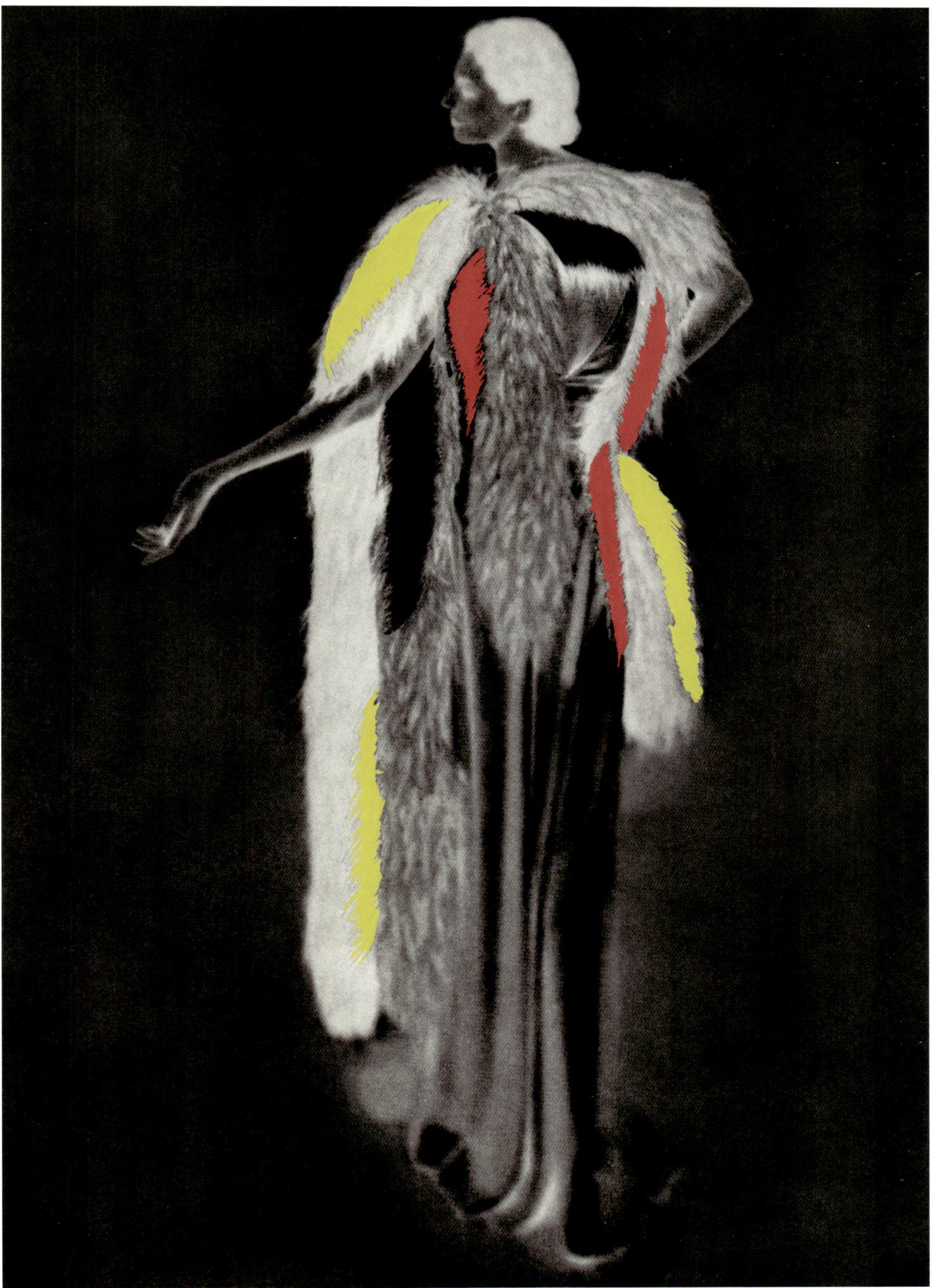

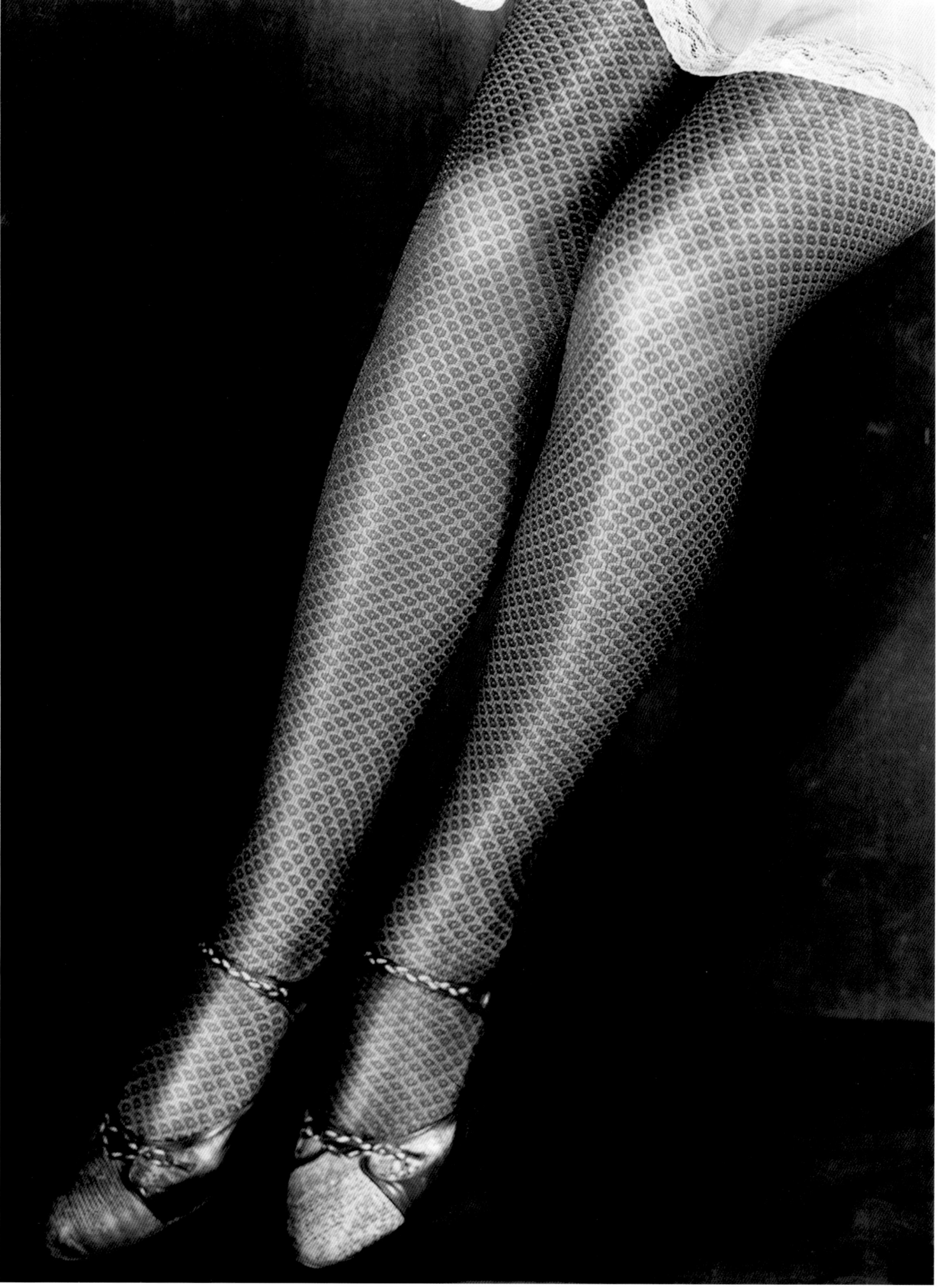

Born in Berlin, 1900;
died in Lublin,
Poland, 1942

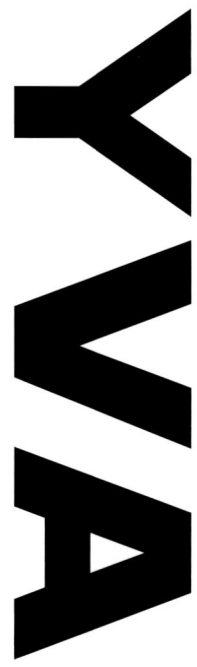

Working under the name Yva, Else Neuländer opened her own photographic studio in Berlin in 1925, with the help of contacts within the industry—her brother Ernst was a partner at a successful fashion house—and went on to become one of the city's most successful commercial photographers. A technically accomplished photographer who often experimented with double exposures, Yva is regarded as a pioneer of advertising photography. By the end of the 1920s, Berlin was a leading fashion center (German *Vogue* published its first issue in 1928), and Yva's first published fashion photographs appeared in the German fashion magazine *Die Dame* in 1927.

Soon, Yva was photographing fashion for magazines such as *Moden-Spiegel*, *Elegante Welt*, and *Sport im Bild*. The modern, clean-lined images of photographers such as Edward Steichen (p. 36) and George Hoyningen-Huene (p. 42) were becoming increasingly popular in Germany, and Yva made her modernist sensibilities clear in her statement for a 1927 exhibition of her photographs: "What matters to me in my pictures is to free the intrinsic essence of photography from all alien embellishments, and at the same time to utilize the artistic possibilities of pure photography more fully." Yva's work also challenged societal norms. Her 1932 photograph of silk stockings was daring for its time: stockings were considered racy, even disreputable, as they evoked nudity, and legs were something of an obsessive subject for photographers.

From 1933 onward, Germany's Nazi government passed increasingly restrictive laws against foreigners and Jews working in publishing and editorial fields. Although individual agencies and publishing houses continued to commission from Yva—who was Jewish—until 1938, work became increasingly scarce. Her last photographs appeared in *Die Dame* in 1937. Helmut Newton (p. 134) joined the studio as an apprentice from late 1936 until early 1938, when the studio was closed. Though Yva and her husband, Alfred Simon, made plans to move to New York, they were arrested by the Gestapo in June 1942 and most likely died in a concentration camp a few weeks later.

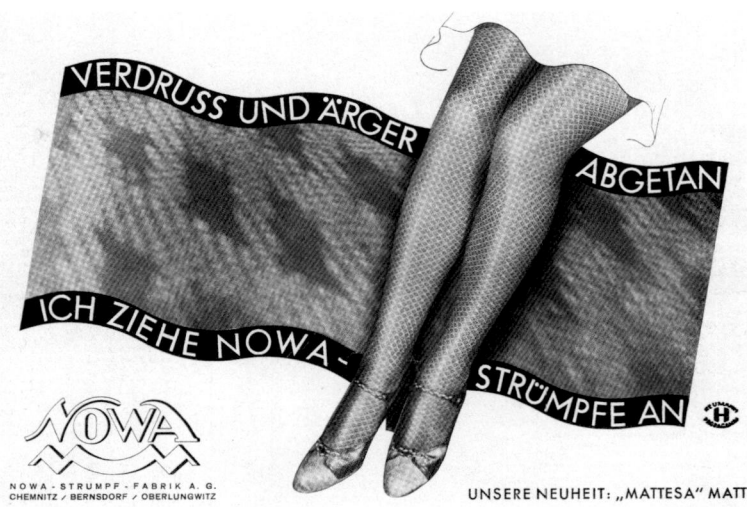

Yva, *Nowa Feinstrumpfhose-Verdruss und Ärger abgetan, ich ziehe Nowa-Strümpfe an [Nowa stocking knitwear— Gone are annoyance and vexation, I am wearing Nowa stockings]*, *Elegante Welt*, September 26, 1932
Left: Yva, *Untitled (woman's legs)*, ca. 1930s

MARTIN MUNKÁCSI

Born in Kolozsvár,
Austria-Hungary, 1896;
died in New York City,
1963

When Carmel Snow took over the editorship of *Harper's Bazaar* in 1932, she was quick to replace Adolph de Meyer (p. 24), who had been the magazine's chief photographer for ten years, with Martin Munkácsi—a Hungarian photojournalist with a passion for motorcycle racing. Munkácsi once said, "All great photographs today are snapshots," a sentiment that he also brought to his fashion work.

Munkácsi moved to Berlin in the late 1920s and rose quickly to the top of his field, ranked alongside members of the photographic avant-garde such as László Moholy-Nagy and André Kertész. Munkácsi's first assignment for *Harper's Bazaar*, shot while he was on a visit to New York in 1933, resulted in some of the most groundbreaking fashion pictures of the era. Invited by Snow to reshoot a bathing-suit feature, Munkácsi photographed the model not in the studio, but outdoors, running along the beach. As Snow later recalled, "Such a pose had never been attempted before for fashion (even sailing features were posed in a studio on a fake boat), but [model Lucile Brokaw] was certainly game and so was I." Outdoor fashion photography was not new, but Munkácsi's images—which evoked the movement and feel of the garment, rather than recording it in intricate detail—turned the industry on its head.

Snow offered Munkácsi a contract immediately, but he had gone back to Berlin and did not return to New York until early 1934, in order to escape the Nazi Party's increasing control of the publishing industry. Versatile and extraordinarily productive, Munkácsi remained on the staff of *Harper's Bazaar* for thirteen years. His best fashion work of this period combines the energy of his photojournalism with the formal virtuosity of American avant-garde photographers such as Alfred Stieglitz, Paul Strand, and Walker Evans.

Martin Munkácsi,
Lucile Brokaw, Harper's Bazaar, December 1933

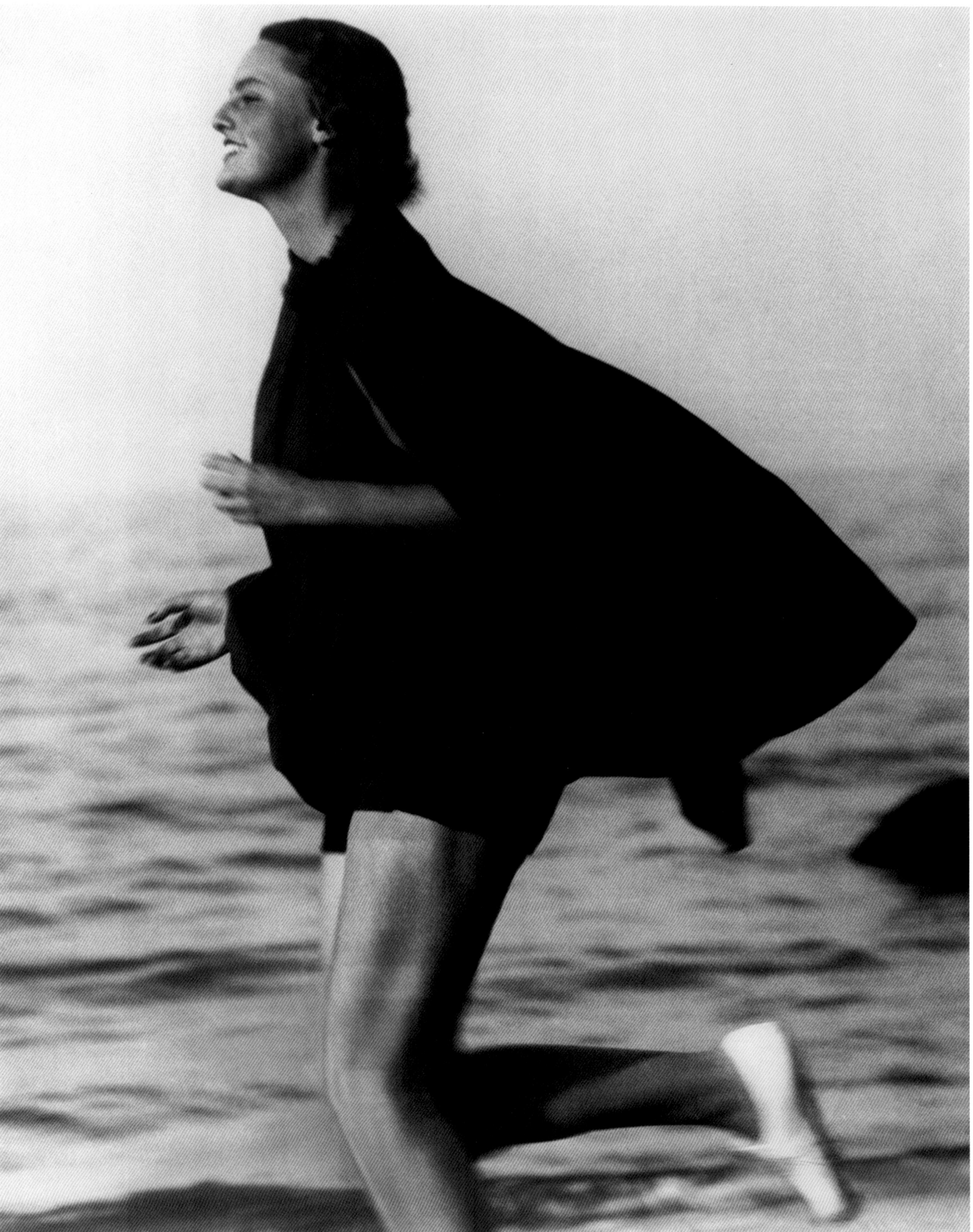

Born in New York City, 1907; died in Saint James, New York, 1988

TONI FRISSELL

Born into an affluent New York family, Toni Frissell spent her childhood and adolescence in privileged surroundings, dividing her time between outdoor pursuits and society events. She began to take photographs around the age of sixteen, taught by her older brother Varick. Fired from an early job writing about fashion for *Vogue* (allegedly because her spelling was so poor), Frissell was encouraged by Carmel Snow, then a fashion editor at the magazine, to pursue photography instead. She took Snow's advice to heart, photographing her society friends in open-air settings and seeking out guidance from luminaries such as Edward Steichen (p. 36) and Cecil Beaton (p. 30), with whom she briefly apprenticed. Her fresh approach to fashion and beauty appealed to *Vogue*'s editors, and her photographic work began to appear in fashion magazines in the early 1930s, around the same time as that of Martin Munkácsi (p. 50).

Like Munkácsi, Frissell was seen as a pioneer of the documentary or "realist" style, moving fashion photography out of the studio and into more natural settings. Despite her admission that this innovation was due in part to her lack of skill at studio lighting, her own plein air lifestyle also provided much of the inspiration for her fashion work: "I try hard to capture atmosphere in the hope the viewer can smell the flowers on a hillside or feel the joy of a windless Alpine day." In the 1940s, Frissell became interested in photojournalism, traveling to England to take photographs for the Red Cross, and later covering the war in Europe as a correspondent for *Harper's Bazaar*. (Her contemporary Lee Miller covered the war for *Vogue* at the same time.) After the war, her interest in fashion photography waned, and her assignments for *Harper's Bazaar* (and, later, for *Vogue*) began to include more reportage. In the early 1950s, Frissell left fashion magazines entirely, and went on to work for the newly launched *Sports Illustrated*.

Toni Frissell,
Vogue, December 1, 1940

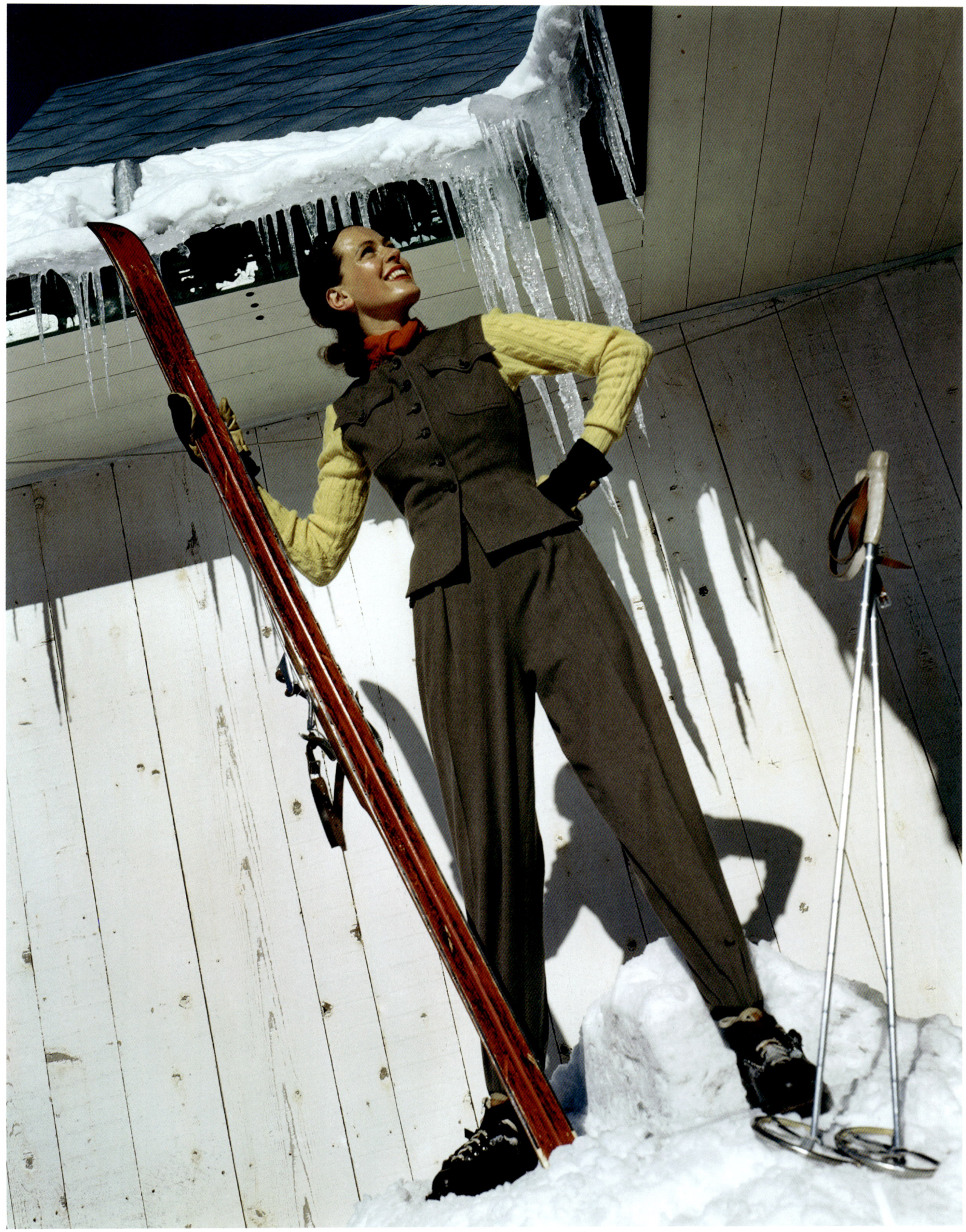

Toni Frissell,
Weeki Wachee Spring, Florida, 1947

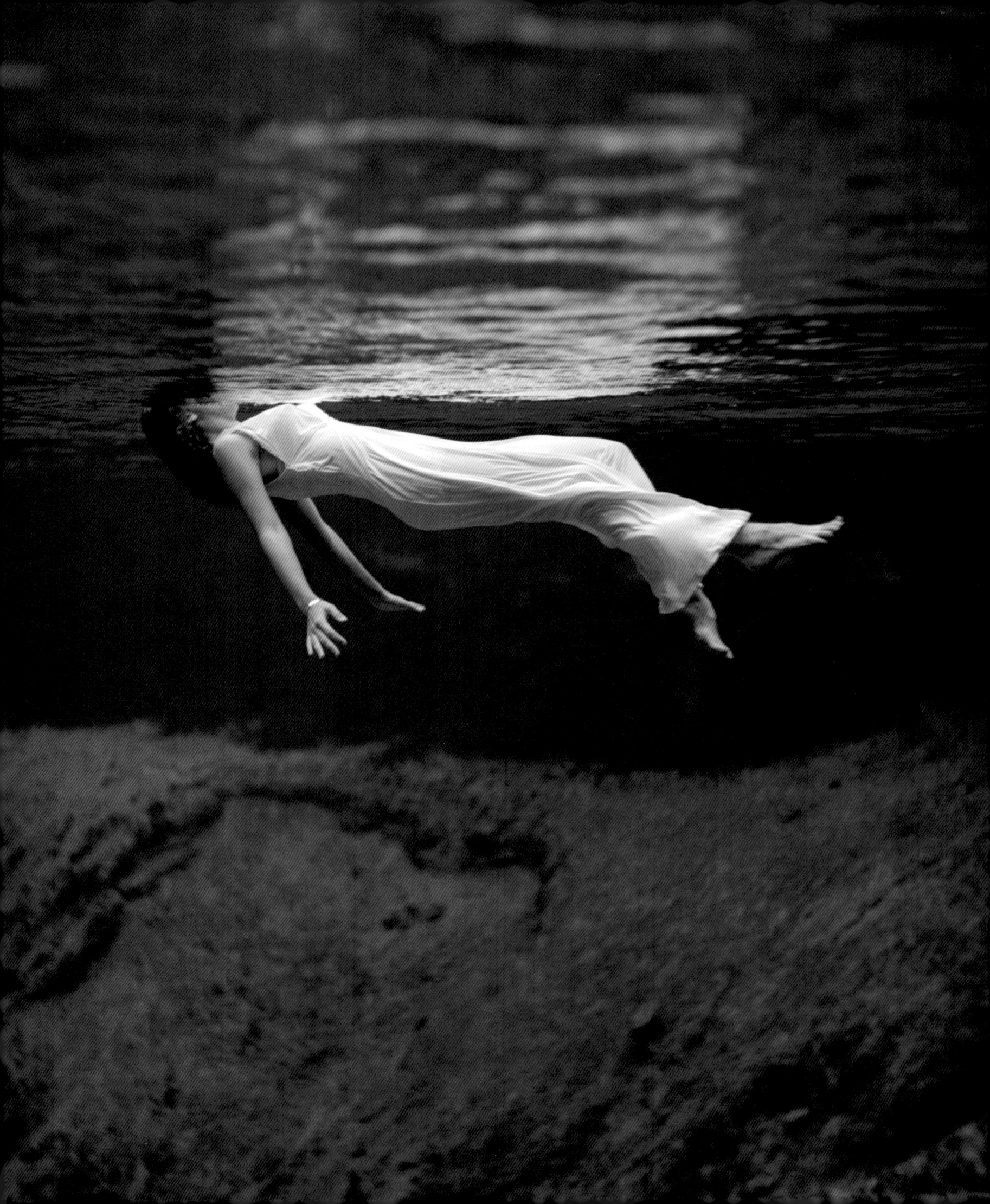

JEAN MORAL

Born in Marchiennes,
France, 1906;
died in Montreux,
Switzerland, 1999

Jean Moral discovered photography in his late teens, and although he lacked formal training, the visual language of early modernism—with its strong perspectives, unusual angles, and abstract compositions—came naturally to him. Moral began taking photographs on the street after he moved to Paris in 1925 to work as a commercial designer, and by 1931, he was publishing his work regularly in *Paris Magazine*. He began photographing fashion in 1933 as one of a number of "realist" photographers working for *Harper's Bazaar* under the editorship of Carmel Snow and the art direction of Alexey Brodovitch; in 1935, he became the only French photographer under contract with the magazine.

Like his colleague Martin Munkácsi (p. 50), Moral came from a documentary background, and his photographs—influenced, like those of Munkácsi, by a love of sport—were sometimes accused of being derivative. Both Moral and Munkácsi combined the spontaneity of the snapshot with the formal rigor of the modernist aesthetic, but Moral's work reflected the uniqueness of young, French style—a more refined, urban image than the sporty American girls photographed by Munkácsi and German expat Hermann Landshoff. By the mid-1930s, Moral was finding fashion work increasingly routine and returned to reportage; however, Snow continued to commission work from him throughout this period, requesting specifically that he photograph fashion in a documentary style. His 1939 series taken on the streets of Paris offers a moment of respite from the city's tense atmosphere, in the months following the outbreak of war.

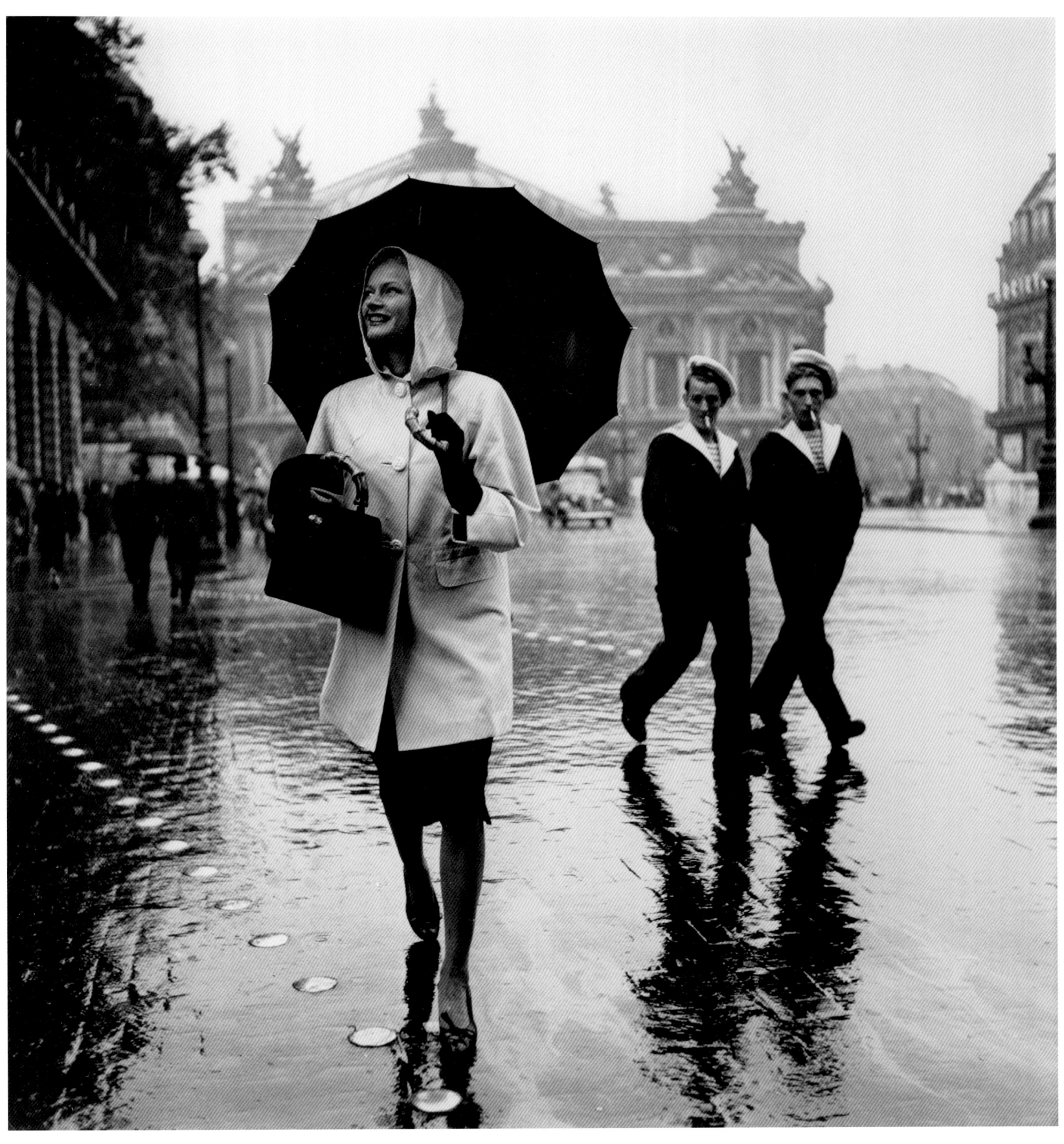

Jean Moral,
Mode, 1938–39, *Harper's Bazaar*, October 1939;
model in raincoat by Schiaparelli, Place de l'Opéra, Paris

HORST P. HORST

HORST

Born in Weissenfels,
Germany, 1906;
died in Palm Beach,
Florida, 1999

Alongside the innovative photojournalistic work of photographers like Martin Munkácsi (p. 50), Jean Moral (p. 56), and Toni Frissell (p. 52), a more classically inspired aesthetic persisted throughout the 1930s and early '40s. Trained in design and construction under Walter Gropius at the Hamburg Kunstgewerbeschule (School of Arts and Crafts), Horst P. Horst had grown up in a post–World War I Germany that was obsessed with the culture and aesthetics of ancient Greece. *Nacktkultur*, or naturism, was a strong influence on his fashion work, which celebrated the lines and shapes of the body as a sculptural object.

Horst arrived in Paris in 1930 at the age of twenty-three to take up a post with the architecture firm of Le Corbusier, but a meeting with George Hoyningen-Huene (p. 42)—then the lead photographer at *Vogue Paris*—led him away from architecture and into photography. Hoyningen-Huene became Horst's mentor, teacher, and lover, introducing him to society and to the editors of *Vogue*, where he published his first (uncredited) pictures in 1931. By 1934, he had taken over from Hoyningen-Huene as *Vogue Paris*'s principal photographer.

Early on, Horst's work closely resembled that of his mentor, but by the late 1930s, he had brought his own, more theatrical twist to Hoyningen-Huene's formal aesthetic—integrating elements from modernist painting, Surrealism, dance, and theater design, as well as his early training in architecture. His work of this period is characterized by classically inspired sets incorporating sculpture and baroque scrolls, and by his characteristic lighting, which was, as *Vogue*'s art director Dr. Mehemed Fehmy Agha remarked, "what the lighting of sculpture in the museums should be . . . three-dimensional and dramatic, striking without harshness." Horst also developed innovative techniques for illuminating pale garments without washing out the fabric, and dark garments without overexposing the model's face. Between 1935 and the 1960s, Horst produced numerous groundbreaking color photographs for *Vogue*, including more than ninety covers.

In 1939, with war imminent, Horst left Paris for New York. He became an American citizen in 1943, when he legally changed his surname from Bohrmann to Horst. He moved away from fashion photography during the 1960s to focus on gardens and interiors for *Vogue*, and later, in the 1970s, for *House and Garden*. The rediscovery of his early black-and-white work in the 1970s prompted a resurgence of his fashion-photography career. In 1978, he was invited to photograph the Paris collections for *Vogue Paris*, invoking his style of the 1930s.

Horst P. Horst, British *Vogue* cover, August 9, 1939
Following pages: Horst P. Horst,
Vogue covers, 1938–52

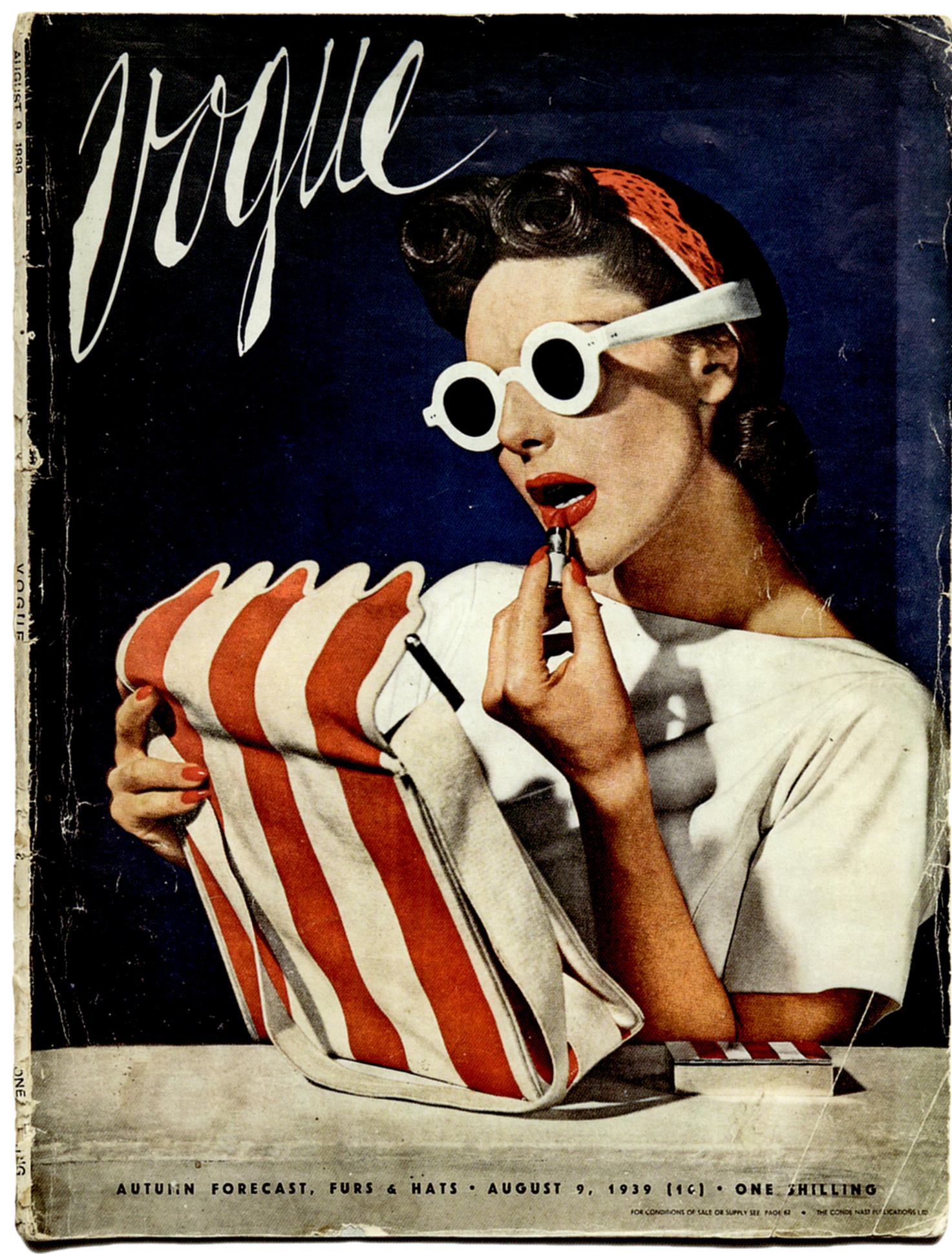

Vogue

AUTUMN FORECAST, FURS & HATS · AUGUST 9, 1939 (16) · ONE SHILLING

FOR CONDITIONS OF SALE OR SUPPLY SEE PAGE 62 · THE CONDÉ NAST PUBLICATIONS LTD

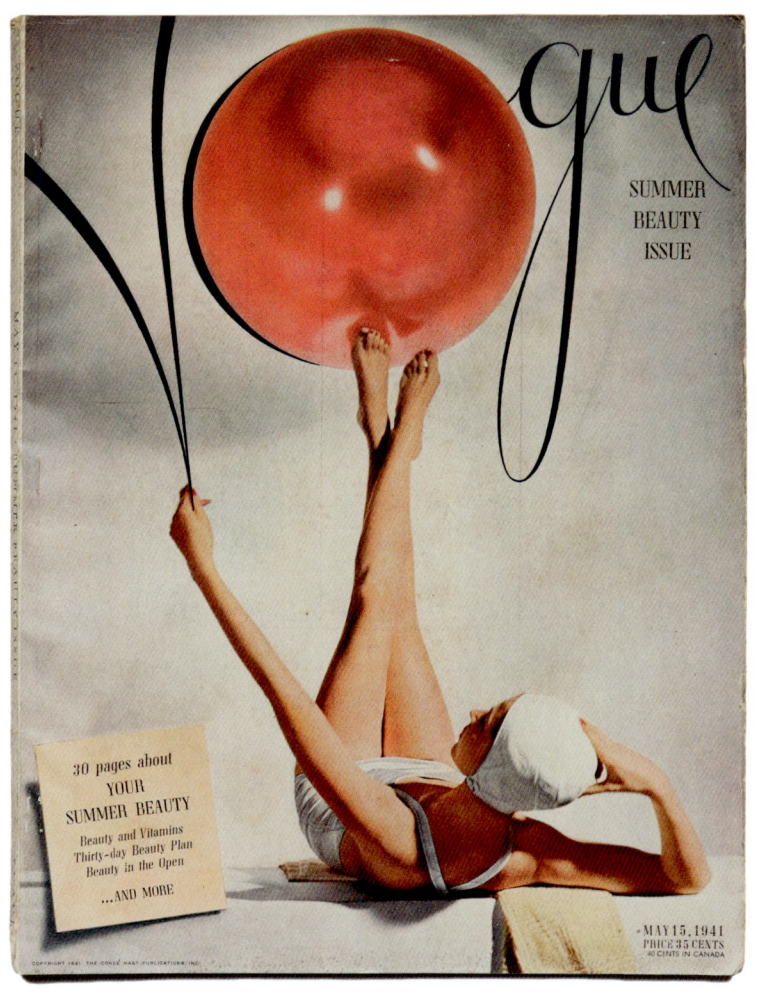

Vogue

SUMMER
BEAUTY
ISSUE

30 pages about
YOUR
SUMMER BEAUTY

Beauty and Vitamins
Thirty-day Beauty Plan
Beauty in the Open

...AND MORE

MAY 15, 1941
PRICE 35 CENTS
40 CENTS IN CANADA

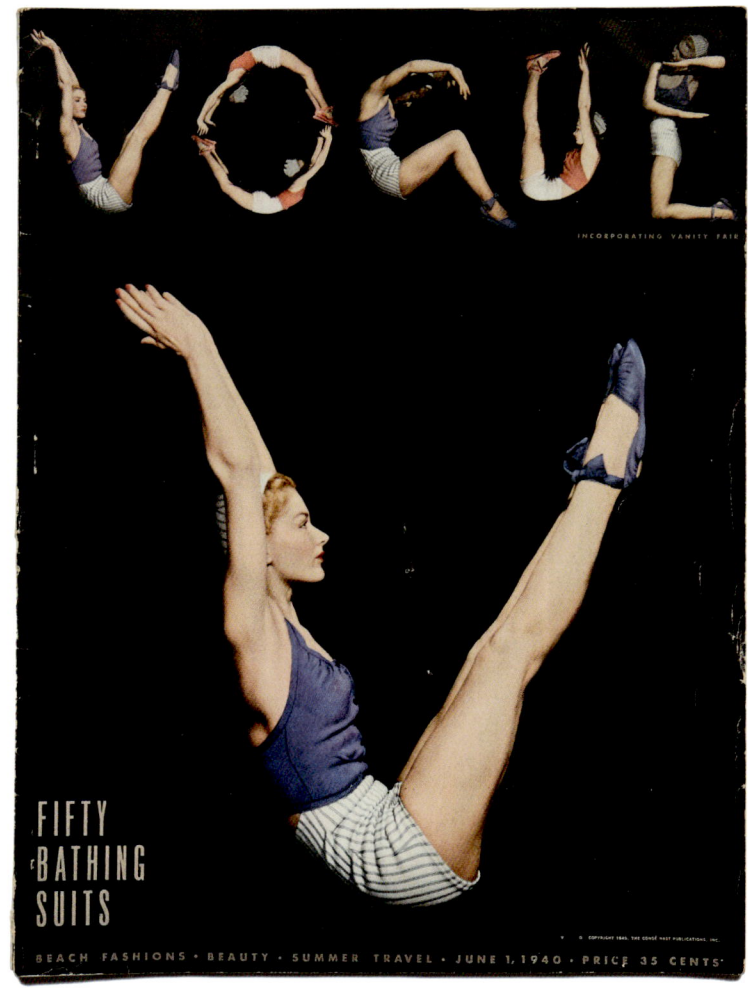

VOGUE

INCORPORATING VANITY FAIR

FIFTY
BATHING
SUITS

BEACH FASHIONS · BEAUTY · SUMMER TRAVEL · JUNE 1, 1940 · PRICE 35 CENTS

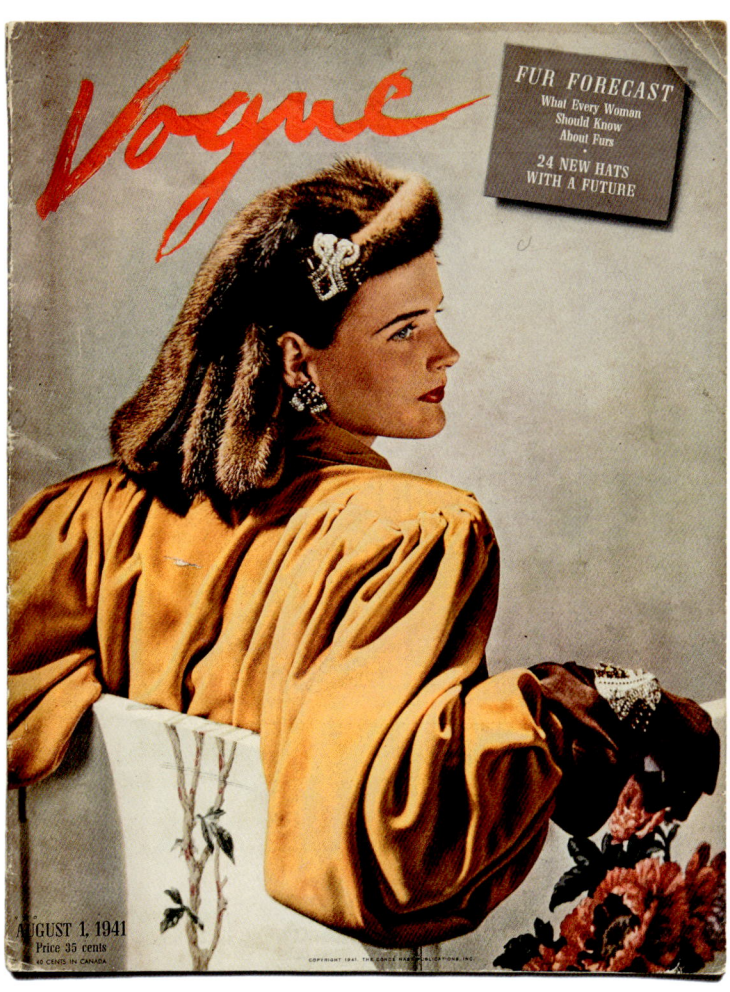

Vogue

FUR FORECAST
What Every Woman
Should Know
About Furs
·
24 NEW HATS
WITH A FUTURE

AUGUST 1, 1941
Price 35 cents
40 CENTS IN CANADA

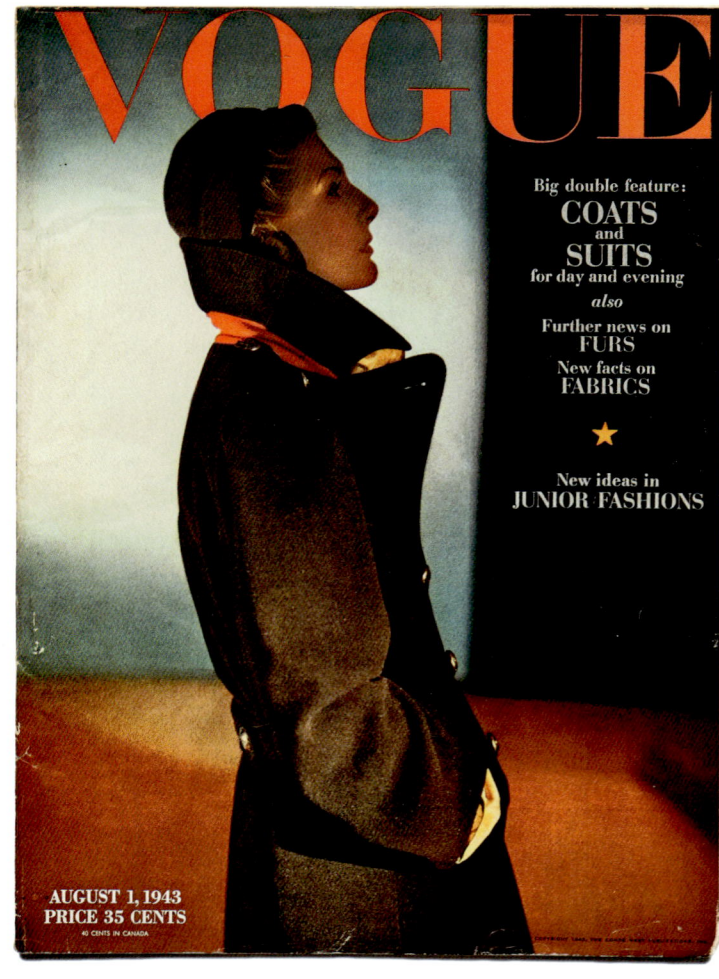

VOGUE

Big double feature:
COATS
and
SUITS
for day and evening
also
Further news on
FURS
New facts on
FABRICS
★
New ideas in
JUNIOR FASHIONS

AUGUST 1, 1943
PRICE 35 CENTS
40 CENTS IN CANADA

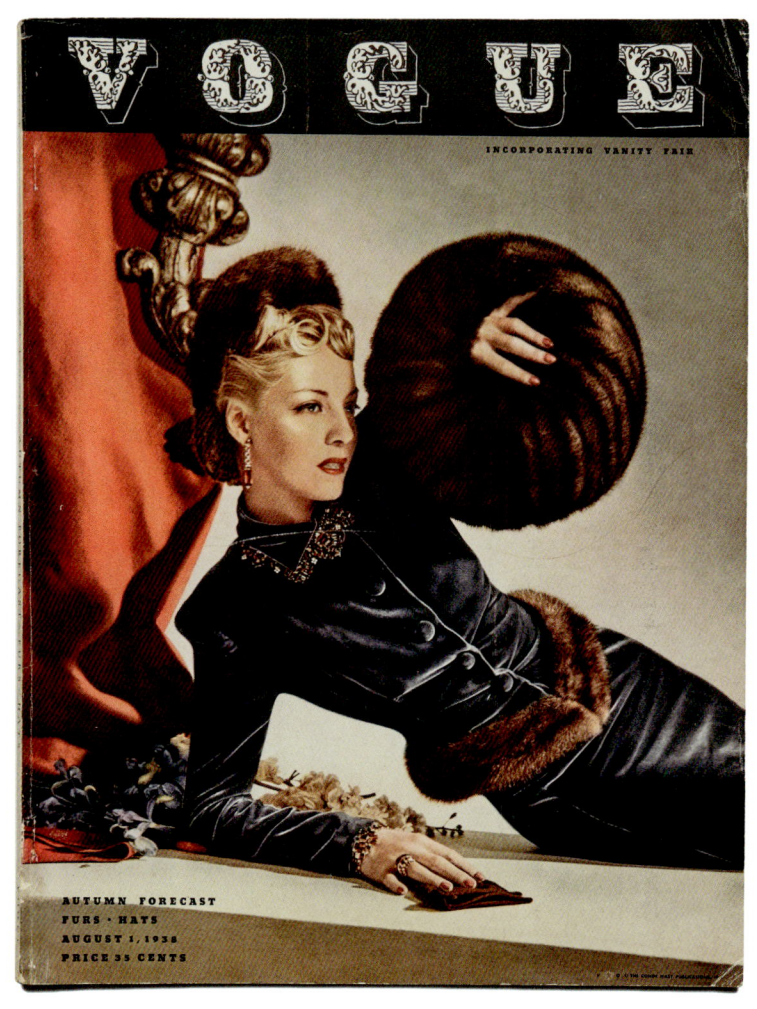

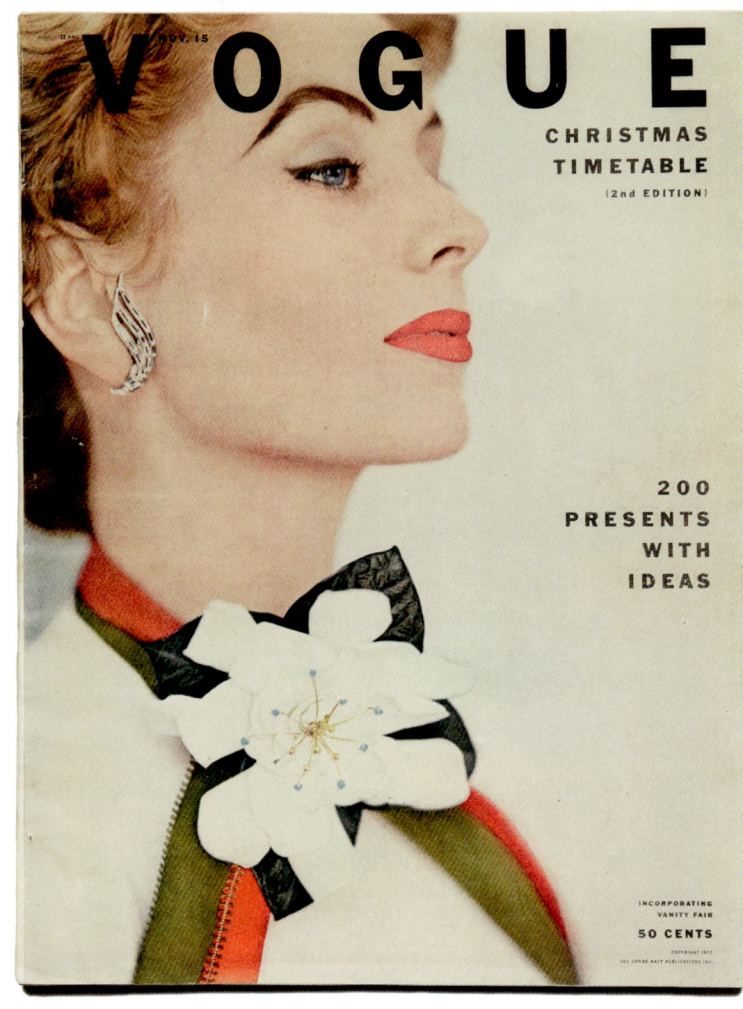

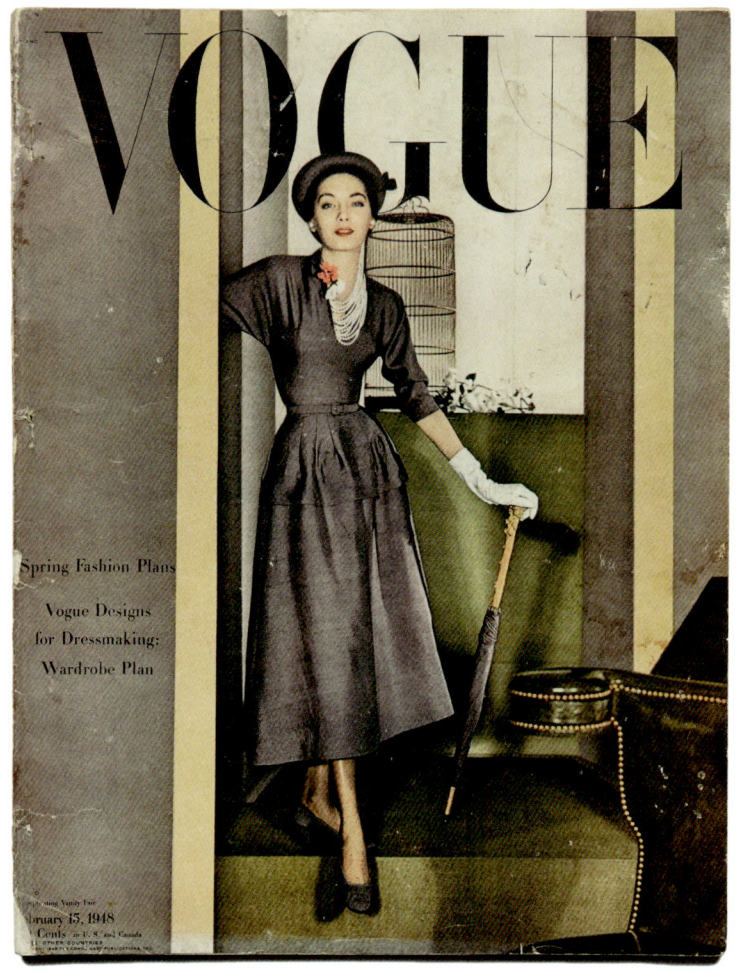

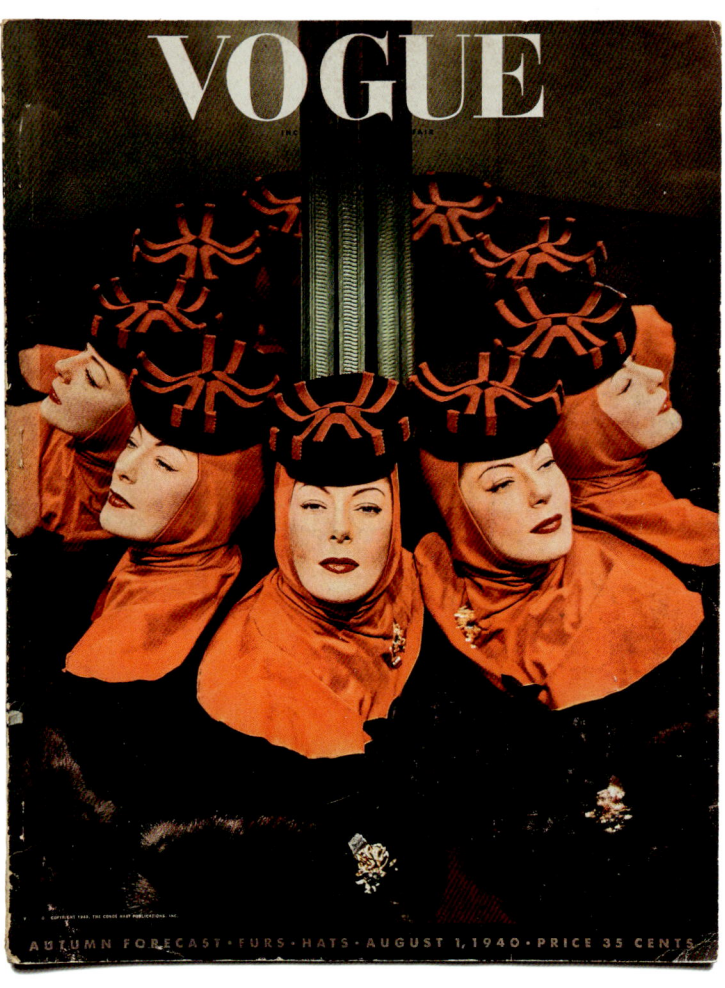

GEORGE PLATT LYNES

Born in East Orange,
New Jersey, 1907;
died in New York City,
1955

The work of George Platt Lynes represented the culmination of the classical and Surrealist-inspired aesthetic that prevailed in fashion photography throughout the 1930s and early '40s. It also marked the beginning of a period of rapid change.

The son of a clergyman, Lynes was blessed with exceptional good looks, which he used to full advantage. On a visit to France in 1925, he met writer Gertrude Stein, who introduced him to her circle of friends in the artistic and literary avant-garde. Lynes returned to Paris in 1928 with the hope of establishing himself as a writer. He took his first photographs that summer—of the writer and artist Jean Cocteau—and soon after, he abandoned writing in order to concentrate on photography.

Lynes's work was well received in both artistic and commercial circles; known for his striking Surrealist compositions, he enjoyed great popularity as a fashion photographer throughout the 1930s. Some of his contemporaries were less enthusiastic: Cecil Beaton (p. 30) once described Lynes's work as "wooden, imitative, and often ridiculous." By the end of the 1930s, Lynes's reputation had also extended beyond fashion photography. In 1933, he took up the post of official photographer for the New York City Ballet, which he held for over a decade, and his work was included in two exhibitions at the Museum of Modern Art, in 1936 and 1938.

The outbreak of World War II had a profound effect on the fashion industry. The poised, elegant femininity embodied in the fashion photography of the prewar years gave way to a fresher, more youthful image and a freer, less controlled photographic style. Lynes's neoclassical aesthetic began to look dated, and although he produced fashion work until the late 1940s, his creative energies were focused on the photography of male nudes. Not wanting to be remembered as a fashion photographer, Lynes destroyed most of his negatives and prints before his early death from cancer in 1955.

George Platt Lynes,
The Three Graces, n.d.

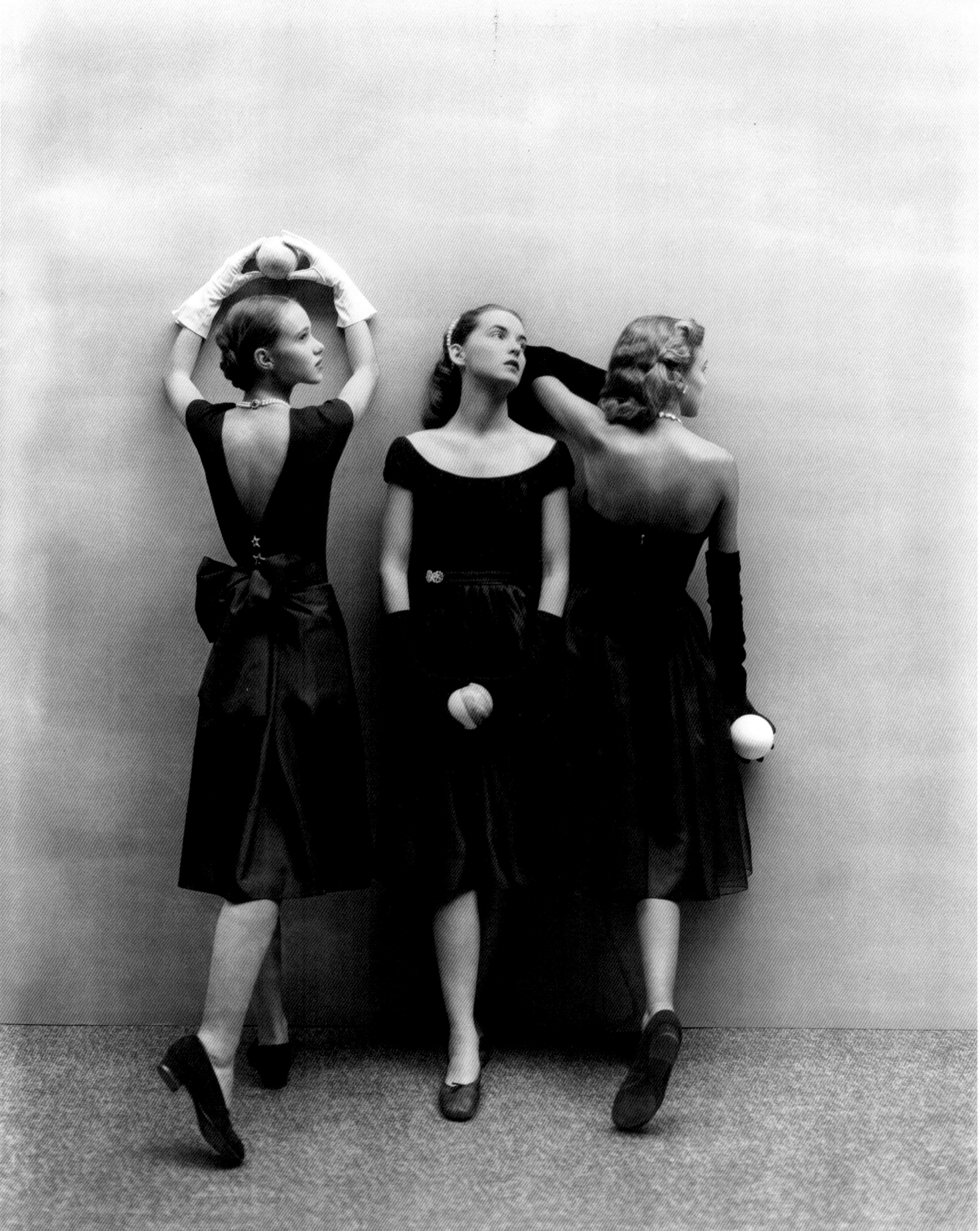

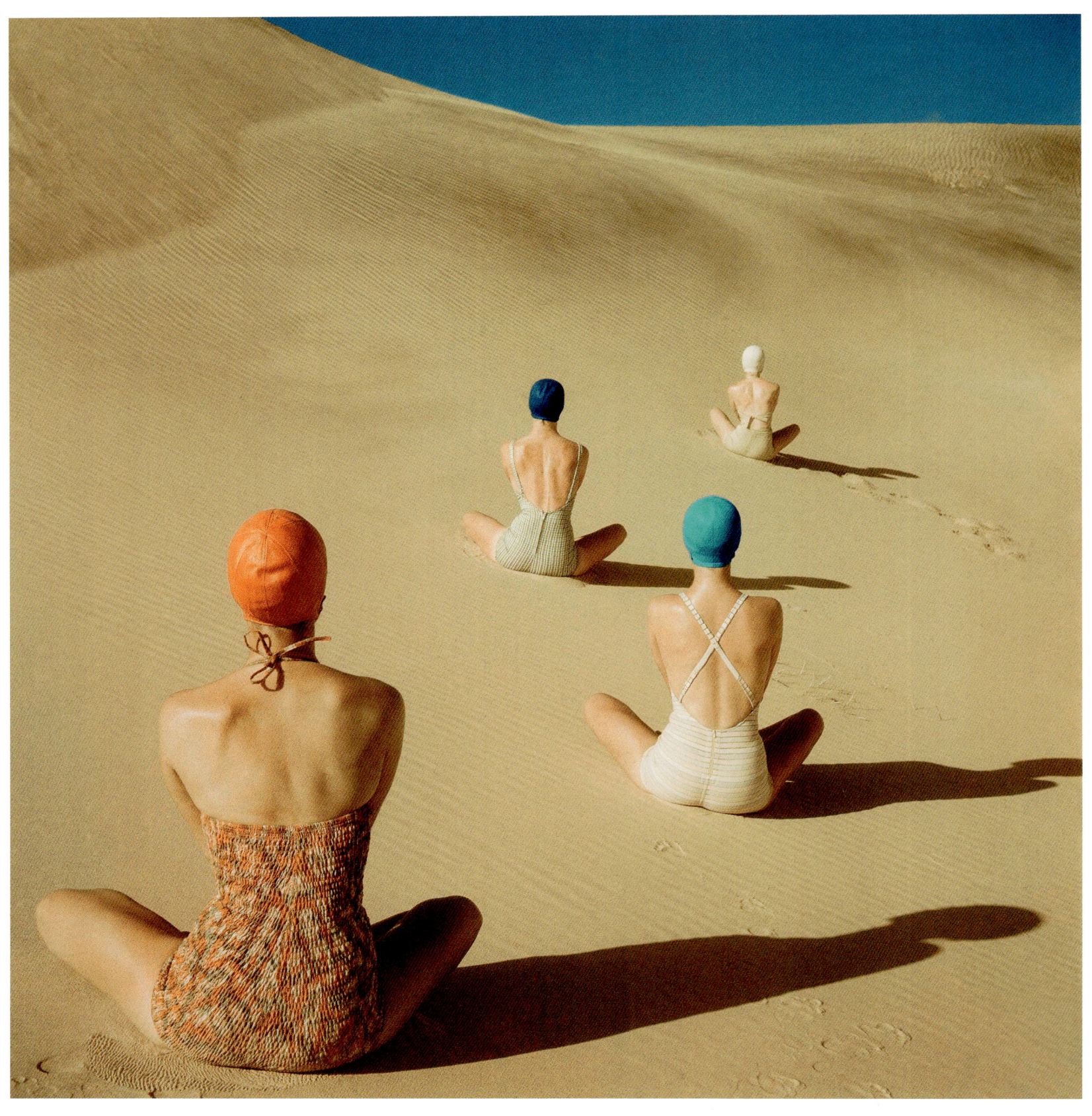

Clifford Coffin,
Back-Views of Four Seated Models in Swimsuits by Cole of California, Mabs, Caltex and Catalina, and Bathing Caps Shot on Location in California Sand Dunes, Vogue, 1949

Though Clifford Coffin always claimed that his magazine work was not art, his expert eye for color and design, as well as his intuitive understanding of fashion, set him apart from most of his peers. In 1939, while working as a financial analyst for Texaco in New York, Coffin decided that he wanted to become a photographer. He studied photography with George Platt Lynes (p. 62), who, along with Cecil Beaton (p. 30), was a key influence on his work. After showing portfolio after portfolio to an art director at *Vogue* (possibly Alexander Liberman), Coffin was finally offered unpaid work with the magazine in 1945.

Coffin's first images were mostly unremarkable studio portraits, but by 1947, the photographer, now working in London, was dominating the pages of British *Vogue*. The next few years were incredibly productive: between April 1946 and April 1948, Coffin undertook 364 fashion shoots and portrait sittings for British *Vogue*, including nearly all of the photographs for the June 1947 issue. He was renowned in the industry for his uncanny insight into the capricious world of postwar fashion, in which silhouettes changed constantly and hemlines rose and fell with every season. Unlike most of his contemporaries, Coffin took a near-obsessive interest in his models' clothes, hair, and makeup, often styling them himself. As one of his peers remarked, "He was the first photographer to actually *think* fashion, sometimes more than the fashion editors."

Recalled to New York in 1949, Coffin did much of his later work for American *Vogue*. His 1954 autumn couture series is considered to be the pinnacle of his later career, although his Jewel series, of evening dresses shot with a low shutter speed that reduced the dresses to abstract blurs of color, was rejected around the same time for being too experimental. His introduction of the ring light into fashion photography has had an enduring legacy: originally used by dentists to photograph patients' teeth, the ring light's clear illumination and distinctive shadow later featured in the work of photographers such as Helmut Newton (p. 134) and David Bailey (p. 122). Erratic, high-strung, and often difficult to work with, Coffin gave up fashion photography in the early 1960s. A disastrous burglary and fire at his New York studio in 1965 resulted in the loss of most of his personal work, including a large collection of male nudes.

Born in Salem, Illinois, 1913; died in Pasadena, California, 1972

CLIFFORD COFFIN

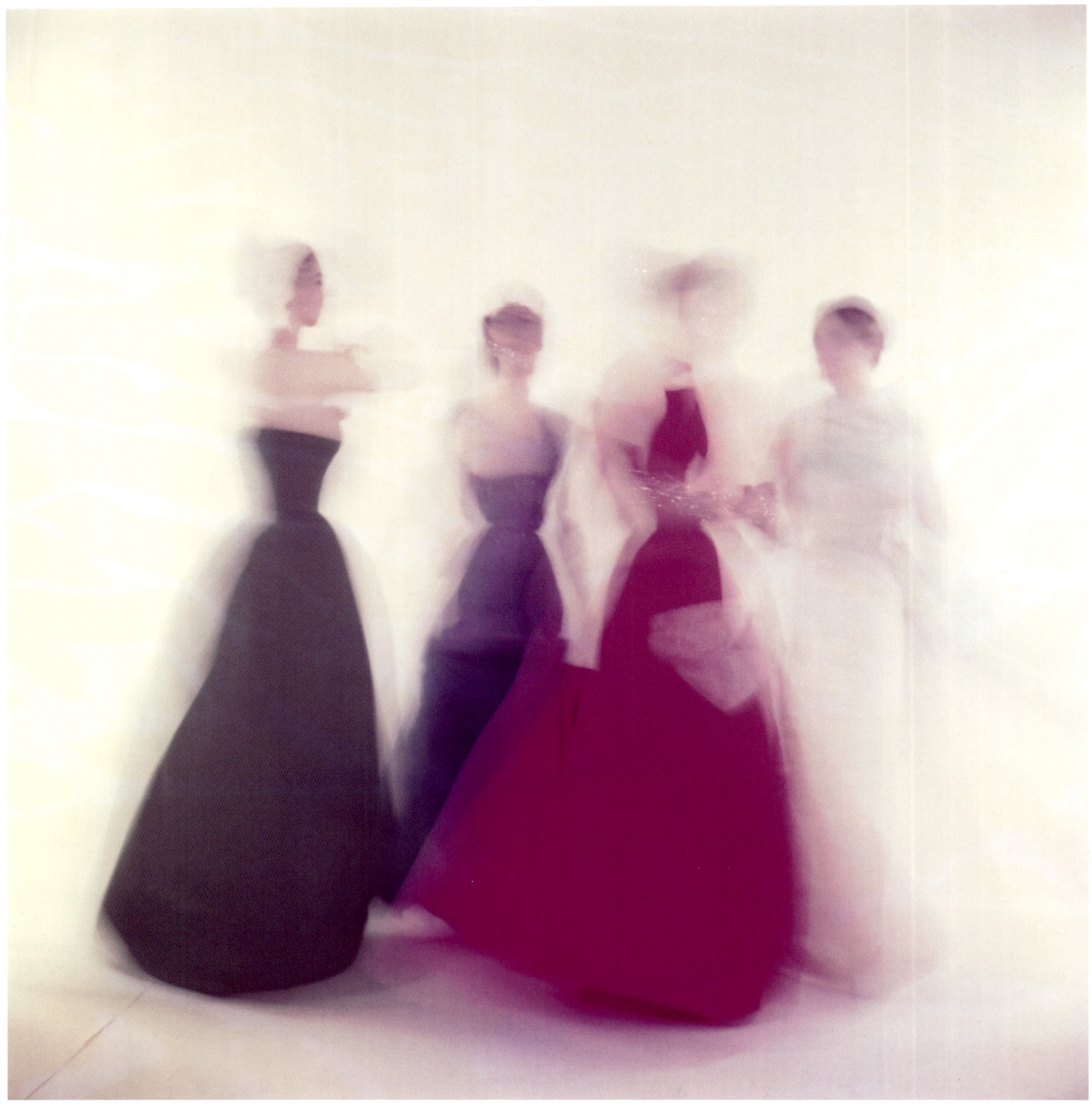

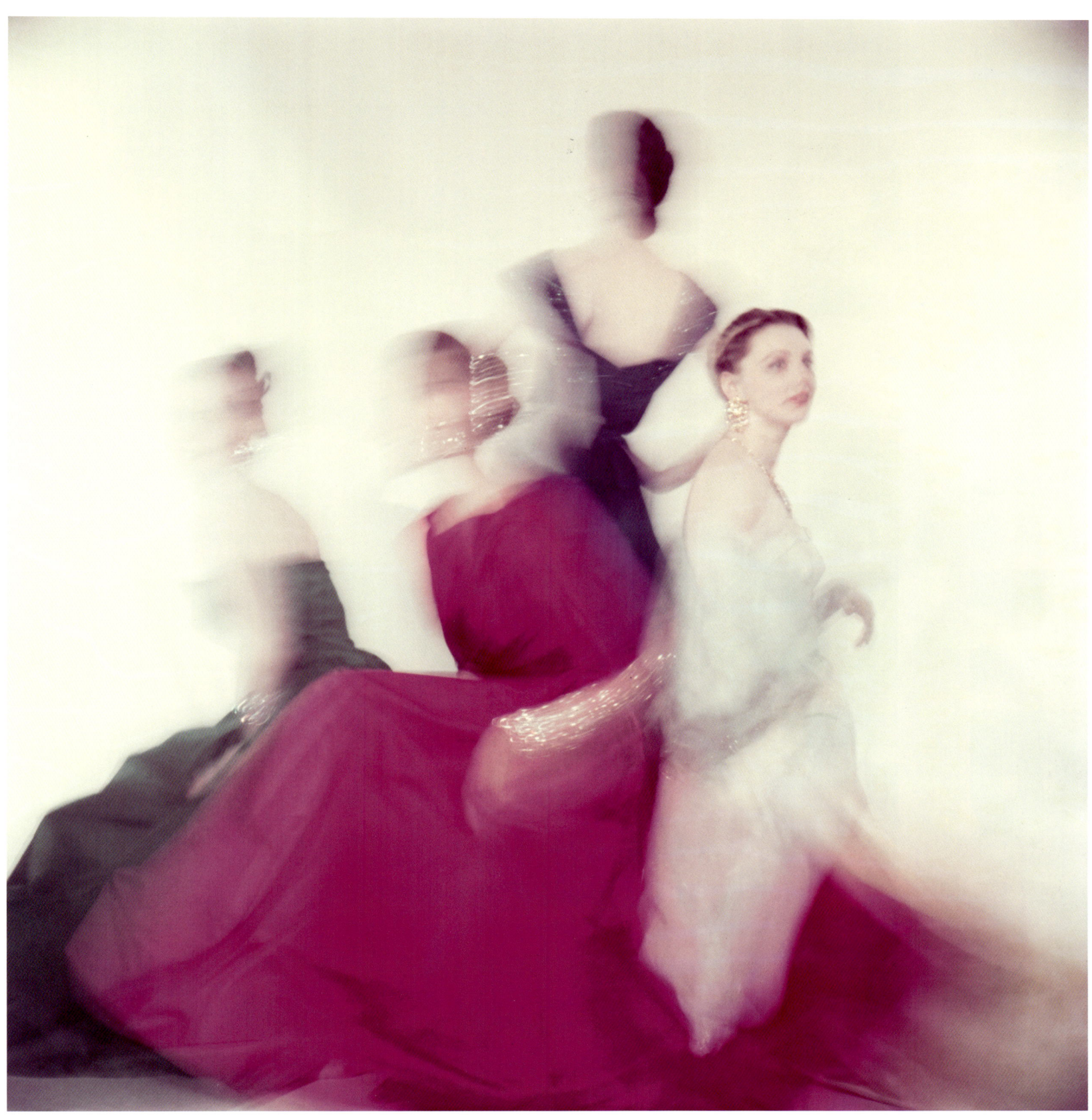

Left and above: Clifford Coffin,
Jewel series, *Vogue*, December 1, 1954

LOUISE DAHL-WOLFE

Born in San Francisco, 1895; died in Allendale, New Jersey, 1989

Along with *Harper's Bazaar* editors Diana Vreeland and Carmel Snow, Louise Dahl-Wolfe is often credited with changing the perception of American fashion, replacing the exclusivity of European couture with a younger, fresher style. Hired by *Harper's Bazaar* in 1936, she remained chief photographer at the magazine until 1948. Dahl-Wolfe studied painting at the San Francisco Institute of Art, and often described herself as a frustrated painter. "The camera may be a third eye, but it has its limitations—you realize that when you've had formal training in drawing and painting," she once said. "I envy the freedom my husband [painter and sculptor Meyer Wolfe] has with his beautiful drawings."

With a background in color theory and an innate feeling for natural light, Dahl-Wolfe was drawn to color photography, and when Kodachrome film became available in 1935, she seized the chance to work with it. Her color photographs were widely acclaimed— as Cecil Beaton wrote in 1975, hers were "the most controlled and exact of the early color plates"—and, along with art director Alexey Brodovitch and photographer Martin Munkácsi (p. 50), she revolutionized the look of *Harper's Bazaar*. Her photographs struck a balance between the formality of studio photography and the spontaneity of a snapshot—"between the elite artistry of European couture and the relaxed accessibility of a more democratic society," as photography critic Vicki Goldberg has written. Dahl-Wolfe was also one of the first fashion photographers to shoot extensively on location, and her postwar work made full use of the increased ease of international travel. The image of femininity that she created was distinctly modern: self-reliant and effortlessly chic, traveling the globe, stylishly clad in American ready-to-wear.

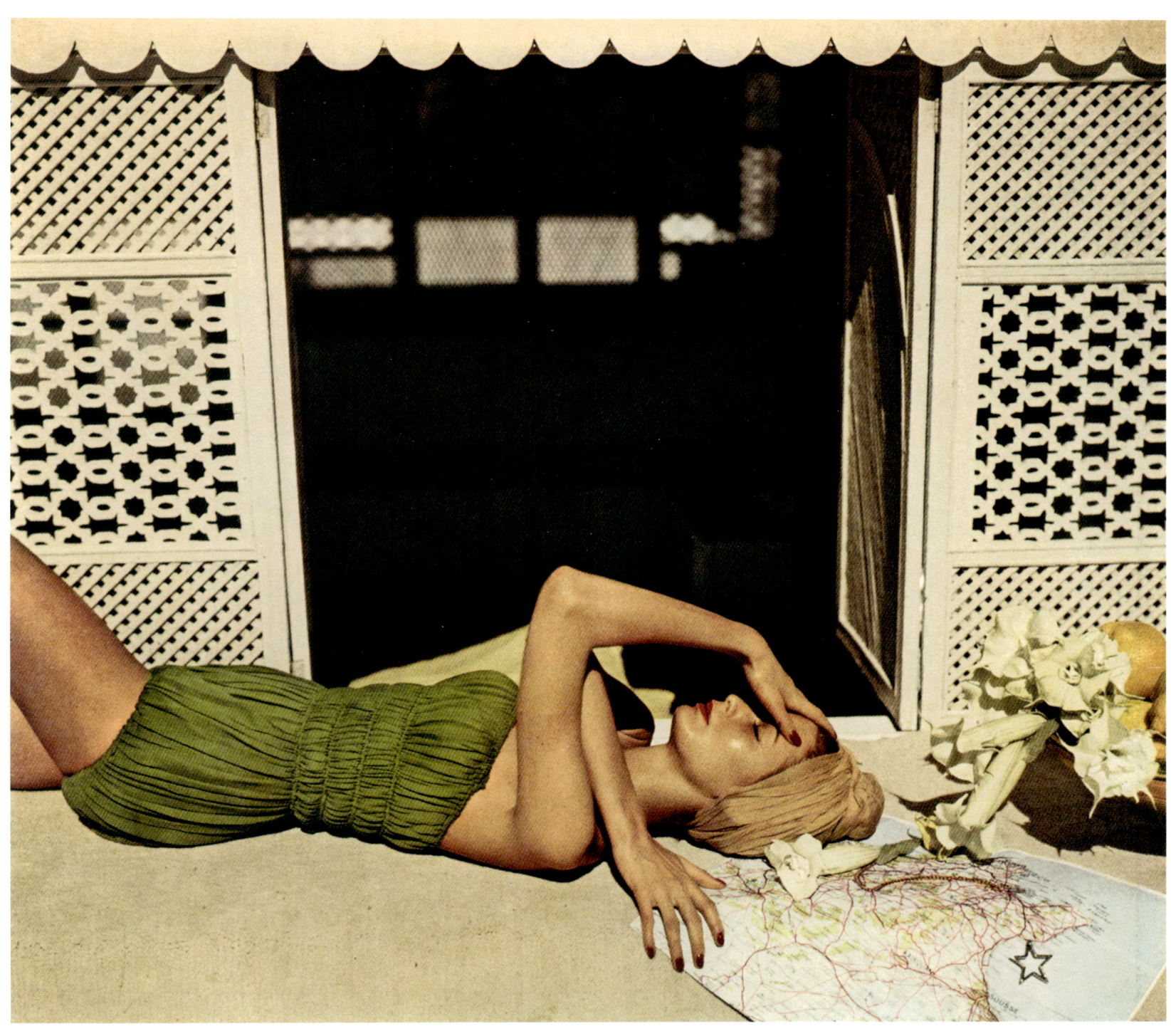

Louise Dahl-Wolfe,
Natalie Paine in Claire McCardell
Bathing Suit, Harper's Bazaar, 1950

IRVING PENN

Born in Plainfield,
New Jersey, 1917; died in
New York City, 2009

The highlight of Irving Penn's postwar fashion work (and, arguably, of his career) was his 1950 photographs of the Paris fall collections. Combining the structured clothing with the precise outline of the model's body, molding the two elements into a series of perfectly poised, almost architectural forms, these photographs were—as curator Martin Harrison has remarked —a melancholic summation of the history of fashion photography up to that point. Like the work of many of his contemporaries, including George Platt Lynes (p. 62), Penn's photographs evoked an image of femininity that was dying out; the polished hauteur that he captured would soon be replaced by a freer, less refined feminine ideal. But for a photographer whose first fashion pictures had been published only seven years earlier, Penn's 1950 series was a remarkable achievement.

Penn attended the Philadelphia Museum School of Industrial Art (now the University of the Arts) in hopes of becoming a painter. While still a student, he interned at *Harper's Bazaar* as an assistant to art director Alexey Brodovitch, taking up the post full-time in 1938. He went to work for art director Alexander Liberman at *Vogue* in 1943, where his austere, clean-lined photographs stood in sharp contrast to the more dynamic style that was increasingly in favor at *Harper's Bazaar*.

In 1950, Penn claimed confidently that the printed page was the ultimate destination for the modern photographer's work. Fourteen years later, he reversed this judgment, deeming the printed page a "dead end." Penn's skill as a fashion photographer was only one aspect of a remarkable and wide-ranging practice that included nudes, still lifes, ethnographic and travel photography, and portraiture—and although his career began with magazine work, it would end on the gallery wall. The last twenty years of his life were increasingly occupied with his personal work, as he experimented in the darkroom and returned to the painting that he had abandoned years earlier.

Penn also continued to work for *Vogue* until shortly before his death in 2009, as well as producing groundbreaking advertising work. His collaboration with Japanese designer Issey Miyake began in 1986 and lasted for thirteen years. Miyake considered Penn a sounding board for his creative vision, calling him "the one person who could look at my clothing, hear my voice, and answer me back through his own creation."

Irving Penn, *Lisa Fonssagrives-Penn
in a Balenciaga Mantle Coat, Vogue*, September 1, 1950
Following pages: Irving Penn, (left) *Model Wearing
Balenciaga Evening Dress and Cape, Vogue*, September 1, 1950;
(right) *Vogue*, September 1, 1947

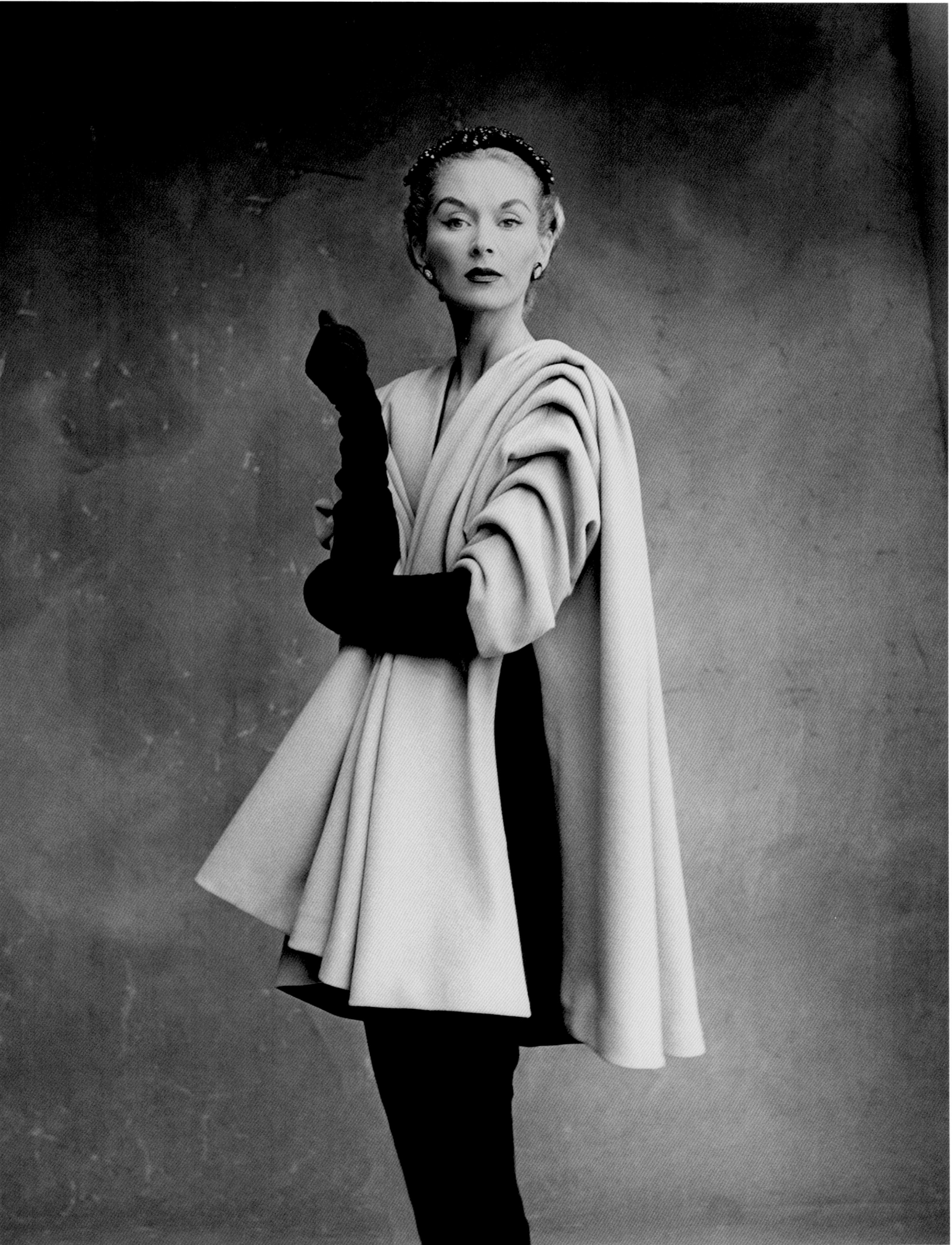

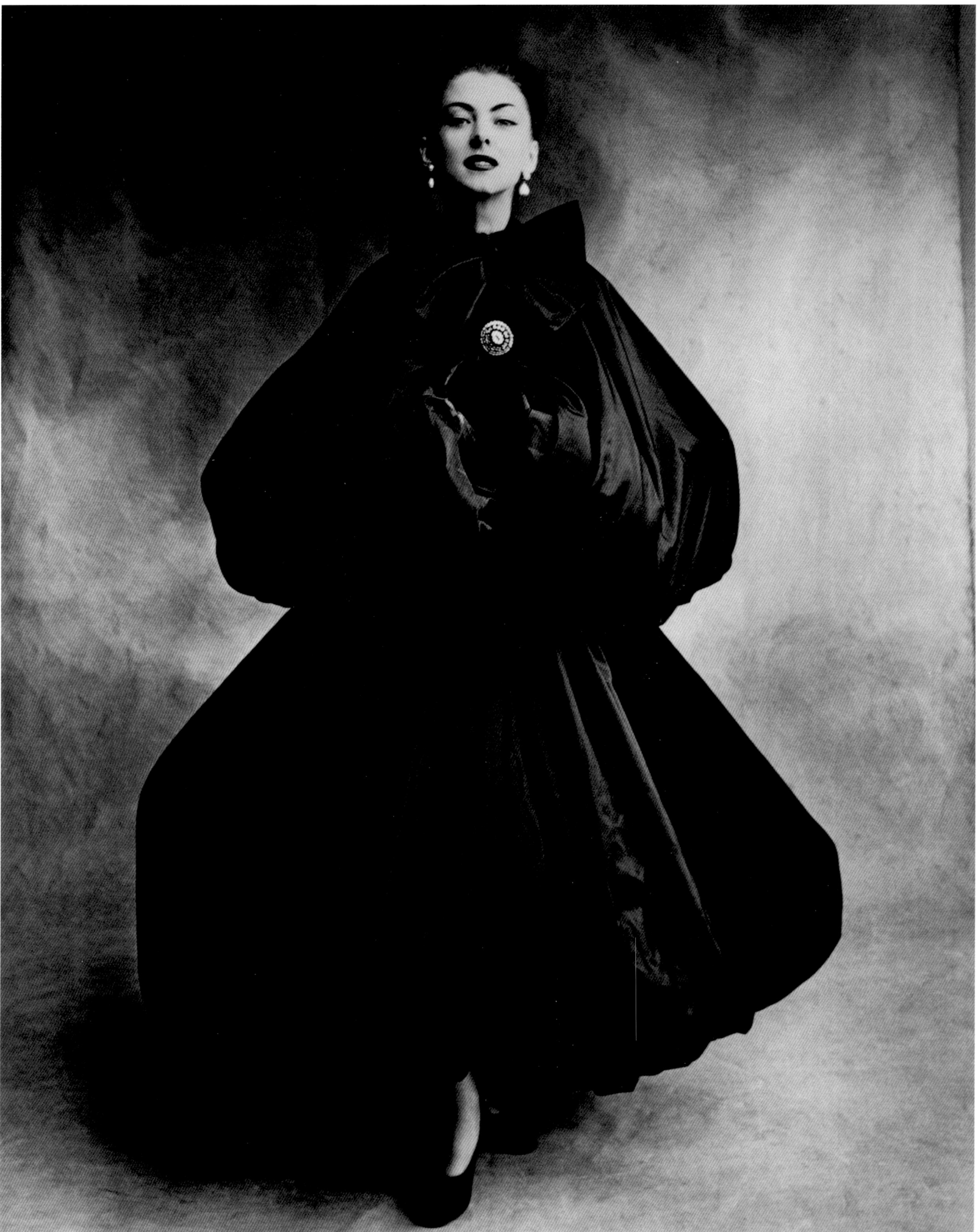

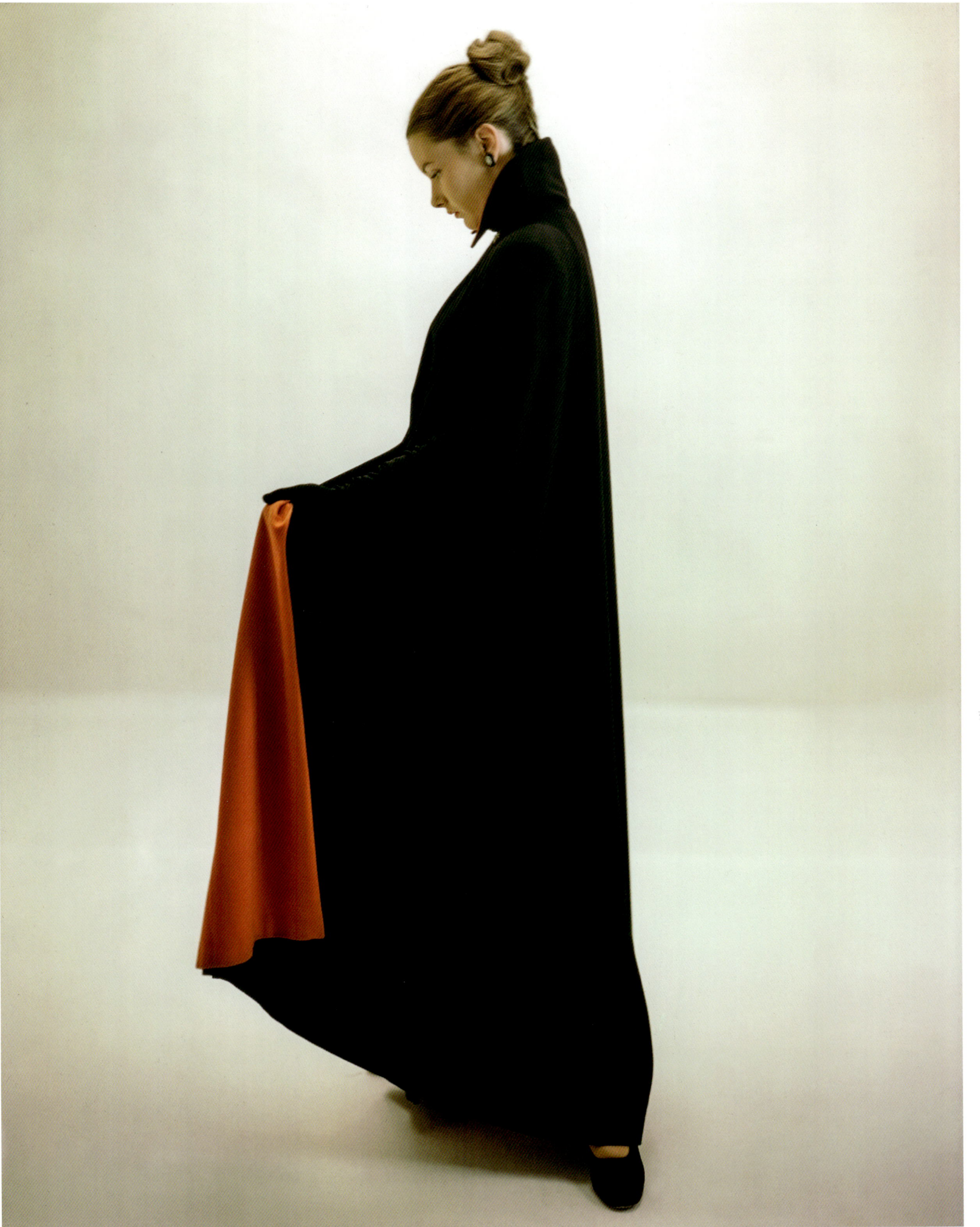

Erwin Blumenfeld's first few years as a fashion photographer were difficult ones. He was over forty and had been working in the womenswear trade since the age of sixteen, before he managed to get his work published in *Vogue*—only to be abruptly dropped within a year, as a result of creative differences with then-artistic director Dr. Mehemed Fehmy Agha. An offer of lucrative work in Paris for *Harper's Bazaar* was interrupted by the outbreak of World War II, and Blumenfeld and his family spent most of the following two years in a series of French internment camps.

Following his release in 1941, Blumenfeld returned to *Harper's Bazaar*, where the creative freedom he was afforded by Carmel Snow and Alexey Brodovitch allowed him to experiment with a range of studio and darkroom techniques, including the recently introduced Kodachrome color process. Blumenfeld, who had established a modest reputation as a photographic artist in the years between the wars, put his extensive darkroom experience to ingenious use, combining negative and positive images, sandwiching color negatives, even freezing developed film to produce crystals on the emulsion.

Blumenfeld's work at *Harper's Bazaar* brought him widespread acclaim and lucrative advertising contracts. He returned to *Vogue* in 1944, and, with the encouragement of the magazine's new art director, Alexander Liberman, pushed the Kodachrome process to its limits, using transparent layers of glass and cellophane to produce spectacular effects. His bold, eye-catching images, with their blocks of brilliant color, were ideal cover shots, and for over a decade, Blumenfeld photographed nearly every cover. When model Jean Patchett turned up for a photographic session on hairstyles, Blumenfeld decided (as he often did) to ignore the fashion editor's instructions and focus on her eye makeup instead. The resulting image—hand-colored by the *Vogue* art department—was one of the most celebrated of his career.

Born in Berlin, 1897; died in Rome, 1969

ERWIN BLUMEN-FELD

Erwin Blumenfeld,
Vogue, March 1, 1950

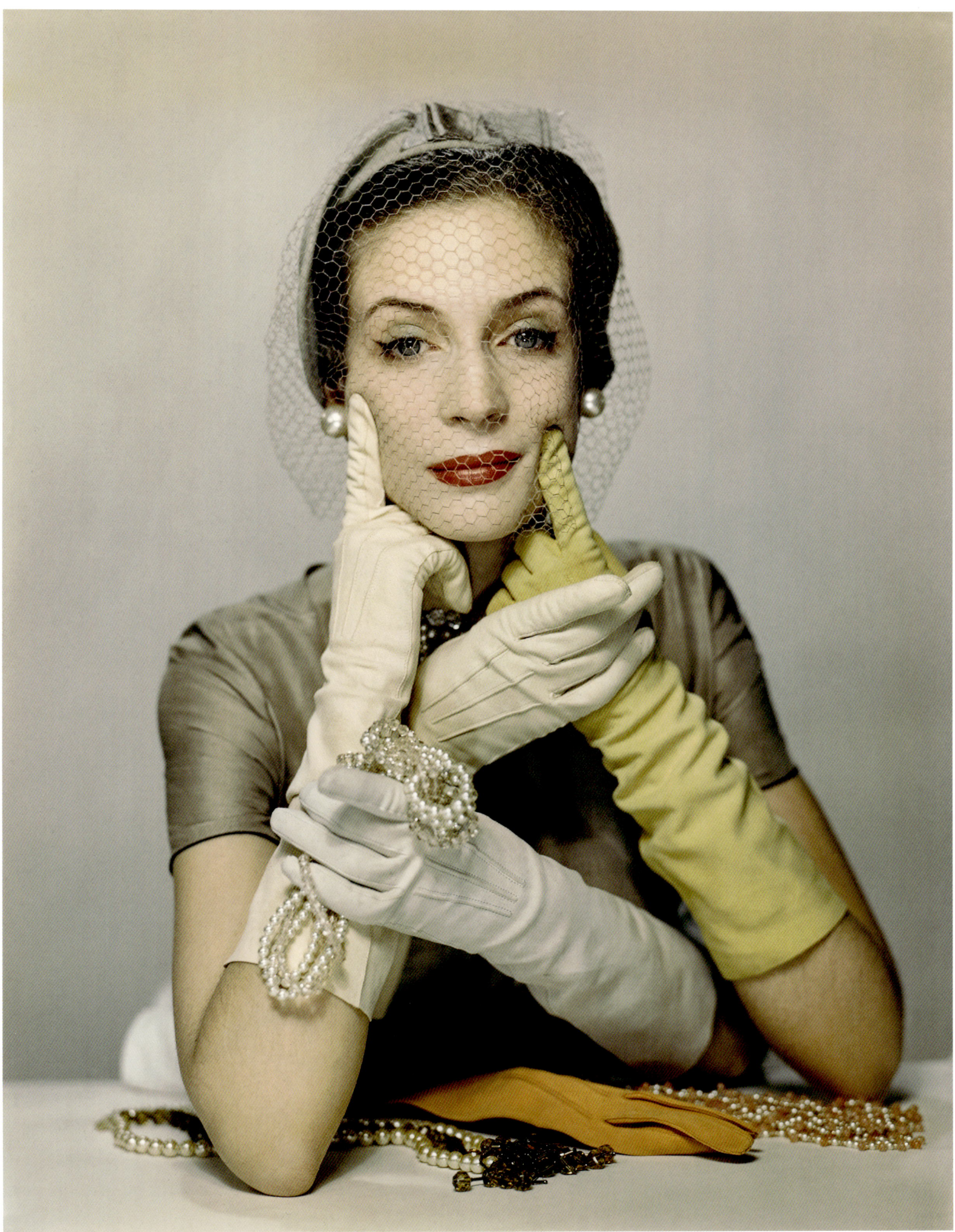

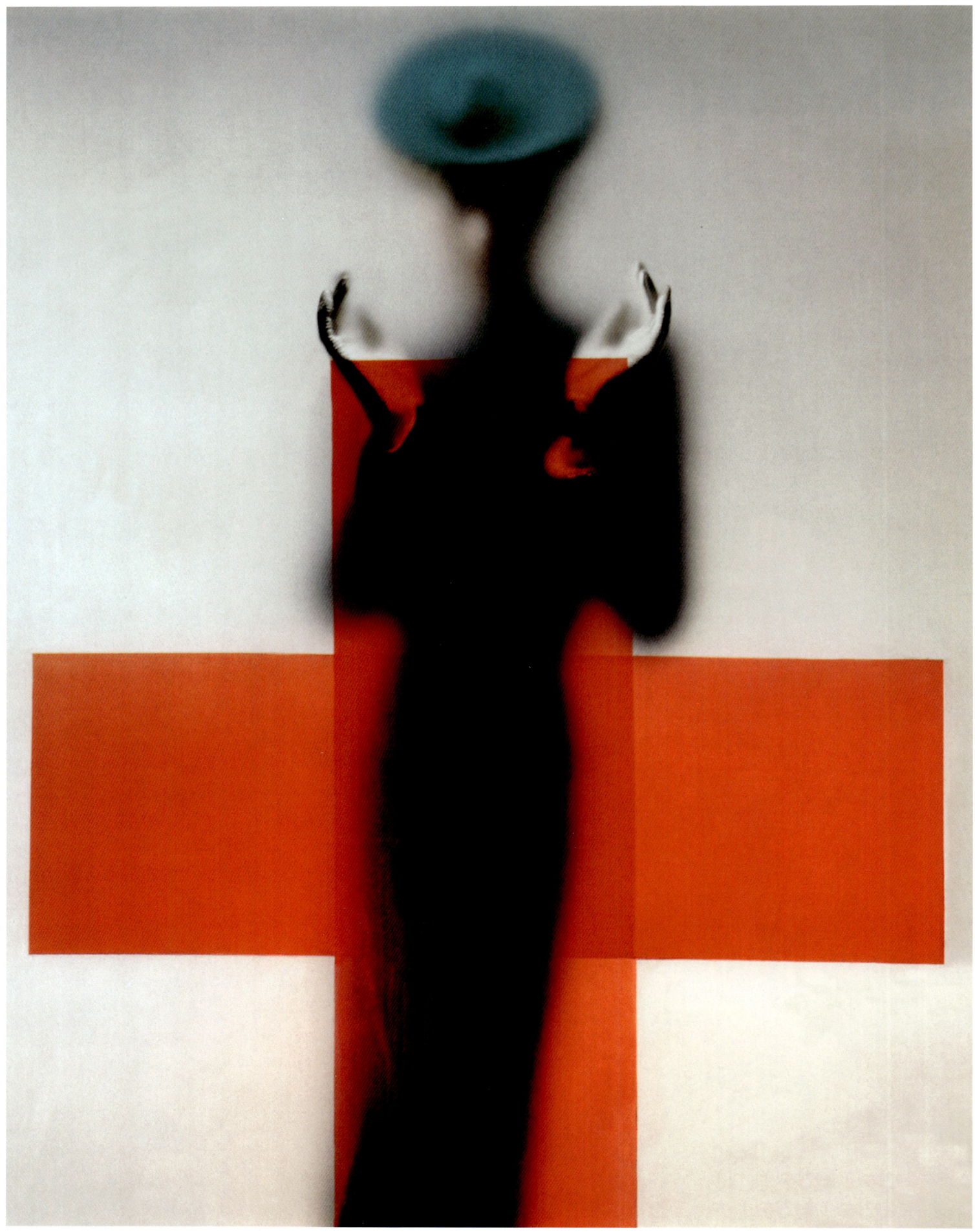

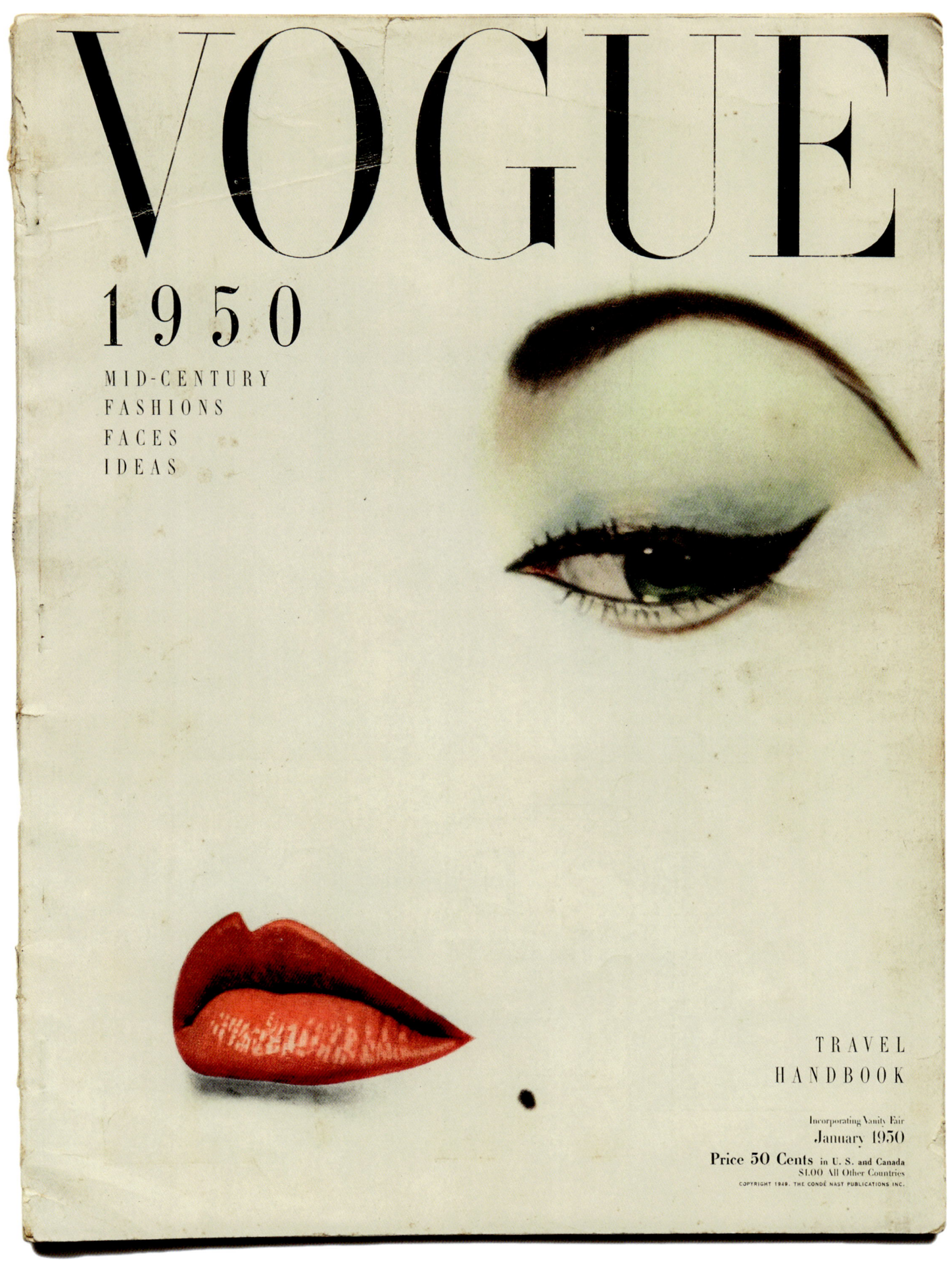

VOGUE

1950

MID-CENTURY
FASHIONS
FACES
IDEAS

TRAVEL
HANDBOOK

Incorporating Vanity Fair
January 1950

Price 50 Cents in U. S. and Canada
$1.00 All Other Countries

COPYRIGHT 1949. THE CONDÉ NAST PUBLICATIONS INC.

Erwin Blumenfeld, *Vogue* cover, January 1950
Left: Erwin Blumenfeld, *Vogue*, March 15, 1945

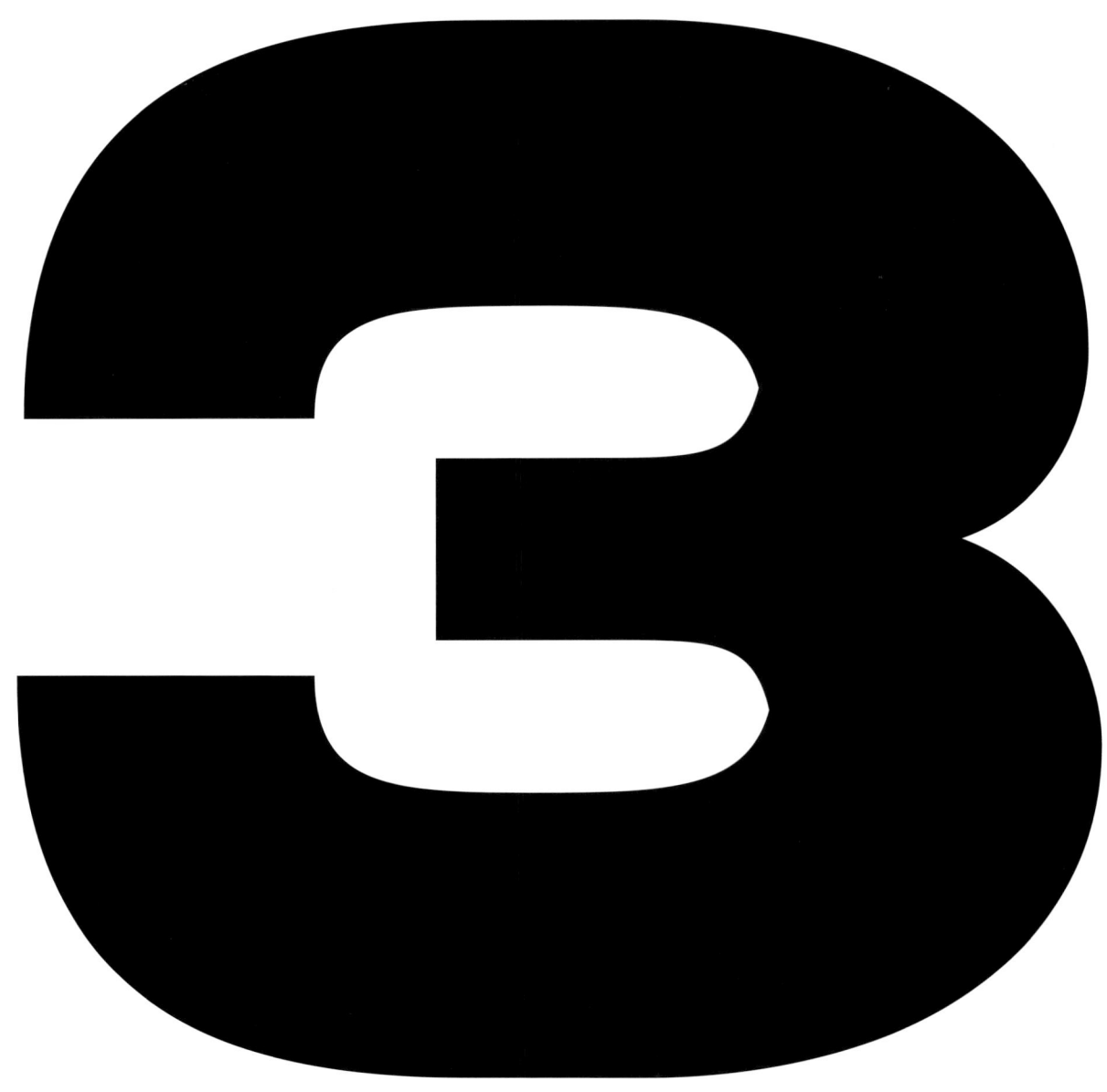

Norman Parkinson,
*After Van Dongen: Adéle Collins
in an Otto Lucas Toque*,
British *Vogue*, 1959

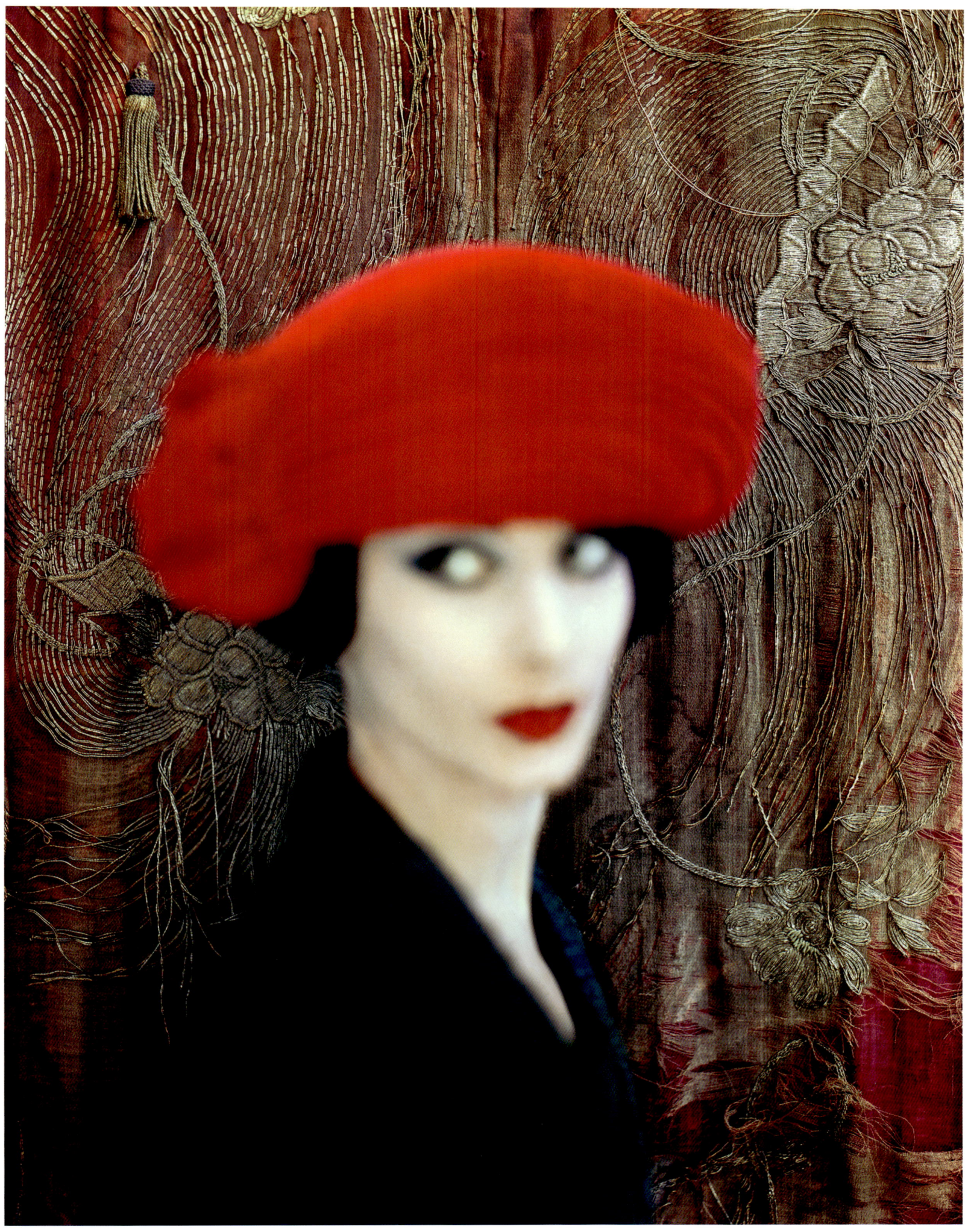

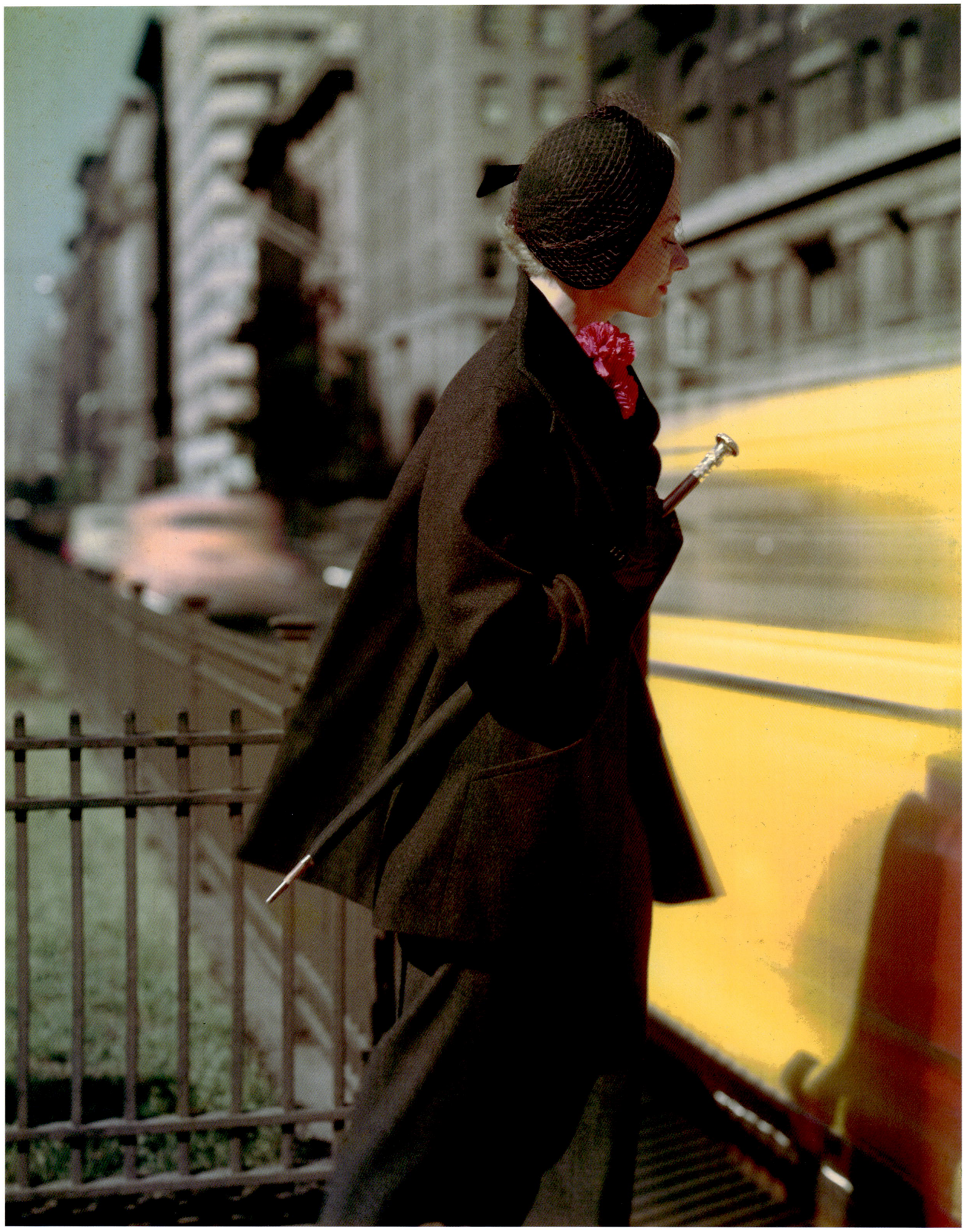

NORMAN PARKINSON

Born in London, 1913;
died in Singapore, 1990

In 1989, a year before Norman Parkinson's death, the National Portrait Gallery, London, proclaimed him "the doyen of British fashion photography." His remarkable range and flexibility as a photographer marked a career that spanned seven decades, including almost forty years with *Vogue*. Born Ronald Parkinson Smith, he learned the craft of photography as an apprentice to court photographers Speaight and Sons, and opened his own portrait studio on Dover Street in London in 1934. Here, he reinvented himself as Norman Parkinson or "Parks"—a wealthy eccentric with a singular dress sense and a flamboyant personality.

Parkinson's first fashion photographs were taken in 1935 for *Harper's Bazaar*, but by 1941, he had left for British *Vogue*. Initially reluctant to shoot on location, Parkinson later embraced the realist style of photographers such as Martin Munkácsi (p. 50) and Toni Frissell (p. 52), drawing on his own affection for the English countryside. As he remarked in 1983, "I wanted [women] out in the fields jumping over the haycocks—I did not think they needed their knees bolted together." This distinctively English aesthetic stood in sharp contrast to the more edgy, urban photographs that he shot for American *Vogue* between 1949 and 1955. His third wife, Wenda Rogerson, was a frequent model in his work from the late 1940s to the early '50s, and she features in some of his best pictures from this period.

Following the expiry of his contract with *Vogue* in 1959, Parkinson went to work as an associate editor and photographer for *Queen* magazine. Some of Parkinson's most memorable work was produced over the next five years, during which he also oversaw *Queen*'s transformation from staid society magazine into an influential fashion glossy. By this time, Parkinson was attracting highly paid advertising commissions alongside his editorial work, and was regarded as one of the top advertising photographers in the world. Parkinson returned to *Vogue* in 1964, where he remained on contract until 1978, reinventing himself yet again as a celebrity and royal portraitist. He spent the final decade of his career doing location work for the society magazine *Town & Country*, dying in 1990 of a cerebral hemorrhage while on assignment in Malaysia.

Norman Parkinson,
*Traffic: Lisa Fonssagrives on
Park Avenue, New York*, Vogue, 1949

LILLIAN BASSMAN

Before taking up fashion photography, Lillian Bassman worked as a graphic designer and assistant to art director Alexey Brodovitch at *Harper's Bazaar*. As the art director for the short-lived *Junior Bazaar*, Bassman gave a young Richard Avedon (p. 94) some of his first assignments. Bassman learned to print before she learned to photograph; experimenting with George Hoyningen-Huene's (p. 42) negatives in the darkroom at *Harper's Bazaar*, she developed innovative techniques (such as printing through tissue paper to achieve soft-focus effects) that were adopted by her contemporaries—and which she went on to use when she began taking her own fashion photographs, in the mid-1940s. Alongside her husband, photographer Paul Himmel, Bassman embraced an experimental approach to picture-making, and high-contrast, painterly images became her signature.

Bassman was a specialist in the photography of lingerie. Early on, she worked alone with her models in domestic settings, creating a relaxed environment free of the sexual tension models often felt when working with male photographers. Her serene, sensual visual language evoked "a woman's experience of undressing" and marked a fundamental shift away from the bland, sexless images traditionally used to advertise undergarments. As Bassman herself remarked in an interview with the *New Yorker* in 2006, "I think my contribution to the genre has been to photograph fashion with a woman's eye for a woman's intimate feelings."

Born in Brooklyn, 1917; died in New York City, 2012

Lillian Bassman,
Betty Threat, New York, 1957; reinterpreted 1994

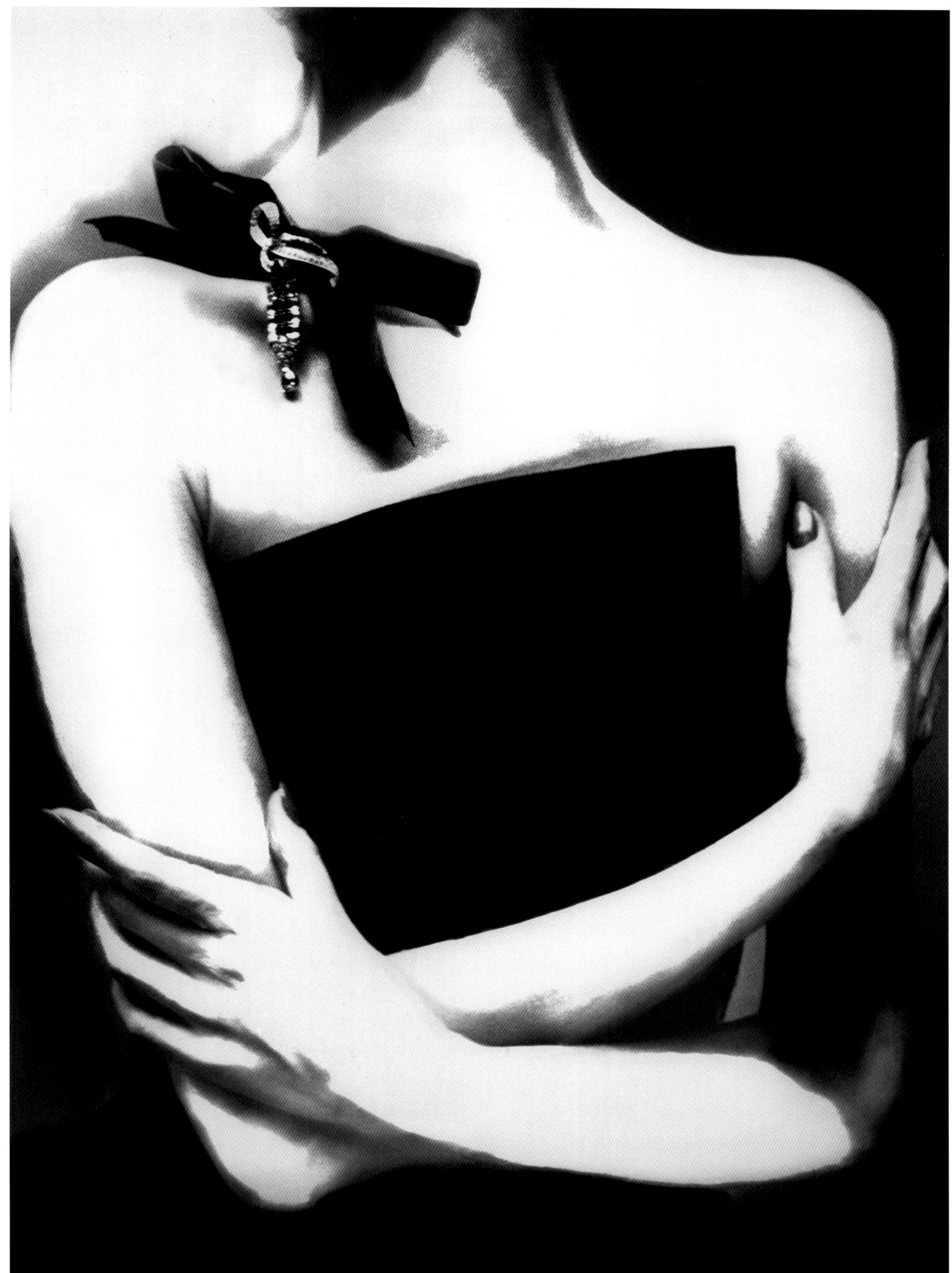

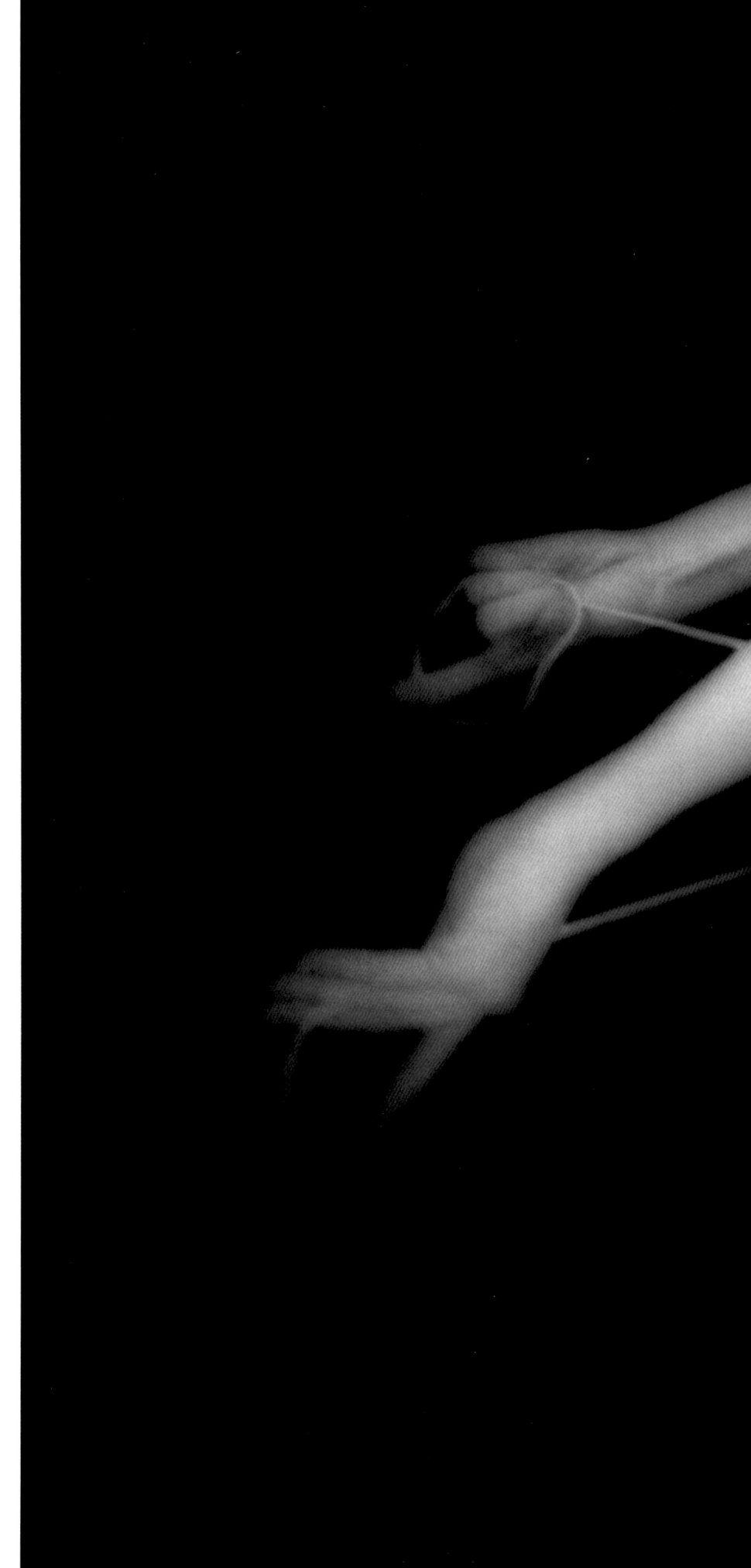

Lillian Bassman,
"It's a Cinch," Carmen, Merry Widow by Warner's, 1951;
alternate version published in *Harper's Bazaar*,
September 1951

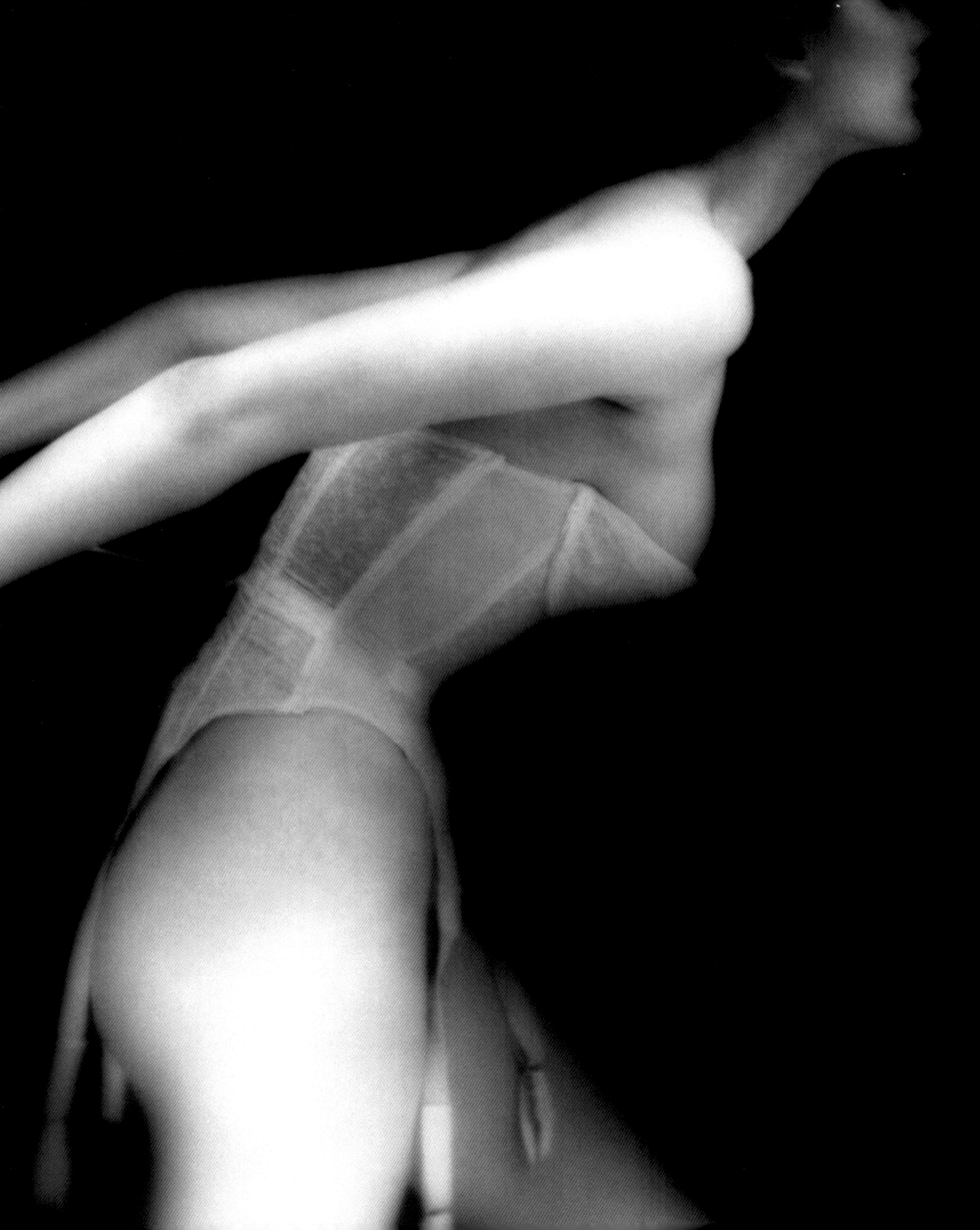

HENRY CLARKE

Born in Los Angeles,
1917; died in Le Cannet,
France, 1996

As the French fashion industry began to recover in the years following World War II, photographers began to return as well. In February 1949, at age thirty-one, American Henry Clarke made the bold decision to move to Paris, where he quickly found work photographing the collections of designers Jacques Fath, Edward Molyneux, and Jean Dessès. Before the year was out, he was publishing his work in *Femina*, British *Harper's Bazaar*, and *L'Album de Figaro*; in 1951, he was offered an exclusive contract with *Vogue Paris*, where he remained for the next twenty years.

Clarke had been introduced to fashion while working at Saks Fifth Avenue in Beverly Hills as a teenager. Relocating to New York at the end of World War II, Clarke was employed as a photographic set dresser at *Vogue*, working alongside the likes of Cecil Beaton (p. 30), Irving Penn (p. 70), and Horst P. Horst (p. 58). It was in the *Vogue* studios that Clarke learned how to take pictures, observing photographers during the day, staying late in the studios to practice his craft, and attending classes with Alexey Brodovitch. His first fashion photographs were published in 1948—one year before he moved to Paris—in a short-lived publication called *Kaleidoscope of American Fashion*.

Clarke was given a great deal of creative freedom at *Vogue*, choosing the locations, accessories, mise-en-scène, and lighting of his shoots. Clarke's signature style—most evident in his black-and-white work of the 1950s—combines the elegance and sophistication of postwar French couture with a keen awareness of the changing role of women in society. His models may have been perfectly turned out, carefully coiffed, and made-up, but they were also independent and in control; when men appear in his images, it is almost always in the background. Shot at dawn on the banks of the Seine, Clarke's 1954 photograph sets the model's spirited gesture against the more passive pose of her male companion.

Henry Clarke,
Dorian Leigh in Jean Dessès, 1954

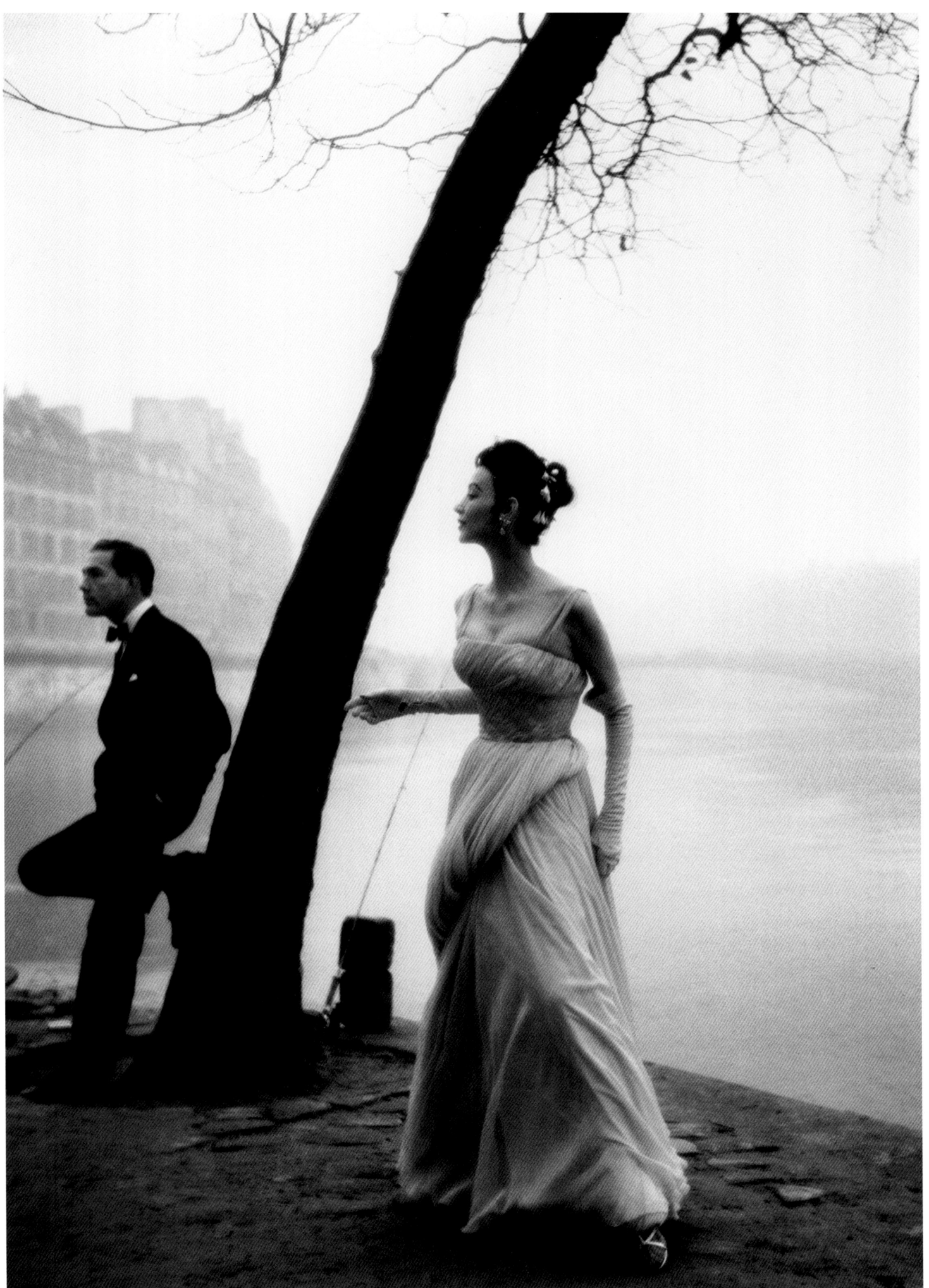

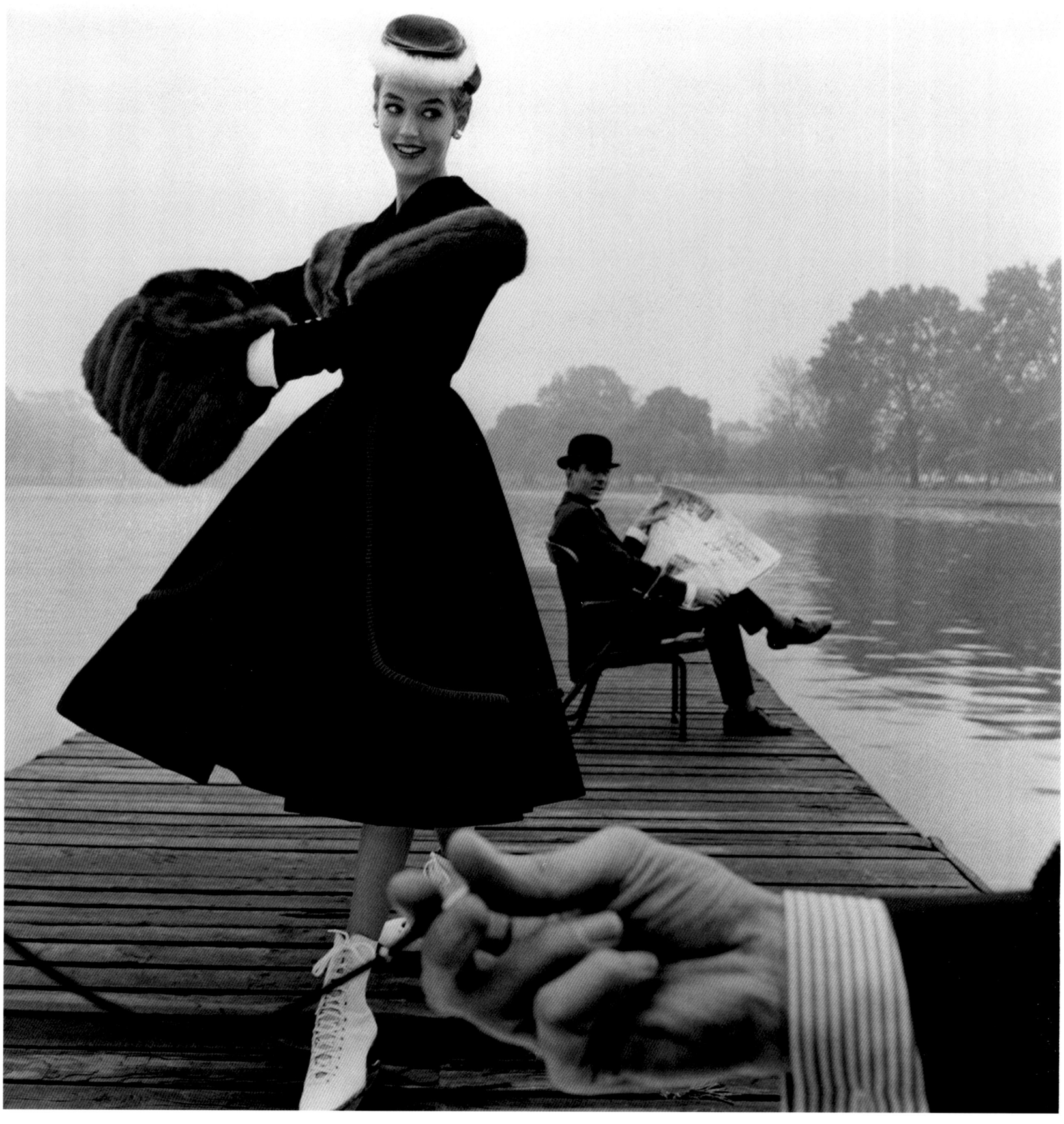

Born in Edmonton,
England, 1907; died in
London, 1966

Described as a "modest genius," John French specialized in the glamorous, ladylike look that was characteristic of postwar fashion. First introduced to photography in the 1930s, French established his own studio in 1948. By the 1950s, his advertising and editorial work was featured regularly in a wide range of English newspapers.

Known for his professionalism and attention to detail, French paid close attention to every element of the model's pose, right down to the position of hands, fingers, and even eyes. Though his models were often photographed in inexpensive ready-to-wear fashions, French styled the outfits to look immaculate, adjusting the shapes with carefully concealed clips, smoothing hemlines with lead weights, and creating the illusion of movement by pulling skirts out with invisible threads. Felicity Green, an assistant editor at the *Daily Mirror* at the time, remarked that "advertising agencies loved his ability to make a three-guinea dress look like a million dollars." When one of French's photographs appeared in the early edition of a national newspaper, the garment in question usually sold out within a few hours.

French was one of the first fashion photographers to use bounced light, surrounding the model with reflectors to create a soft, almost shadowless illumination that was flattering to skin and fabric. He also preferred to work with natural light and a medium-format Rolleiflex camera, rather than the more conventional studio setup of an 8-by-10 plate camera and tungsten lighting. French continued working until the 1960s, launching the careers of David Bailey (p. 122) and Terence Donovan, both of whom worked for him as assistants.

JOHN FRENCH

John French,
Skater in a Digby Morton Coat, London, 1955

GORDON PARKS

Born in Fort Scott, Kansas, 1912; died in New York City, 2006

Gordon Parks's life was marked by a long list of groundbreaking achievements. He was the only black photographer to shoot for the Farm Security Administration, the first black staff photographer for *Life* and *Vogue* magazines, and, in 1969, the first African American filmmaker to direct a mainstream Hollywood motion picture, *The Learning Tree*.

Although his powerful social documentary work has been his greatest legacy, Parks began his career in fashion photography. He learned his craft leafing through magazines—including copies of *Vogue*—that had been left behind on the passenger train between Chicago and Seattle, where he worked as a porter and car waiter: "Along with its fashion pages I studied the names of its famous photographers —Steichen, Blumenfeld, Horst, Beaton, Hoyningen-Huene, thinking meanwhile that my own name could look quite natural among them."

Soon after buying his first camera in 1937, Parks convinced the owners of the Frank Murphy fashion store in St. Paul, Missouri, to let him photograph some dresses. He managed to produce a single perfect shot and was hired again. Shortly after, he relocated to Chicago and established a successful business as a society portraitist. It was there, amid the grinding poverty of Chicago's South Side, that he began to take an interest in photojournalism, eventually securing an apprenticeship with the Farm Security Administration in 1942. His talent blossomed under the tutelage of photography project head Roy Stryker, and in 1943, Parks approached *Harper's Bazaar* art director Alexey Brodovitch seeking work at the magazine, only to be turned down because the Hearst corporation had a policy against hiring African Americans. At Condé Nast, Alexander Liberman was more receptive, and Parks was soon shooting for *Glamour* and *Vogue*.

Parks's fashion photography was spontaneous and inventive, capturing the intensity of city life with a unique sensibility that married documentary realism and soft romanticism. He continued to freelance for *Vogue* until the early 1960s, although by 1948, his work for *Life* magazine had begun to take precedence. Hired on the strength of his reputation as a fashion photographer, Parks soon proved himself to be a master of the photo-essay form. For the next twenty years, his work for *Life* would lay bare the harsh realities of racism and segregation in the United States. Reflecting on the difference between documentary and fashion photography, he remarked, "In one lay the responsibility to capture a prevailing mood, while in the other was the obligation to create a mood."

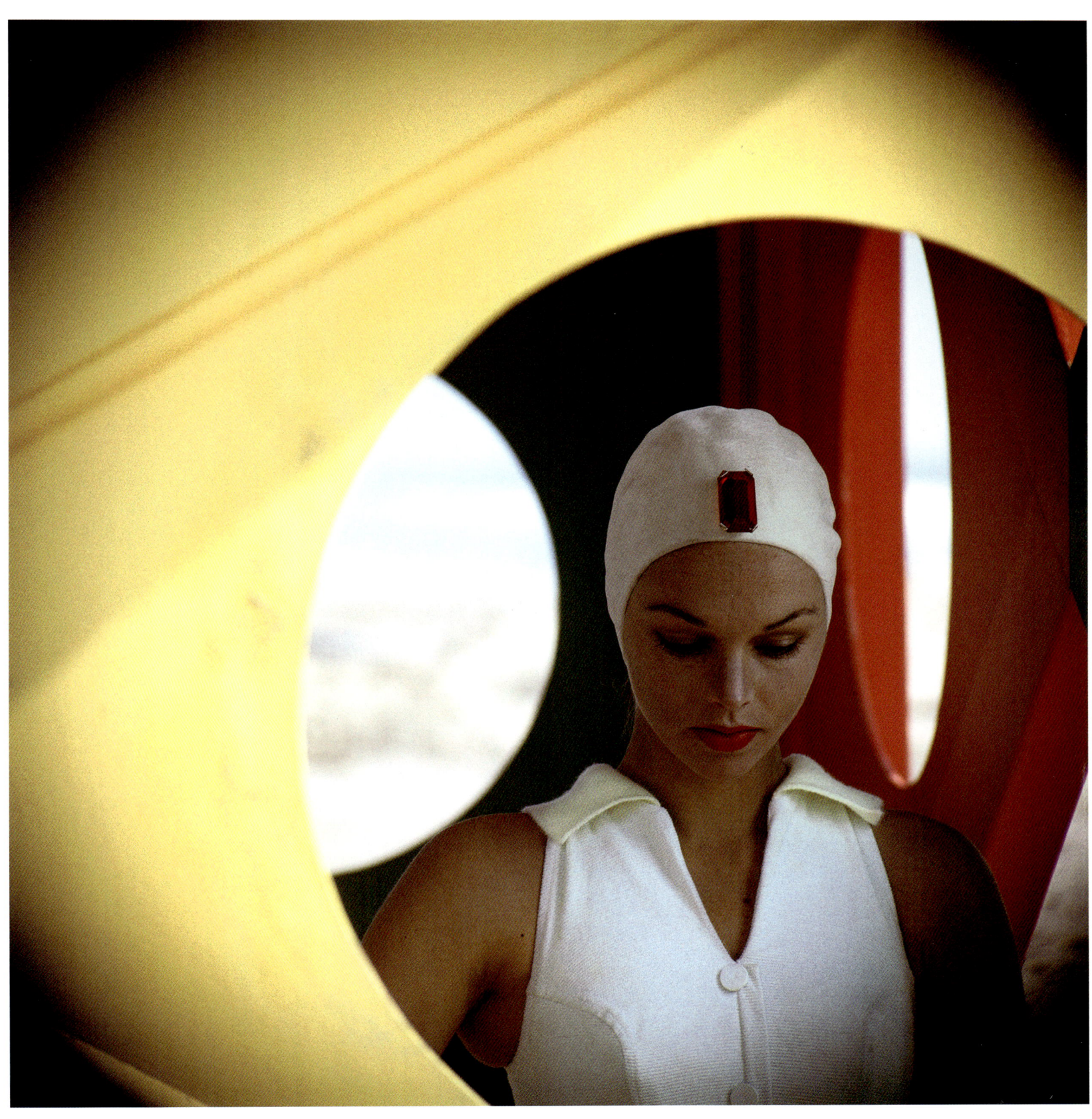

Gordon Parks, *Jeweled Cap, Malibu, California*, 1958
Following pages: Gordon Parks,
James Galanos Fashion, Hollywood, California, 1961

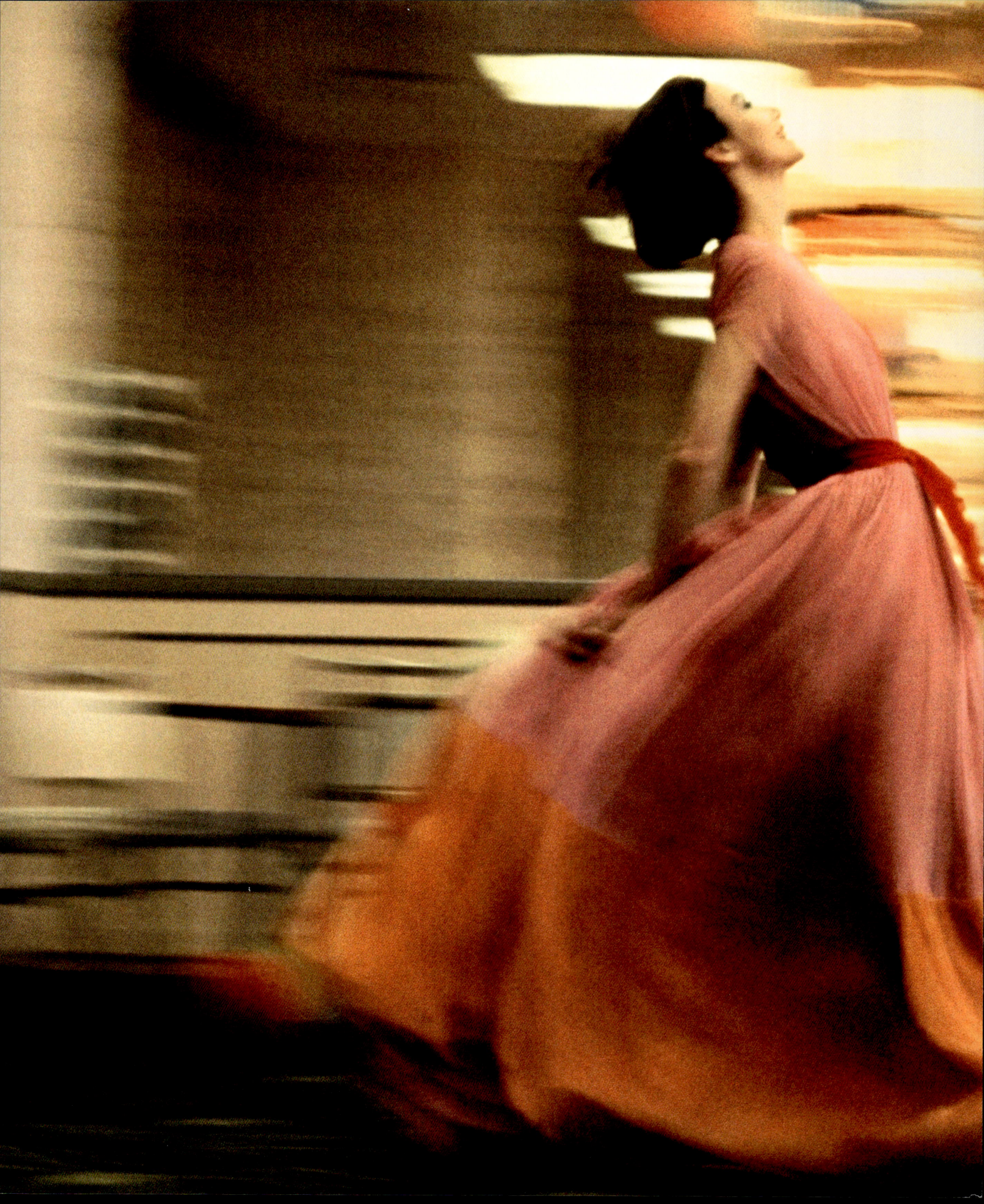

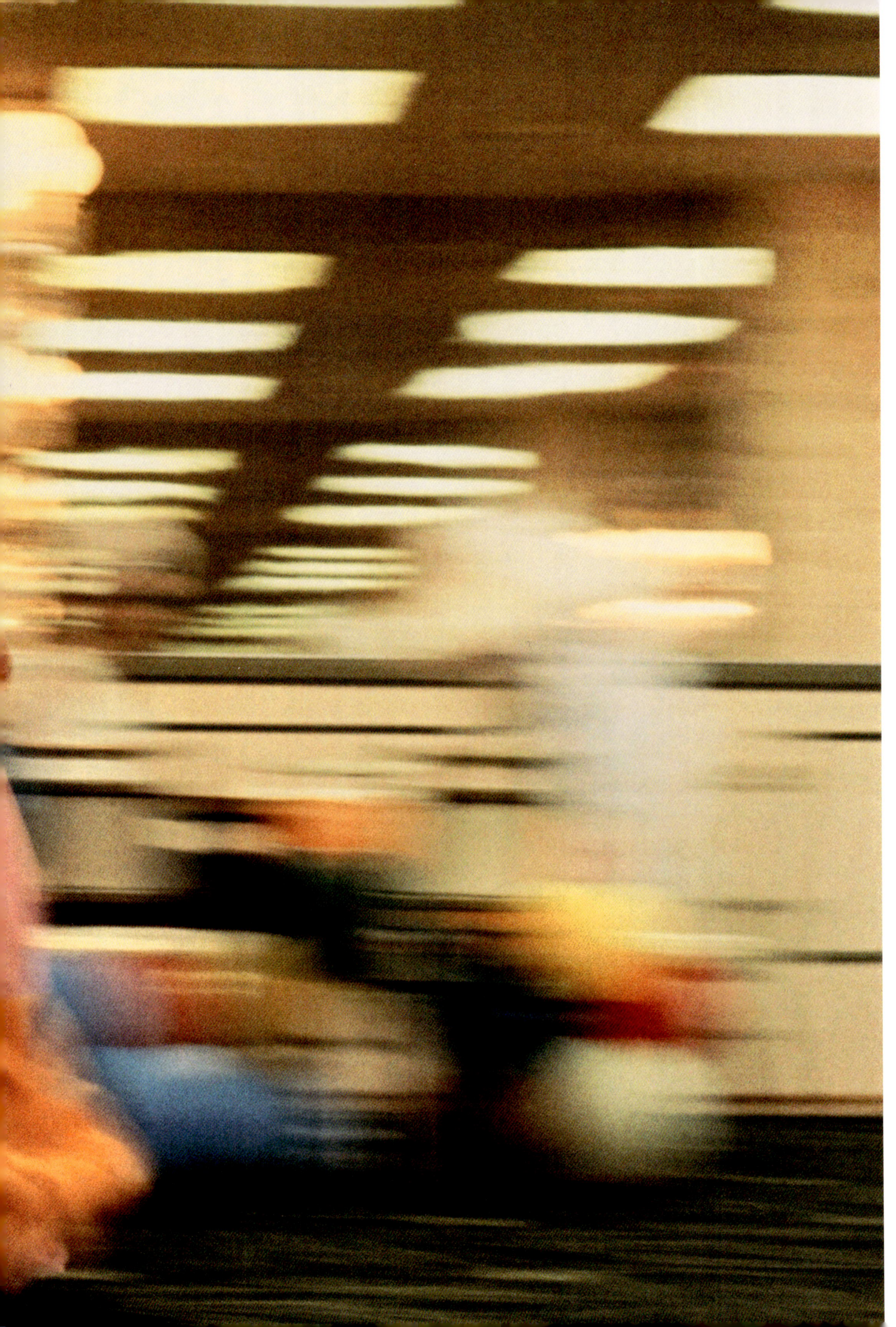

RICHARD AVEDON

Born in New York City, 1923; died in San Antonio, Texas, 2004

Within a year of his discharge from the Merchant Marine in 1944, Richard Avedon had his first photographs published in *Harper's Bazaar*. Under the tutelage of the magazine's art director Alexey Brodovitch, Avedon developed a fresh and spirited style—incorporating variable focus, dynamic camera angles, and blurring—that epitomized postwar optimism and changing ideals of femininity. He photographed his models laughing and smoking, without hats or gloves—a lapse in the decorum that was expected of fashionable women of the era. And although the influence of photographers such as Martin Munkácsi (p. 50) and Jacques Henri Lartigue is clear, Avedon combined this spontaneity with the glamour and polished elegance of earlier work by photographers such as Horst P. Horst (p. 58), Cecil Beaton (p. 30), and George Hoyningen-Heune (p. 42).

From 1947 through to the late 1950s, Avedon worked extensively in Paris, where the fashion industry was playing a key part in the postwar revival of the French economy. The streets and cafés of Paris provided the backdrop for some of his most memorable early work, although one of his best-known images, *Dovima with Elephants*, was shot at a Paris circus: "I saw the elephants under an enormous skylight and in a second I knew . . . there was a potential here for a kind of dream image," Avedon later recalled.

In the late 1950s, both Carmel Snow and Alexey Brodovitch left *Harper's Bazaar*. Standards of beauty were changing as more and more women entered professional life, and the top models of the 1950s were being replaced by younger women such as Twiggy, Jean Shrimpton, and Penelope Tree, who embodied an independent lifestyle and a more natural kind of beauty. Avedon decided that it was time to reinvent himself.

In the early 1960s, he began combining the seamless white background typically used in advertising work with dramatic, dynamic poses, shot from a low angle. This "studio leap" evoked exuberant motion, rather than suggesting mood or narrative, and it was widely imitated.

As the civil rights movement gathered strength in America, Avedon also pushed to change attitudes toward race in fashion publishing. His insistence on featuring Portuguese-Chinese model China Machado in the 1959 collections issue of *Harper's Bazaar* almost resulted in his resignation. Later, in March 1964, his photographs of a young model named Rebecca Hutchings would be the first images of a black model to appear in the magazine. In April 1965, Avedon left *Harper's Bazaar* for *Vogue*, after more than twenty years at the vanguard of his profession. Shortly after, he moved away from editorial work to focus on advertising.

Richard Avedon, *Dovima with Elephants, Evening Dress by Dior, Cirque d'Hiver, Paris*, August 1955, *Harper's Bazaar*, September 1955

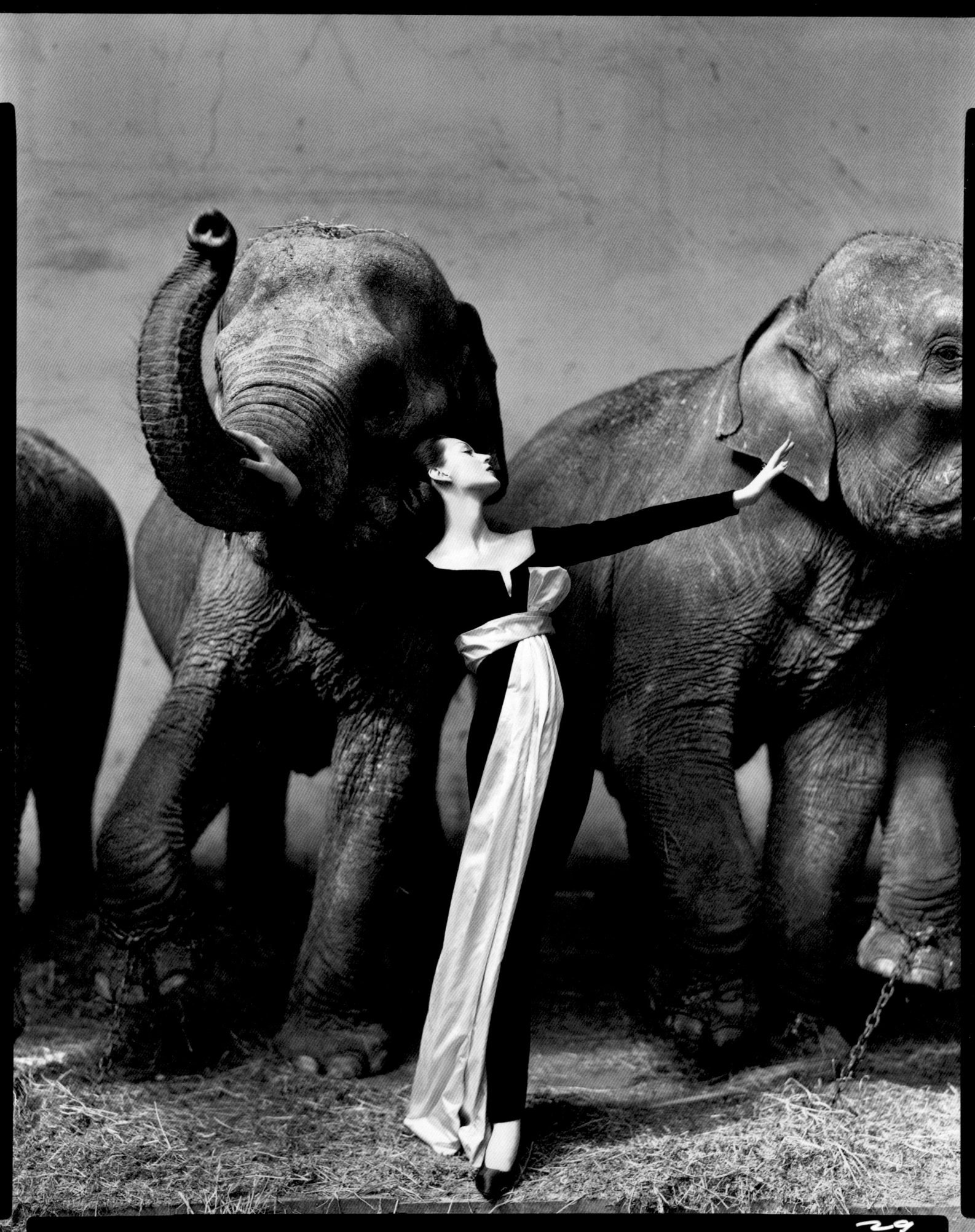

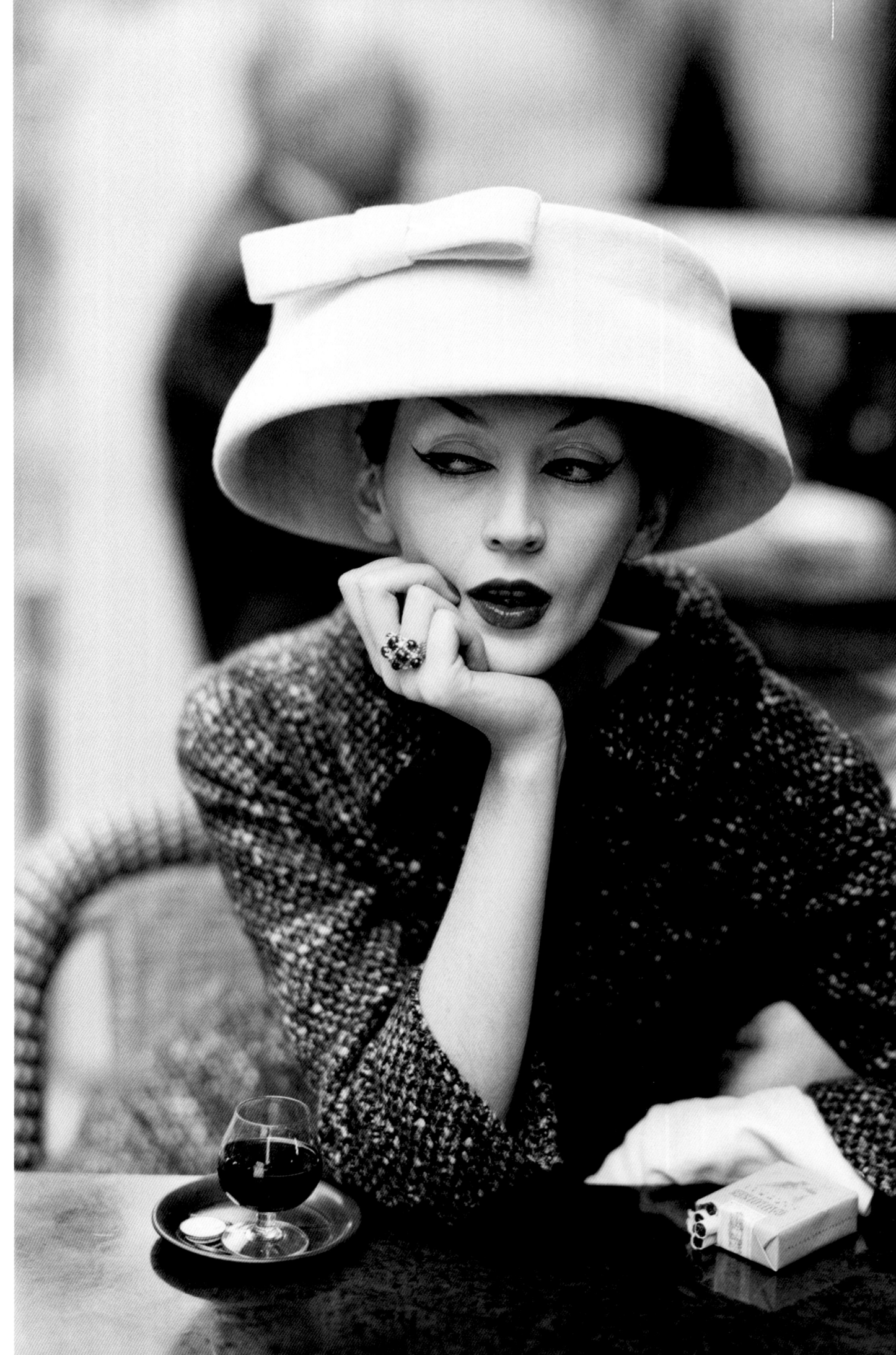

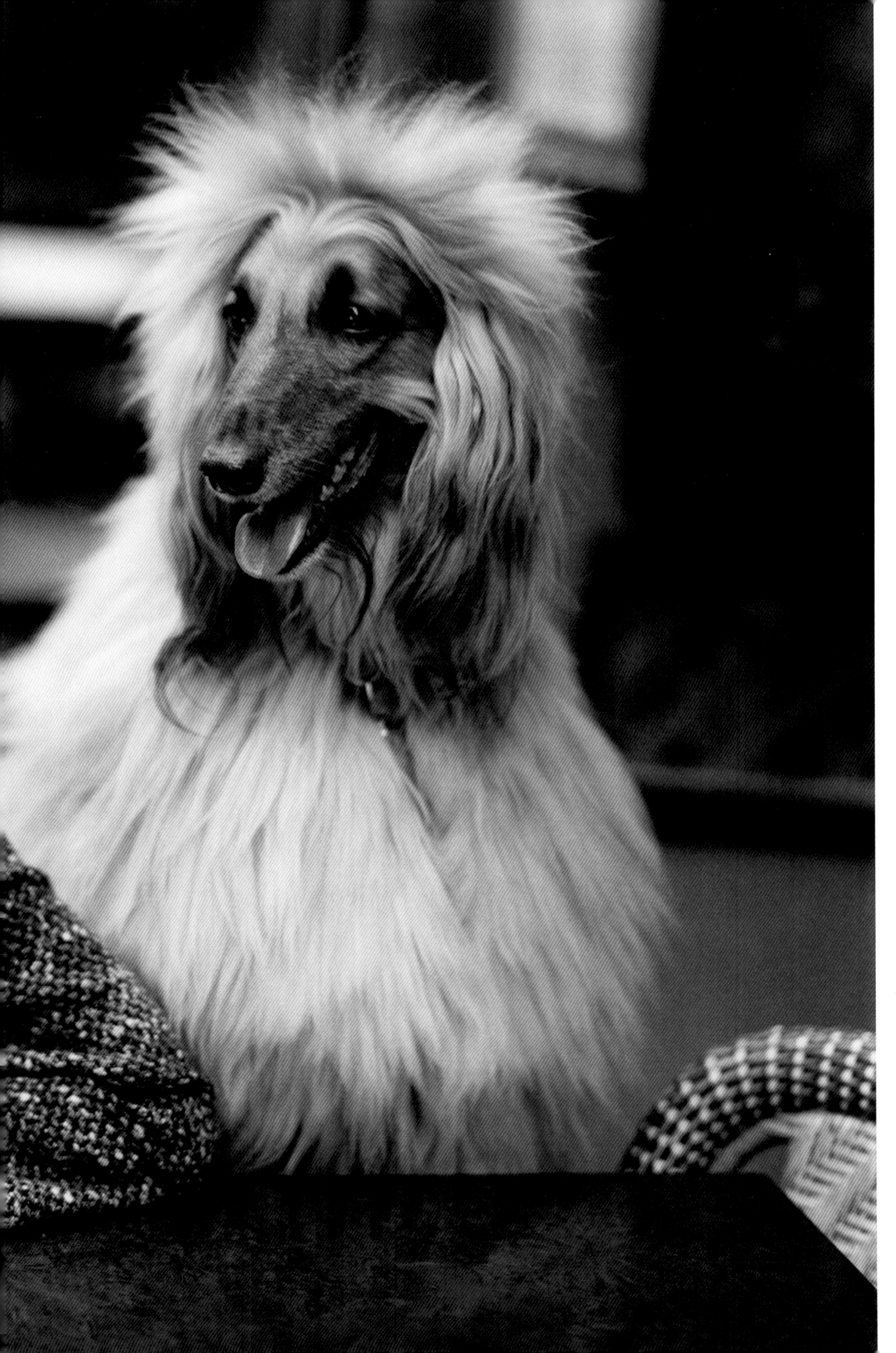

Richard Avedon,
*Dovima with Sacha, Cloche
by Balenciaga, Café les Deux
Magots, Paris,* August 1955

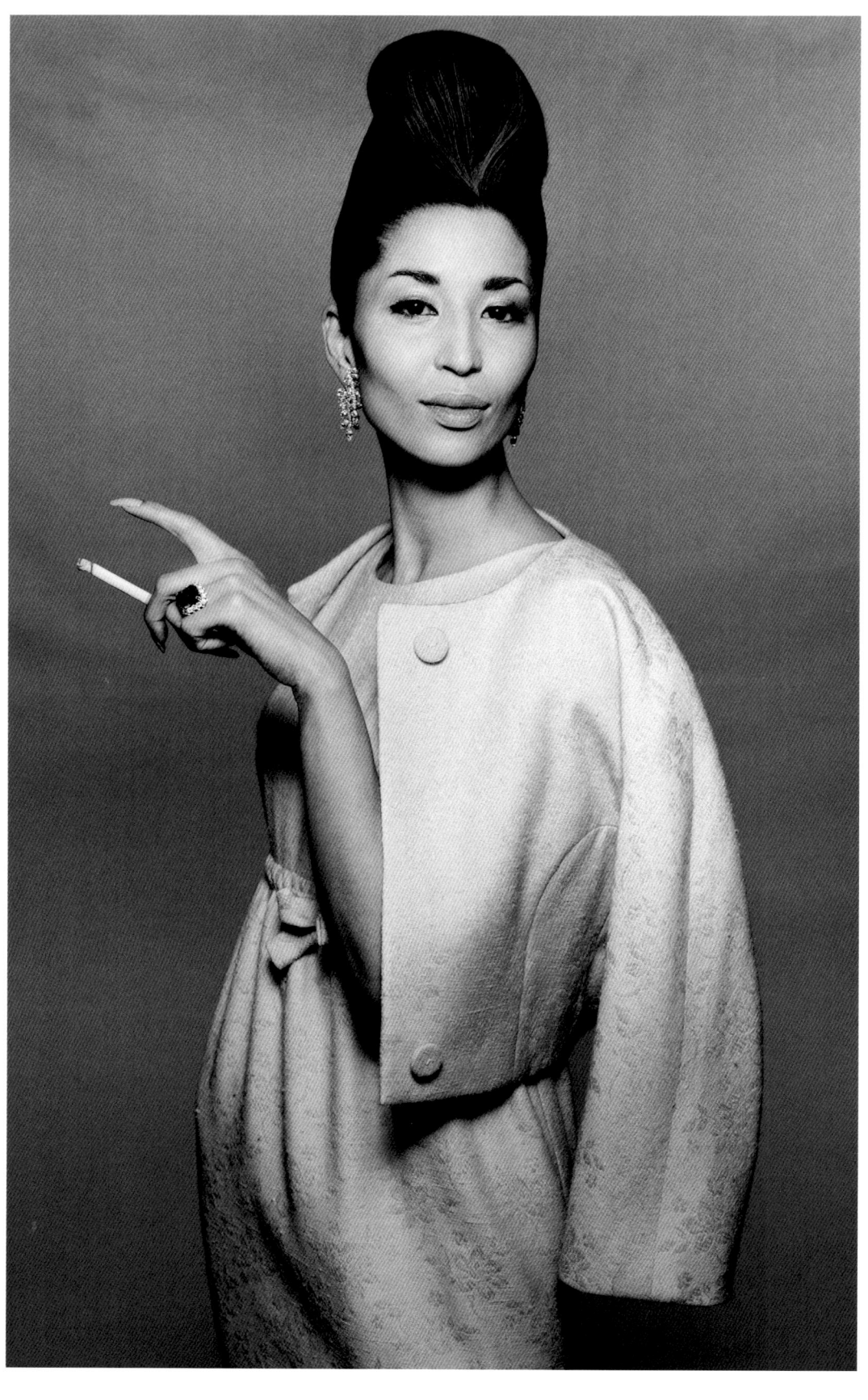

Richard Avedon, *China Machado, Dinner Dress
and Jacket by Ben Zuckerman, New York*, November 1958
Right: Richard Avedon, *Veruschka, Dress by Bill Blass,
New York*, January 1967

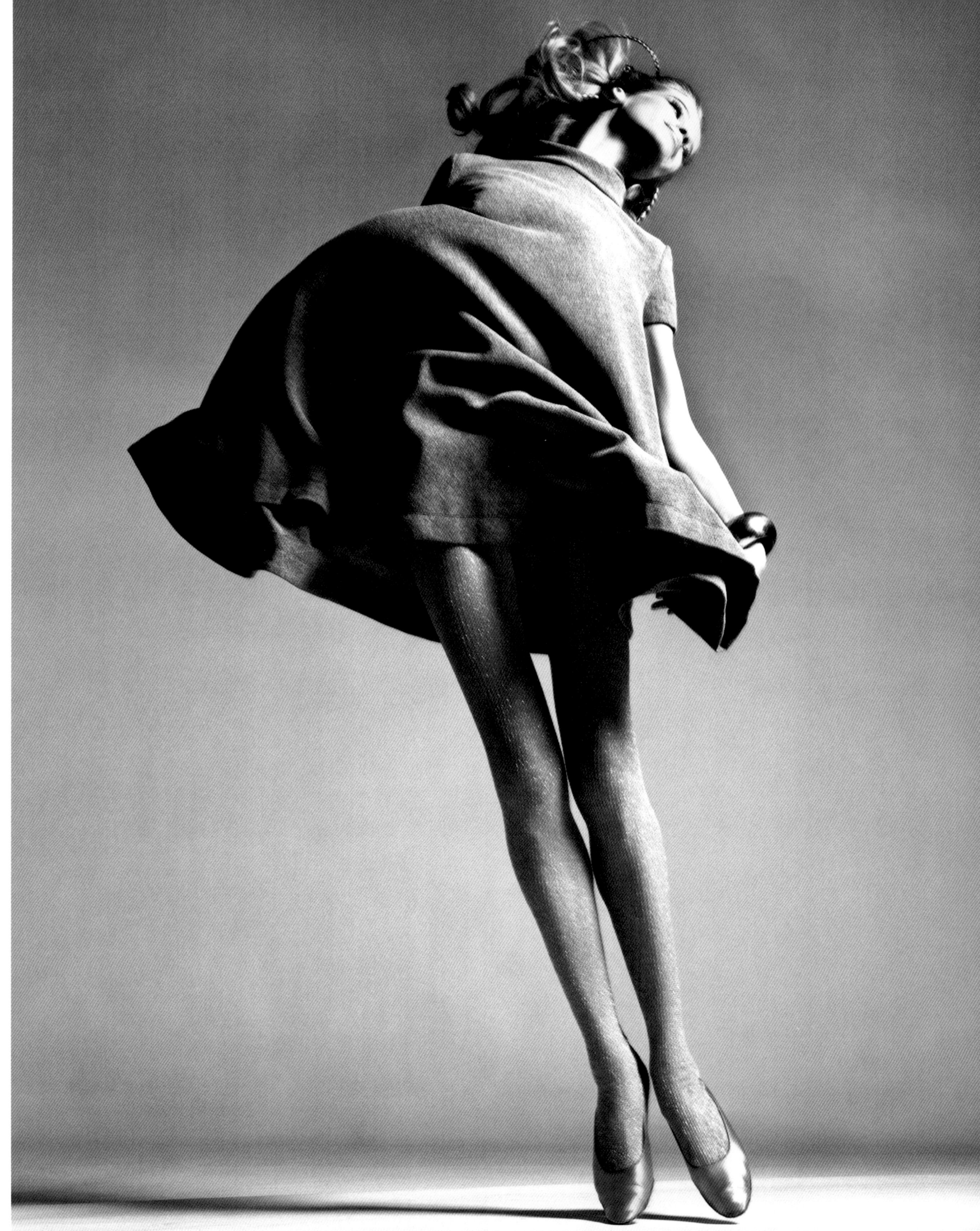

SAUL LEITER

Born in Pittsburgh,
1923; died in New York City,
2013

Abandoning his training to be a rabbi, Saul Leiter arrived in New York in 1946 with the intention of becoming a painter. He was introduced to photography by his friend, the Abstract Expressionist painter Richard Pousette-Dart, who was experimenting with large photographic prints. Leiter began taking photographs on the street soon after, using his painter's intuition to create complex, layered images full of rich yet subtle colors and textures. Unlike contemporaries such as Diane Arbus, Leiter's attention was not focused exclusively on people, but on the complexity of visual experience and the way that the life of the city could be condensed into near-abstract compositions.

Leiter opened a small photographic studio and began photographing for *Harper's Bazaar* in 1957. As curator Martin Harrison remarks, Leiter's work "brought a quietly subversive note into *Harper's Bazaar*," exploring color with a depth and rigor that was new to fashion photography. The visual simplicity of his 1959 photograph of a model in a Seymour Fox coat masks a sophisticated pictorial structure. The image is divided into two rectangular sections, the deep perspective on the left side contrasting sharply with the two-dimensional volume on the right. The entire composition consists almost entirely of soft shades of green and blue, offset by flashes of bright red, along with the straw-like tones of the model's hat and skin, and the worker's hand in the foreground. Like much of Leiter's work, the photograph also reflects his fascination with New York's rich street life.

When his editorial and advertising commissions began to slow down in the 1970s and '80s, Leiter returned to painting and fell into relative obscurity until the early 2000s, when the rediscovery of his early work—including thousands of unprinted images—prompted the release of a number of books and monographs.

Saul Leiter,
Harper's Bazaar, 1959

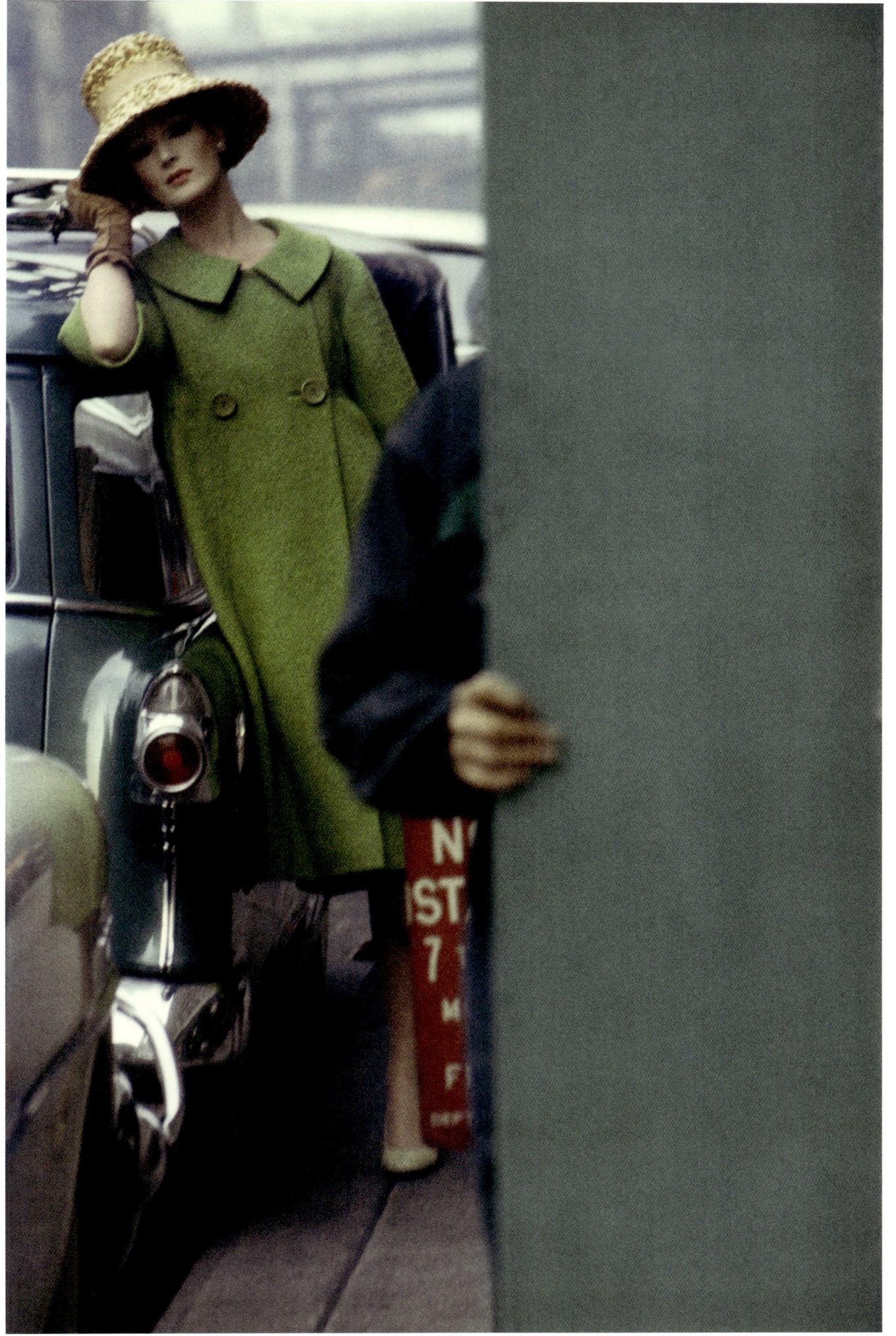

WILLIAM KLEIN

Born in New York City,
1928

After training as a painter, William Klein turned to photography in the 1950s and began working at *Vogue* in 1954, on the invitation of art director Alexander Liberman. Klein initially took on fashion work as a means of subsidizing his artwork; he had, by his own admission, mixed feelings about it. Self-taught as a photographer, he found fashion work did not come naturally to him: "How to light? What camera? What was the model supposed to be doing? How not to make both of us look like fools?" It was by embracing and exaggerating the artificiality of the fashion image, and drawing on his own penchant for experimental and abstract imagery, that he began to develop a personal style.

Klein's 1958 Paris fashion report for American *Vogue* is a tour de force of photographic styles and techniques: blurring and double exposures, low-angle street photographs, poised studio portraiture, and radiant nighttime images. *Simone and Nina, Piazza di Spagna, Rome*, 1960, was shot with a telephoto lens from a high viewpoint. The models, their dresses mirroring the horizontal stripes of the pedestrian crossing, stand out sharply against the cropped forms of onlookers moving in and out of the frame. Klein consistently broke the rules of fashion photography, parodying its conventions and poking fun at the attitudes of the fashion world. While many of his more extreme images went unpublished, his work had a significant influence on his contemporaries, encouraging not just technical experimentation, but a more self-critical and satirical approach to the genre of fashion photography.

William Klein,
Simone and Nina, Piazza di Spagna, Rome, Vogue, 1960

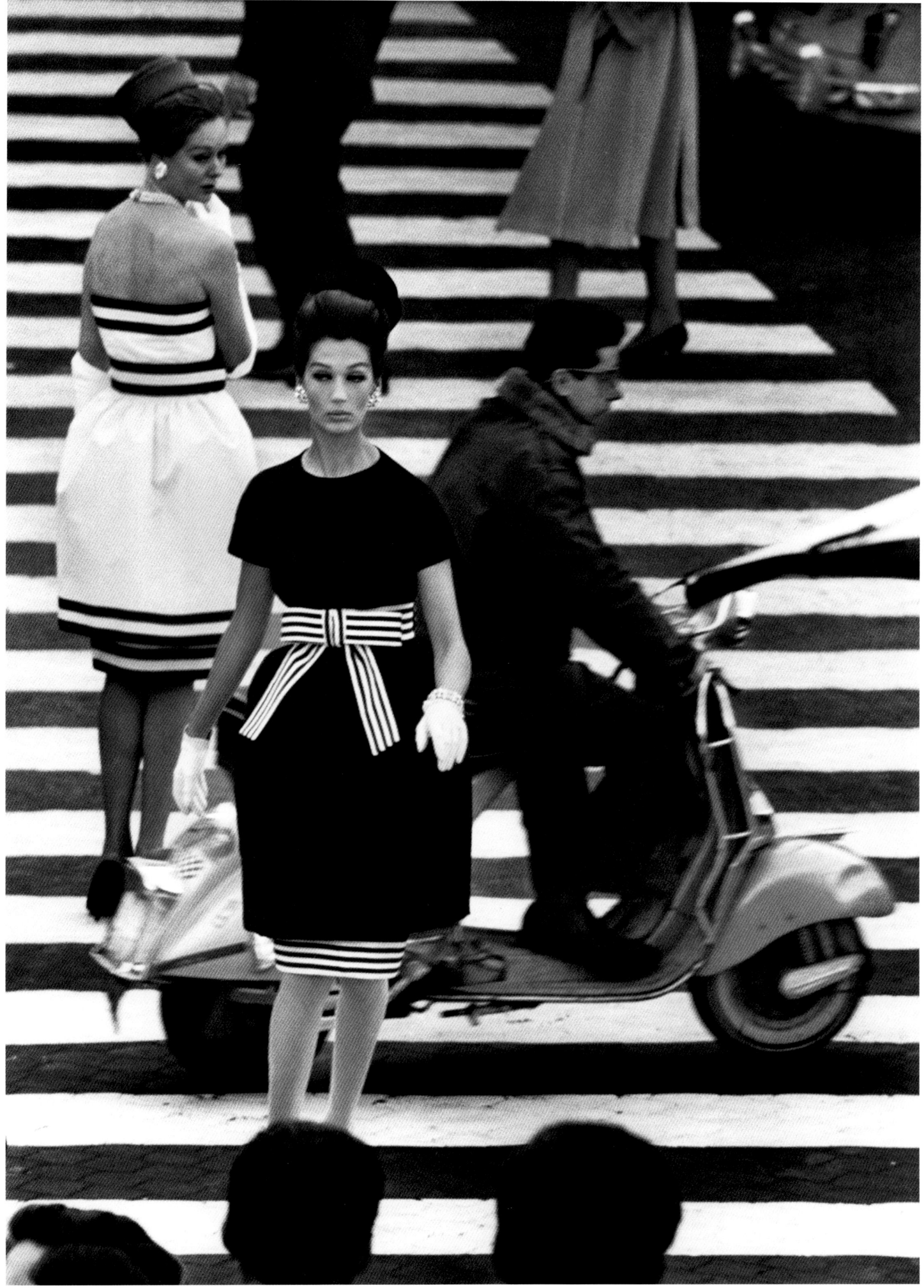

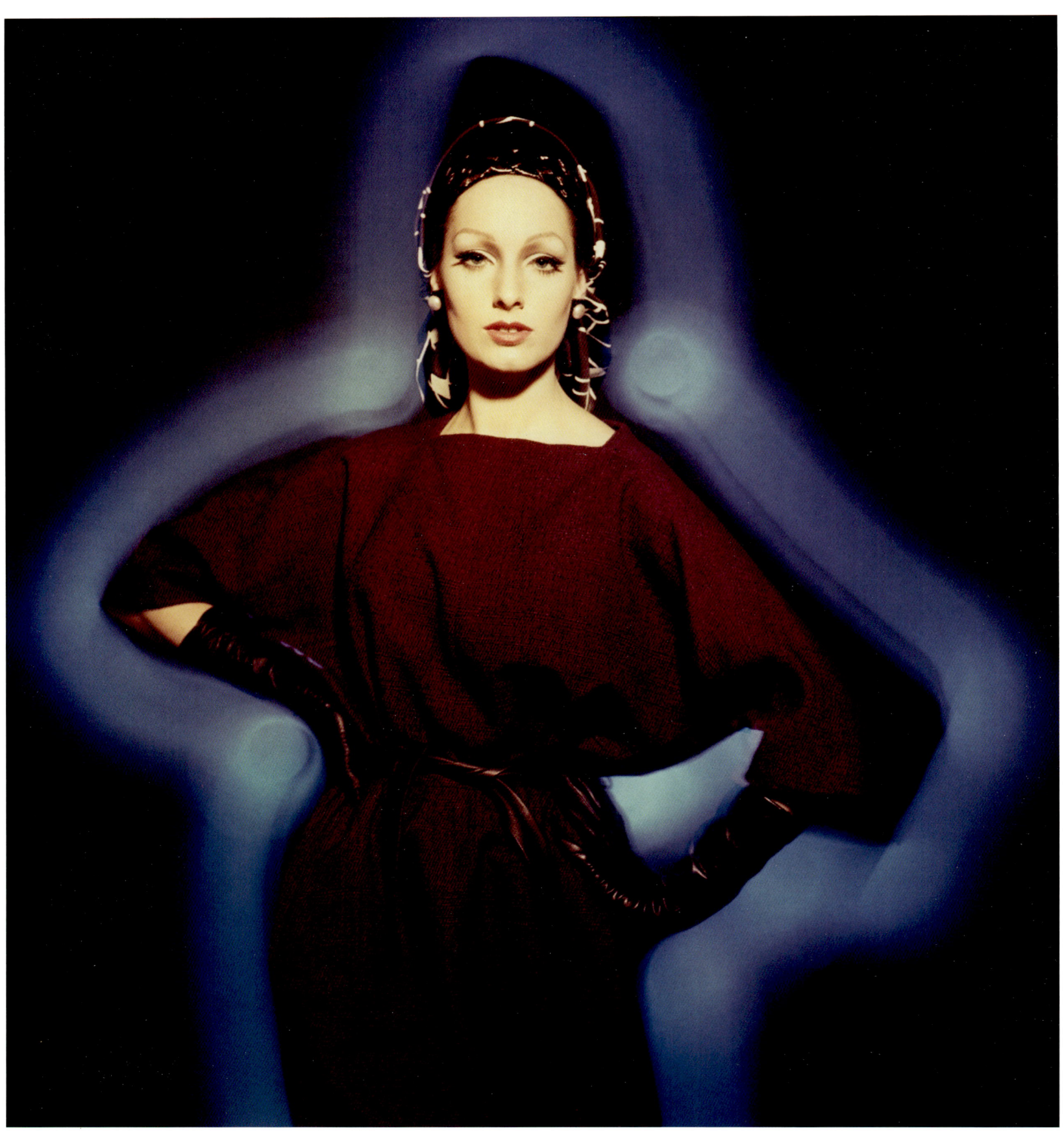

William Klein, *Antonia, Purple and Blue,*
Yves Saint Laurent, Paris, Vogue, 1962
Right: William Klein, *Evelyn Tripp,*
Quai de Seine, Dior, Paris, Vogue, 1958

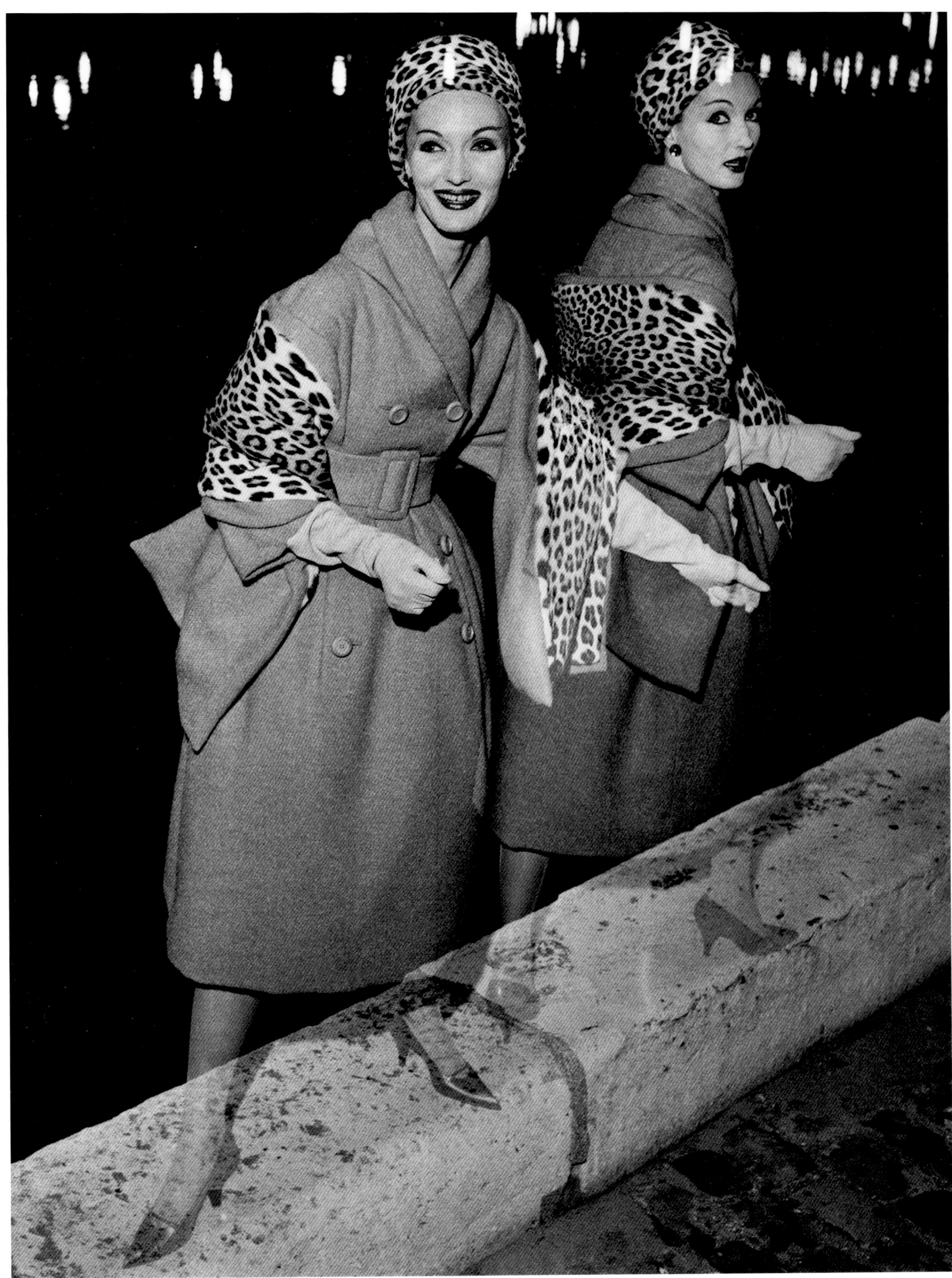

FRANK HORVAT

Born in Abbazia, Italy,
1928

Frank Horvat was part of a new wave of European photographers who brought a fresh feeling to American fashion photography in the 1960s. Horvat studied drawing at Milan's Brera Academy and began his photographic career as an aspiring photojournalist, presenting himself at the Magnum Photos offices in 1952. Following Henri Cartier-Bresson's advice to "stop viewing the world from [his] belly," Horvat abandoned his Rolleiflex camera and bought a 35 mm Leica.

After several years spent working for *Paris Match*, *Picture Post*, and *Life*, Horvat was introduced by William Klein (p. 102) to Jacques Moutin, editor of French fashion magazine *Le Jardin des Modes* in 1957. The magazine had just changed hands, and the new editor was eager to update its image, which Horvat later recalled in less than flattering terms: "Young women loaded with makeup, in front of gray or white backgrounds, in conventional poses, some of them with their eyes turned skyward, others with robotic smiles on their faces." Horvat brought his Leica and his photojournalist's sensibility to his fashion commissions, and his work—shot in a realist style that combined the language of fashion photography with that of photojournalism—was immediately successful.

In 1961, Horvat moved to New York and was soon offered work by Marvin Israel, the new art director at *Harper's Bazaar*. Poised somewhere between Klein's raw experimentation and Avedon's polished spontaneity, Horvat's aesthetic was perfectly aligned with the postwar shift from haute couture to ready-to-wear. Like many of the new wave, including Jeanloup Sieff (p. 110) and David Bailey (p. 122), Horvat also rejected the heavily made-up look that had been in favor throughout the 1950s, and his work made a strong impression on a younger generation of fashion photographers. Throughout the 1960s and '70s, Horvat continued to challenge the stereotypes that pervaded fashion photography, rejecting conventional poses and gestures, and often refusing to work with professional models. A remarkably versatile photographer, Horvat created an oeuvre that also includes social documentary, landscapes and cityscapes, nudes, and portraits.

Frank Horvat, *French High Fashion, Carol Lobravico at Café Flore, Paris, Harper's Bazaar*, 1962
Following pages: Frank Horvat, *Fashion in the Metro, Paris, Jours de France*, 1958

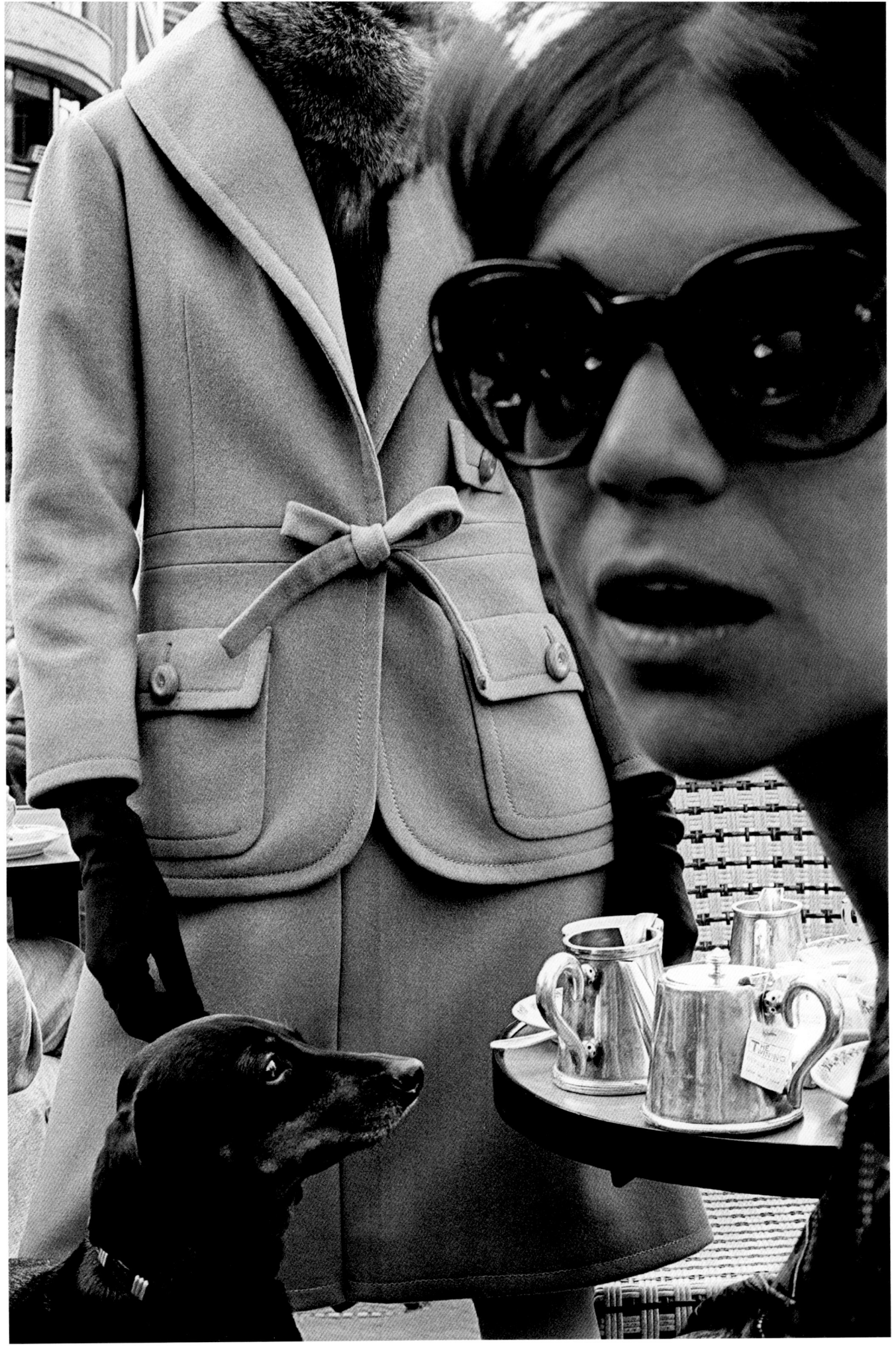

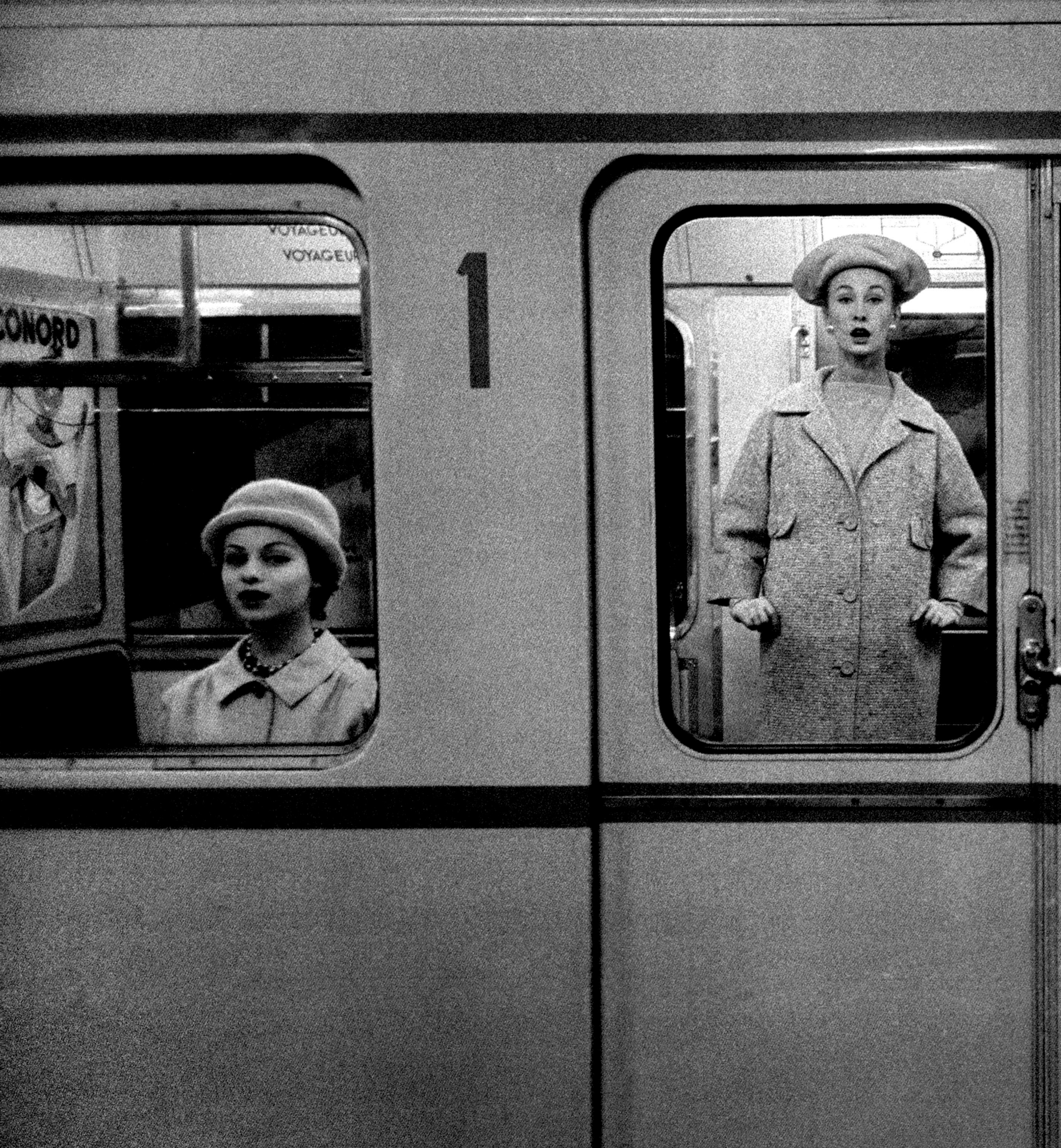

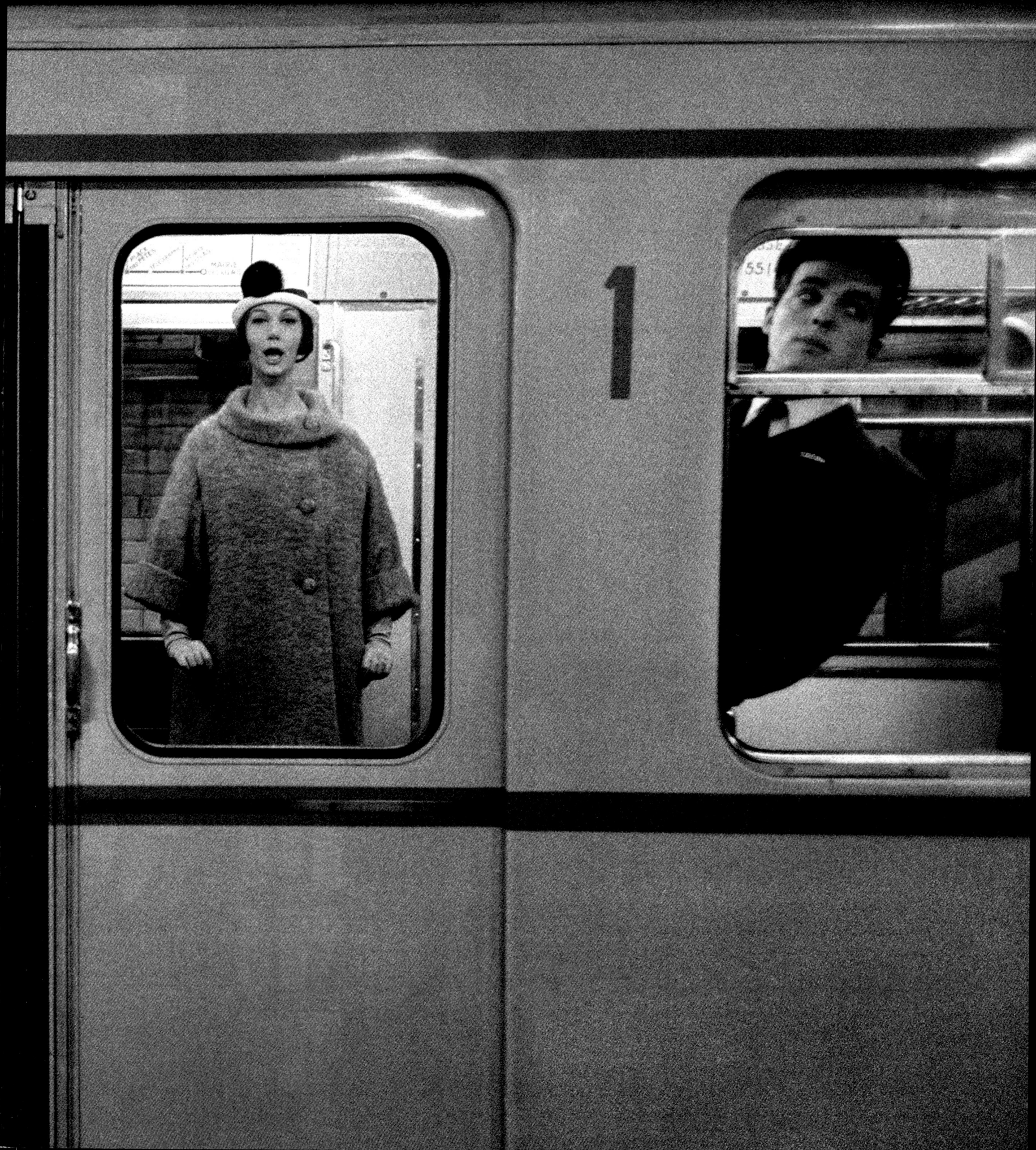

Jeanloup Sieff first took up photography as a teenager and began working as a freelance photojournalist in Paris in 1954. The following year, he published his first photographs in *Elle*, and soon became a regular contributor of portraits and articles. He later moved into fashion photography after the departure of fashion photographer Lionel Kazan, who had worked extensively for the magazine throughout the 1950s.

After a short stint with the Magnum Photos agency in the late 1950s, Sieff returned to fashion photography, shooting for *Le Jardin des Modes*. At the time, the magazine was attempting to rebrand itself along the avant-garde lines of *Harper's Bazaar*, and Sieff was given a lot of creative freedom. One of the key photographers of the "new realist" movement, Sieff had a playful, surreal style that was influenced by the films of Michelangelo Antonioni and Ingmar Bergman, making frequent use of the fish-eye effect introduced by very short lenses. In 1961, Sieff departed for New York, where he briefly shared a studio with Frank Horvat (p. 106). For the next five years, Sieff moved back and forth between New York and Paris, shooting fashion for magazines, including *Queen*, *Vogue*, *Harper's Bazaar*, and *Esquire*, before returning to Paris permanently in 1966.

Sieff's suggestive 1964 image of model Astrid Heeren smoking, photographed for *Harper's Bazaar*, raised the eyebrows of the magazine's editor, Nancy White. As Sieff later recalled, "This series of fashion photographs was to be called 'Chic is . . .' The editor of the magazine thought that this picture was not at all 'chic,' and it took Richard Avedon's friendly insistence to mellow her reticence."

Born in Paris, 1933; died in Paris, 2000

JEANLOUP SIEFF

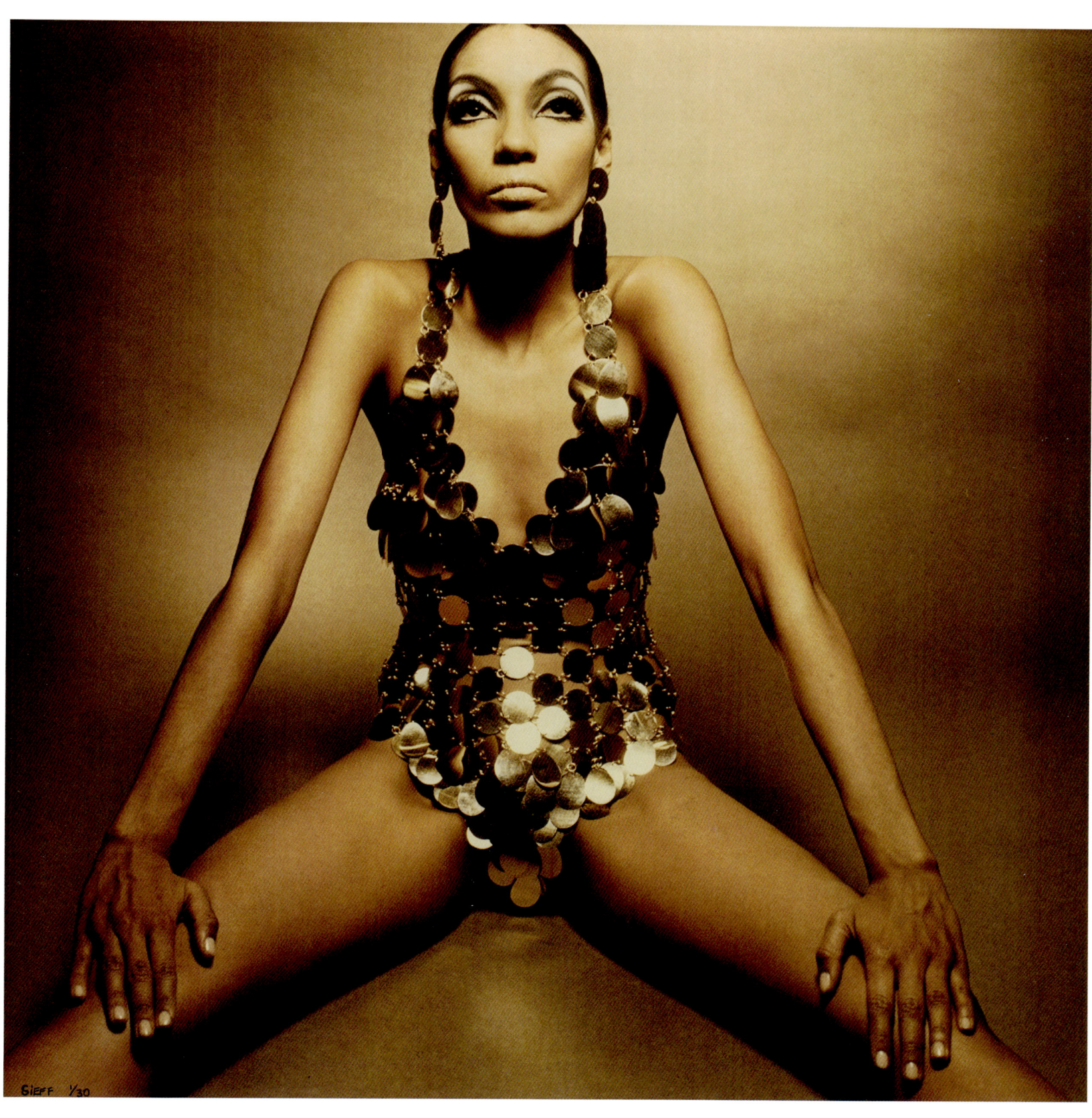

Jeanloup Sieff,
Model Kellie Wilson Wearing an Outfit
by Paco Rabanne, Nova, 1966

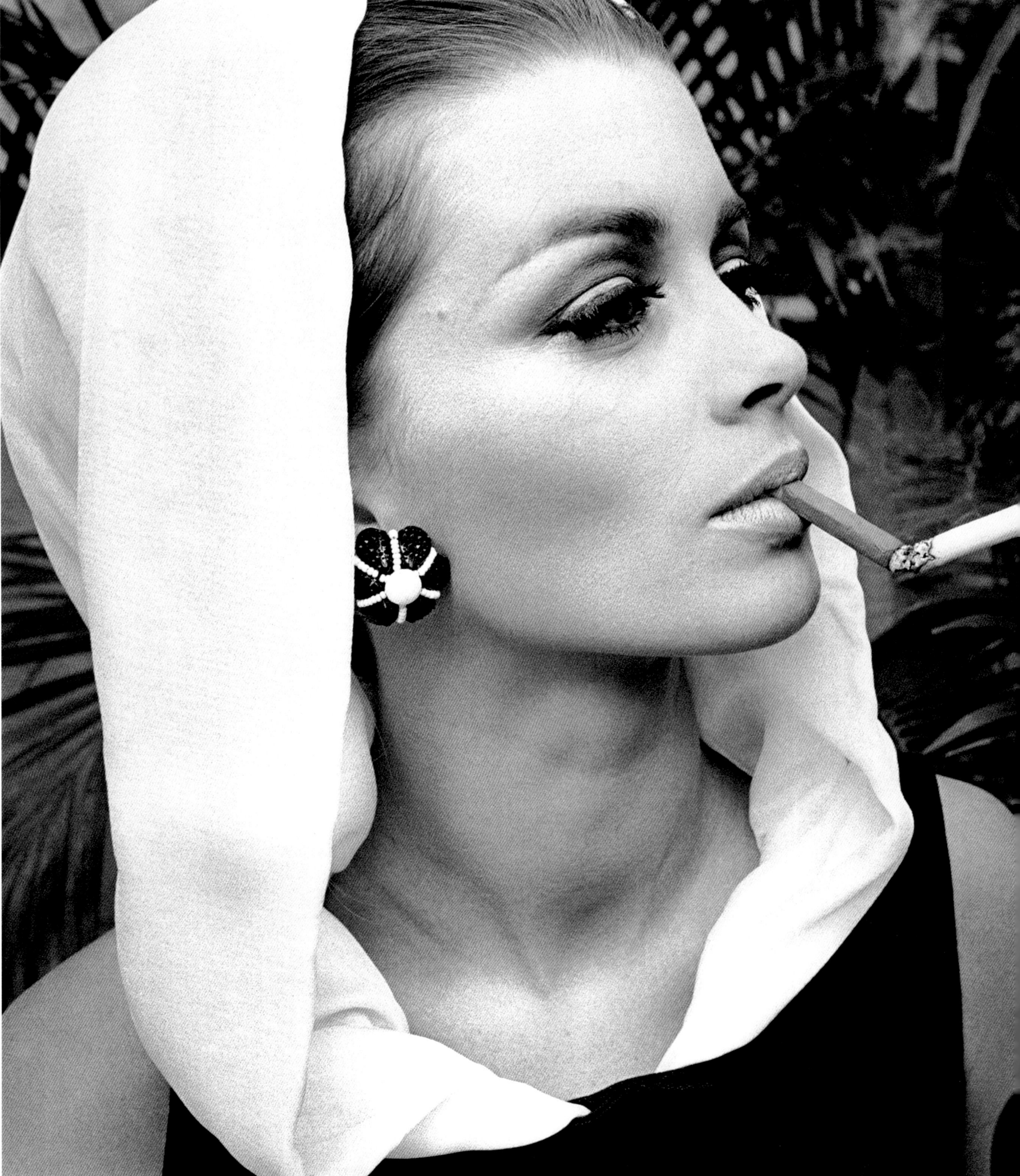

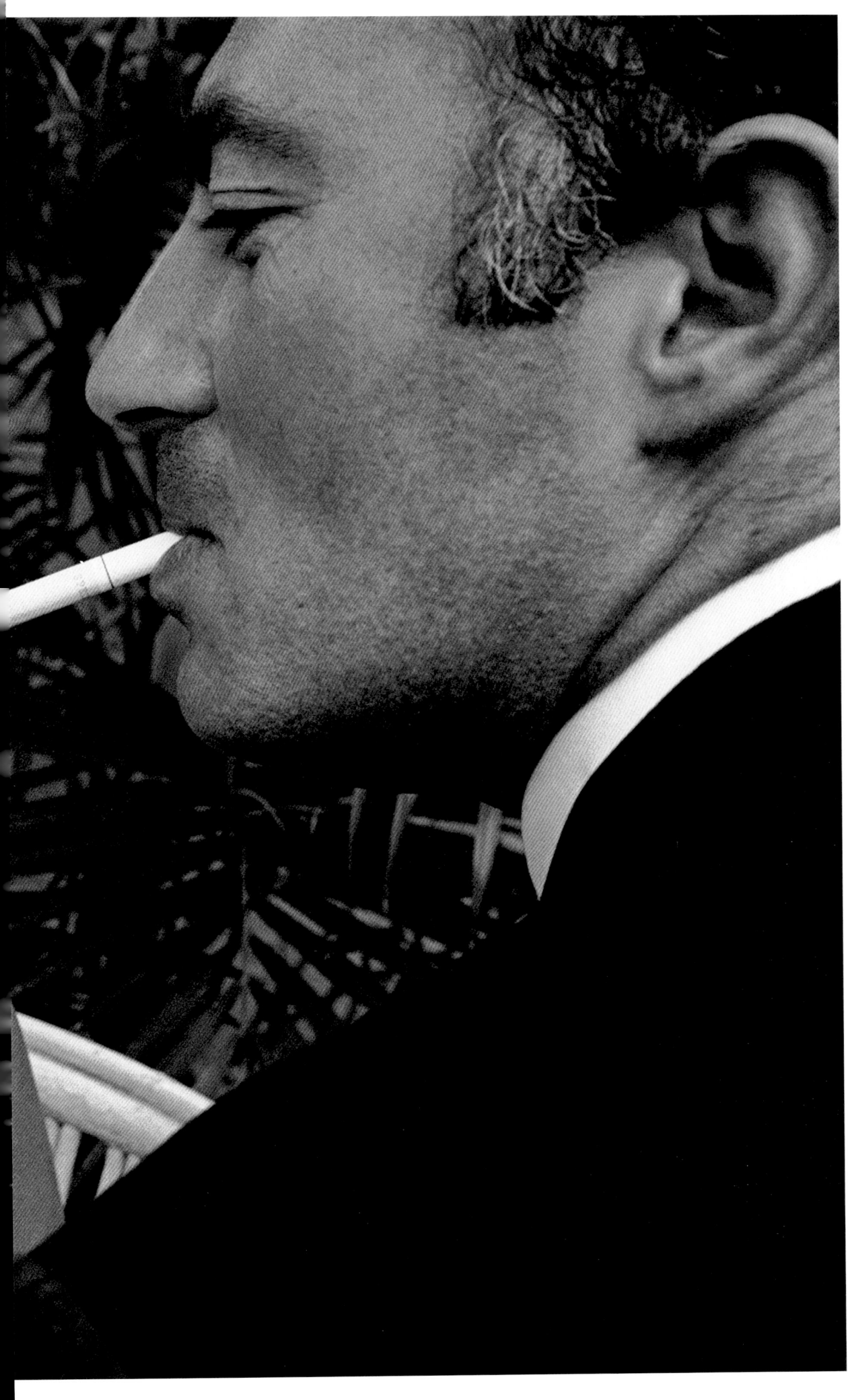

Jeanloup Sieff,
Palm Beach, Harper's Bazaar, 1964

HIRO

Born in Shanghai,
1930

Born into a distinguished Japanese family, Yasuhiro Wakabayashi was brought up in China, returning to Japan after World War II. His early ambitions to become a doctor were set aside when he encountered the work of Richard Avedon (p. 94) and Irving Penn (p. 70) in American fashion magazines. Around the same time, Hiro acquired a Minoltaflex camera, and in 1953, the twenty-three-year-old left Japan for New York with the aim of working for Avedon or Penn. Once there, he briefly took classes at the School of Modern Photography, before leaving to assist still-life photographers Lester Bookbinder and Rouben Samberg.

In 1956, Hiro, as he was known professionally, finally went to work for Avedon, where he was encouraged to use the studio to learn his craft. It was under the critical eyes of Avedon and, later, Alexey Brodovitch that Hiro refined the skills he'd learned working under Bookbinder and Samberg into a unique personal style. Fashion photographers had been making use of still life since the 1920s, but Hiro's bold geometric shapes, strong colors, and frequent use of close-ups lent the genre a graphic punch that invited comparisons to Pop art. By 1957, Hiro was sharing Avedon's studio, and in early 1958, Brodovitch offered him an exclusive contract at *Harper's Bazaar*, where he remained until the mid-1970s.

Hiro's innovative photographs were carefully planned and visualized in advance. For *Harry Winston Necklace, New York*, 1963, the steer's hoof was obtained from a slaughterhouse and left in a freezer overnight to ensure that it remained in the pose Hiro had envisioned. The surreal juxtaposition—a whimsical twist on the classic tale of the beauty and the beast—was typical of his work. Renowned for his technical expertise and his inventive use of lighting, Hiro experimented with black light, neon, light painting, sequential strobe lighting, and multiple flashes, working for months and sometimes years to develop particular techniques. As he remarked to photography writer Owen Edwards in a 1982 interview, "Technique can be fascinating. But you've got to apply it to an idea. It's a language, and it's no good unless you have something to say."

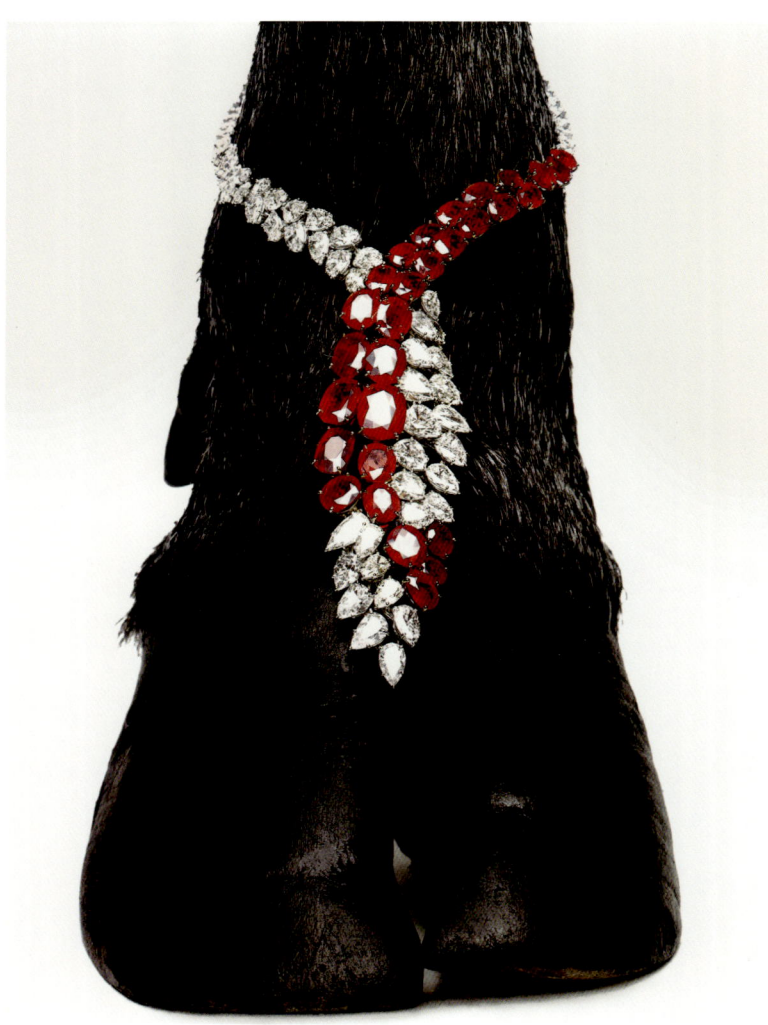

Hiro, *Harry Winston Necklace, New York*, 1963
Right: Hiro, *Tilly Tizzani with Acetate Visor, New York*, 1966

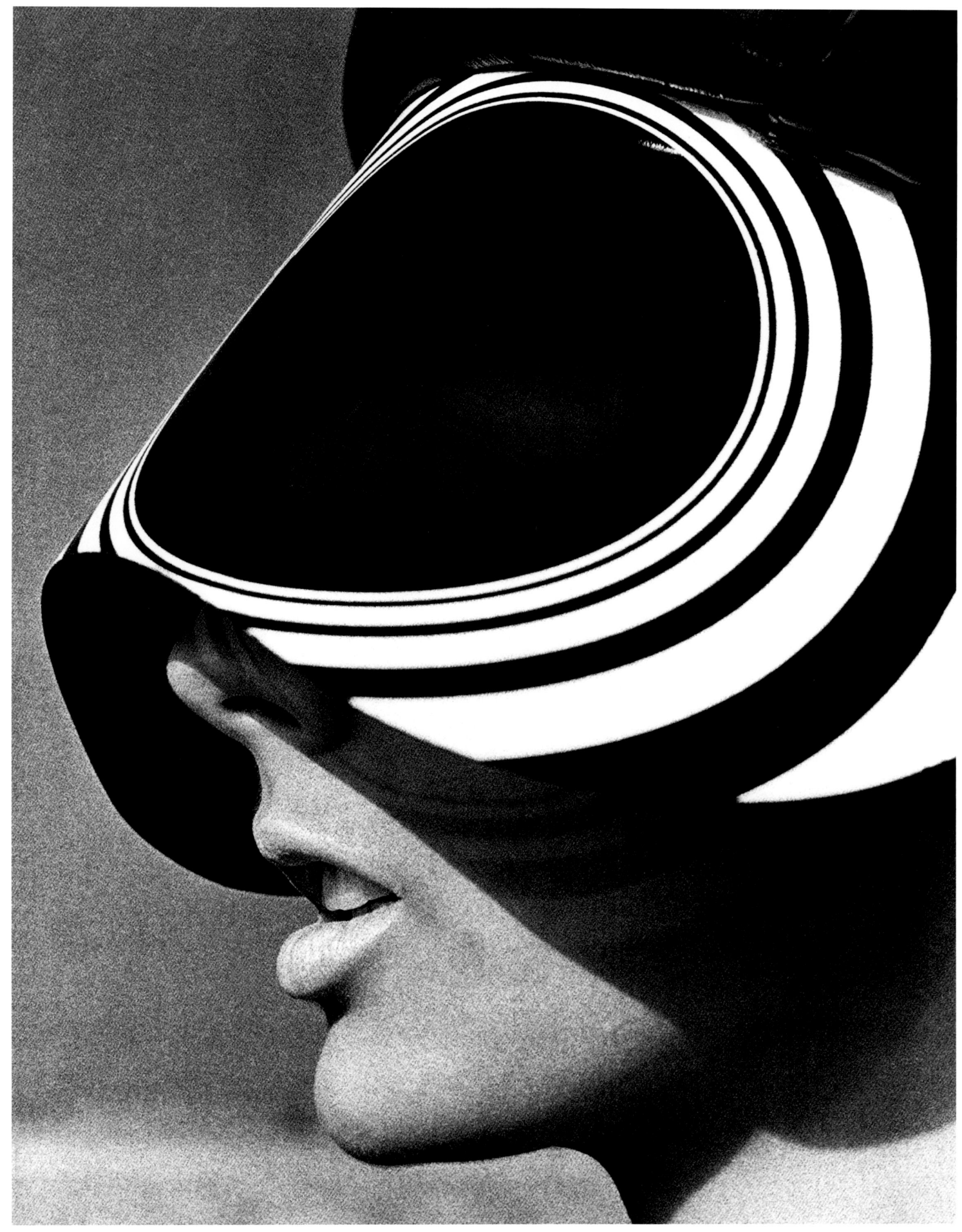

BERT STERN

Born in Brooklyn,
1929; died in
New York City, 2013

Bert Stern's name is synonymous with Madison Avenue's "golden age" of advertising photography—the creative revolution of the 1950s that transformed advertisements from fact-laden screeds into lavish, provocative sales pitches. Stern learned to use a camera in the army. At nineteen, he got a job in the mail room of *Look* magazine, where he met art director Hershel Bramson. When Bramson left to become the art director of the short-lived *Flair* magazine, he took Stern with him as his assistant.

It was Bramson, later working in an advertising agency, who also gave Stern his first break as a photographer, in the form of an account for Smirnoff vodka. Stern's witty, conceptual images redefined the look of advertising photography. By the late 1950s, Stern was regarded as one of the most successful advertising photographers in the country, with a roster of lucrative commercial contracts. Enormously productive and in huge demand, at one point he employed a staff of thirty in his studio, shooting as many as seven campaigns simultaneously.

Stern joined *Vogue* in 1962. Although he worked frequently for fashion magazines and was regarded as a go-to photographer of women, Stern didn't regard himself as a fashion photographer, per se. Nonetheless, he shared the fashion world's then passion for realism in photography: "I don't take models leaping, gesturing, and posturing," he said in 1968. "I am interested only when I can show a model looking like a real woman." If Stern's popularity as a fashion photographer was a testament to his creative vision and versatility, it also signaled a shift in the relationship between editorial and advertising photography. Fashion magazines had long relied on income from advertising clients, but as this revenue stream grew exponentially throughout the 1950s, fashion brands began to demand that their products also be featured in editorials. From this point on, advertisers would exercise increasing control over the look of not just their own advertising campaigns, but of fashion editorials as well.

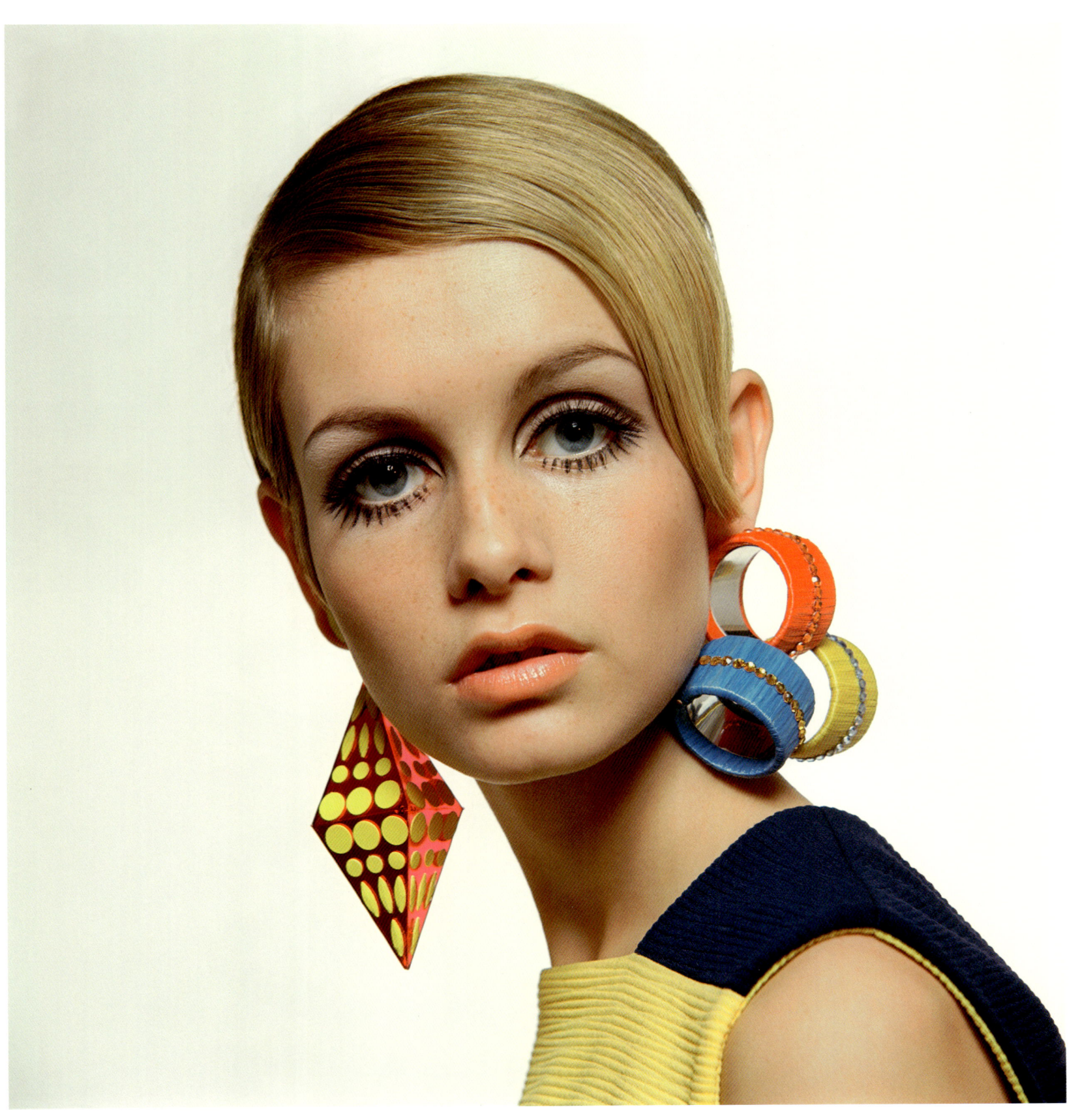

Bert Stern,
Twiggy, 1967

John Cowan was the archetype of the young fashion photographer as a womanizing enfant terrible, bringing a distinctly ungentlemanly energy to the previously staid pages of the fashion glossies. Known in the industry for being brash, energetic, and adventurous, Cowan did his best work in collaboration with model and girlfriend Jill Kennington, whose athletic beauty became the symbol of young, fashionable London. As Kennington recalled, "Our teamwork elevated the usual status of model from clothes horse to action art form."

Cowan found his place in fashion photography after spending a number of years drifting through a variety of jobs that included shop assistant, chauffeur, and travel agent. By the late 1950s, he had ended up in the advertising office of a heavy-equipment company. It was at this point that Cowan, dissatisfied with the quality of the photographs provided to the company, took up a camera. Not long after, he decided to leave his job and strike out on his own as a society photographer.

Cowan's charisma and natural talent, combined with his willingness to take chances, swiftly earned him a reputation. By the end of the 1950s, commissions were flooding in. Throughout the 1960s, Cowan shot for a host of daily newspapers and magazines, including *Le Jardin des Modes*, *Elle*, *Vogue*, and *Queen*, where his photograph *Flying High* appeared in June 1966. This image, a collaboration with Kennington, is typical of Cowan's dynamic style: he liked to shoot from unusual angles, usually without a tripod, and often pushing his models to the limits of their endurance. By the end of the 1960s, however, the innocent, girlish sexuality of both models and fashions had shifted into something more mature and aggressive. Cowan found himself unable to adapt, and his career as a fashion photographer came to an end.

Born in Gillingham, England, 1929; died in 1979

JOHN COWAN

John Cowan, *Flying High*, *Queen*, June 8, 1966; dress by Rosalind Yehuda

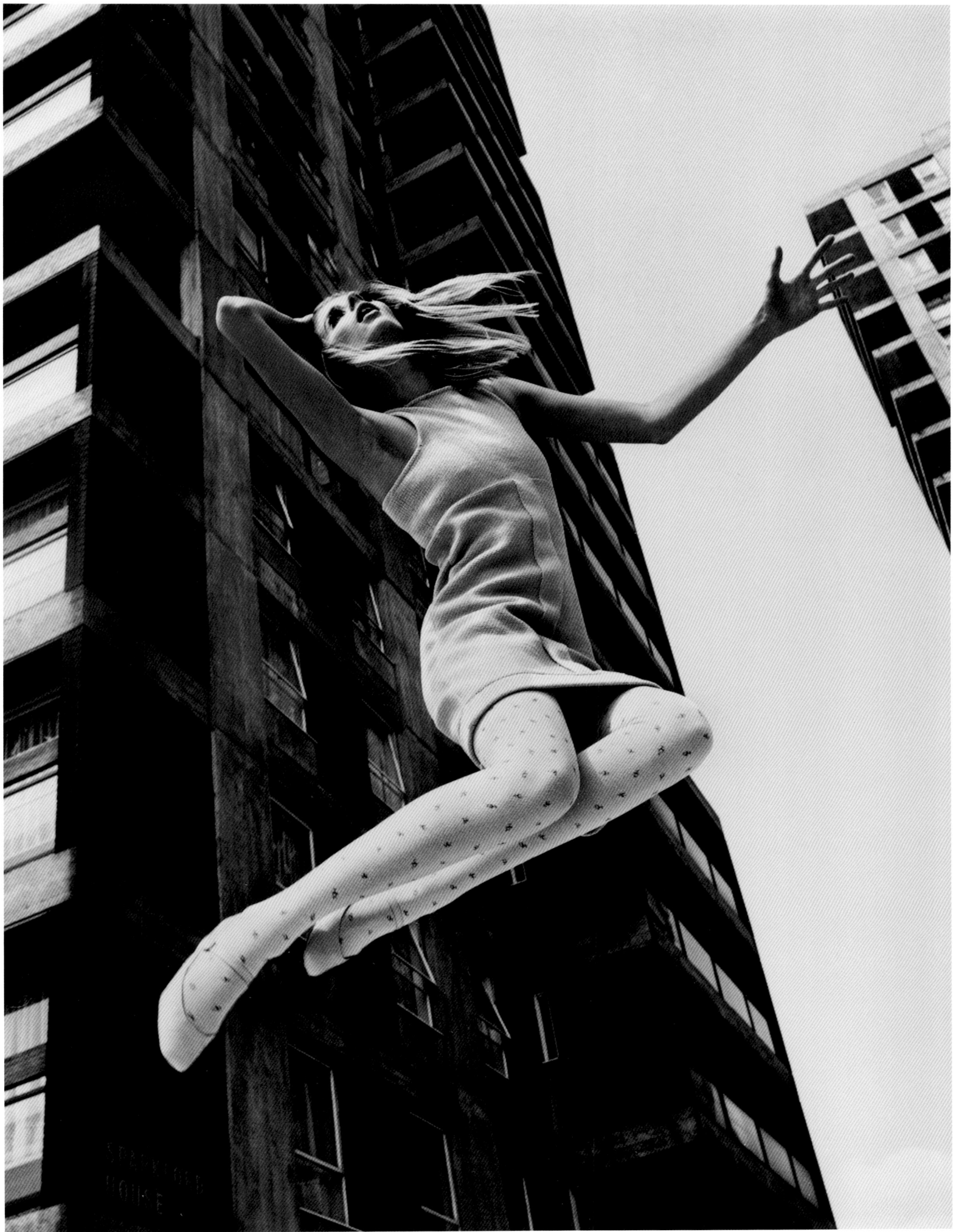

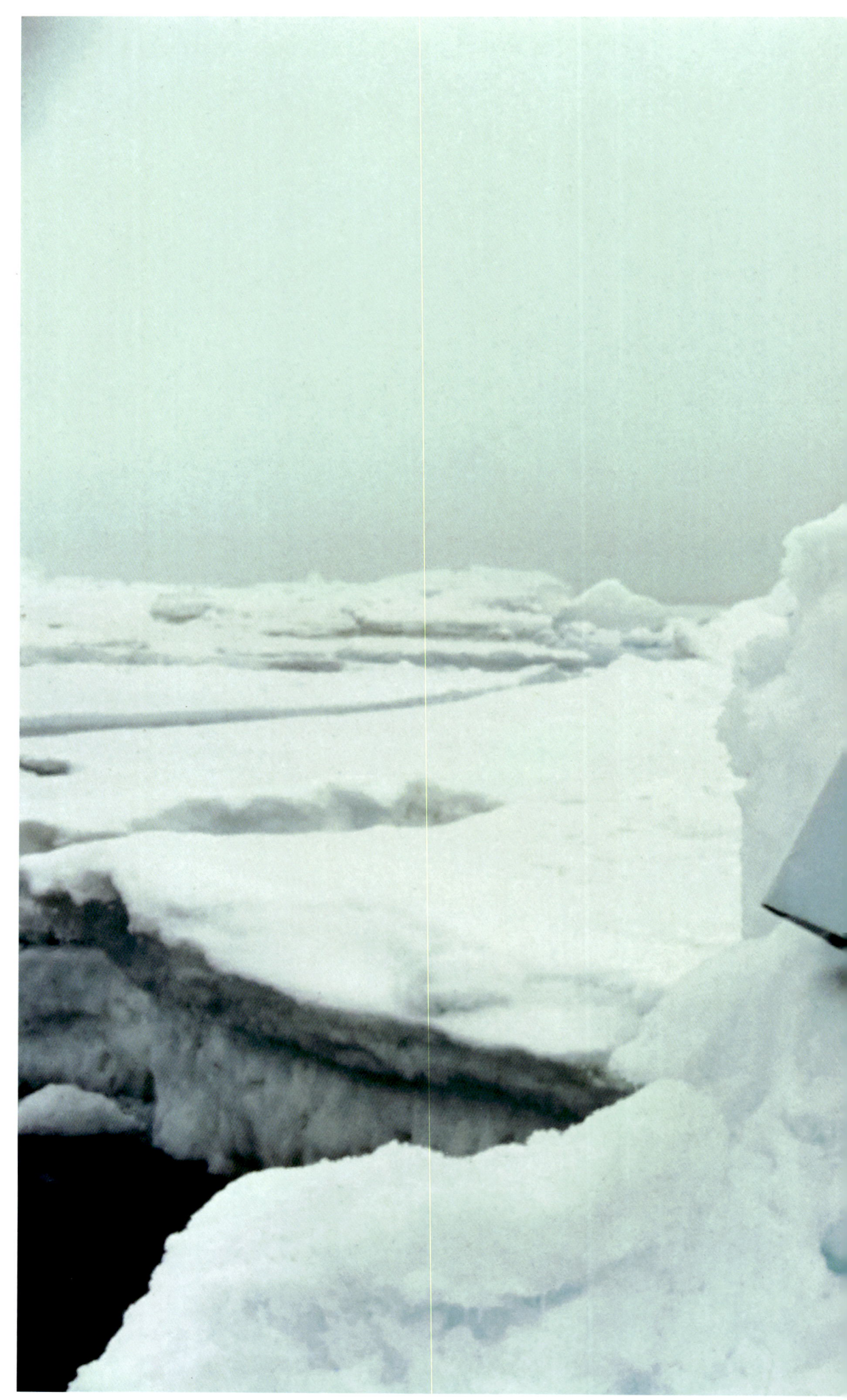

John Cowan,
"The Girl Who Went Out in the Cold,"
Vogue, November 1, 1964

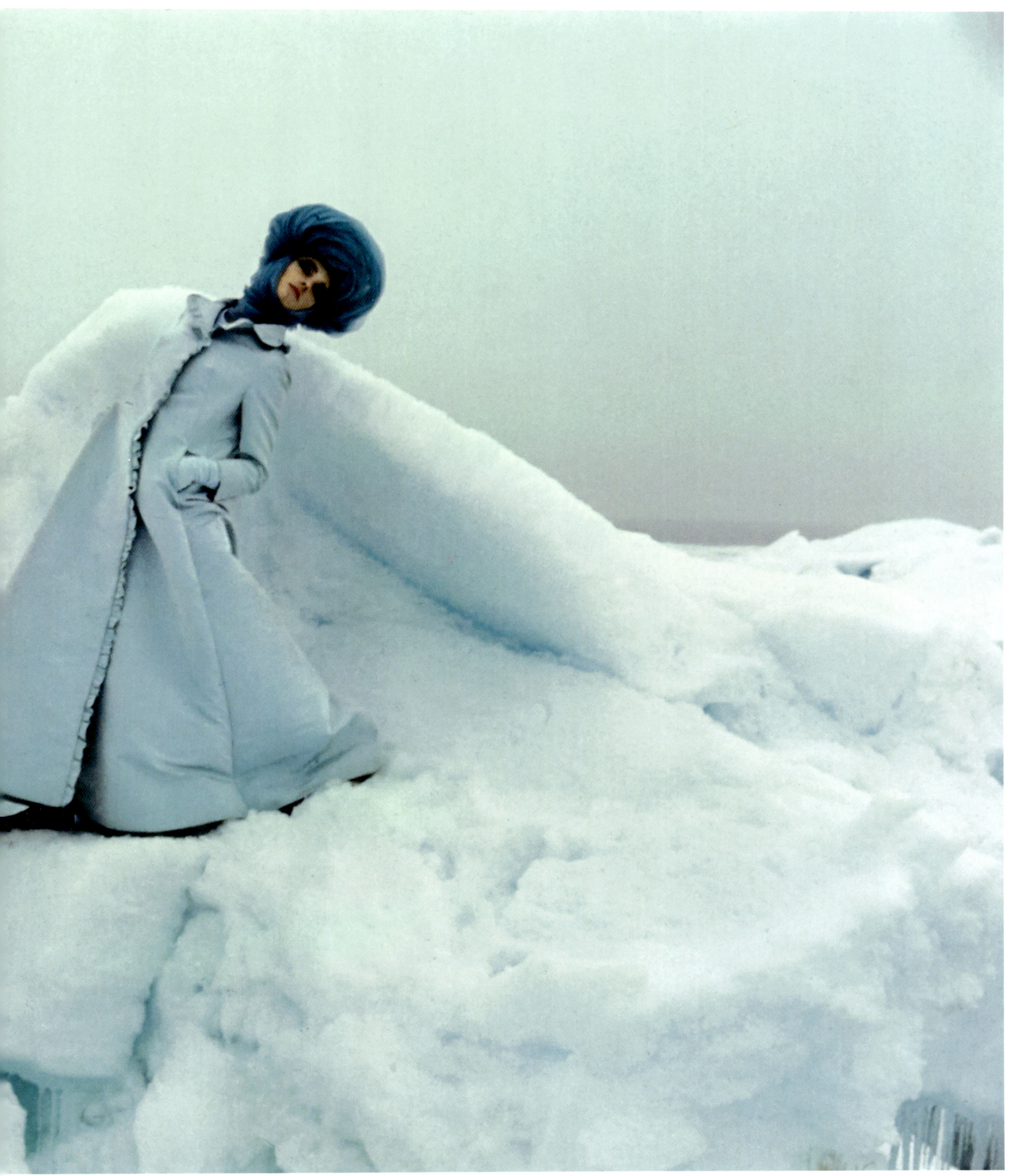

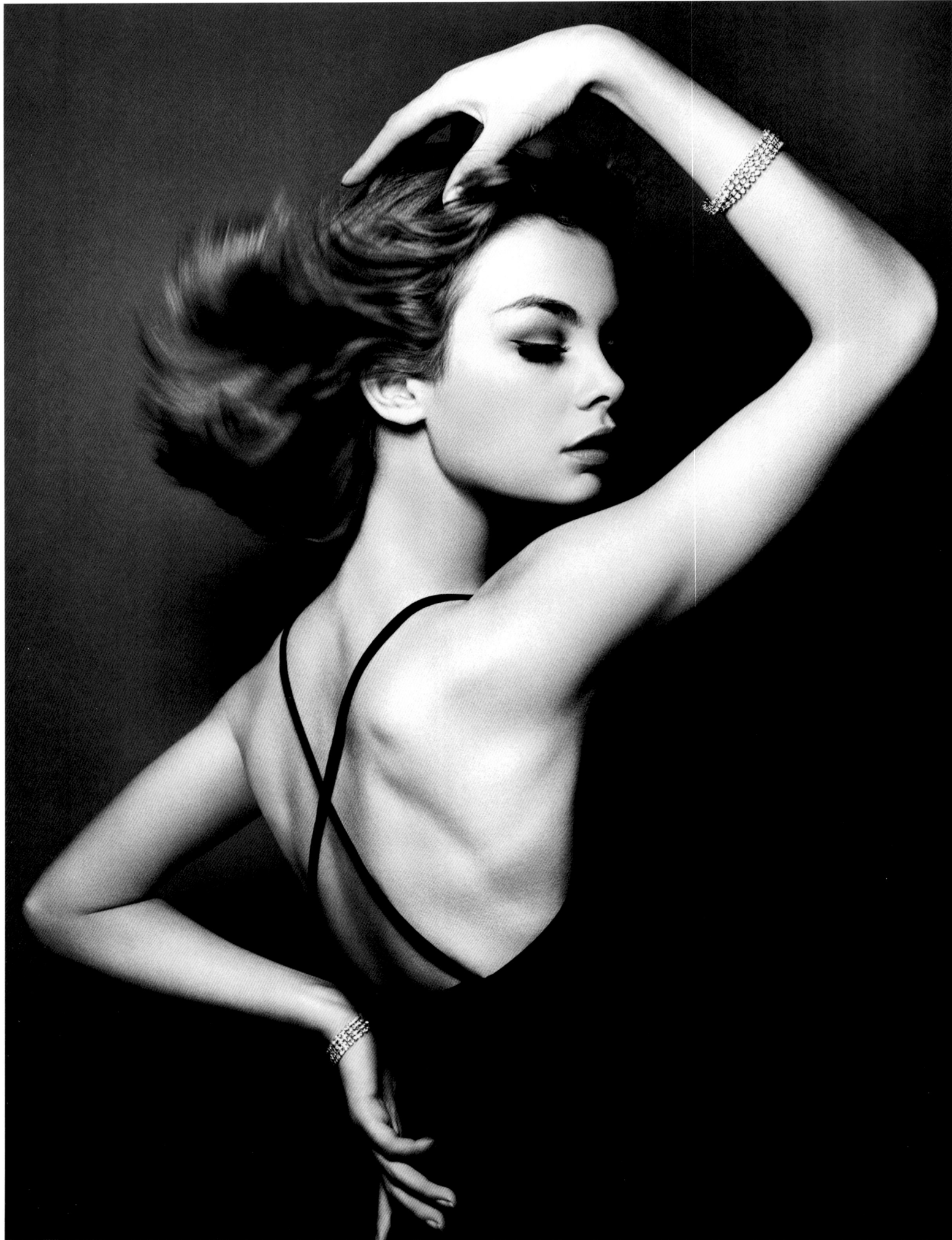

Born in London,
1938

DAVID BAILEY

David Bailey was part of a new generation of young English fashion photographers that also included Brian Duffy and Terence Donovan. Collectively, they broke the class barrier in fashion photography, shattering its elitist aura and putting British fashion photography—whose only international stars prior to the 1960s were Cecil Beaton (p. 30) and Norman Parkinson (p. 80)— back on the map.

The son of a tailor, Bailey was born in London's East End just before the beginning of World War II. He bought his first camera in Singapore in 1956 while serving in the Royal Air Force, and returned to London in 1958 determined to become a photographer. After trying unsuccessfully to join a photography course at the London College of Printing, Bailey sought work as an assistant, finally landing a job with John French (p. 88) in 1959. French was a generous teacher and, within a year, Bailey's fashion and portrait photographs were being published in daily newspapers and magazines, including *Man About Town*, *Flair*, and *Vanity Fair*. Offered a contract with *Vogue* in 1960, Bailey shot his first cover for the magazine in 1961.

Bailey's early fashion photographs combined the formal rigor of Irving Penn (p. 70) and Richard Avedon's (p. 94) styles with a sexual frisson that made the latter photographers' work look prudish by comparison. His highly publicized relationship with model Jean Shrimpton through-out this period resulted in some game-changing images: his 1961 photograph transformed Shrimpton's girl-next-door looks into a kind of beauty that was both classic and utterly of its time. As Bailey later remarked, "What attracted me to her was that she genuinely didn't care how she looked. She honestly never understood what all the fuss was about."

Bailey's early, realist style became increasingly polished throughout the 1960s, as he abandoned the 35 mm camera and began to focus more closely on other genres, including portraiture, reportage, travel photography, and still life. In 1967, he met seventeen-year-old Penelope Tree—whom he described as "an Egyptian Jiminy Cricket"—and she became his model and muse for the rest of the decade.

David Bailey,
Jean Shrimpton, 1961

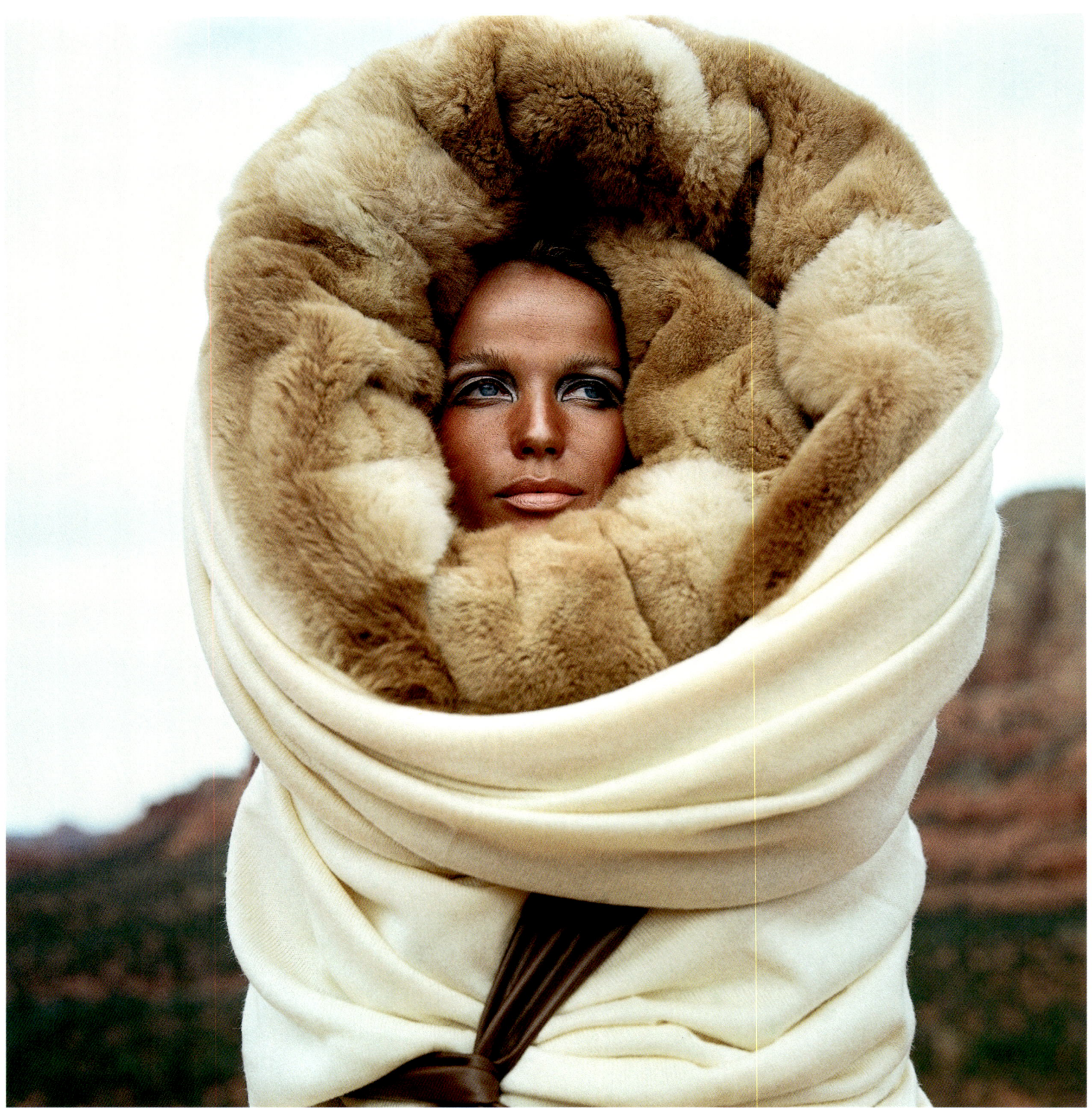

Born in Florence,
1937

FRANCO RUBARTELLI

Expelled from his early training to be an officer in the Italian navy, Franco Rubartelli studied social and political science at the University of Rome, with the intention of preparing himself for a diplomatic career. Later, he traveled to Cambridge, England, to learn English, where he met and married an English woman. His account of his introduction to fashion photography is a mysterious one: upon learning that his wife Francoise, an aspiring model, intended to leave him for a photographer, he awoke from a nap one day to find a camera on the table in front of him: "No one in the house was a photographer, nobody had brought a camera. . . . Maybe an angel brought it, I don't know, but the fact is that there was an old Leica."

Rubartelli's very first photographs—of his wife running on the beach—were unconventional by the standards of the day, but they found their way onto the desk of American *Vogue* editor Diana Vreeland, who offered him work. Although Francoise was his first model and muse, it was his discovery of German model Veruschka in the early 1960s that propelled both to fame. The pair went on to become lovers and creative collaborators for the next nine years.

"The Magnificent Mirage," which appeared in the July 1968 issue of American *Vogue*, was originally intended as a preview of fall and winter fabrics. Vreeland sent Rubartelli, Veruschka, and designer Giorgio di Sant' Angelo into Arizona's Painted Desert with four suitcases full of fabric, tape, and cord, with instructions to wrap the model in the materials. Sant' Angelo's extravagant, tribal-inspired styling—dramatically different from the structured outlines that had been so prevalent in fashion until the late 1960s—was the perfect foil for Veruschka's Amazonian looks and Rubartelli's lush, saturated images. The resulting editorial personified the exoticism that defined American *Vogue* in the late 1960s, and hinted at the sexually charged glamour that would come to define fashion photography in the 1970s.

Franco Rubartelli,
Vogue, July 1, 1968

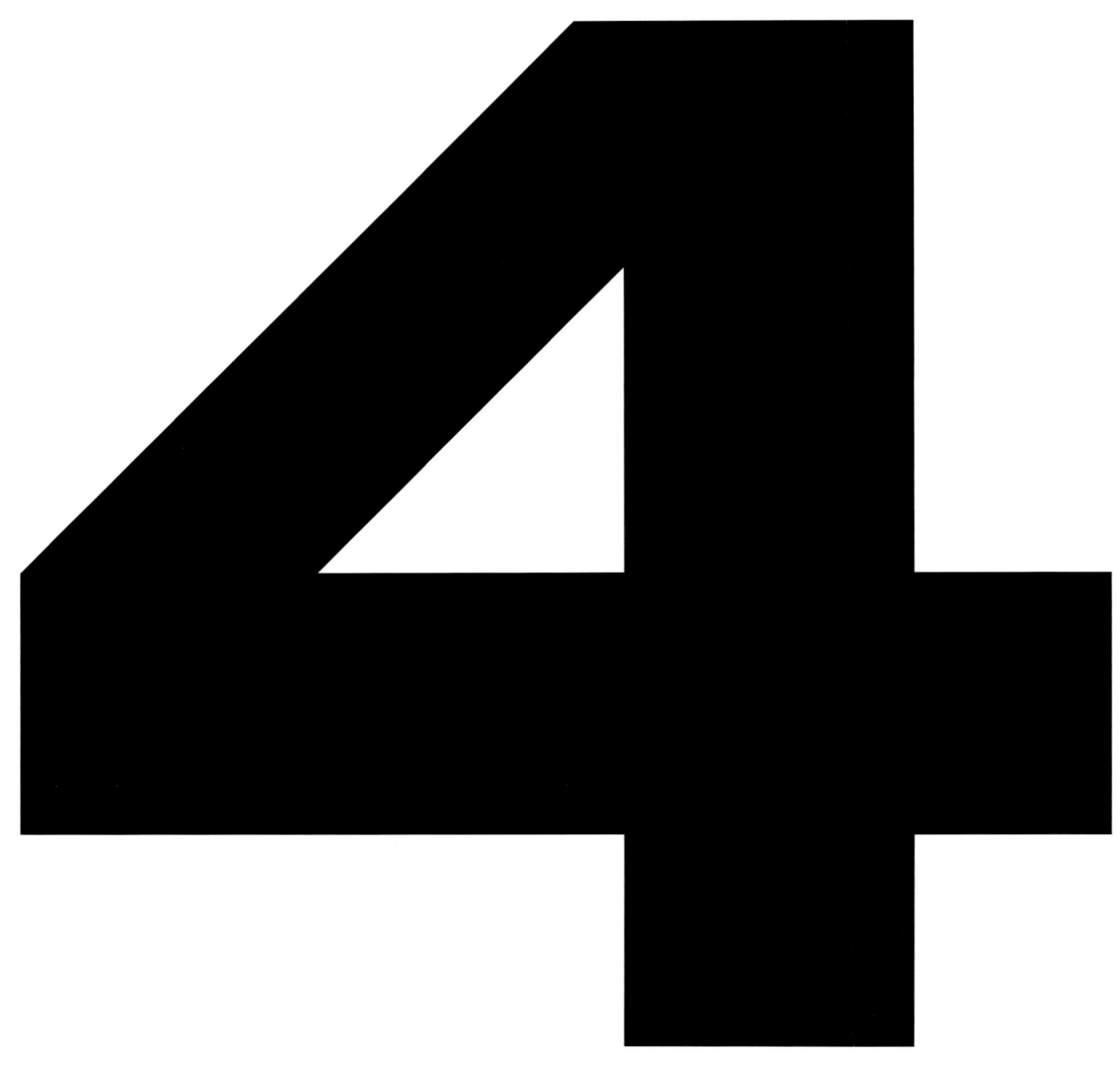

Deborah Turbeville,
*Stigmata: Isabella at École
des Beaux-Arts, Paris*, 1977

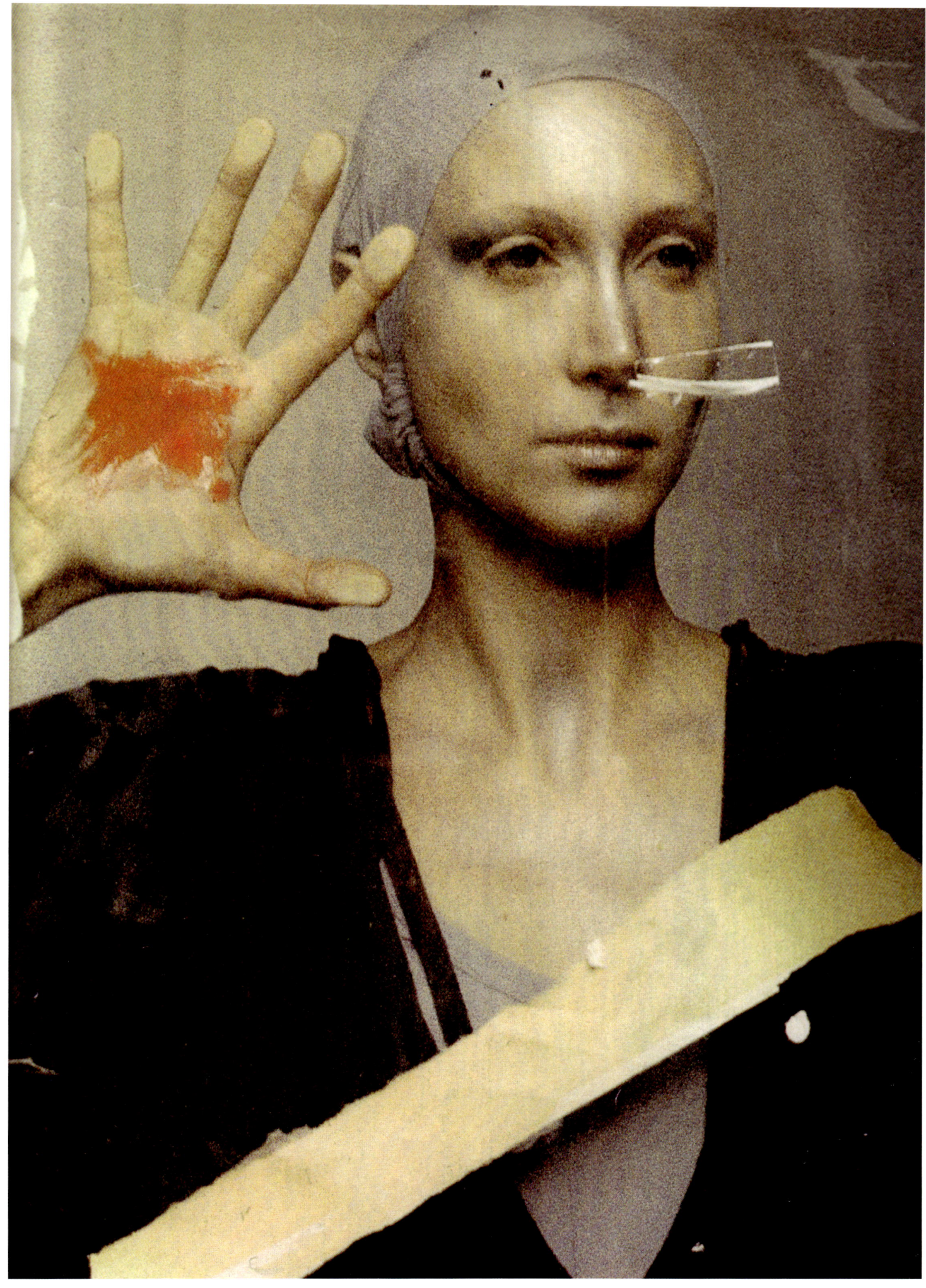

DEBORAH TURBEVILLE

Born in Stoneham,
Massachusetts, 1932;
died in New York City,
2013

Deborah Turbeville's photographs—like those by her contemporary Sarah Moon (p. 130)—stood out amid the work of her male colleagues throughout the 1970s and '80s. Rather than the romanticism of Moon's work, however, Turbeville's softly focused images suggested darker, more introspective narratives. Raised by bohemian parents in a small town outside of Boston, Turbeville began photographing as a teenager. For one of her first projects, The Maine Story, she documented a local family for an entire year. "I'd hang around every day, catching them in various activities," she later said. "If things got dull, I'd invent little scenes that didn't exist." The desire to tell stories, and to create mystery in her photographs, would stay with Turbeville throughout her career. "At their best, I feel my pictures have this quality," she wrote, "films you might have missed but would liked to have seen."

Turbeville began working in fashion in the 1950s as an assistant and sample model for American designer Claire McCardell. She went on to work as a stylist and editor at magazines, including *Harper's Bazaar* and *Mademoiselle*, before starting to take her own photographs in the 1960s. In 1966, she enrolled in a photography workshop taught by Richard Avedon (p. 94) and art director Marvin Israel. By her own admission, Turbeville's fashion photographs were always more about atmosphere than clothes. Her lack of technical skill became a vital part of her signature style: she used faded color and sepia tones, overexposure and blurred outlines, with dust and scratches on the negatives.

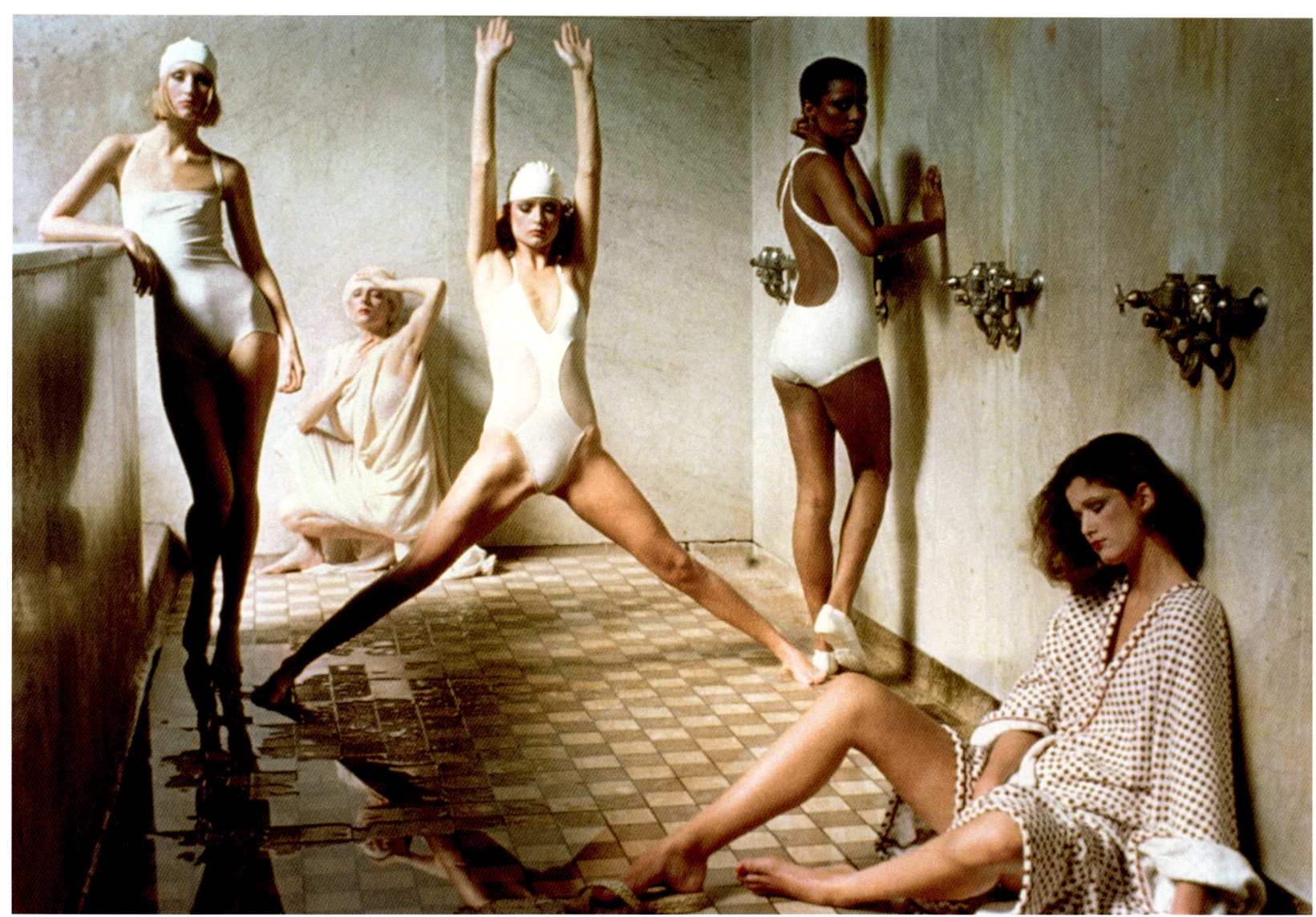

Her best-known work, the May 1975
bathhouse editorial, started with a request from
Vogue editorial director Alexander Liberman
to shoot ten pages of bathing suits on five models,
to be printed as double-page spreads. Rather
than a conventional location such as the beach,
however, Turbeville decided to shoot the spread
in a run-down nineteenth-century bathhouse
on New York's Lower East Side. "Something in
the atmosphere began to dictate the pictures,"
she recalled. "As the sitting progressed they
became increasingly surreal, bizarre, Marquis
de Sade in feeling, particularly the black-and-white
images. Each photograph took almost a full day
to work out." The spread generated a good deal
of controversy, due not just to the extreme
thinness of some of the models, but to their expres-
sionless faces and dingy surroundings: "People
started talking about Auschwitz and lesbians
and drugs . . . and all I was doing was trying to
design five figures in space."

Deborah Turbeville,
Vogue, 1975; from the Bathhouse series

Born in Vichy,
France, 1941

SARAH MOON

Although it was her male contemporaries—including Helmut Newton (p. 134), Chris von Wangenheim (p. 138), and Guy Bourdin (p. 144)—who would lead fashion photography into increasingly controversial terrain throughout the 1970s, it was Sarah Moon's first major magazine assignment that is often said to have ushered in the "age of decadence" that marked the end of the 1960s. Hinting at drug use and pedophilia, her photographs for the March 1969 edition of British *Harper's Bazaar* led to the firing of the editor who had commissioned them.

Moon began her career as a model, but she was never comfortable in front of the camera. She first began taking her own photographs in the 1960s, photographing models as they waited in the studio, and later, shooting portfolios for friends. In 1968, a friend asked Moon to shoot a collection that she was designing for fashion house Cacharel. Together with publicist and publisher Robert Delpire, Moon carried on working for the brand for the next twenty years. Her early photographs, mostly shot in black and white (often on Polaroid film), have a distinctive look and feel: melancholic and dreamlike, they offered a softer and more romantic—though equally suggestive—vision of femininity than that of her male colleagues.

In the 1980s, Moon began shooting almost exclusively in rich, saturated color, and the mood of her work changed profoundly. "For me, black and white is closer to introspection, to memories, to loneliness and loss," she has said. "I don't see the same in color—it's another language, a living language." Moon's process has remained the same for many years: she rarely plans her shoots, preferring to work intuitively, drawing inspiration from the atmosphere on set. "I usually have the impression that sometimes there's a sort of collaboration with my unconscious, which has a life of its own, and therefore, I can only be the reflection, the sounding board, for something I cannot say with words."

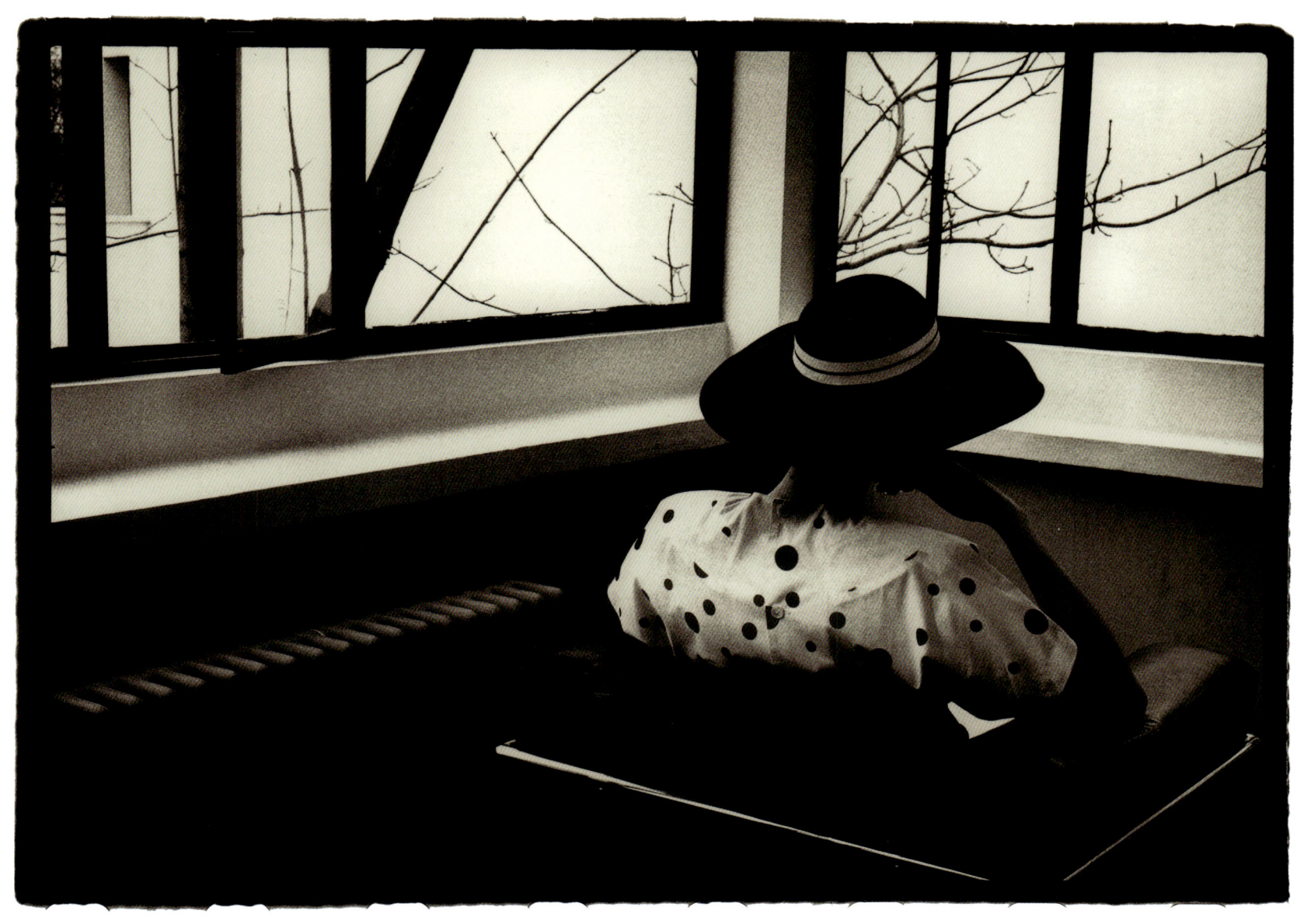

Sarah Moon, *Robe à pois*, 1979
Following pages: Sarah Moon, (left) *Adriana pour Watanabe*,
2000; (right) *Sveta pour Hussein Chalayan*, 2000

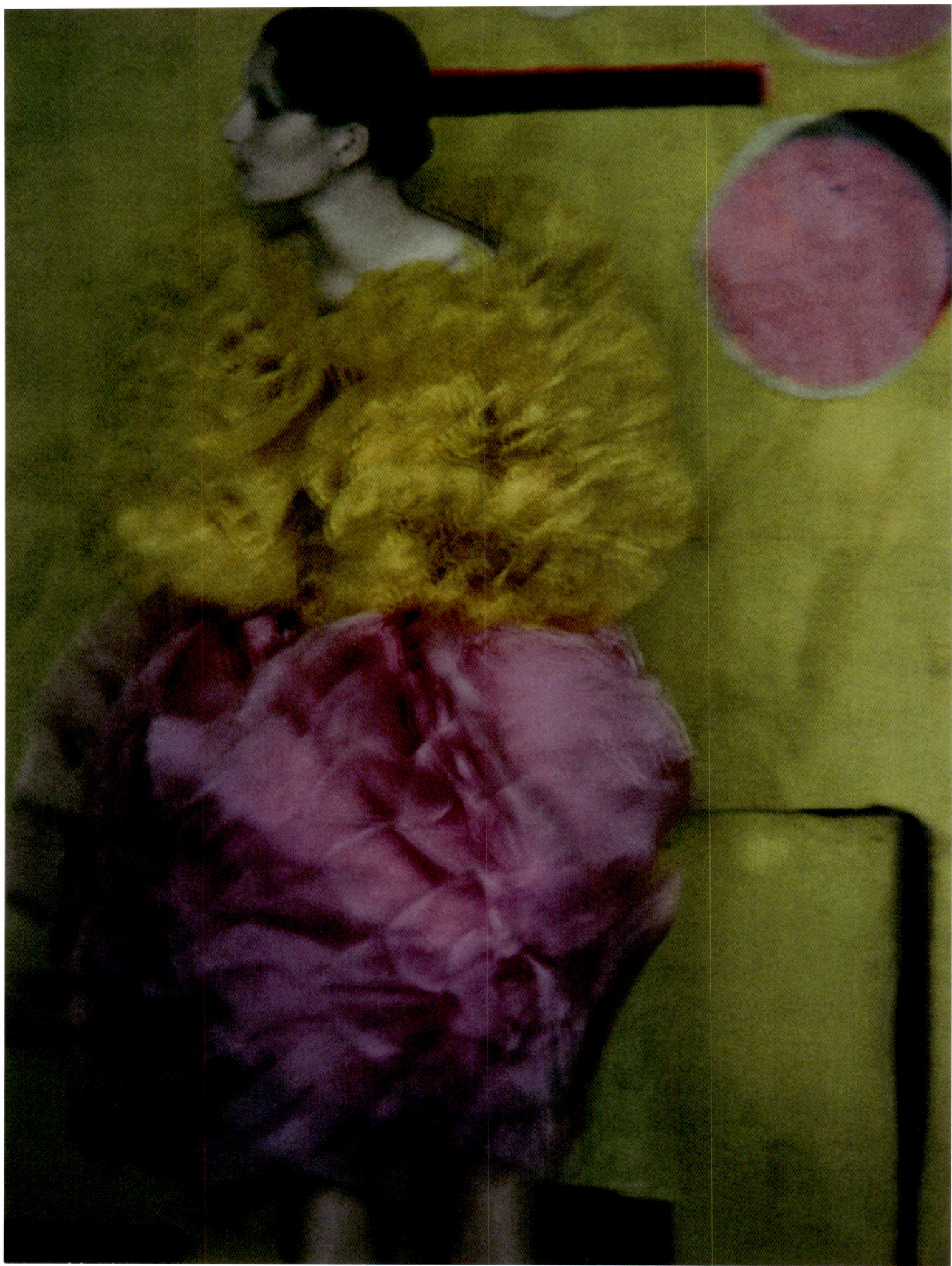

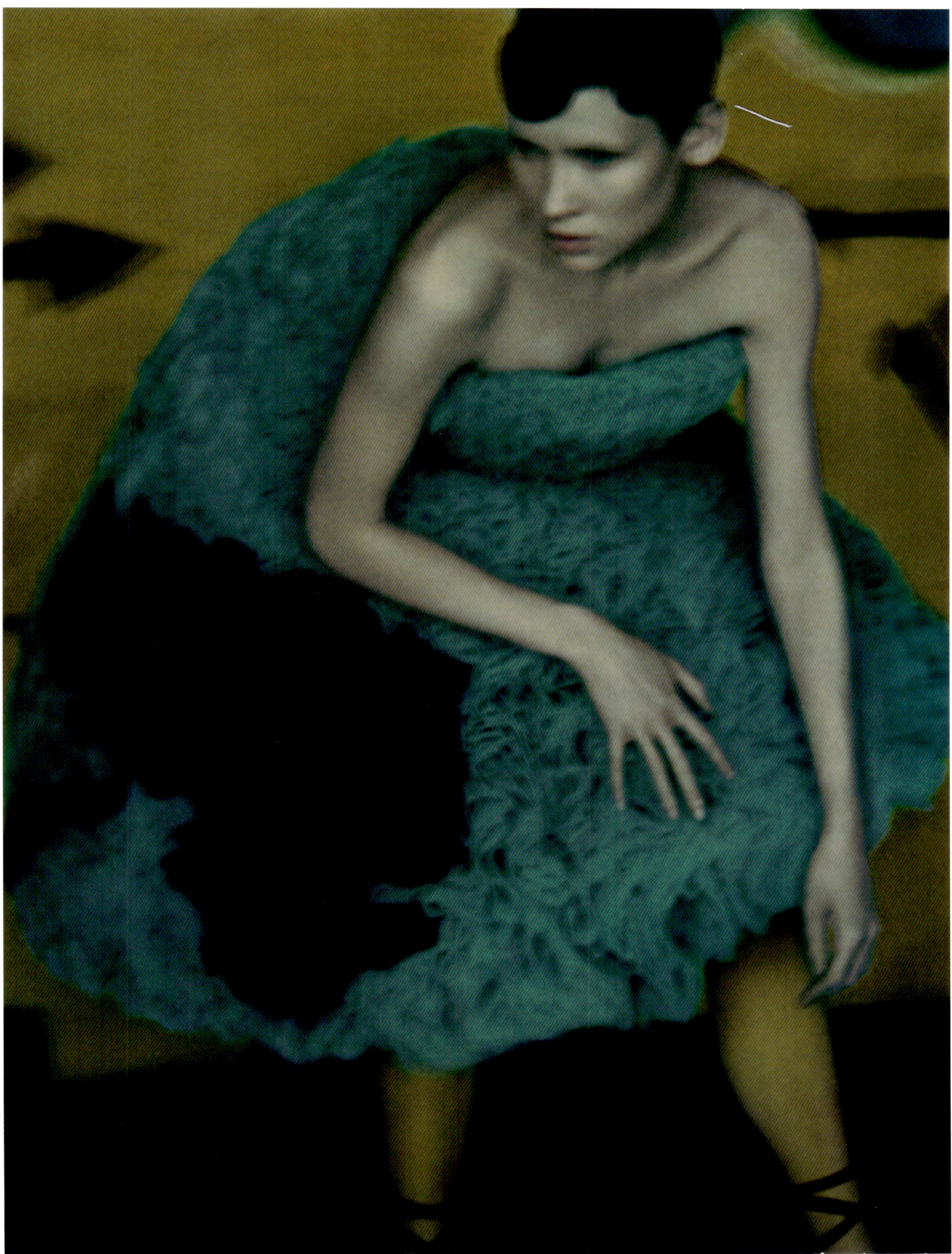

Born to a wealthy German Jewish family, Helmut Newton—né Neustädter—apprenticed with fashion photographer Yva (p. 48) at the age of sixteen. In 1938, amid growing discrimination against Jews, Newton left Germany, working briefly for a local newspaper in Singapore before being sent to an internment camp in Australia and eventually enlisting in the Australian army. Upon discharge in 1946, Neustädter opened a wedding photography studio and changed his surname to Newton. It wasn't until the 1950s that Newton took his first fashion photographs.

His early assignments for British and French *Vogue* failed to impress the editors, so Newton returned to Australia, where he finally found steady work with Australian, and, later, American *Vogue*. It wasn't until the 1970s, however, that Newton hit his stride. In 1972, Hugh Hefner launched *Oui* magazine, targeted at a younger, more educated audience than his first publication, *Playboy*. Hired by fashion director Tina Bossidy, Newton was given total creative freedom. "He got to play with sex with *Oui*," Bossidy recalled. "He didn't get to do that with French *Vogue*."

Sleek eroticism, lavishly mixed with wealth, luxury, and decadence, would become the hallmark of Newton's work—and of 1970s fashion photography in general. His style landed Newton in hot water more than once: "The Story of Ohhh," which appeared in the May 1975 issue of *Vogue* alongside Deborah Turbeville's notorious bathhouse spread (p. 129), generated a storm of debate and subscription cancellations.

The less controversial YSL Le Smoking editorial was shot in Paris's Rue Aubriot for the September 1975 issue of *Vogue Paris*. Although the photograph that appeared in the magazine featured model Vibeke Knudsen standing on her own under the streetlights, a second image—shot the following evening—has become even more iconic. As Knudsen recalled, "It was about 2 a.m. when we pulled up in front of Helmut's studio to do this last shot in the street. . . . Helmut insisted on shooting with the streetlight only, which meant I had to stand completely still for two seconds—that's a long time in stilettoes on cobblestones! . . . While he was shooting, Helmut asked us all to come back the following night. He was already planning his next shot. He wanted me to use the same pose with a nude model (Aya) standing next to me. I was asked to wear the same suit."

Born in Berlin, 1920; died in Los Angeles, 2004

Helmut Newton, *Le Smoking, YSL, Rue Aubriot, Paris*, 1975

HELMUT NEWTON

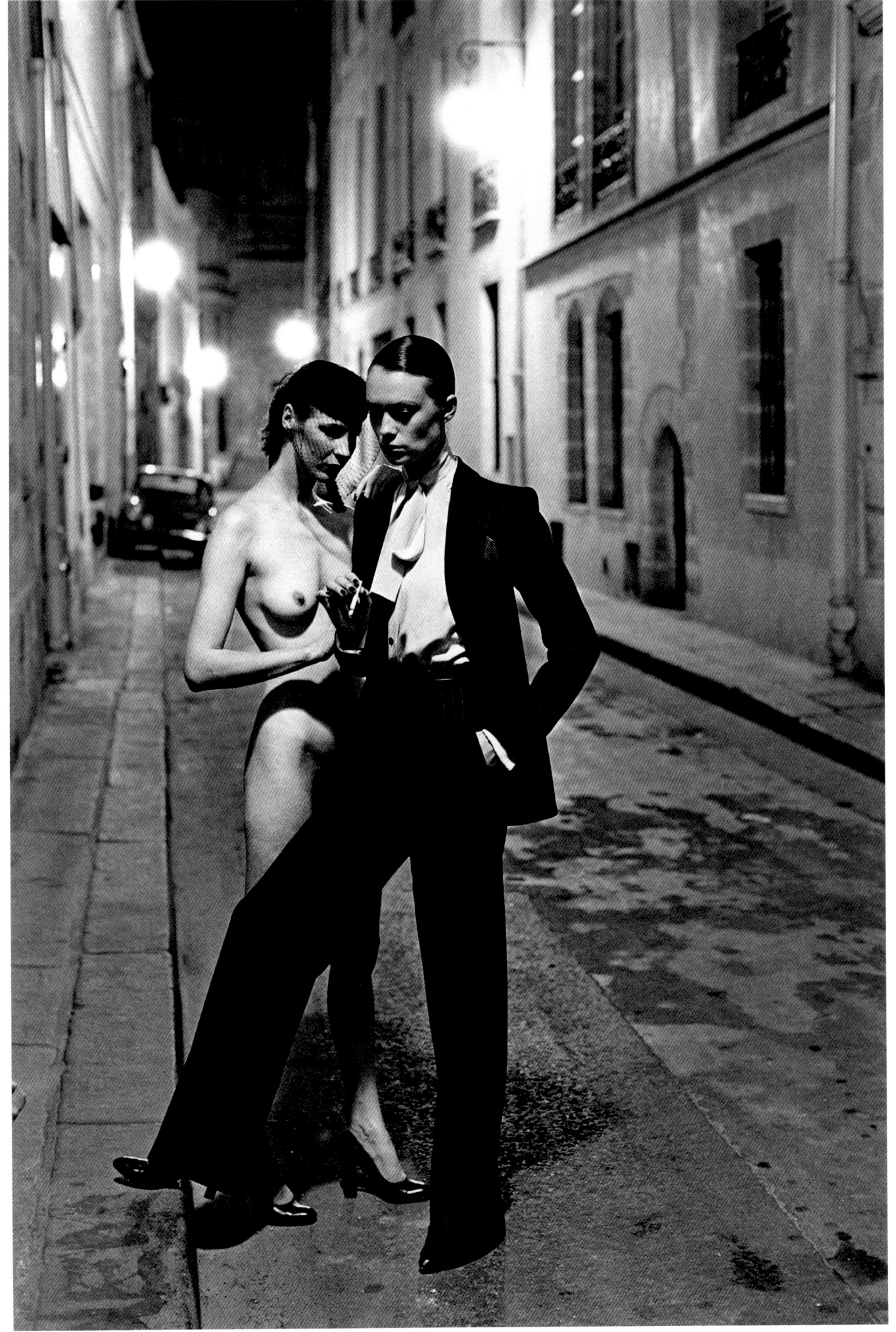

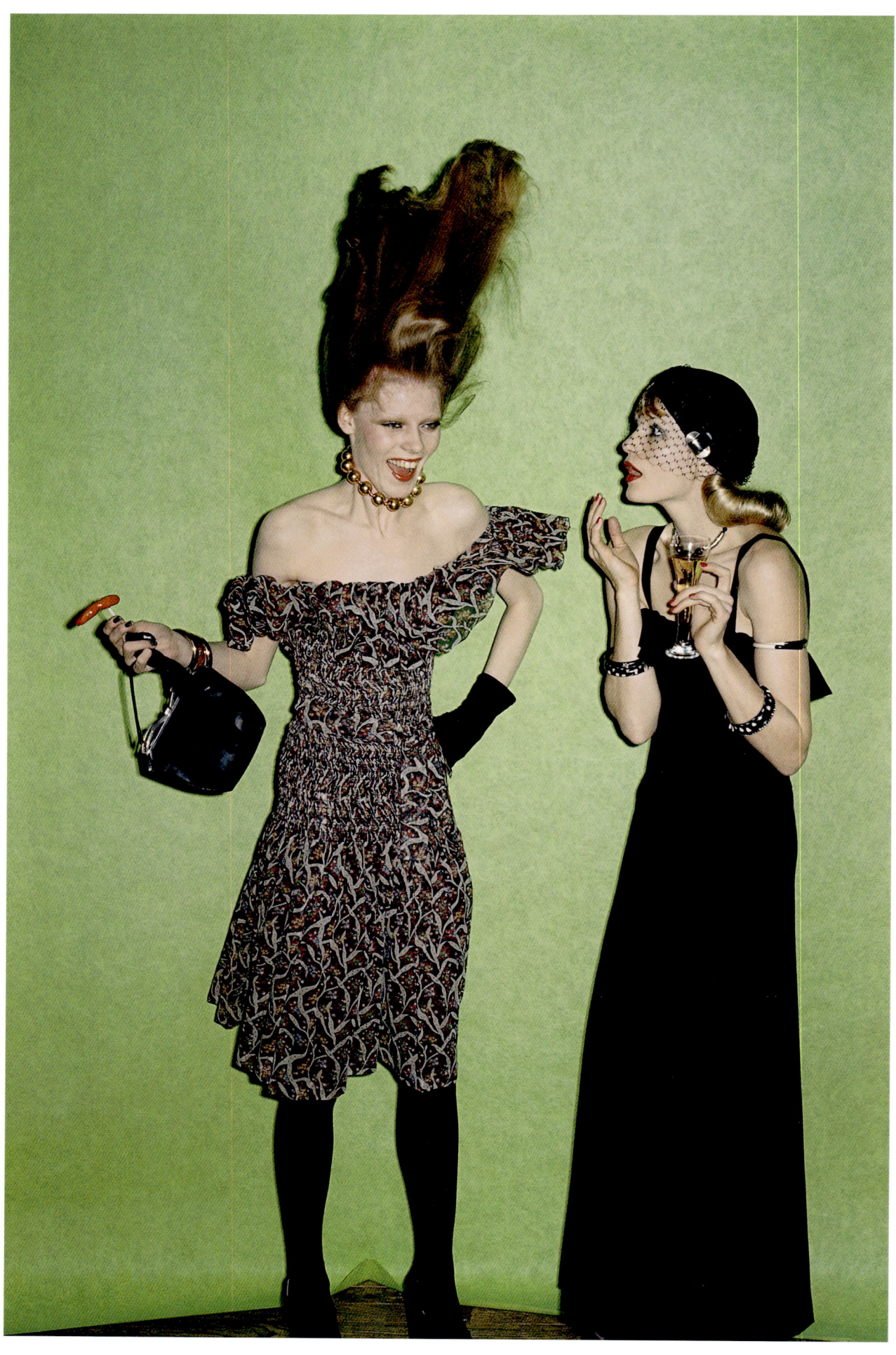

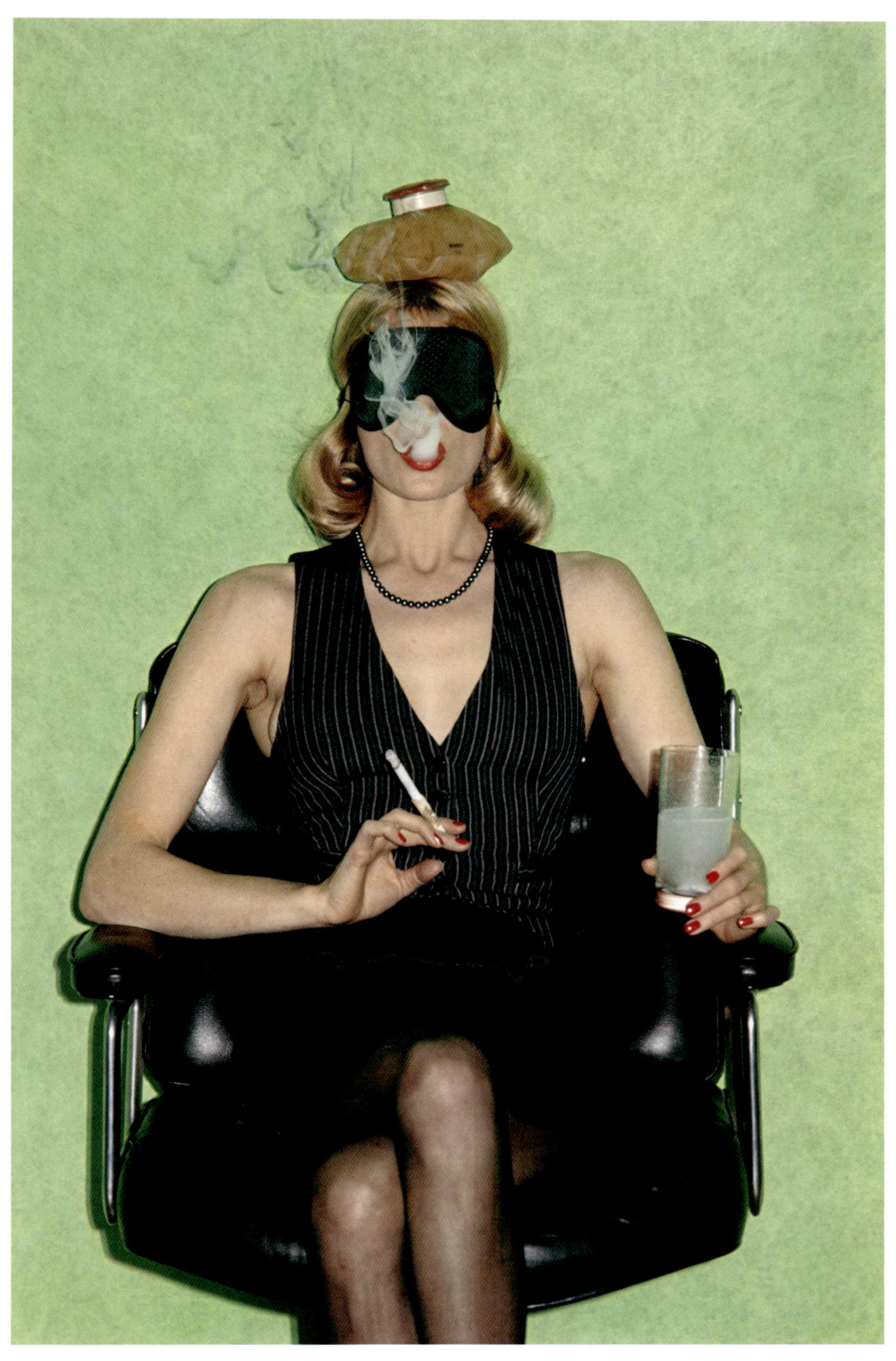

Left and above: Helmut Newton,
Nova, Paris, 1973

CHRIS VON WANGEN- HEIM

Born in Breig, East Prussia, 1942; died in Saint Martin, 1981

Chris von Wangenheim's legacy—according to photographer Steven Klein—is the edge he brought to fashion pictures, "creating a conduit for the violence and sexuality emerging within the context of their turbulent times." However, to Wangenheim's detractors, he was simply the "king of porno chic."

He was drawn to fashion photography from an early age. In 1965, at the age of twenty-three, he moved from his native Germany to New York, where he supported himself doing darkroom work and assisting. He eventually landed a job with fashion photographer James Moore. In 1968, Wangenheim shot his first story for *Harper's Bazaar*—but it was not until 1969, when he began working with *Vogue Italia* features editor Anna Piaggi, that he began experimenting with the disquieting imagery that would become his trademark.

Wangenheim's mature work embodied the turmoil of New York City in the 1970s, where the violence and corruption of a crumbling metropolis sat alongside the hedonistic glamour of nightclubs such as the legendary Studio 54. His Dior campaign—which Wangenheim conceived, and for which he wrote the copy—also owed a creative debt to Andy Warhol's silkscreen works of the early 1960s, which combined celebrity portraits with graphic images of death. His photographs hinted at decadence and intrigue, with models firing guns, diving through showers of banknotes, reclining in luxury hotel rooms, and being mauled by Dobermans. "The violence is in our culture," he once remarked to an interviewer, "so why shouldn't it be in our pictures?" Wangenheim's untimely death in a car crash in 1981 brought to an abrupt end a career that had been marked by a love of extremes.

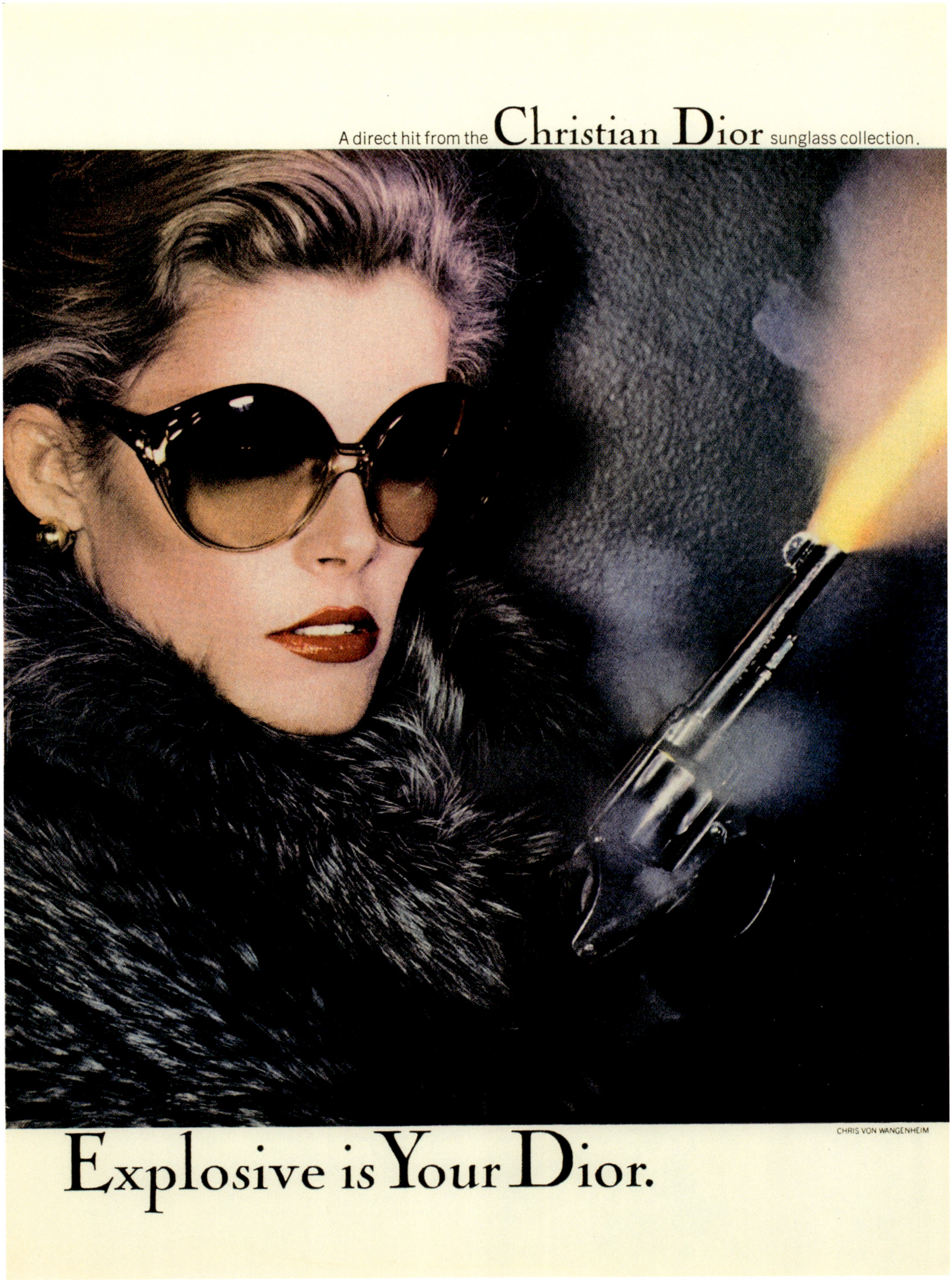

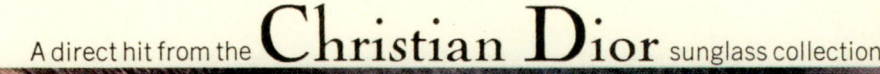

CHRIS VON WANGENHEIM

Explosive is Your Dior.

Chris von Wangenheim,
Dior Campaign, 1977

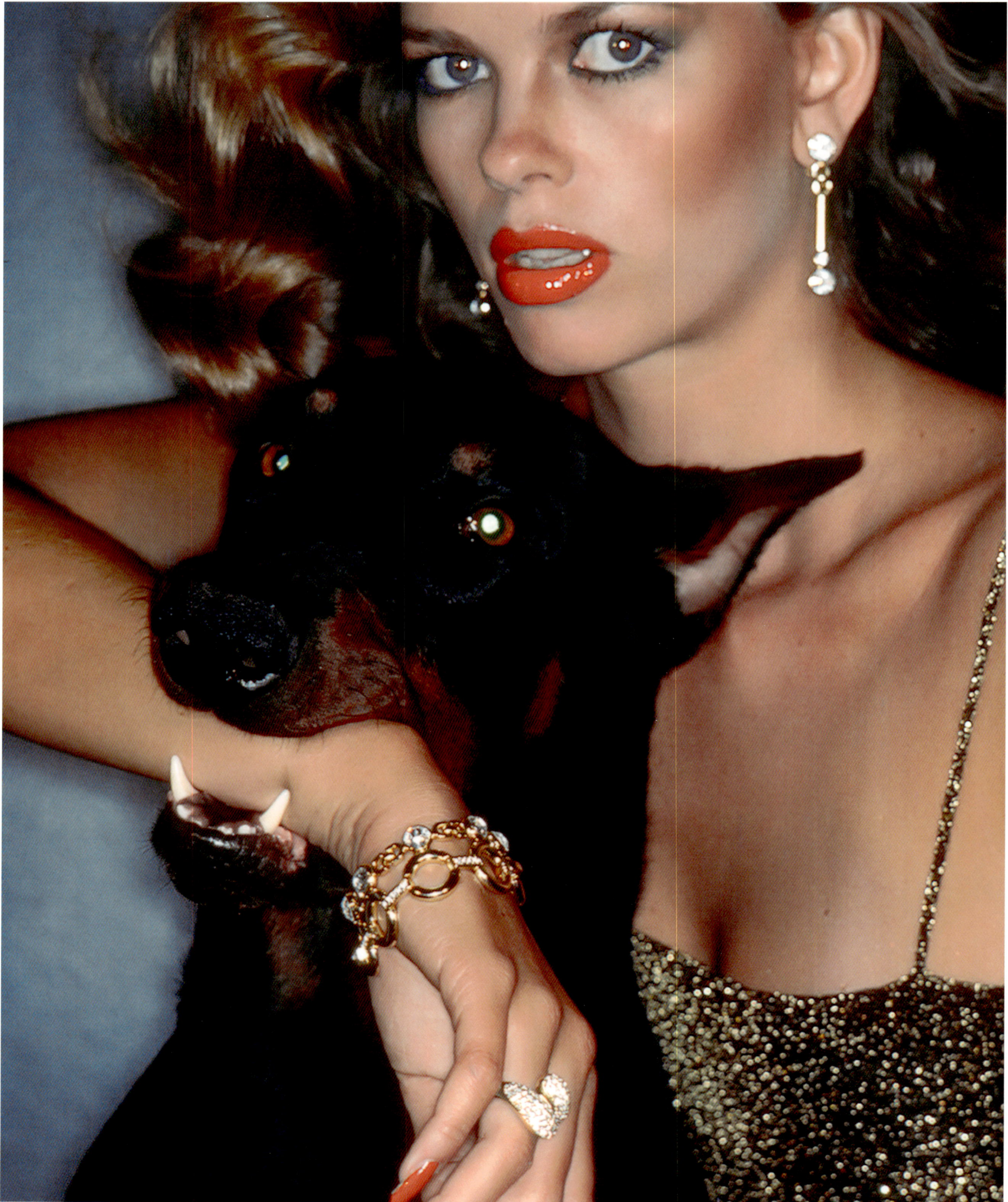

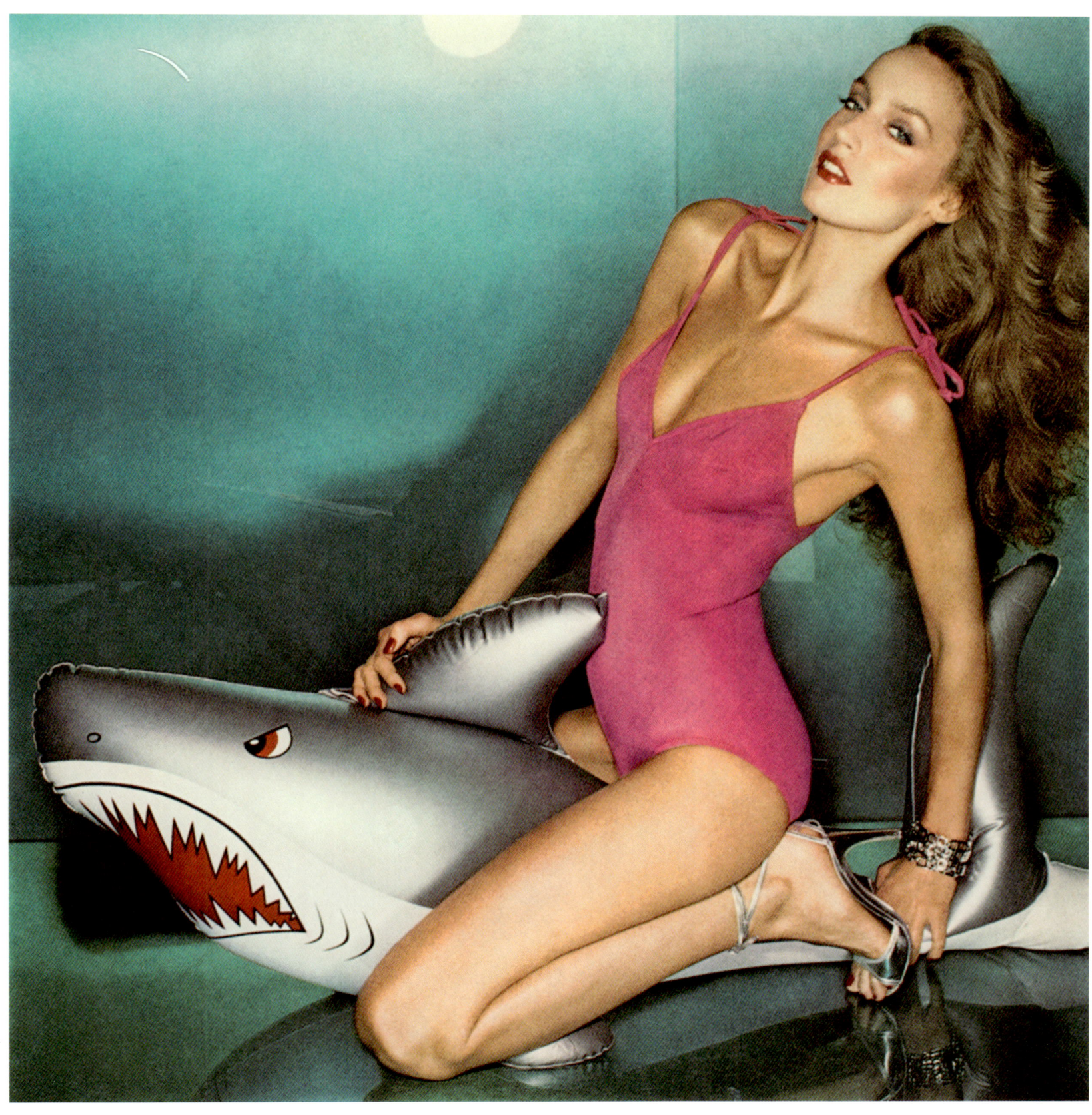

Chris von Wangenheim, *Dior Campaign*, 1977
Left: Chris von Wangenheim, *Dior Campaign*, 1976

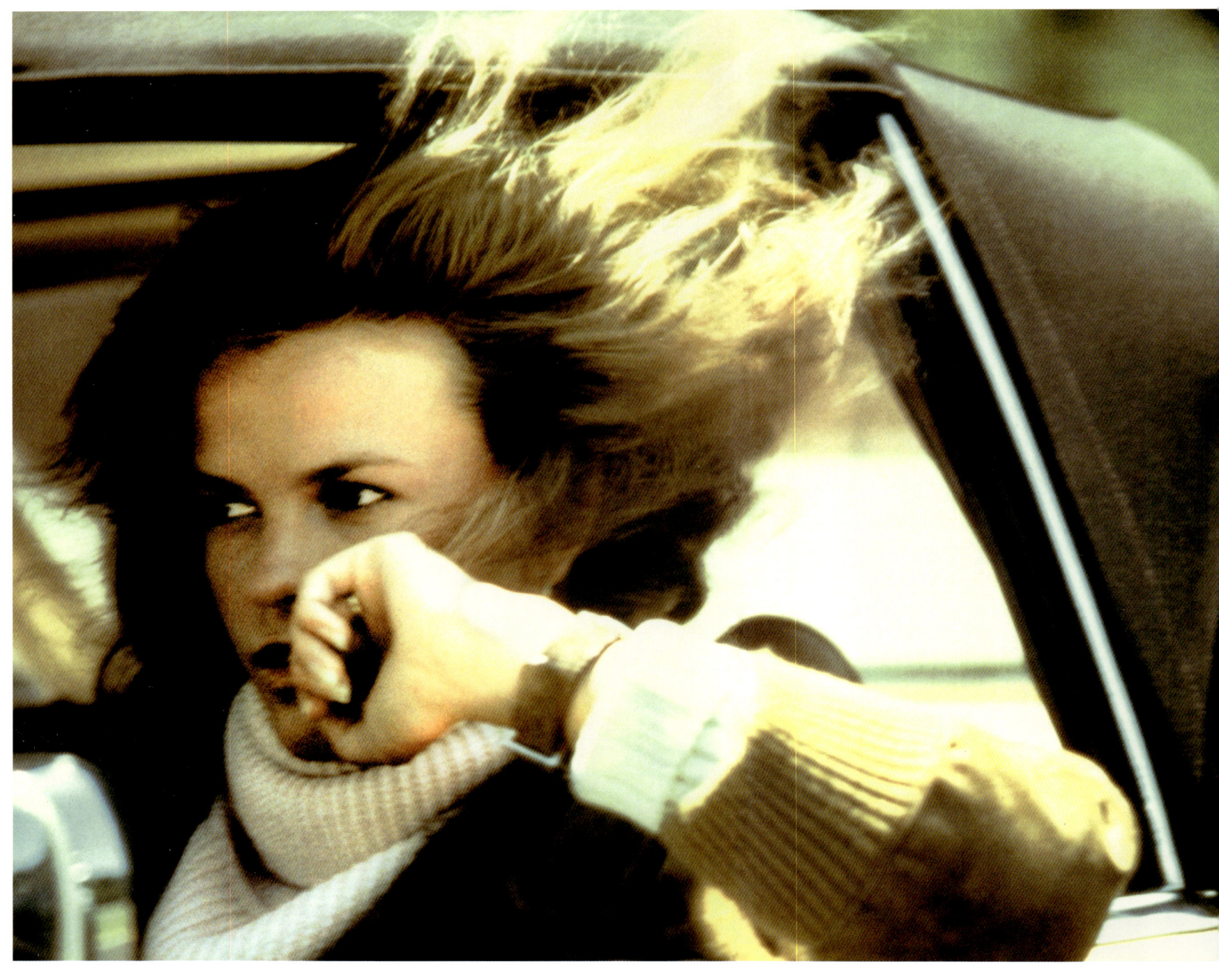

Arthur Elgort,
Lisa Taylor, George Washington Bridge, Vogue, 1976

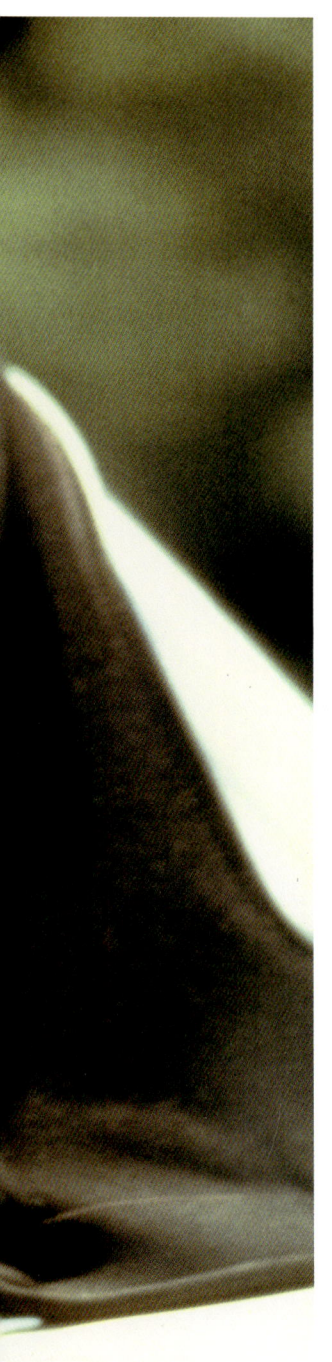

Born in New York City,
1940

ARTHUR ELGORT

Early in his career, Arthur Elgort decided to take his models out of his small, dark studio so that he could work outdoors. His mastery of natural light, along with the warmth and humor of his snapshot style, made his name. Self-taught, Elgort began taking photographs in 1960 while studying painting at Hunter College in New York. He credits the now-defunct magazine *Mademoiselle* for giving him his break in fashion photography: in the late 1960s, after viewing a portfolio of his work (delivered by one of his friends, as Elgort was too shy to do so himself), *Mademoiselle* gave the virtually unknown photographer twelve pages and a cover. In 1970 Elgort moved to Paris, where he was loosely associated with a group of French plein air photographers known in fashion circles as the "Paris Mob."

Elgort's photograph of the model Lisa Taylor driving a Mercedes convertible over New York's George Washington Bridge was taken for the October 1976 issue of *Vogue*. "My assistant drove our car, with me leaning out the window of the passenger side and Polly [Mellen, fashion editor] sitting in the back seat. [Hairstylist] Christiaan was lying down in the back of Lisa's Mercedes and would pop up in between shots to fix her hair," he recalled. Elgort's photograph was trailblazing not just for its departure from the rules of traditional beauty photography, but for the confidence that Taylor exuded. Her image—sporty, ambitious, and fiercely independent—was a perfect embodiment of 1970s American femininity.

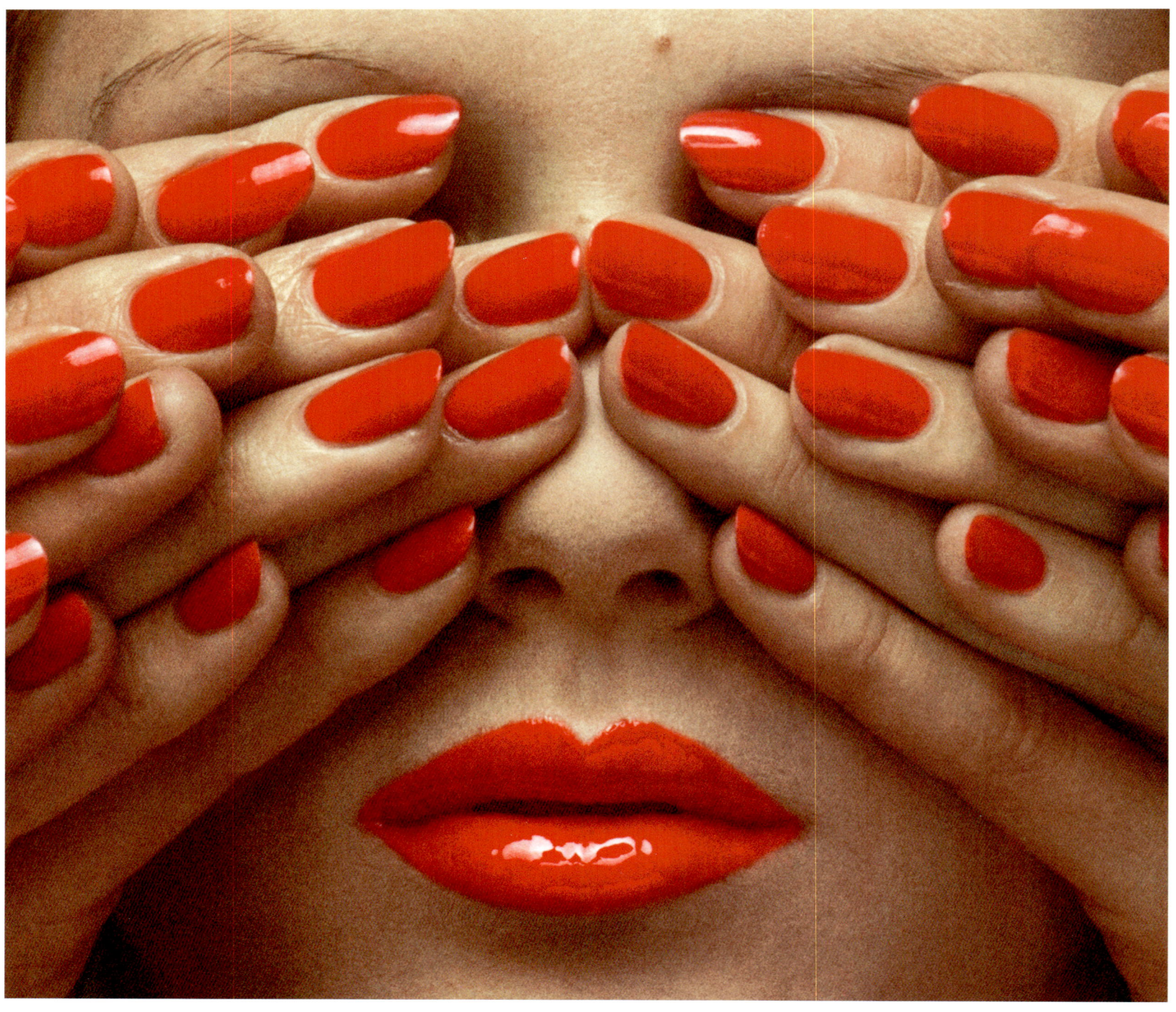

Born in Paris, 1928;
died in Paris, 1991

GUY BOURDIN

"I have never perceived myself as responsible for my images," Guy Bourdin once said. "They are just accidents. I am not a director, merely the agent of chance." Bourdin's enigmatic statement draws on the sensibility of one of his earliest influences, the photographer and Surrealist Man Ray (p. 46); in 1951, at the age of twenty-two, Bourdin even convinced Man Ray to write an introduction for his first exhibition of photographs. Although he would continue to invoke Surrealist motifs throughout his career as a fashion photographer, Bourdin is better known for his later style, which fused anxiety, eroticism, and psychological tension with glamour and decadence.

In 1954, Bourdin knocked on the door of *Vogue Paris* with portfolio in hand and was hired immediately; his first photographs appeared in the magazine in February 1955. It wasn't until the 1970s, however, under the editorship of Francine Crescent, that he was free to let his often-macabre imagination run wild. The sharp, hard shadows, supersaturated colors, and high glamour in Bourdin's images defined the decade's fashion photography, as did the suggestions of illicit desire, dark humor, and death. Some of Bourdin's best-known work was produced for footwear label Charles Jourdan between 1967 and 1981; his 1979 advertising image for Jourdan is characteristically simple in its design, with blocks of rich color setting off the model's black shoes and stockings. Psychologically, it is rich and complex, marrying sexual fetishism with slapstick humor.

Guy Bourdin,
Vogue Paris, May 1970

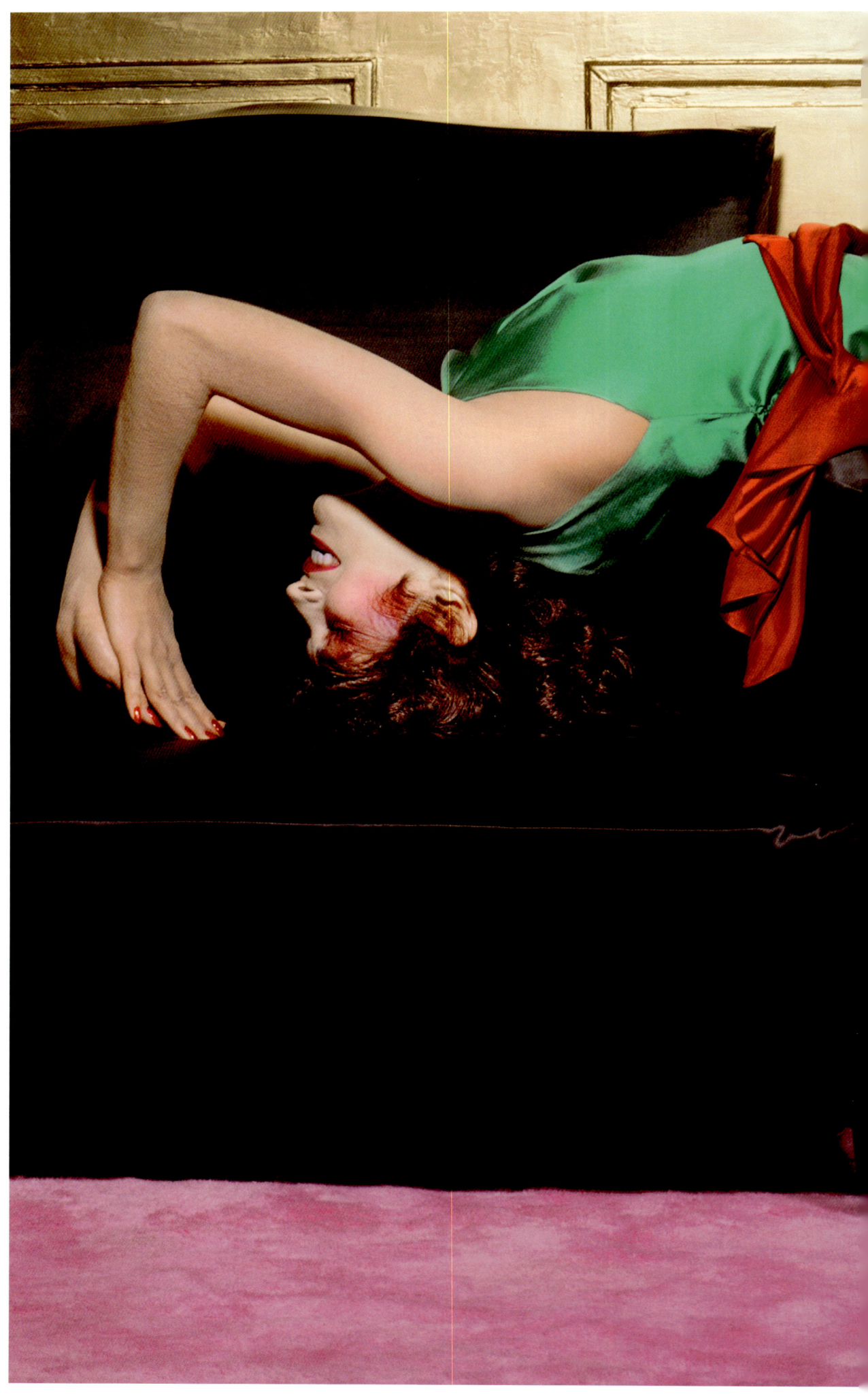

Guy Bourdin,
Charles Jourdan, Spring 1979
Following pages: Guy Bourdin,
Charles Jourdan, Spring 1979

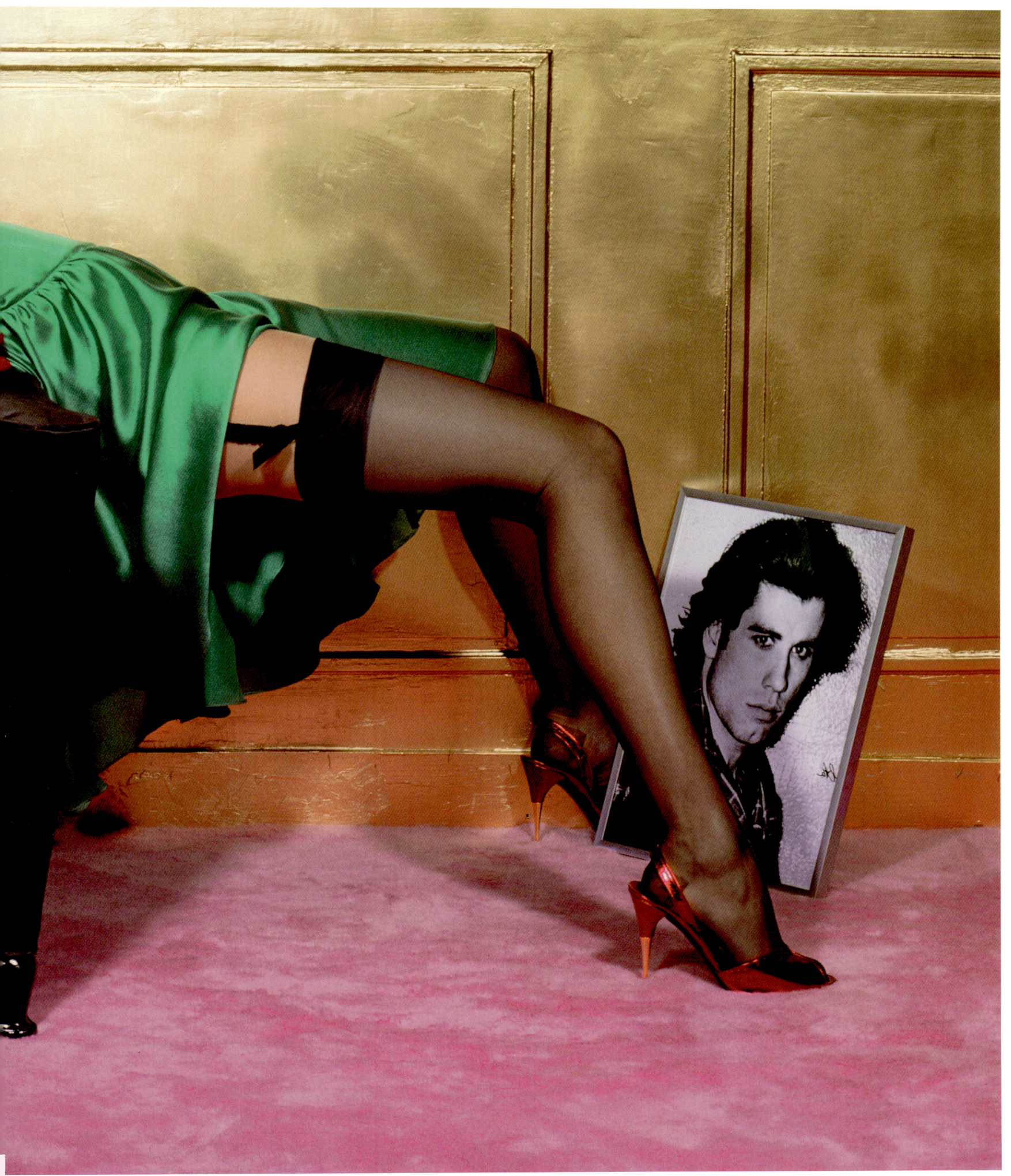

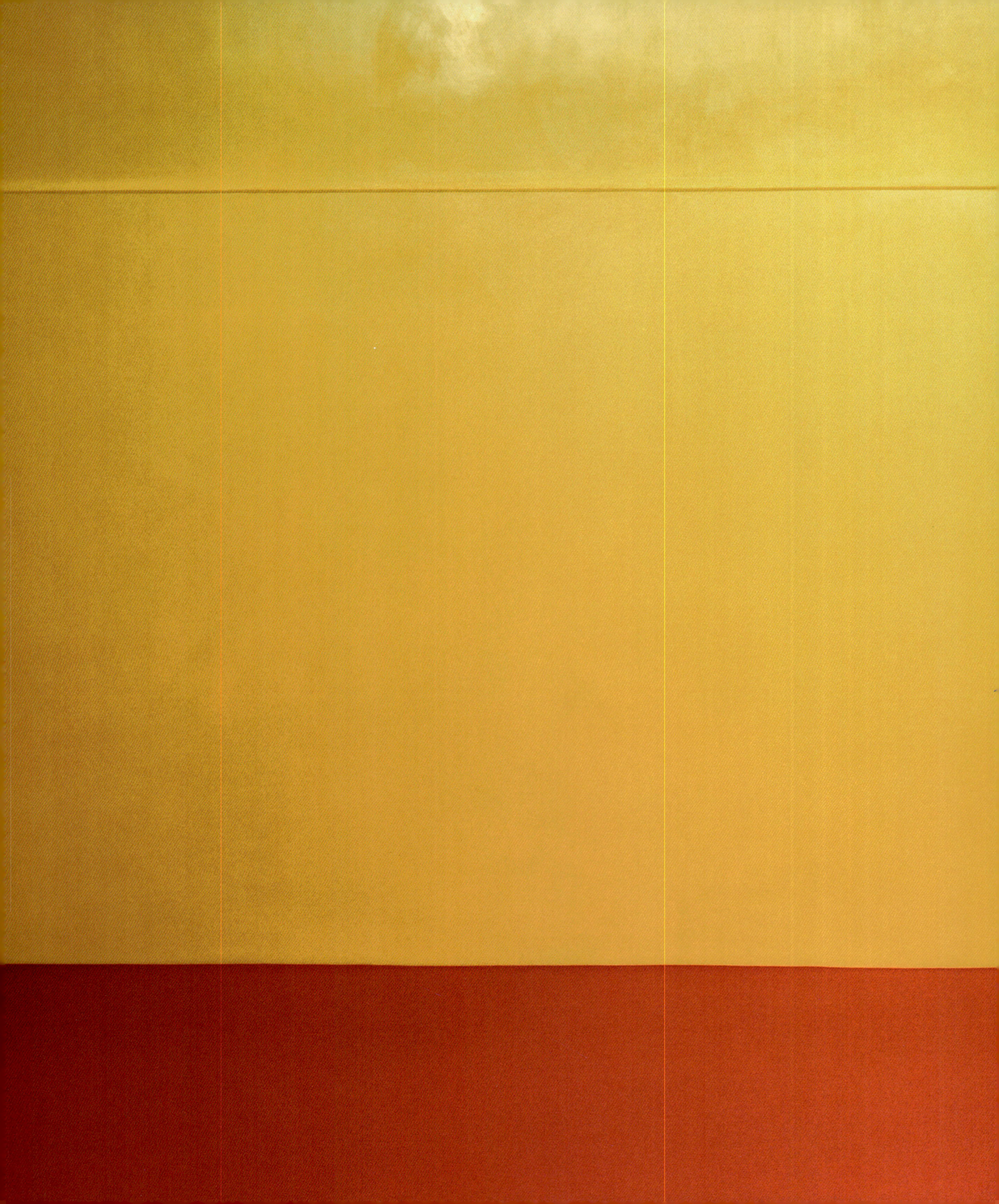

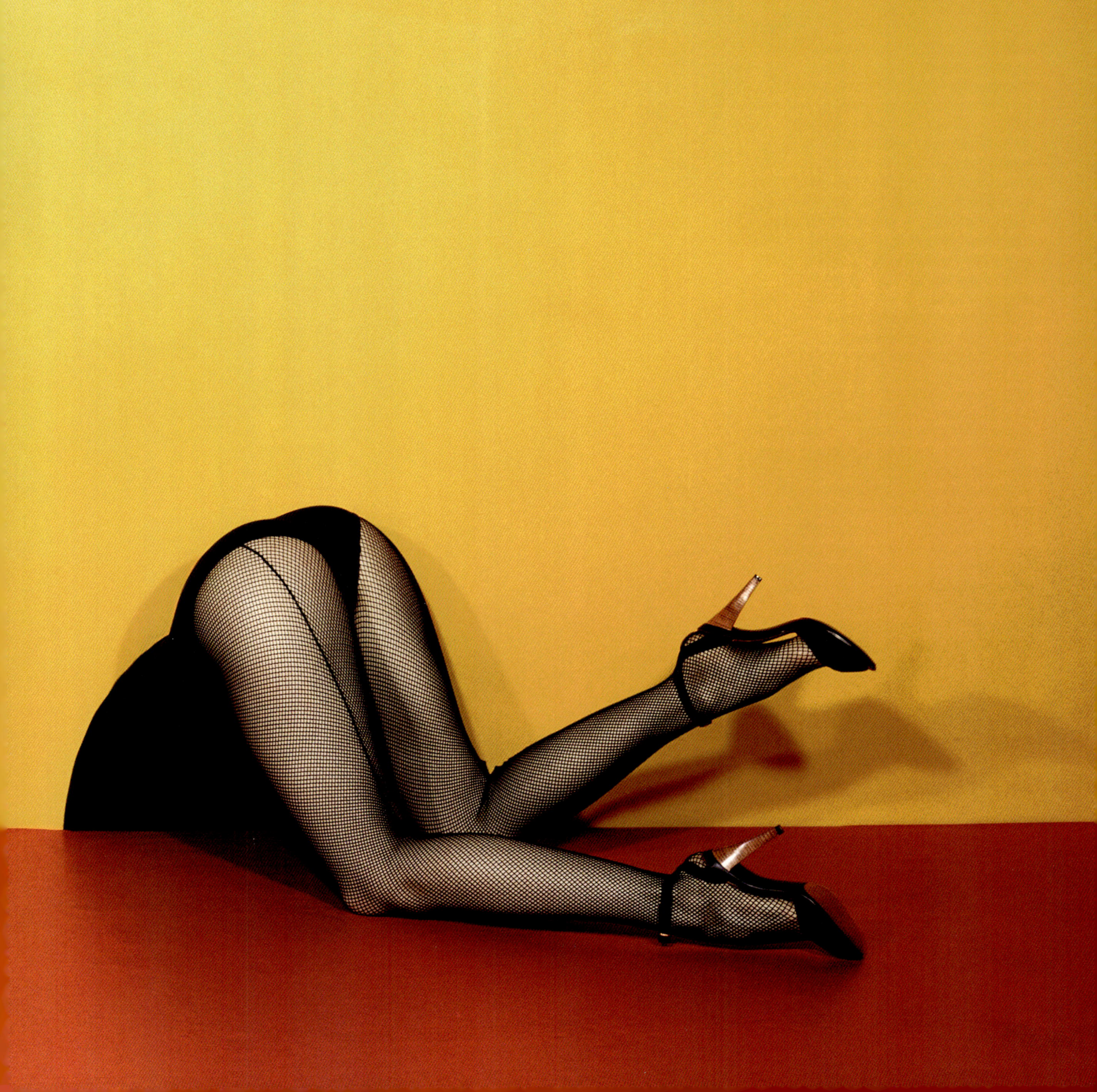

Born in Switzerland,
1939

Hans Feurer doesn't identify as a fashion photographer, preferring to describe himself as an "artisan mercenary" whose job is to project the dreams and desires hidden in clothing. A talented artist from a young age, Feurer was introduced to the world of fashion in his twenties, while working as an art director for an advertising agency in Paris and collaborating with photographers such as Helmut Newton (p. 134), William Klein (p. 102), and Frank Horvat (p. 106). A move to London followed, where he worked as creative director for a large advertising agency.

In 1966, Feurer gave up his advertising job and spent the next two years traveling through Africa. The experience had a profound effect on his creative vision: "These two years traveling around Africa marked me tremendously in many ways, but also visually, in terms of what I see and how I see things. . . . [I] started to develop a feeling and understanding for the magic of light and shadow." By the time he returned to London, Feurer had made up his mind to become a fashion photographer.

Despite having no formal training in photography, Feurer's career took off, in his words, "like a rocket." Although he found himself shooting for major publications almost immediately, some of his most exciting early work was done for *Nova* magazine, with fashion editor Caroline Baker. However, his best-known work, shot in outdoor locations with vivid color and movement, was done in the 1980s with fashion designer Kenzo.

Feurer's approach to photography is Zen-like in its simplicity: he only shoots in natural light, prefers film to digital, and never uses filters or reflectors. He often works with telephoto lenses, in order to "have in the picture only the essence of what matters and leave out all the rest."

HANS FEURER

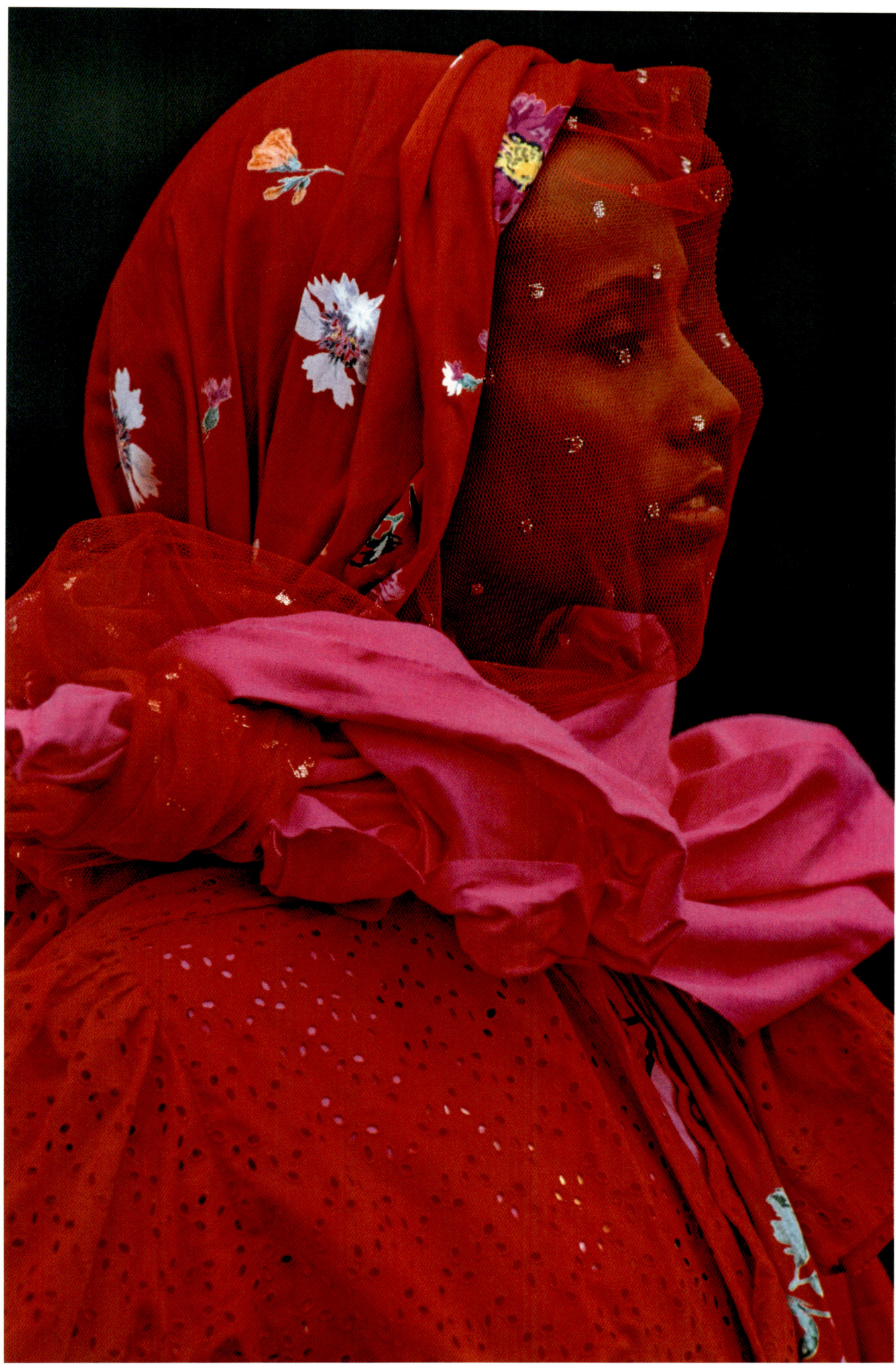

Hans Feurer,
Kenzo, 1983

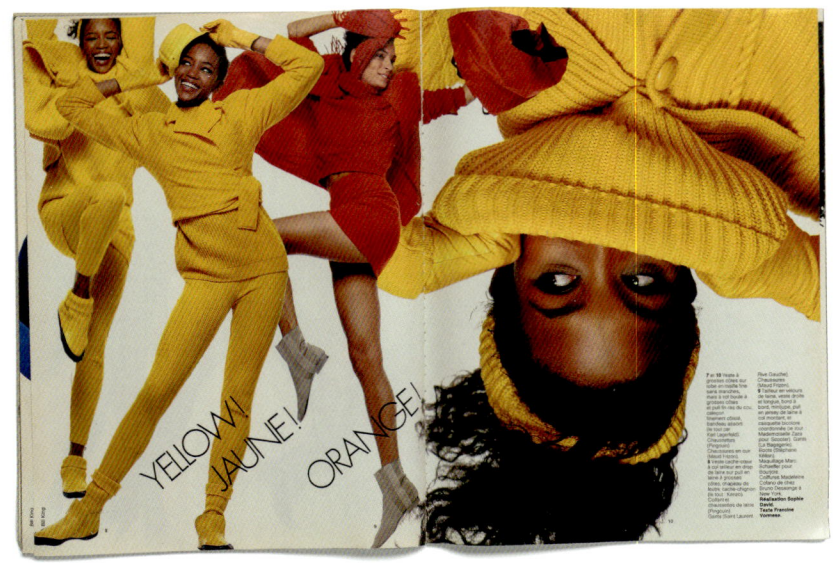

YELLOW! JAUNE! ORANGE!

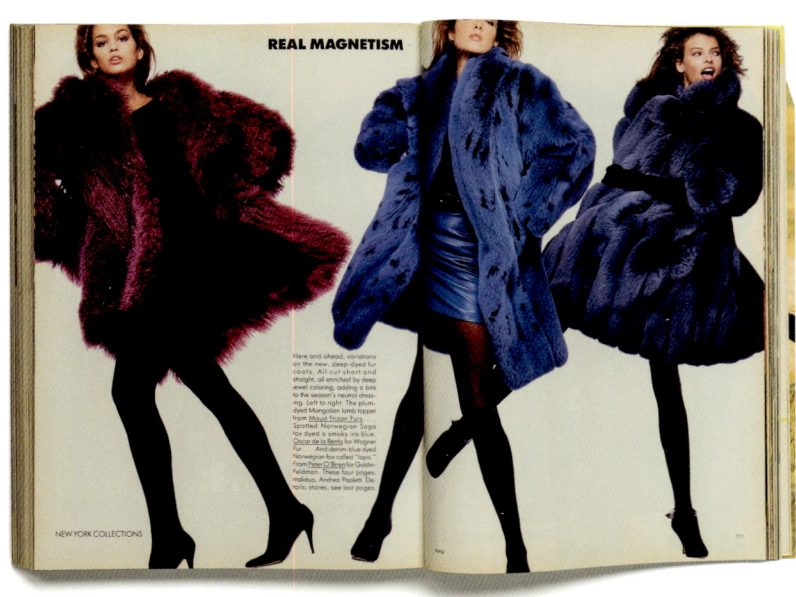

REAL MAGNETISM

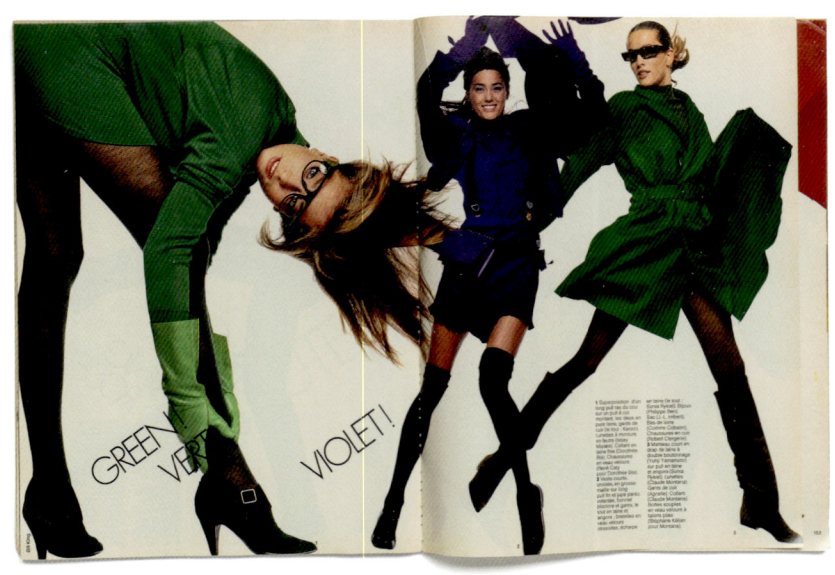

GREEN! VERT! VIOLET!

BILL KING

Born in the Netherlands
Antilles in 1939; died in
New York City, 1987

Hugely successful during his lifetime, Bill King has been largely forgotten since his death from AIDS in 1987. Raised in Cliffside Park, New Jersey, King studied painting at New York's Pratt Institute. He began taking fashion photographs "almost accidentally," while on a visit to London in the early 1960s, and his star rose rapidly. At *Queen* magazine, working with newly appointed men's fashion editor Erica Crome, King was given free rein to experiment. "The question was always, 'How can we subvert this?'" Crome recalled. "You could be as brave as you liked at *Queen*."

Between 1965 and 1968, King shot nearly every cover for British *Harper's Bazaar*, including one of the first covers to feature a black model. Returning to New York in 1968, King set up a studio on Fifth Avenue, where he worked closely with Bea Feitler, American *Harper's Bazaar*'s new art director. The style that he became known for featured models leaping exuberantly around the set—a technique he first used during his final photo shoot for *Queen*, in September 1970. Whether it was the influence of Richard Avedon's "studio leap" (p. 99) or, as some suggest, an idea proposed by Feitler, King's ability to capture energy and movement brought him huge success. "Bill King's pictures were a party you longed to join," as fashion writer Michael Gross has remarked. In 1972, King succeeded Avedon as the photographer behind the prestigious advertising campaign for Blackglama fur, "What Becomes a Legend Most?" By 1980, his work was appearing regularly in *Vogue*, *Rolling Stone*, and *Vanity Fair*, and he was shooting campaigns for Lancôme, Max Factor, Revlon, and Enrico Coveri.

From the late 1970s onward, King's excessive lifestyle was almost as famous as his work. Shy, gentlemanly, and spotlessly efficient in his professional life, he was well-known in the fashion world for his drug-fueled sex parties, many of which ended in photo sessions. Diagnosed with HIV in 1985, he continued working despite his failing health, until shortly before his death. King's estate was left in disarray and much of his archive remains in limbo. A decade's worth of early work, stored at his parents' home, was thrown away by his father after his mother's death. Several planned books failed to materialize during his lifetime, and most of his nudes have been lost.

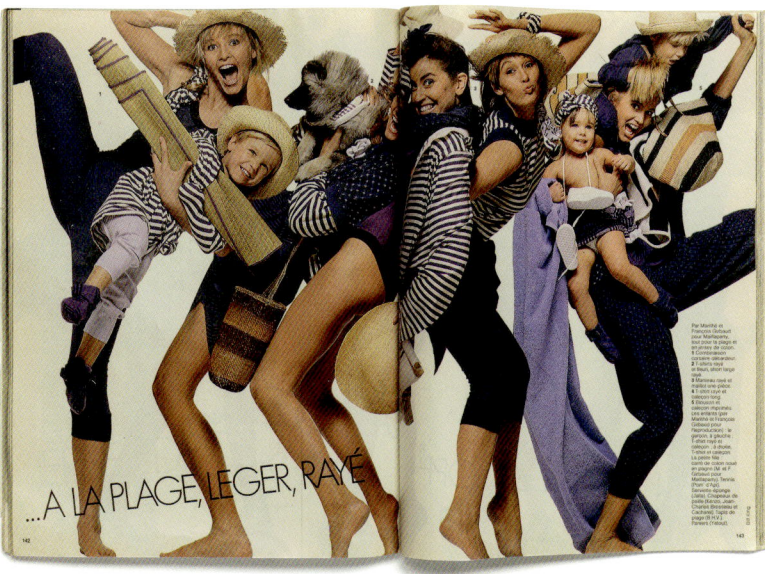

...A LA PLAGE, LEGER, RAYÉ

Bill King, clockwise from top left: *Elle France*, September 1987; *Elle France*, March 1986; *Elle France*, September 1987; *Vogue*, September 1987

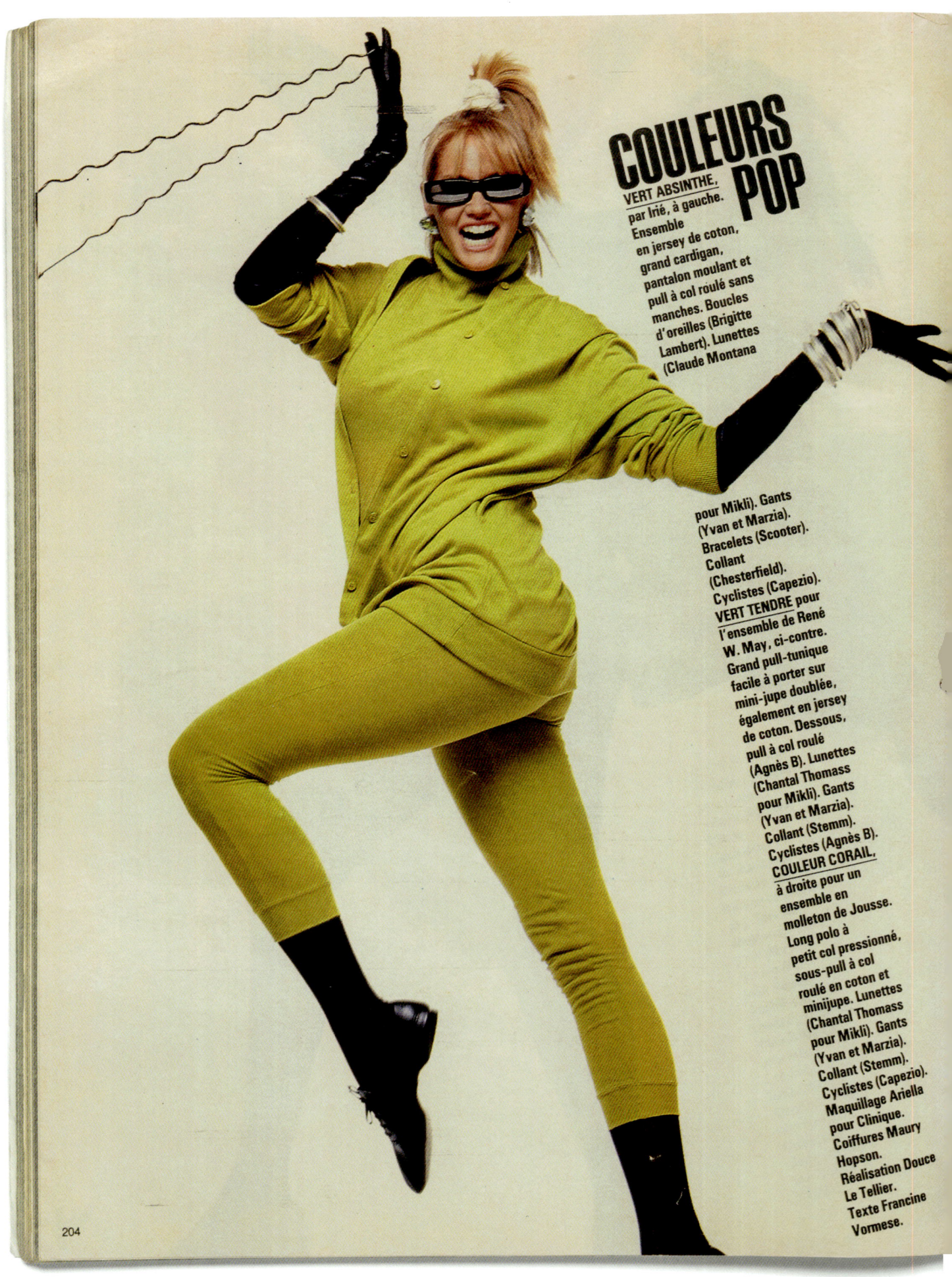

COULEURS POP

VERT ABSINTHE, par Irié, à gauche. Ensemble en jersey de coton, grand cardigan, pantalon moulant et pull à col roulé sans manches. Boucles d'oreilles (Brigitte Lambert). Lunettes (Claude Montana pour Mikli). Gants (Yvan et Marzia). Bracelets (Scooter). Collant (Chesterfield). Cyclistes (Capezio). VERT TENDRE pour l'ensemble de René W. May, ci-contre. Grand pull-tunique facile à porter sur mini-jupe doublée, également en jersey de coton. Dessous, pull à col roulé (Agnès B). Lunettes (Chantal Thomass pour Mikli). Gants (Yvan et Marzia). Collant (Stemm). Cyclistes (Agnès B). COULEUR CORAIL, à droite pour un ensemble en molleton de Jousse. Long polo à petit col pressionné, sous-pull à col roulé en coton et minijupe. Lunettes (Chantal Thomass pour Mikli). Gants (Yvan et Marzia). Collant (Stemm). Cyclistes (Capezio). Maquillage Ariella pour Clinique. Coiffures Maury Hopson. Réalisation Douce Le Tellier. Texte Francine Vormese.

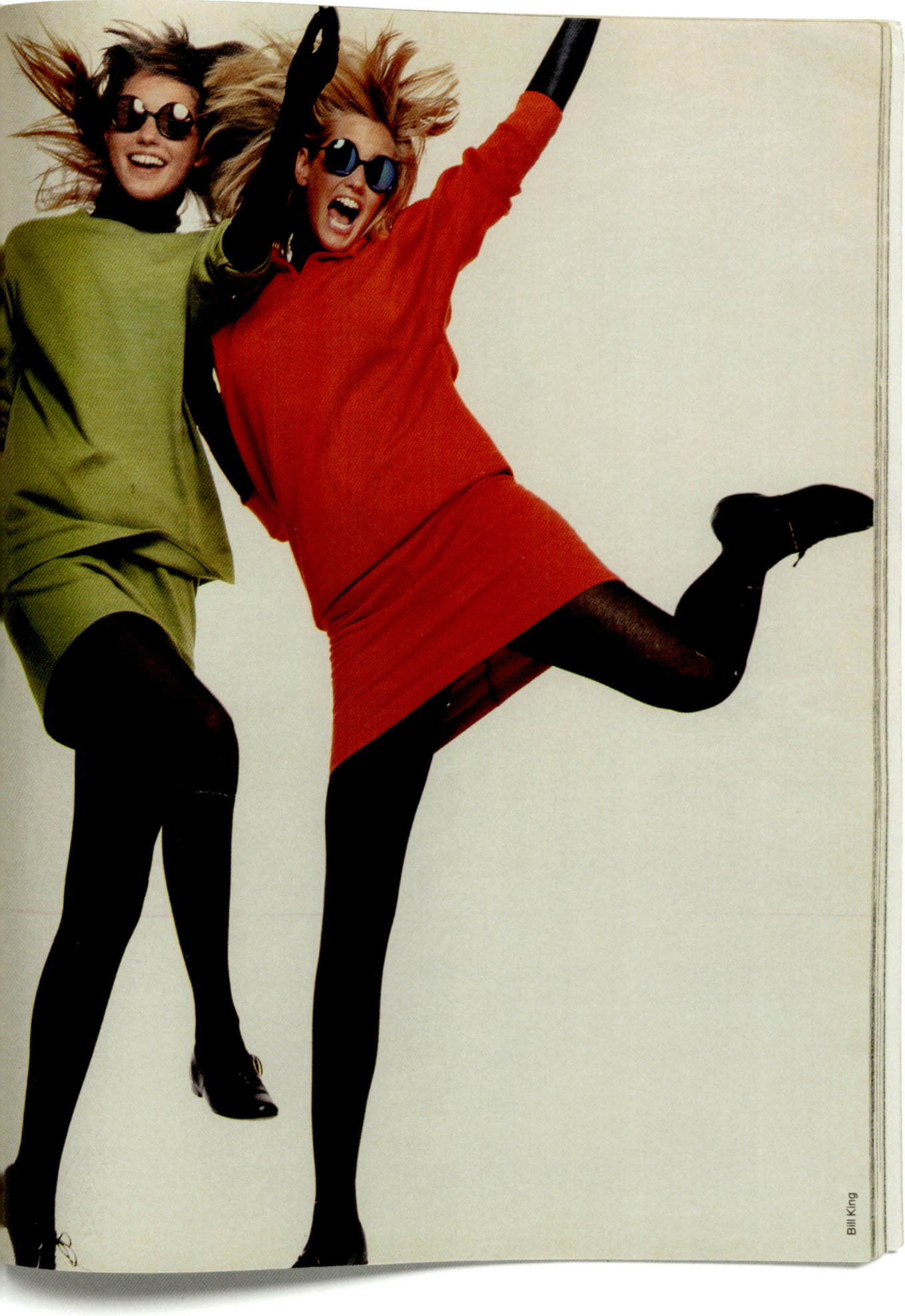

Bill King,
Elle France, September 1985

STEVE HIETT

Born in England,
1940

Steve Hiett came to photography via painting and graphic design, studying at the Brighton School of Art and the Royal College of Art in England. His training exposed him to a wide range of influences, including Pop art and abstract painting, Constructivist poster design, and typography. In 1968, acting on a friend's suggestion that he try fashion photography, Hiett gathered some friends and a collection of clothing from Woolworth's department store, and did an impromptu fashion shoot at designer Zandra Rhodes's flat. Shortly afterward, he began shooting stories for *Nova*.

In 1972, while living in Paris, Hiett was asked to shoot for *Marie Claire* while the rest of the magazine's staff photographers were on vacation. His work went on to feature in every issue for the next two decades. Hiett's preferred style, with its bold shapes, strong light, and suburban settings, took shape early in his career, but it was his use of Kodachrome film—intensified with the use of outdoor flash lighting, which he pioneered in the 1980s—that gave his images the intense, saturated color for which he is best known.

By the early 1990s, with the growing popularity of the grunge aesthetic in fashion photography, Hiett's style began to look tired, and he was forced to support himself doing graphics and typography for magazines, including *Mirabella*. He still continued to take photographs throughout this period, and in the late 1990s, a chance meeting with *Vogue Italia* editor Franca Sozzani revitalized his career: "Three weeks later I had a phone call," he said, "and I was back on a plane to France doing Italian *Vogue*."

Steve Hiett,
Lise, Sri Lanka, 1979

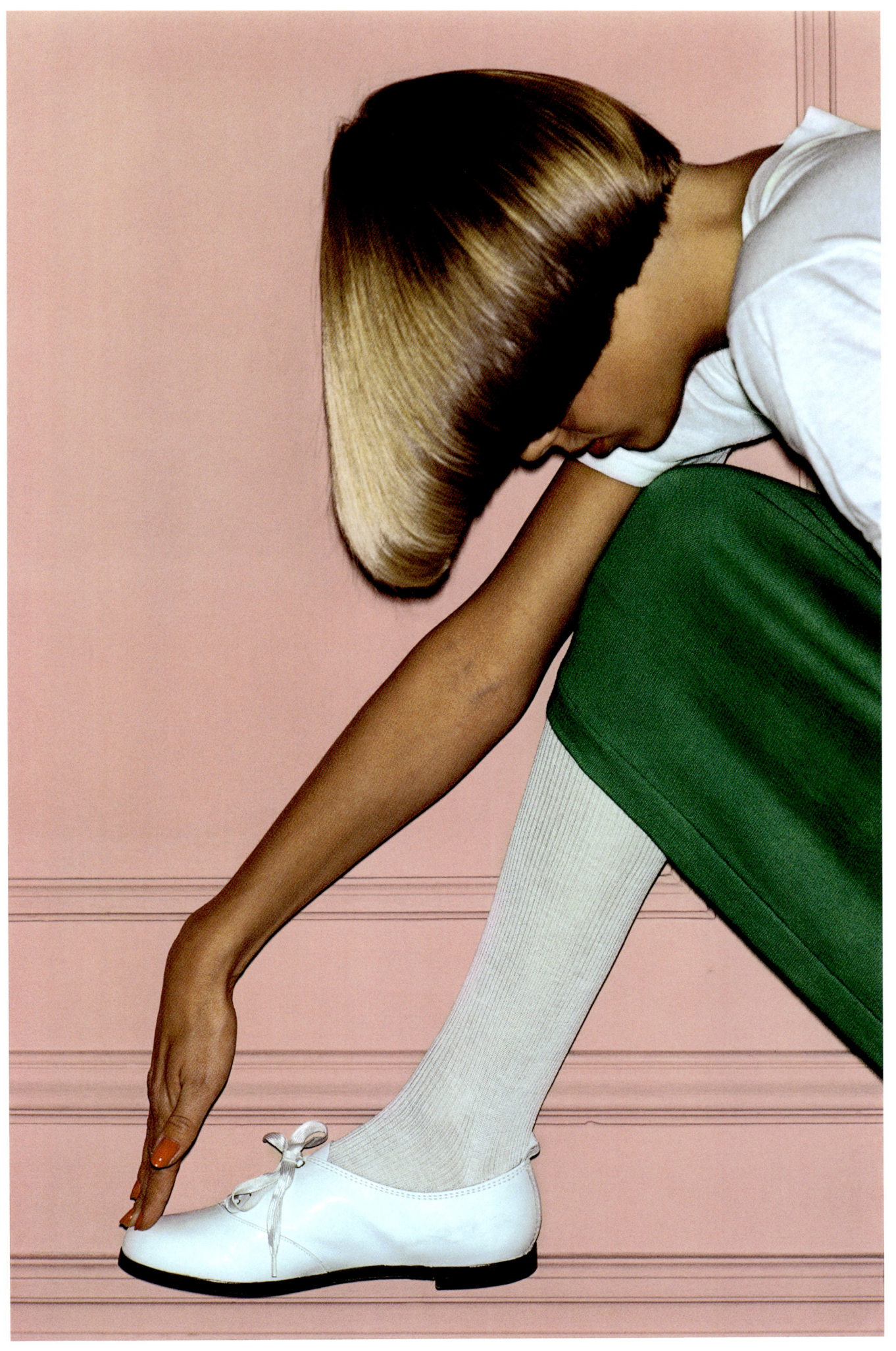

COREEN SIMPSON

Born in New York City,
1942

Before turning to photography, Coreen Simpson had pursued a career as a freelance writer, working for lifestyle magazines such as *Essence* and *Unique New York* from the early 1980s onward. Simpson first learned how to use a camera as an editor at *Unique New York*: "I didn't like the photographs taken by the photographers, and I thought I could do better. I called a friend of mine who loaned me a camera and showed me how to use it in about half an hour. That started me."

Simpson later took lessons in darkroom processing at the Studio Museum in Harlem, studying under jazz photographer Frank Stewart. Along the way, she amassed a diverse mix of influences, including Diane Arbus, Weegee, Adolph de Meyer (p. 24), and Joel-Peter Witkin. Her photographs—which included documentary images, fashion, and portraiture—appeared in numerous publications, such as the *New York Amsterdam News* and the *Village Voice*.

From an early age, Simpson had been drawn to individual and street style, and in 1982 she began her B-Boys series: "I wanted to photograph these kids and the whole break-dancing/rap genre," she recalled. "I wanted to really key in on what these people look like, what they are about, and how they put themselves together." She set up a studio in a club called the Roxy, where she went every Friday and Saturday night, drawn to the "tribal" culture of the B-boys and the women in their circle—their immaculate outfits and sense of style born out of their alienation from mainstream American culture.

Although it was shot with a fashion sensibility, the B-Boys series had a more personal focus, exploring the poise and self-possession of her subjects and the way that they expressed themselves through dress: "Even people who have very little can control how they present themselves to the world. If you have no money, no nothing, you can throw on a scarf, put your hat to the side and walk out into the street and feel good. It's style."

Coreen Simpson,
Artist Eve Sandler, ca. 1980s

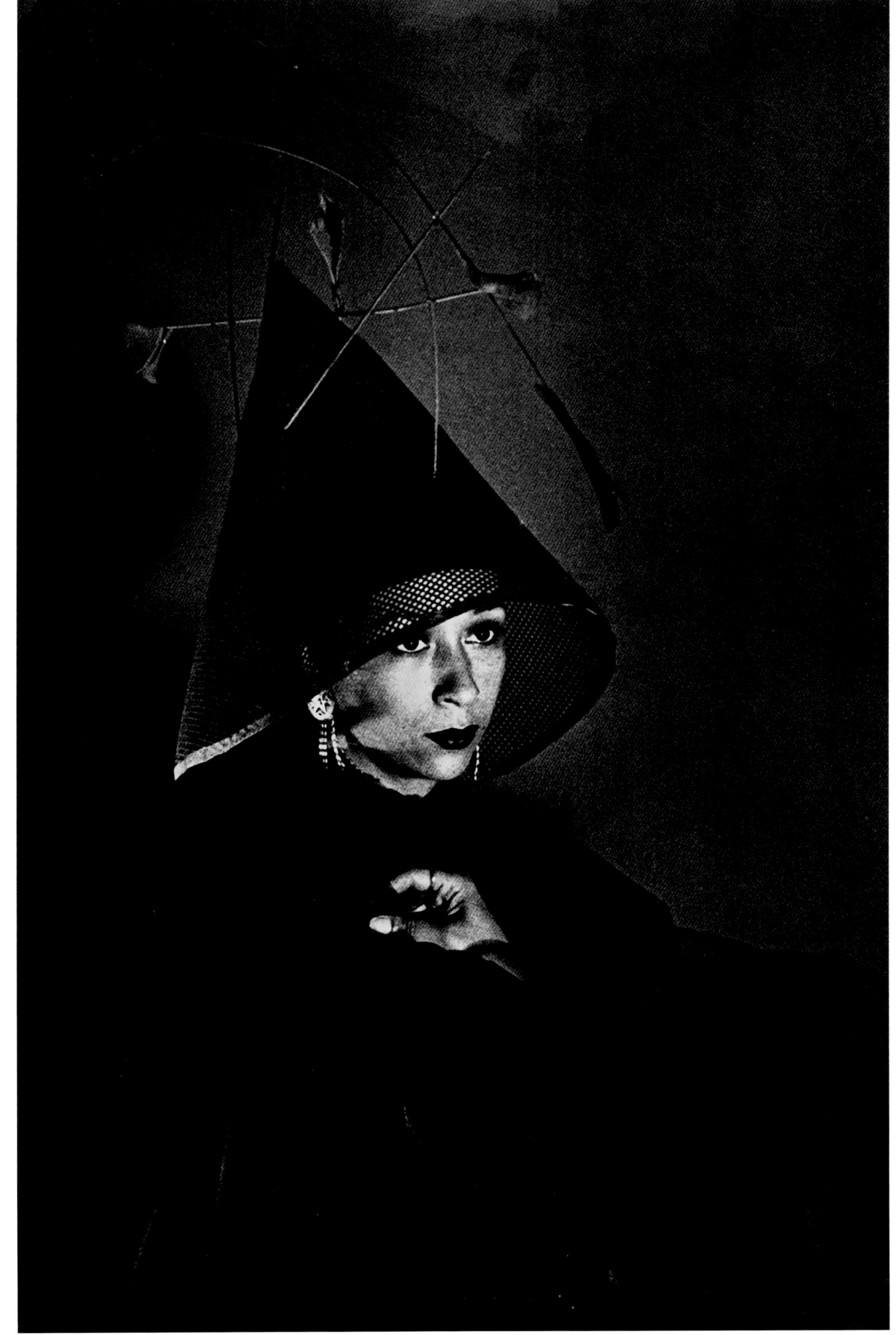

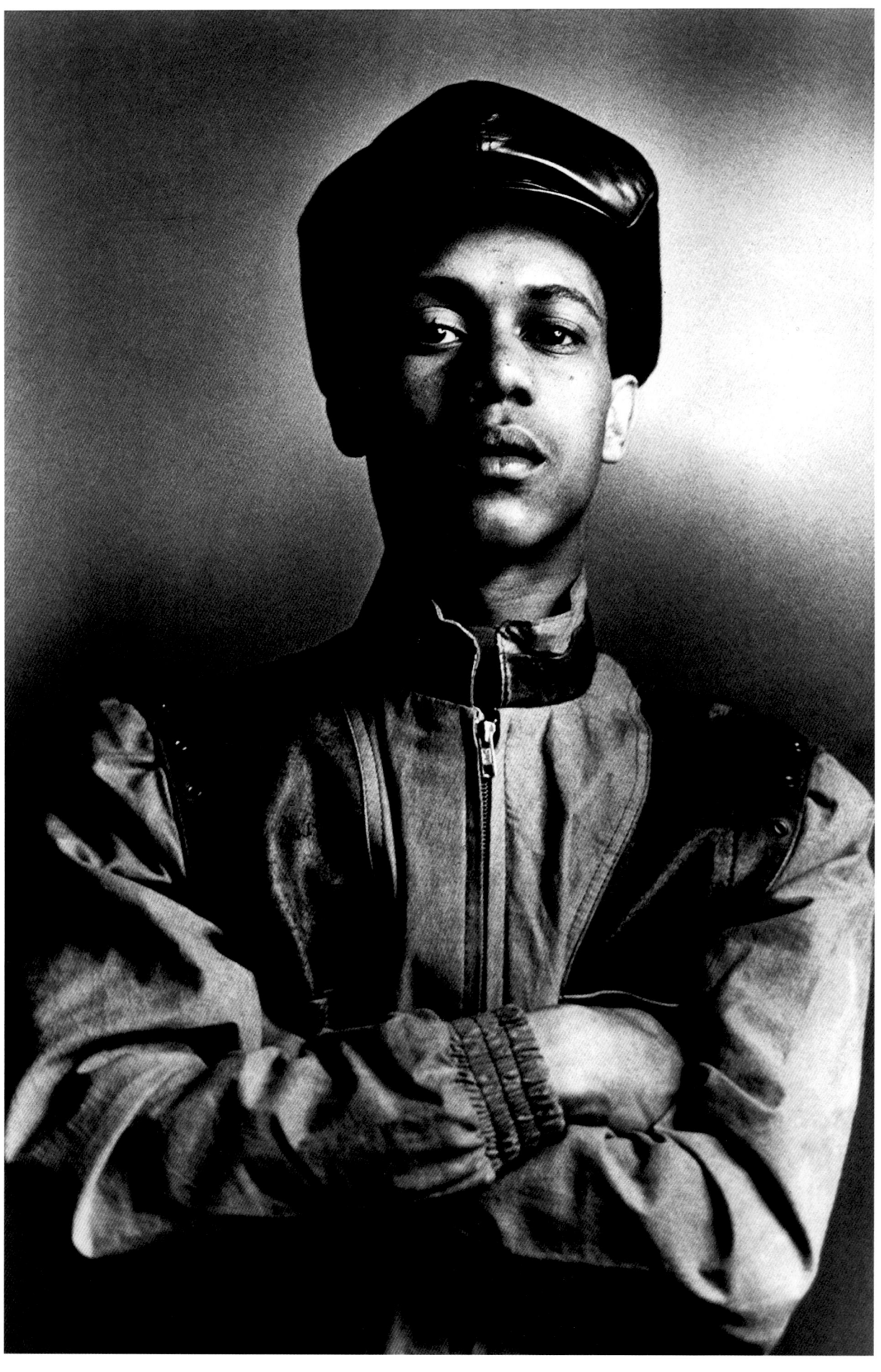

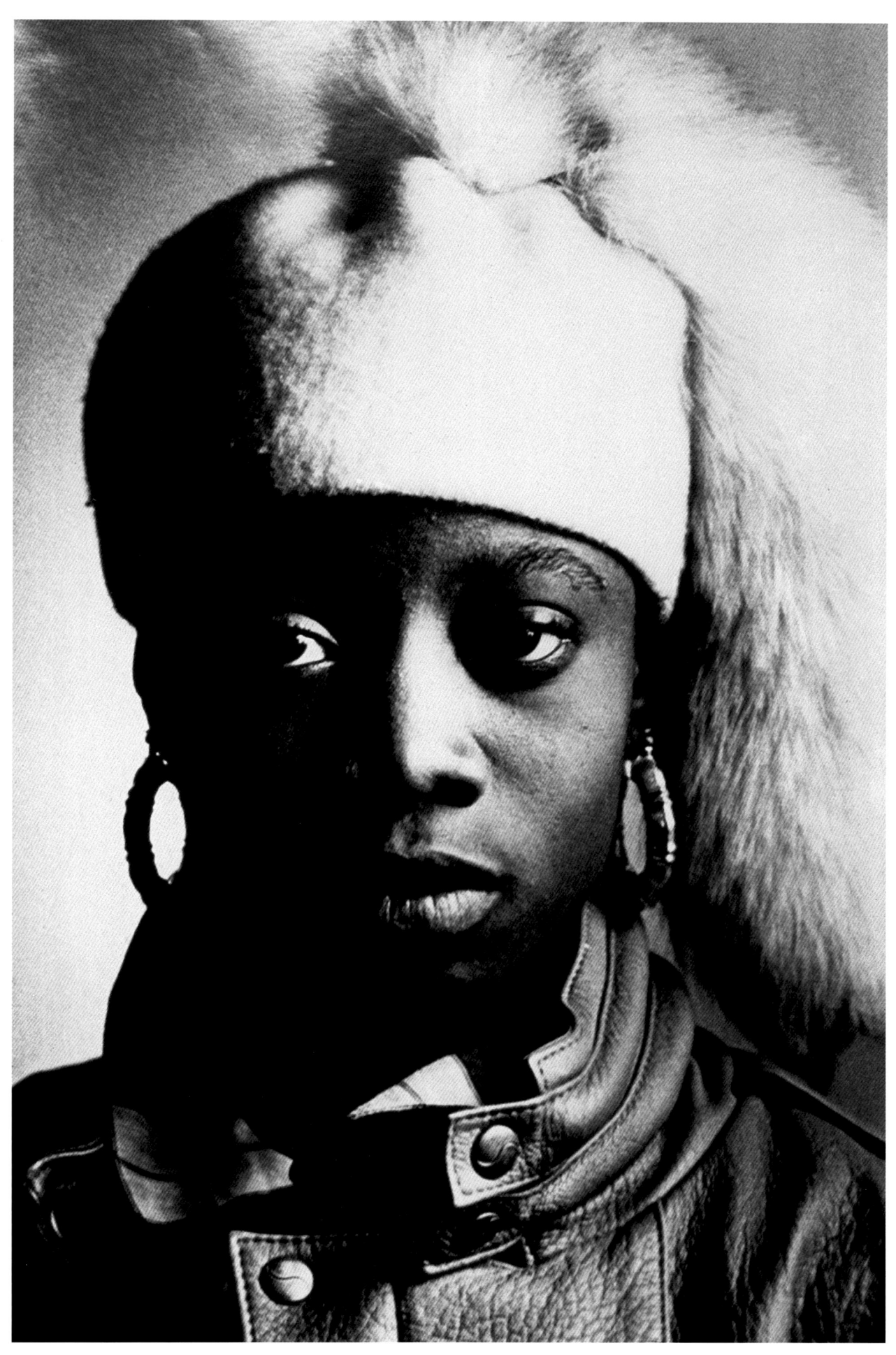

Coreen Simpson, *Helene*, 1985
Left: Coreen Simpson, *Robert, The Roxy Club,*
NYC, 1985; from the series B-Boys

RAY STEVENSON

Born in London,
1949

By the 1970s, a culture of independent street fashion was emerging alongside the underground art and music scenes on both sides of the Atlantic. Positioned well below the radar of the popular fashion press, the British counterculture scene relied on weekly music broadsheets such as *Sounds* and *New Musical Express* (*NME*) for visual expression of the latest trends.

In 1976, impresario Malcolm McLaren put together a band called the Sex Pistols as a subversive marketing tool for Sex (renamed Seditionaries in December 1976), the King's Road boutique that he owned with designer Vivienne Westwood. "We decided we needed mannequins to model our clothes, and that was when we invented the Sex Pistols, with Johnny [Rotten] doing his audition there in the shop," McLaren said. *Anarchy in the UK* was a one-off broadsheet fanzine, published by McLaren to accompany the Sex Pistols' first UK tour in 1976.

Ray Stevenson was the band's official photographer at the time, a post he held for about eighteen months starting in January 1976, before being driven away—like many others— by McLaren's laissez-faire approach to the payment of accounts. Stevenson took all of the photographs for the *Anarchy in the UK* fanzine, including the iconic cover image of Pistols follower Soo Catwoman, which was shot in a flat at the St. James's Hotel in London, with a group of Pistols fans known as the Bromley Contingent. As Stevenson recalled, "Soo got a reluctant Ealing barber to cut that style as a way of frightening off unwanted male attention. For me (and others), it made her more attractive."

Very few of the clothes in the zine were actually from Sex, but by that time, the punk look was firmly linked to McLaren's boutique. Stevenson's photographs of the Bromley Contingent anticipated the style and mood of the images that would appear, just a few years later, in trailblazing alternative fashion and lifestyle titles such as *BLITZ*, *i-D*, and *The Face* (the latter launched by former *NME* editor Nick Logan).

Ray Stevenson,
Anarchy in the UK magazine, 1976

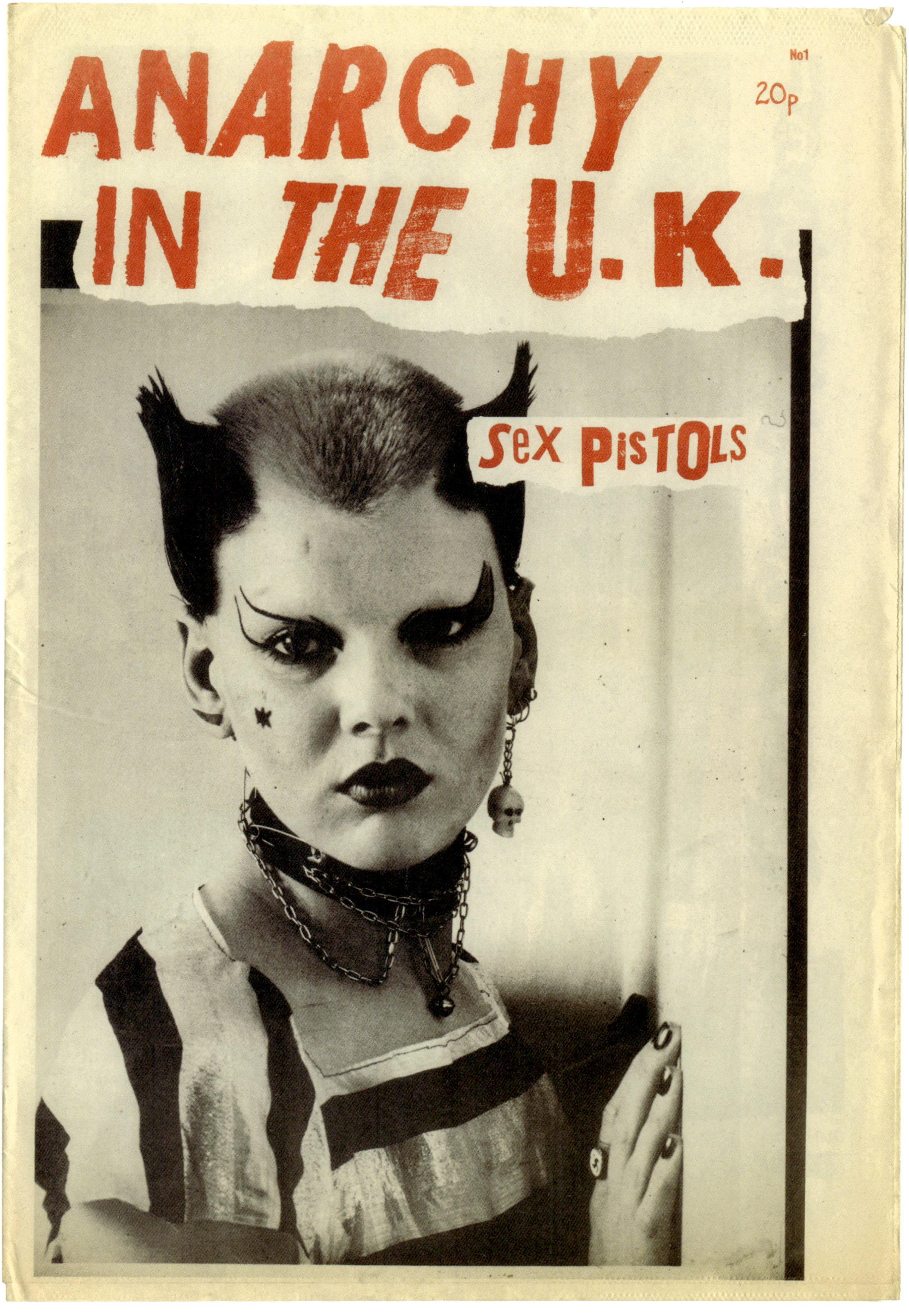

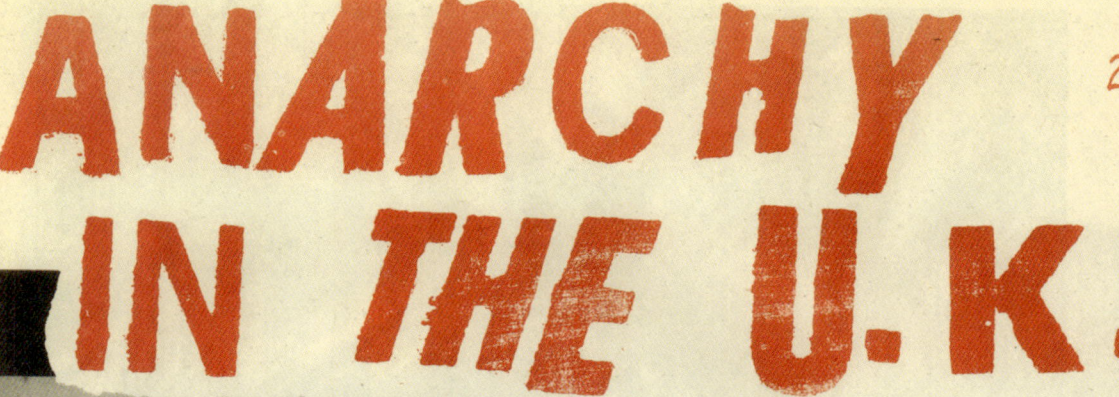

ANARCHY
IN THE U.K.

No1
20p

SeX PisTOLs

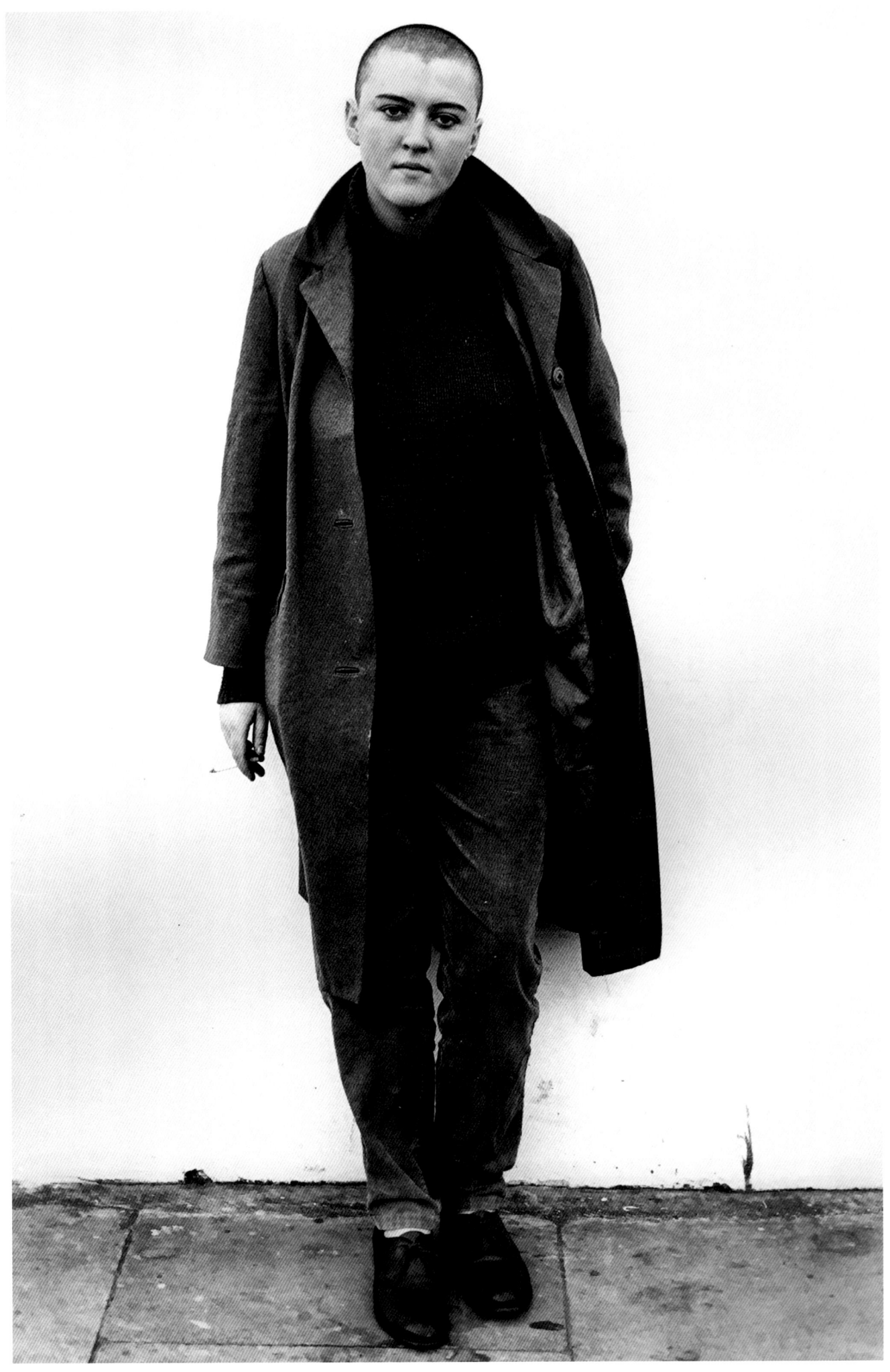

Terry Jones:
born in Northampton,
England, 1945

Steve Johnston:
born in Glasgow,
1956

STEVE JOHNSTON

Terry Jones, who would go on to found *i-D* magazine, studied commercial art at the West of England College of Art in the 1960s. He began his career in fashion as an art director at *Vanity Fair*, moving to the art department at British *Vogue* in 1971. Never fully comfortable with *Vogue*'s hierarchical studio system and social conservatism, Jones left in 1977 due to creative differences. Jones had worked on side projects throughout his time at *Vogue*, including *Not Another Punk Book* (1978) with photographer Steve Johnston. Increasingly estranged from the high glamour and excess of mainstream fashion magazines, Jones started up *i-D* in 1980 with money from his advertising work.

i-D's mission was to document street style, club culture, and music, and the first few issues looked a lot like the punk fanzines that had inspired it, using photocopies and collage, experimental typefaces, and an anarchic layout. In place of carefully curated fashion spreads, *i-D* featured page after page of "straight-ups"—documentary images of fashion shot on the streets and in clubs, little of it haute couture, and all of it styled uniquely by the wearer. The straight-up aesthetic had been a feature of Johnston's work from early on—his first street portraits, taken on London's Kings Road in 1976, were inspired by the work of Irving Penn (p. 70) and August Sander—and it became the magazine's trademark, capturing the vitality of street style. Individuality was at the heart of *i-D*'s manifesto: "Style isn't what but how you wear clothes. Fashion is the way you walk, talk, dance, and prance."

i-D's renegade spirit anticipated the era of "grunge" photography, and launched the careers of a generation of photographers and stylists, including Juergen Teller (p. 208), Nick Knight (p. 218), Judy Blame, Simon Foxton, Corinne Day (p. 188), Ray Petri, Craig McDean (p. 216), and Mark Lebon.

Steve Johnston,
Untitled, Kings Road, London, 1980

BUFFALO

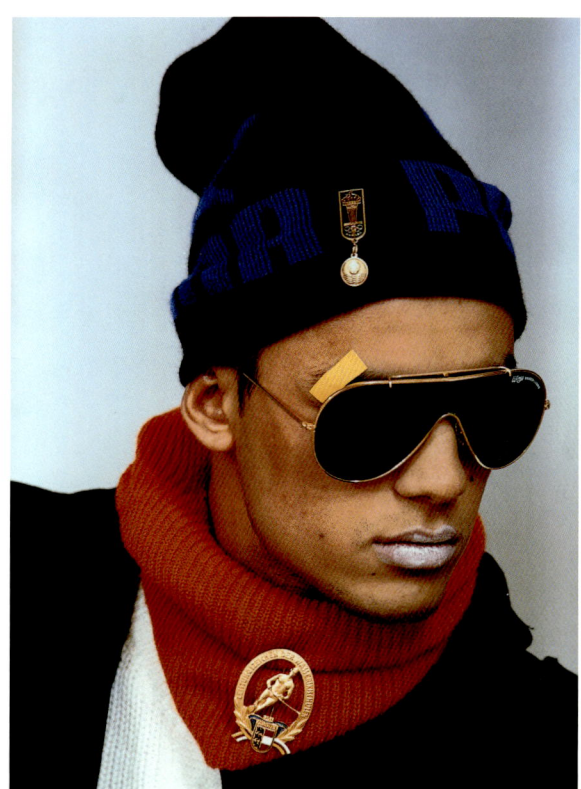

Ray Petri:
born in Dundee,
Scotland, 1948; died
in London, 1989

Mark Lebon:
born in London,
1957

Jamie Morgan:
born in London,
1959

Buffalo was a close-knit group of stylists, models, musicians, and photographers (including Mark Lebon, Roger Charity, and Jamie Morgan) who gathered around the charismatic figure of stylist Ray Petri. The Buffalo look had its roots in street style, the sharp-dressing legacy of the mod movement, and the tough, gender-bending attitude of the 1980s London club scene. Petri cast black and mixed-race models, and blended haute couture with sportswear, at a time when doing either was rare in the fashion world. He created a cutting-edge vision of urban masculinity that mixed the iconography of the modern male hero (the cowboy, the athlete, the soldier) with lavish hints of homoeroticism.

The first cover Petri styled for *The Face*, in January 1984, featured Burmese-Irish model Nick Kamen, photographed by Jamie Morgan in aviator sunglasses, a ski hat, and vintage jewelry. Petri's hand in creating the characteristic Buffalo look, and his expert eye for casting, also signaled the growing importance of the stylist in fashion photography—a role that would become increasingly significant through the 1990s. As Morgan recalled, "Styling became a career by accident . . . Ray created the space for it." Between 1983 until his untimely death in 1989, Petri worked for magazines such as *i-D*, *The Face*, and *Arena* (which he helped to launch in 1986), transforming the representation of men's fashion.

Jamie Morgan, (above) *Nick Kamen* and (right) *Men in Skirts*, for "Winter Sports," *The Face*, January 1984; styling by Ray Petri for Buffalo

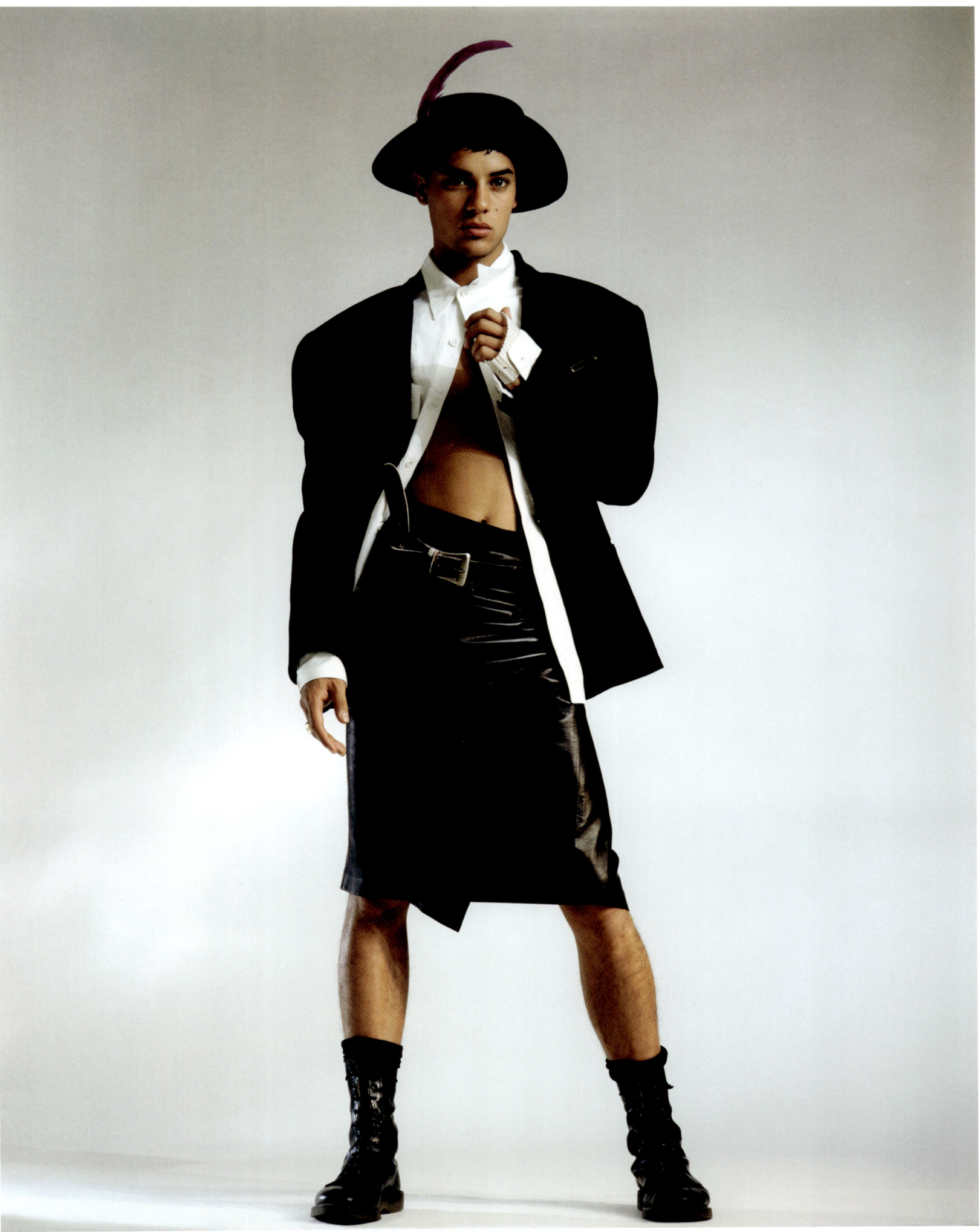

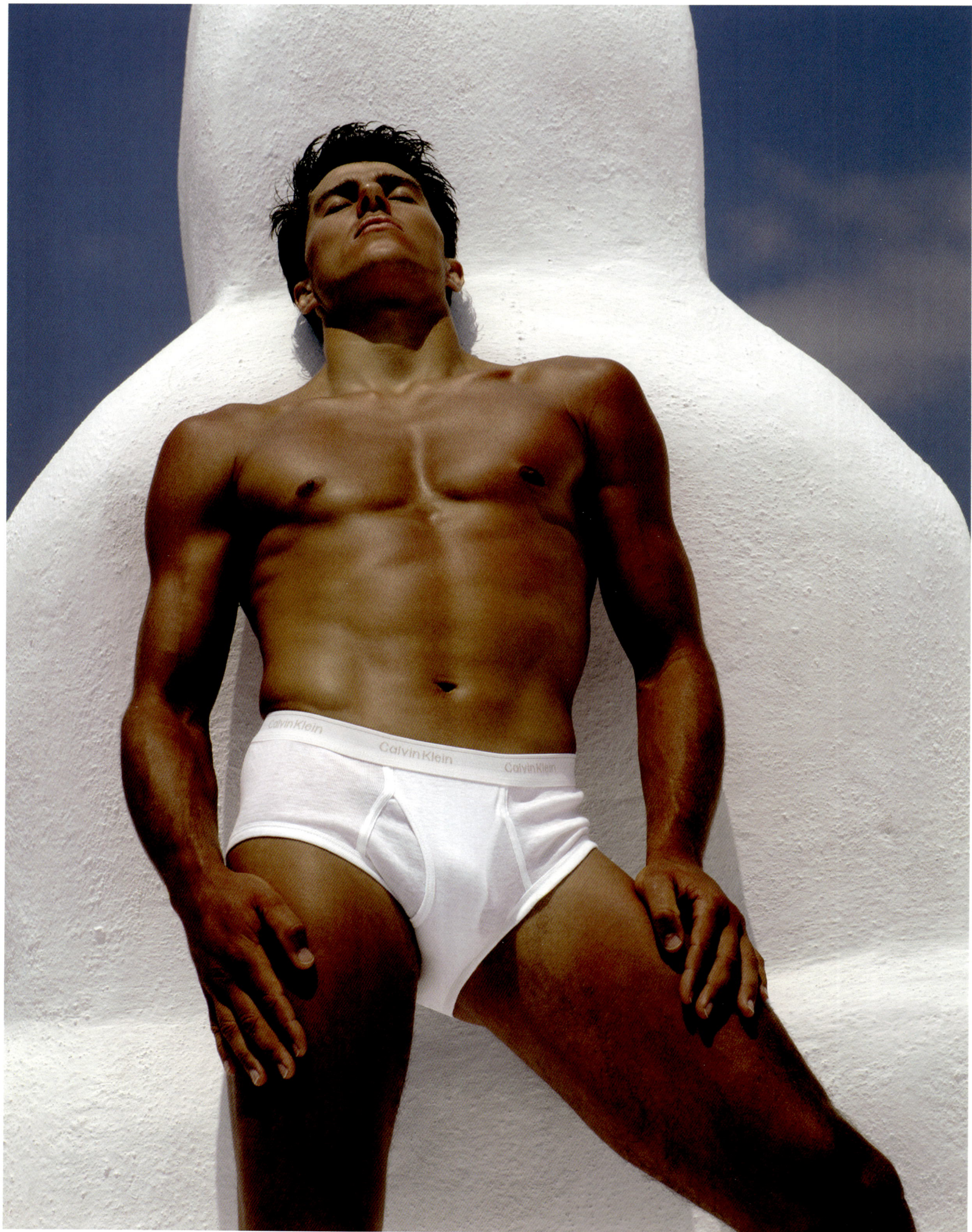

Born in Greensburg,
Pennsylvania, 1946

Bruce Weber's infamous image of Olympic pole-vaulter Tom Hintnaus—bronzed, sensual, and clad in nothing more than a pair of Calvin Klein briefs—was radical for its time. Displayed on an enormous billboard in Times Square in 1982, the image signaled a shift in Western cultural values and a growing acceptance of homoeroticism and male nudity in an industry that had, up until that point, tended to keep its male models fully clothed and conspicuously straight.

By the time that Calvin Klein campaign first appeared, Weber was already recognized as one of the most influential fashion photographers of his generation. Weber had taken photographs from an early age, but his first encounter with fashion photography was as a model in the 1960s, posing for photographers, including Melvin Sokolsky, Saul Leiter (p. 100), Richard Avedon (p. 94), and Art Kane. On Avedon's advice, he went on to study photography under Lisette Model at the New School for Social Research in New York. His first fashion photographs were published in the early 1970s.

Weber is a contemporary of—and was close friends with—Herb Ritts (p. 176), to whom he is often compared. However, Weber's style is less formal and often more brashly sexual. His relaxed attitude to nudity and eroticism, combined with references to an outdoorsy and slightly nostalgic, all-American lifestyle, has come to define the image of some of his best-known advertising clients, including Ralph Lauren, Calvin Klein, and Abercrombie & Fitch.

BRUCE WEBER

Bruce Weber,
Tom Hintnaus, Santorini, Greece, 1982

Born in Washington, DC, 1953

NAN GOLDIN

In 1985, the *Village Voice* launched a short-lived fashion supplement called *View* (retitled *Vue* after the first edition). Although it only lasted six issues, *View*'s approach—driven by photography, art, and design rather than fashion trends—anticipated the philosophy of many of the independent lifestyle magazines that launched in the 1990s, including *Dazed & Confused*, *Purple*, *Dutch*, and *Self Service*. Rather than using established fashion photographers and professional models, the editorial staff commissioned photographic artists to create stories based around their own practices.

Photographer Nan Goldin was approached by *View* around the same time that her slide show *The Ballad of Sexual Dependency* was gaining widespread public attention. Goldin first exhibited her work—a series of a group of drag queens—at age fifteen. Stolen copies of French and Italian *Vogue* were a source of inspiration; "All I knew about photography came from the fashion magazines," she recalled. Larry Clark's 1971 book *Tulsa*—which documented the lives of a group of young drug users in his hometown—was also a key influence, and when Goldin graduated from Boston's School of the Museum of Fine Arts in 1977, she moved to New York and began photographing her friends in the underground club and drug scene. Shot in a loose and seemingly amateurish style, Goldin's photographs were a powerfully intimate record of the lives—and, often, the tragically early deaths—of the people closest to her.

Goldin also used her friends as models for the *View* shoot. Printed on newsprint rather than glossy paper, laid out in a scrapbook style, *Vue* was a radical departure from traditional fashion glossies, riffing on the iconoclastic design of publications like *i-D* and infusing it with a characteristic mix of art and cultural criticism. It was also a perfect vehicle for Goldin's images, some of which went on to be added to *The Ballad of Sexual Dependency*. Raw and unpolished, her snapshot aesthetic anticipated the work of the grunge photographers who would rock fashion photography to its foundations only a few years later.

Nan Goldin,
Rebecca at the Russian Baths, NYC, 1985

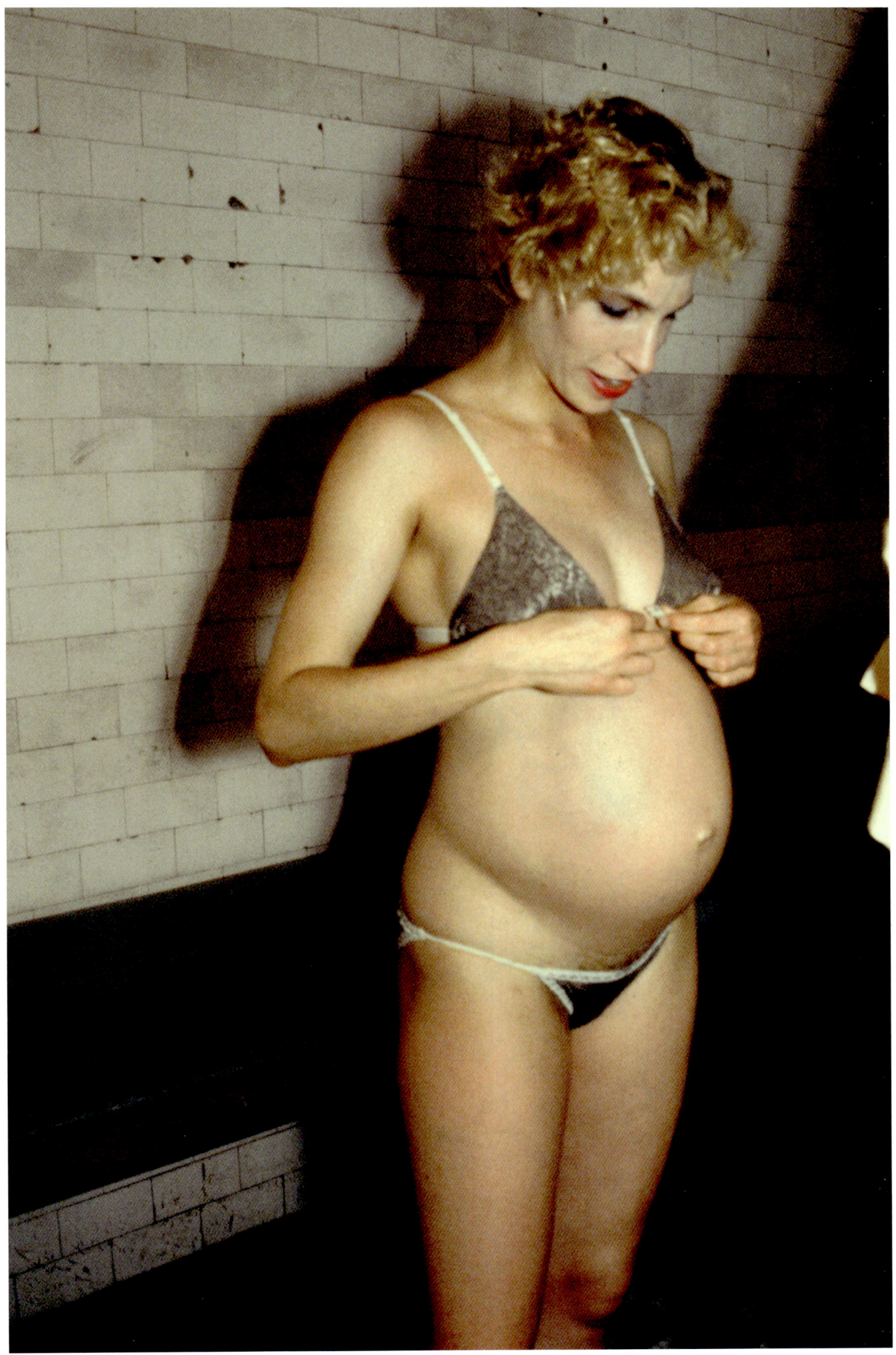

MARK LEWIS

Born in Johannesburg,
South Africa, 1954

In the early 1980s, South African photographer Mark Lewis moved to London and began taking fashion photographs for magazines, including *BLITZ*, *The Face*, and *Vogue*. *BLITZ* had been started by Simon Tesler and Carey Labovitch in 1980 while both were still university students. At the time, fashion magazines for a younger UK audience were limited to mainstream titles for teenage girls, while it was left to music journals like *NME* to report on the experimental style of the club and music scenes. Along with *i-D* and *The Face*, *BLITZ* filled a gap in the market, covering music, film, art, fashion, and design for an audience in their late teens and twenties, and providing a platform for young creatives who were having trouble breaking into the more established fashion glossies. Of the three titles, *BLITZ* had the most artistic and experimental approach to fashion photography. The magazine's fashion pages, as Tesler remarked, were meant "to inspire artistically, not to serve as a shopping guide."

Lewis shot "No Nukes Is Good News" for the September 1986 issue of *BLITZ*. Inspired by the pervasive threat of nuclear war and the dystopian vision of the future in films such as *Blade Runner*, "No Nukes" was both menacing and romantic. Its post-punk vibe featured hand-painted T-shirts, bondage trousers, and accessories by stylist and jewelry designer Judy Blame. Lewis, still early in his career, later showed the spread to horrified fashion editors at *Marie Claire* in Paris: "It was then that I realized that we were quite radical," he said, "and how conservative the rest of the fashion world was—and how I would struggle to fit into the world of fashion."

BLITZ published its final issue in 1991, but the critical, conceptual voice that it brought to fashion photography would become an increasingly significant difference between the alternative and mainstream fashion press.

Mark Lewis,
"No Nukes Is Good News," *BLITZ*, 1986

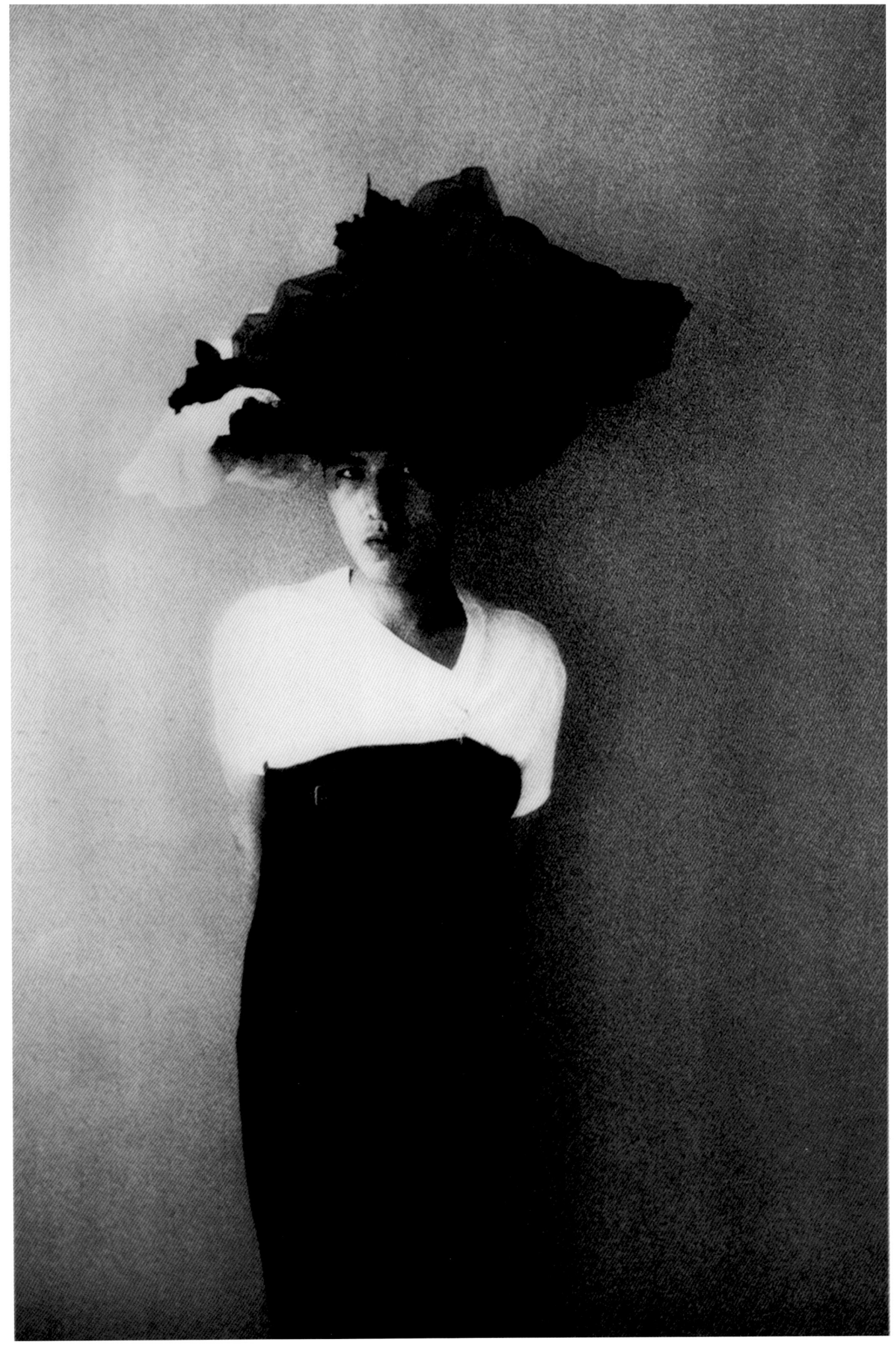

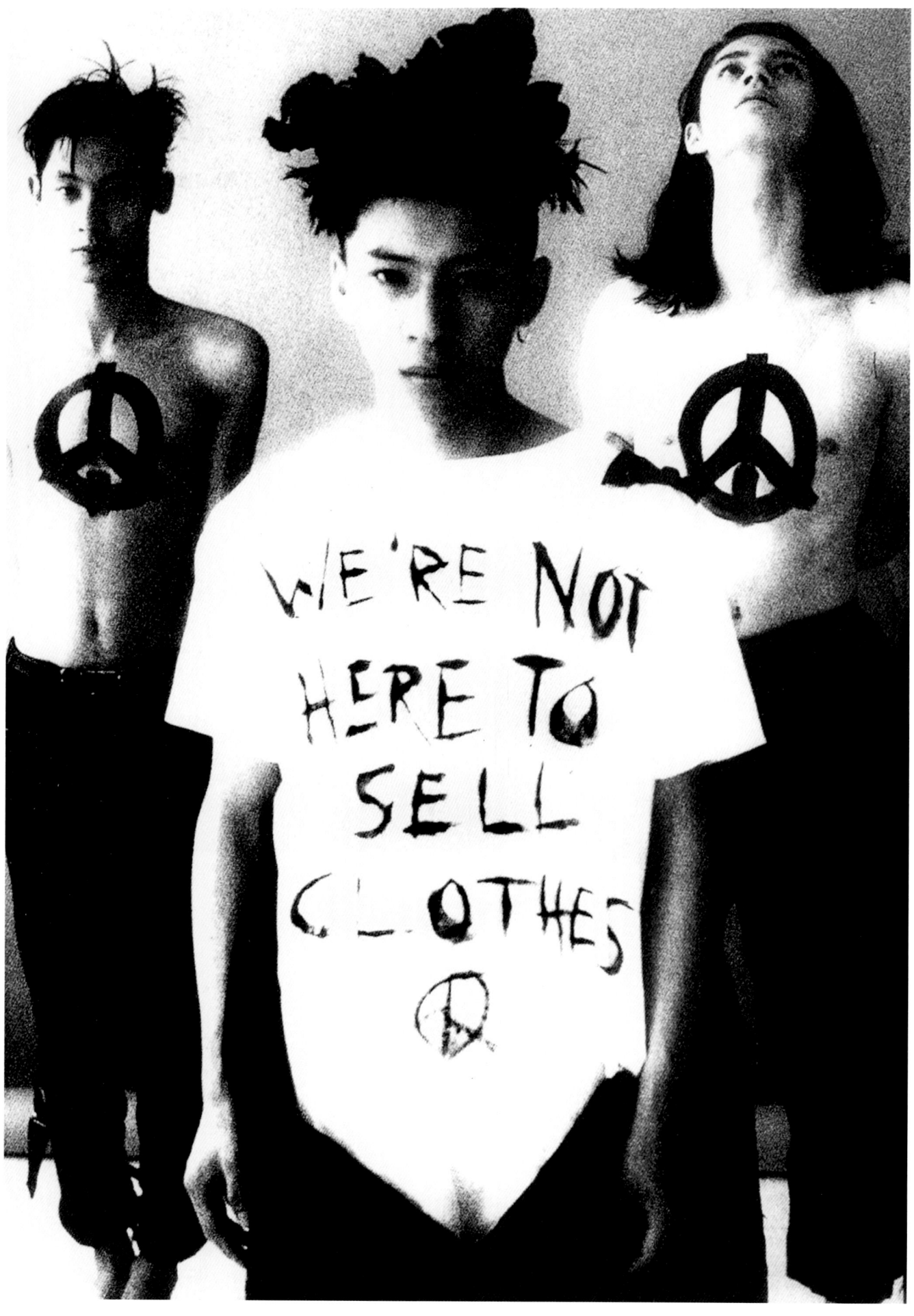

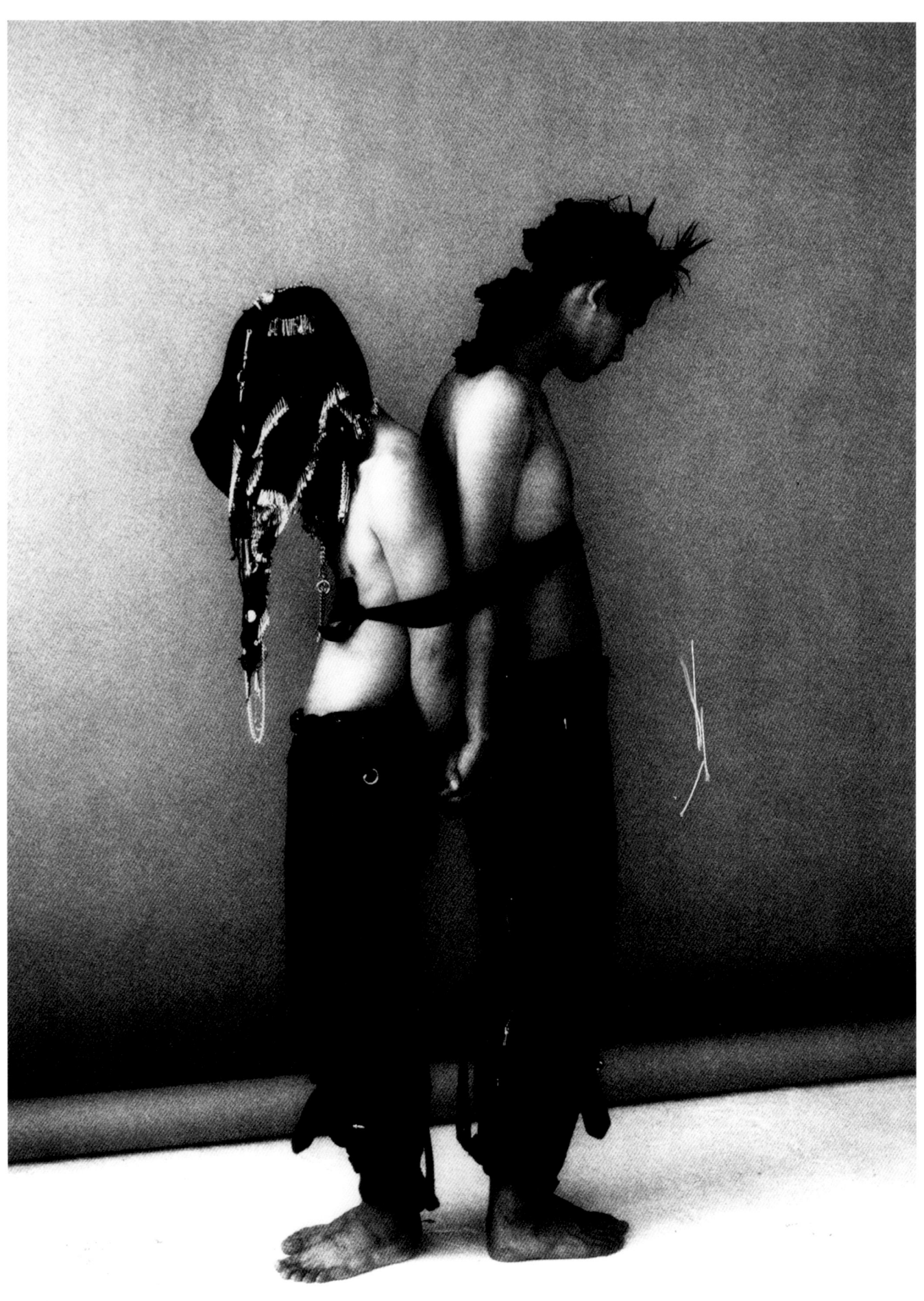

Left and above: Mark Lewis,
"No Nukes Is Good News," *BLITZ*, 1986

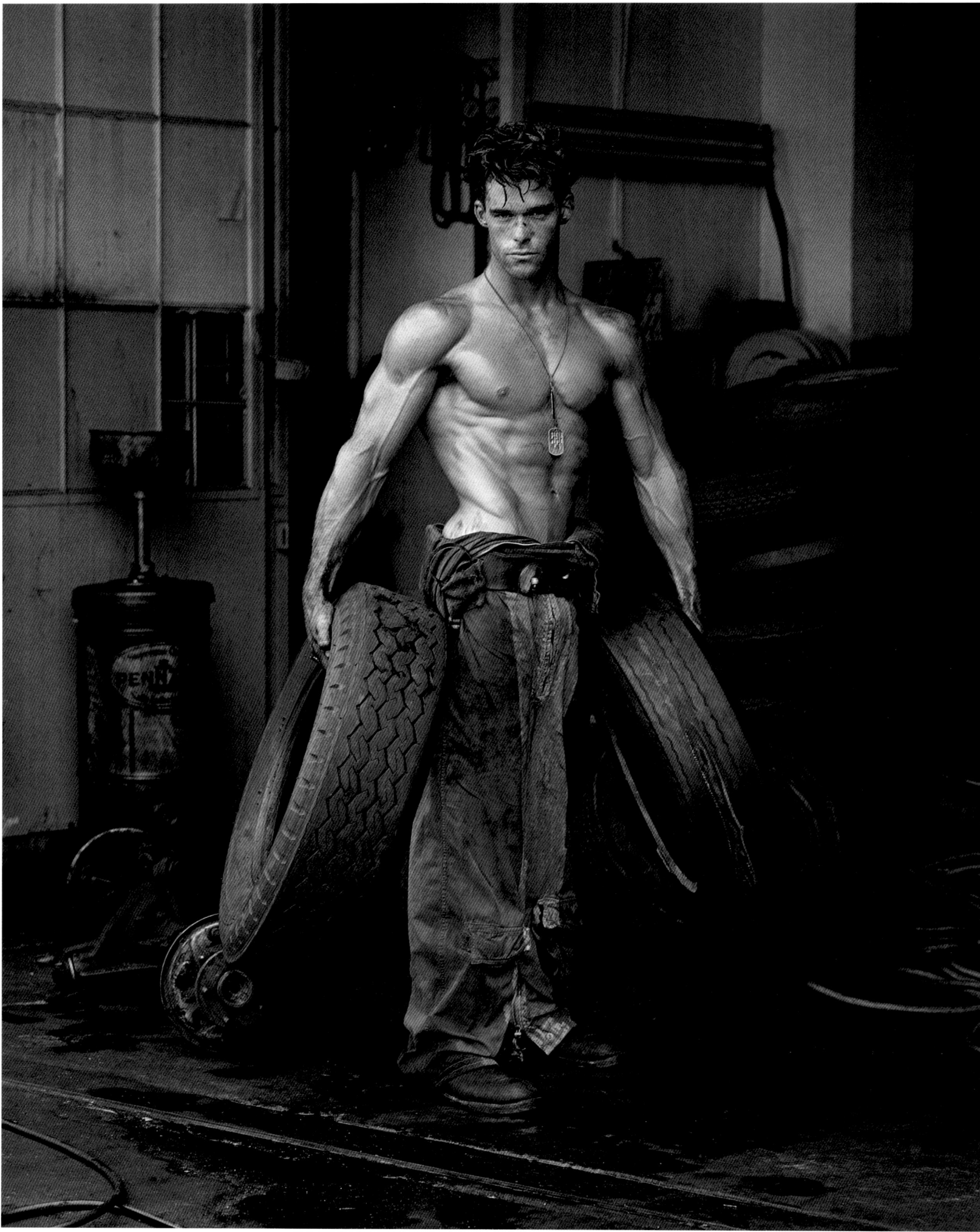

Born in Santa Monica,
California, 1952;
died in Los Angeles, 2002

Despite lacking any formal training in photography,
Herb Ritts bought a simple camera in 1976
and began making portraits of his friends in LA's
art scene. His first fashion photographs were
published in *Mademoiselle* in 1979. An avid collector
of photography since early in his professional
career, Ritts's collection included work by Man Ray
(p. 46), Paul Outerbridge, Louise Dahl-Wolfe
(p. 68), Irving Penn (p. 70), and Richard Avedon
(p. 94). However, it was the male nudes shot by
Horst P. Horst (p. 58), George Hoyningen-Huene
(p. 42), and George Platt Lynes (p. 62) that would
have the most profound influence on Ritts's style,
with his preference for formal composition and
classical, elegant lines.

Often shot in bright sunlight to emphasize
form, Ritts's images of the unclothed body
highlighted a growing emphasis on the nude as
a form of fashion photography in its own right.
He was especially attracted to toned, athletic bodies
and unblemished skin—more so, as *Vogue* editor
Anna Wintour once remarked, than he was to
the clothes themselves. *Fred with Tires, Hollywood*
was the outcome of a 1984 shoot for *Per Lui* magazine:
"Franca [Sozzani, the editor at the time] had sent
these really hideous raincoats, and I just hated
them. . . . We ended up going to Western Costumes
and getting vintage jeans and overalls. . . . We
turned in the pictures, and Franca almost had a heart
attack. But she ran it, and it was a huge success. . . .
Poor Fred, who was a student, had to swing
these heavy tires around, and at one point he was
so tired he just turned around and stood there.
It was the last frame of the shoot."

Along with his contemporaries Bruce Weber
(p. 168)—an early mentor and, later, close friend—
and Robert Mapplethorpe, Ritts presented the
male body in an unabashedly homoerotic light,
changing perceptions of masculinity in mainstream
advertising and editorial imagery.

HERB RITTS

Herb Ritts,
Fred with Tires, Hollywood, 1984

PATRICK DEMARCHELIER

Born in Le Havre,
France, 1943

Patrick Demarchelier's career began in the darkroom in 1963—first as a printer and retoucher of passport photos, and later as a printer of news photos. He began assisting shortly after moving to Paris at age twenty, eventually landing a job with Hans Feurer (p. 150). Demarchelier soon began to produce his own work for *Elle* and *Marie Claire*, becoming part of a loosely knit group of young fashion photographers—including Uli Rose, Arthur Elgort (p. 142), Alex Chatelain, and Mike Reinhardt—who were known as the "Paris Mob." Rejecting studio photography and heavily made-up models for a more spontaneous, plein air style, the work of the Paris Mob contrasted sharply with the harsh colors and flash favored by contemporaries such as Laurence Sackman, Helmut Newton (p. 134), and Guy Bourdin (p. 144).

In 1974, with his reputation established in France, Demarchelier moved to New York, and by the end of the 1970s he was a regular contributor to American *Vogue*. Some of Demarchelier's best-known work was produced with fashion editor Grace Coddington at British *Vogue* in the early 1980s—a period which marked a turning point in his creative development and launched his international career.

"The Ebb and Flow of Fashion" includes a number of remarkable location shots posed against a painted backdrop. "We asked a London-based painter to create a romantic seascape and ship it over to us," Demarchelier explained. "Some of these photos were made on the beach in East Hampton, New York, in natural outdoor light, and others were made in the studio. For the outdoor shots, model Cecilia Chancellor posed before the ten-foot-high painting. I used Polaroid Polachrome 35 mm film and the seaside environment—the wind, the high grasses, and the sand—to create the soft ambience we wanted." Demarchelier's embrace of a more wholesome, natural kind of beauty marked a decisive end to the decadent and often disturbing themes that had been so central to the fashion photography of the 1970s.

Patrick Demarchelier,
Cecilia, New York, 1986

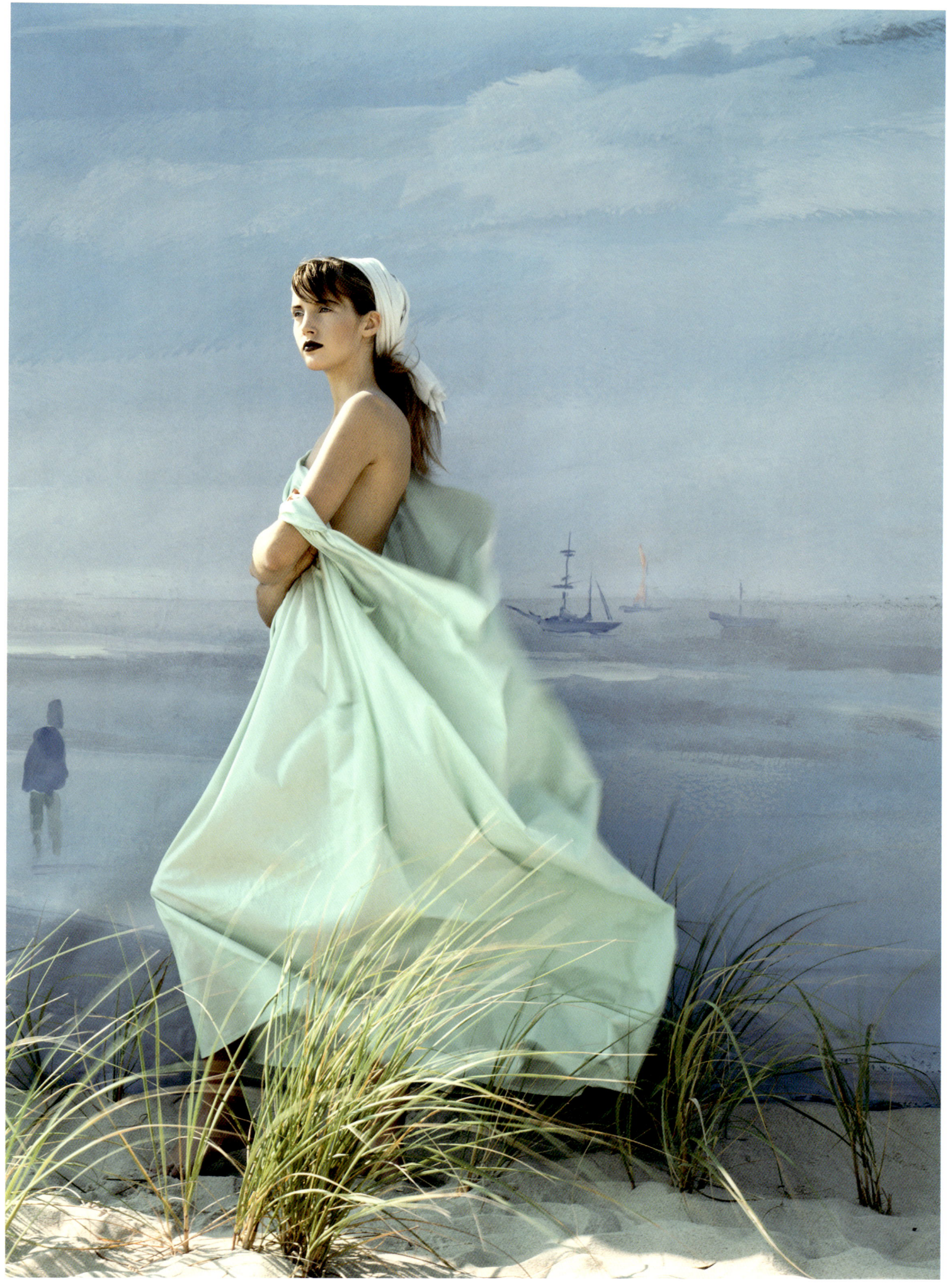

Paolo Roversi discovered photography as
a teenager and opened his first studio in Ravenna
in 1970. A chance meeting in 1971 with Peter
Knapp, then art director of *Elle*, brought Roversi
to Paris, where he worked for a short time as
a reporter for the Huppert photo-news agency.
Then, a nine-month stint assisting British
photographer Laurence Sackman introduced
Roversi to the fashion world. "Sackman was very
difficult. Most assistants only lasted a week
before running away," Roversi said. "But he taught
me everything I needed to know in order to
become a professional photographer. Sackman
taught me creativity."

In 1980, Roversi began working with
the large-format 8-by-10 Polaroid camera
that would become his trademark. The slow speed
and saturated colors of Polaroid film allowed
Roversi to create remarkable, painterly effects
using long exposures and a combination of light
sources, including natural light, colored gels,
and "light painting" with a handheld flashlight.
"The light is something alive; it's always changing,"
Roversi has said.

During that decade, Roversi produced
groundbreaking campaigns for Romeo
Gigli, Comme des Garçons, and Yohji Yamamoto.
Recently, with large-format Polaroid film
becoming increasingly difficult to find, Roversi
has turned to other formats, including digital—
but he still prefers the slowness and sensuality
of his wooden Deardorff camera and the
materiality of the Polaroid process. "I always say
photography is not all about view," Roversi
has said. "It's all five of our senses—the view, the
smell, the taste, everything. . . . [Digital] images
are just numbers appearing on a screen—you don't
touch them, you don't smell them. In this,
I am very traditional. For me photography is not
an image floating on a screen, it's an object,
a format with weight that you can put in your
pocket, your wallet, your family album."

Born in Ravenna,
Italy, 1947

PAOLO ROVERSI

Paolo Roversi,
Kirsten Owen for Romeo Gigli,
A/W 1988

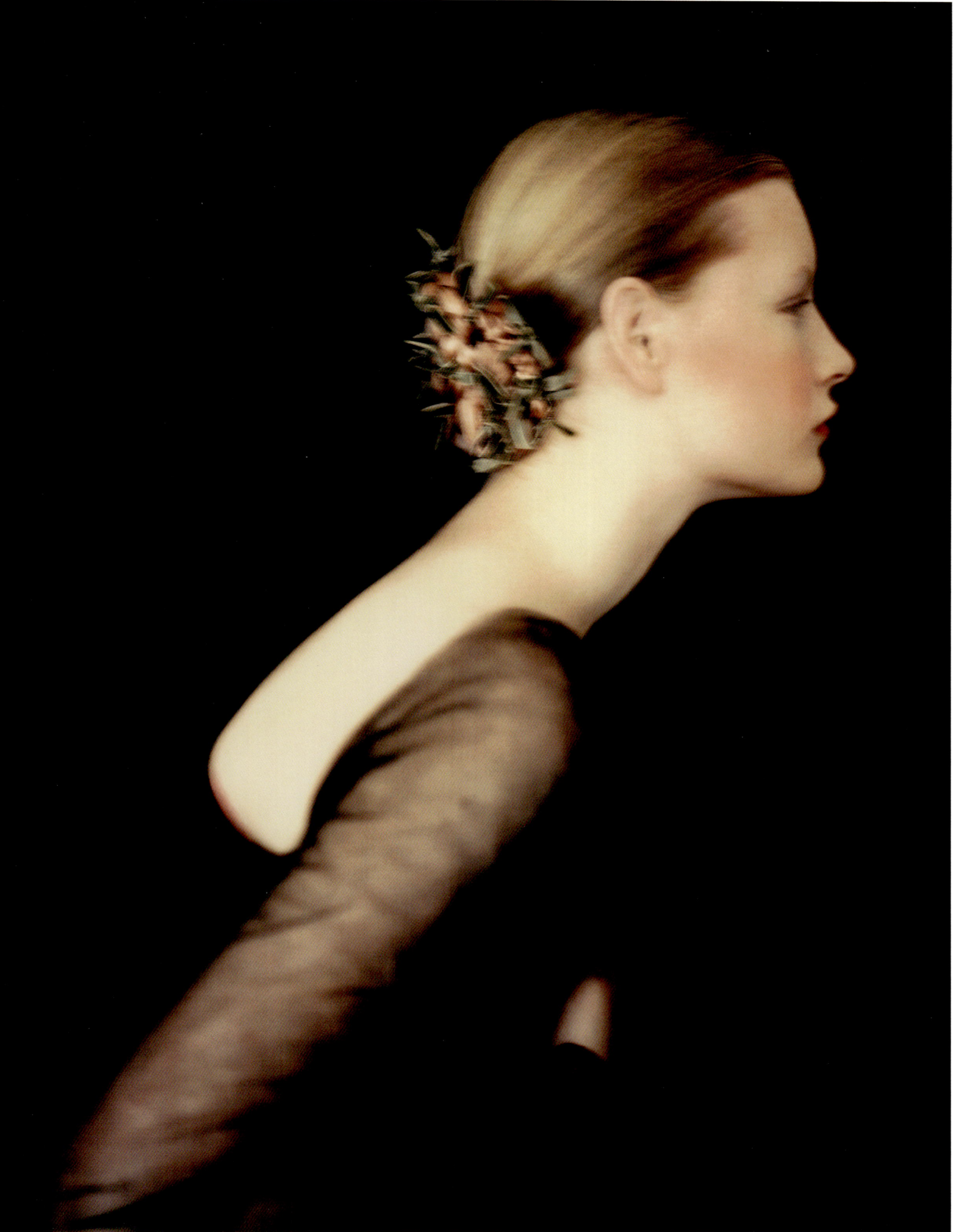

BILL CUNNING-HAM

Born in Boston, 1929;
died in New York City,
2016

When he died in 2016, Bill Cunningham's *New York Times* column "On the Street" had been running for nearly forty years. Part street photographer, part anthropologist, Cunningham was an obsessive chronicler of style, photographing everything from fashion's most outré trends to its subtler details: a trending color, a clever cut, a new style of heel. Perched on his bicycle, wearing his blue worker's jacket, khakis, and trainers, Cunningham was a familiar figure in midtown Manhattan, where he did most of his research.

Cunningham first arrived in New York in 1948, working in the advertising department at the Bonwit Teller department store, and later, under the name "William J," as a designer of hats. Following a stint in the army during the Korean War, Cunningham returned to New York and the hat trade. His first work for the fashion press came in 1953, when he was invited to cover fashion for *Women's Wear Daily*, and later, the *Chicago Tribune*. In 1966, Cunningham was given a camera by photographer David Montgomery. "He said 'Here, use it like a notebook,'" Cunningham recalled. "And that was the real beginning."

Cunningham was drawn to the street, and to fashion as it was worn not just by celebrities and models, but by real people. "The main thing I love about street photography is that you find the answers you don't see at the fashion shows," he said. "You find information for readers so they can visualize themselves." Cunningham began shooting street style for the *New York Times* in 1978, and his column became a weekly fixture in 1989.

His work with *Details* magazine is less well-known but equally important: after helping editor Annie Flanders to launch the magazine in June 1982, Cunningham wrote fashion criticism and shot the biannual collections issues until the mid-1990s. He is credited, in his 1989 report on Martin Margiela's collection, with introducing the term "deconstructivist" into fashion criticism.

A modest and unassuming man, Cunningham shunned publicity. He was given privileged entry to New York's most exclusive fashion and society events, but insisted on treating them as work assignments, refusing even a glass of water. Emptied of fittings and furniture, his apartment in the Carnegie Hall Artist Studios (where he lived until 2010) was filled with the filing cabinets that held his negatives. (At the time of his death, there were over a million of them.) Though Cunningham's sister column, "Evening Hours," launched at the same time, "On the Street" remains his true legacy: a record of Cunningham's encyclopedic knowledge of dress and fashion, and his devotion to the project of chronicling fashion as a mirror of the times. "I'm a record keeper," he remarked. "More than a collector. I'm very aware of things not of value, but of historical knowledge."

On the Street
Bill Cunningham

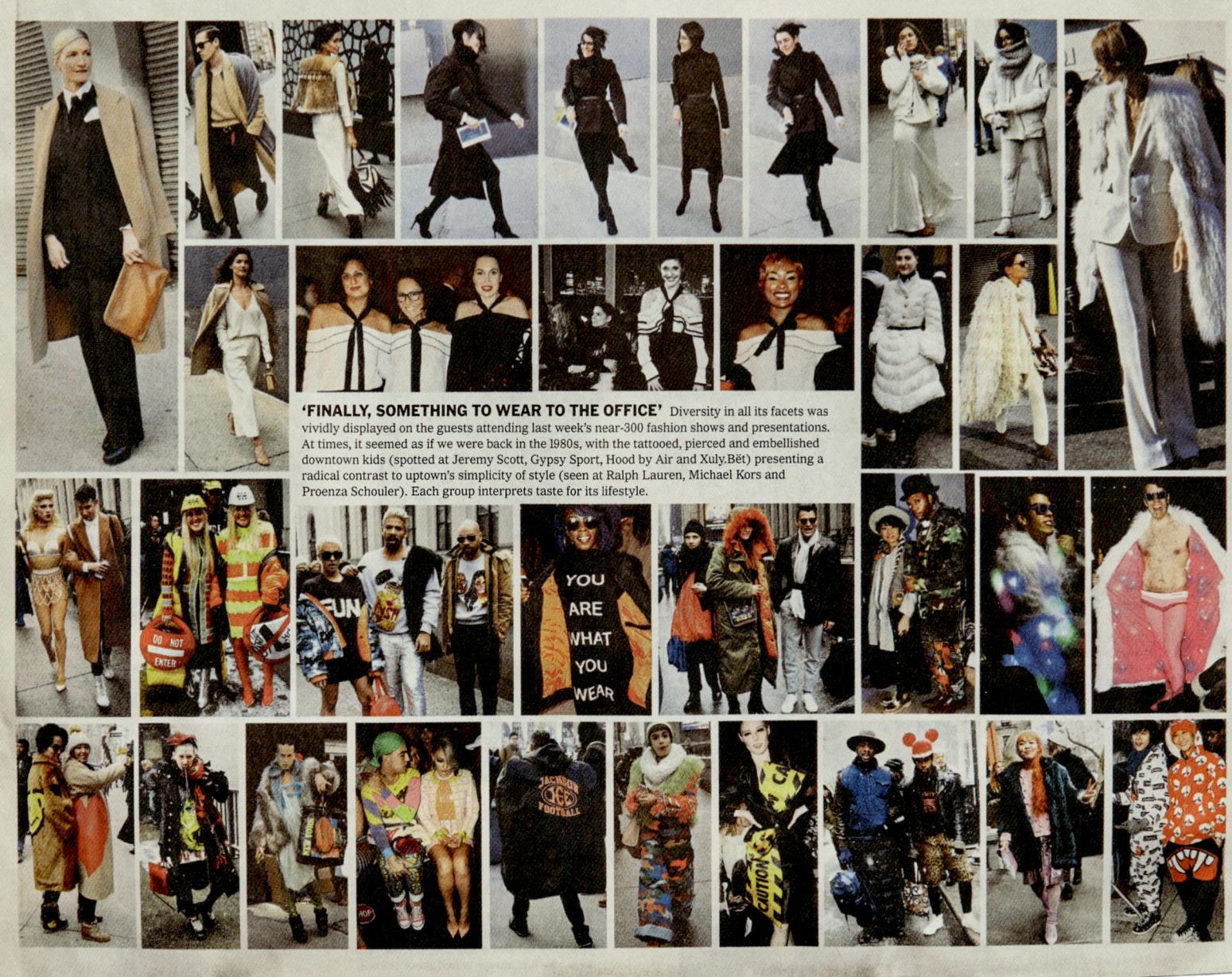

'FINALLY, SOMETHING TO WEAR TO THE OFFICE' Diversity in all its facets was vividly displayed on the guests attending last week's near-300 fashion shows and presentations. At times, it seemed as if we were back in the 1980s, with the tattooed, pierced and embellished downtown kids (spotted at Jeremy Scott, Gypsy Sport, Hood by Air and Xuly.Bët) presenting a radical contrast to uptown's simplicity of style (seen at Ralph Lauren, Michael Kors and Proenza Schouler). Each group interprets taste for its lifestyle.

Bill Cunningham, "On the Street,"
New York Times, February 21, 2016
Following pages: Bill Cunningham,
pages from *Details*, September 1986

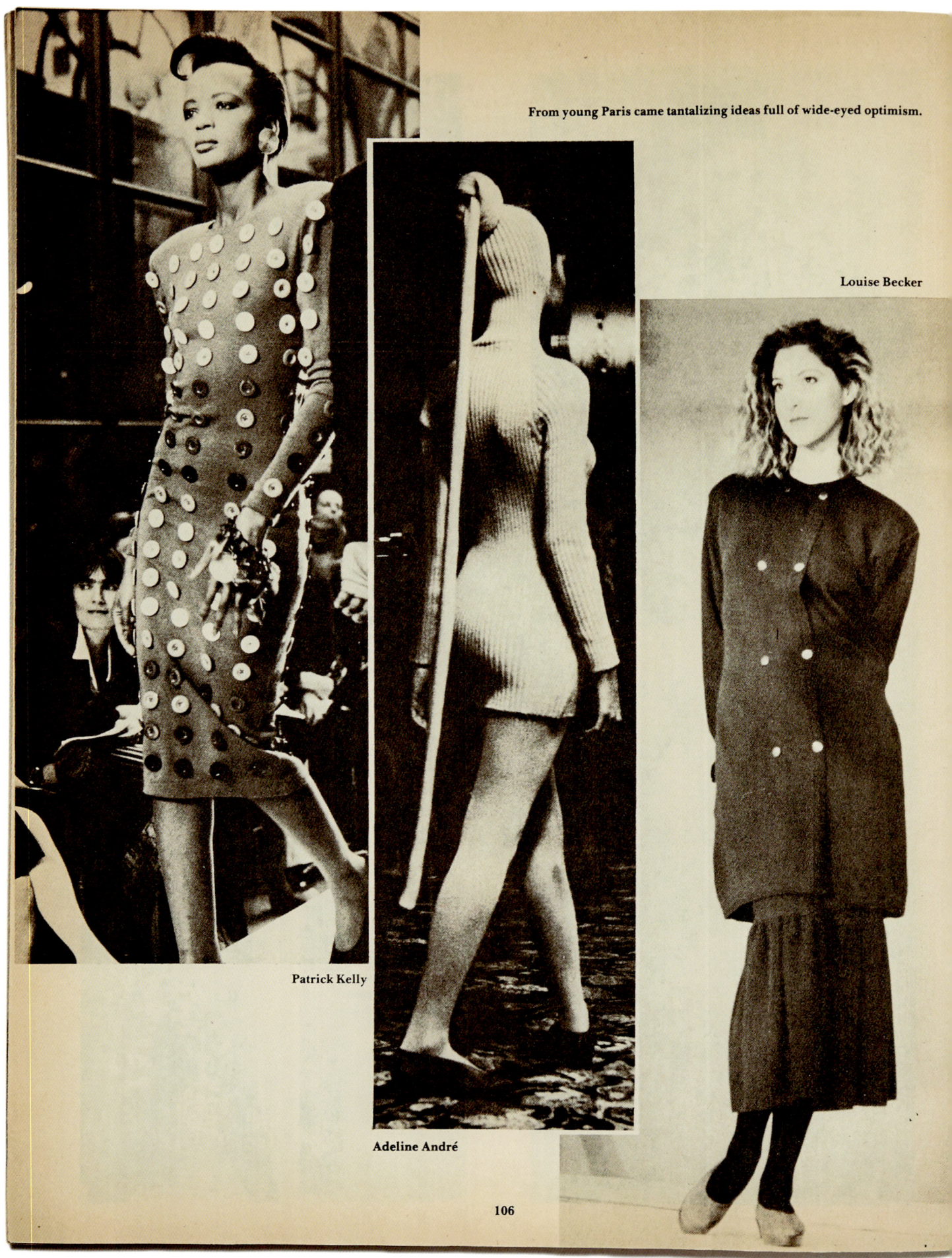

From young Paris came tantalizing ideas full of wide-eyed optimism.

Louise Becker

Patrick Kelly

Adeline André

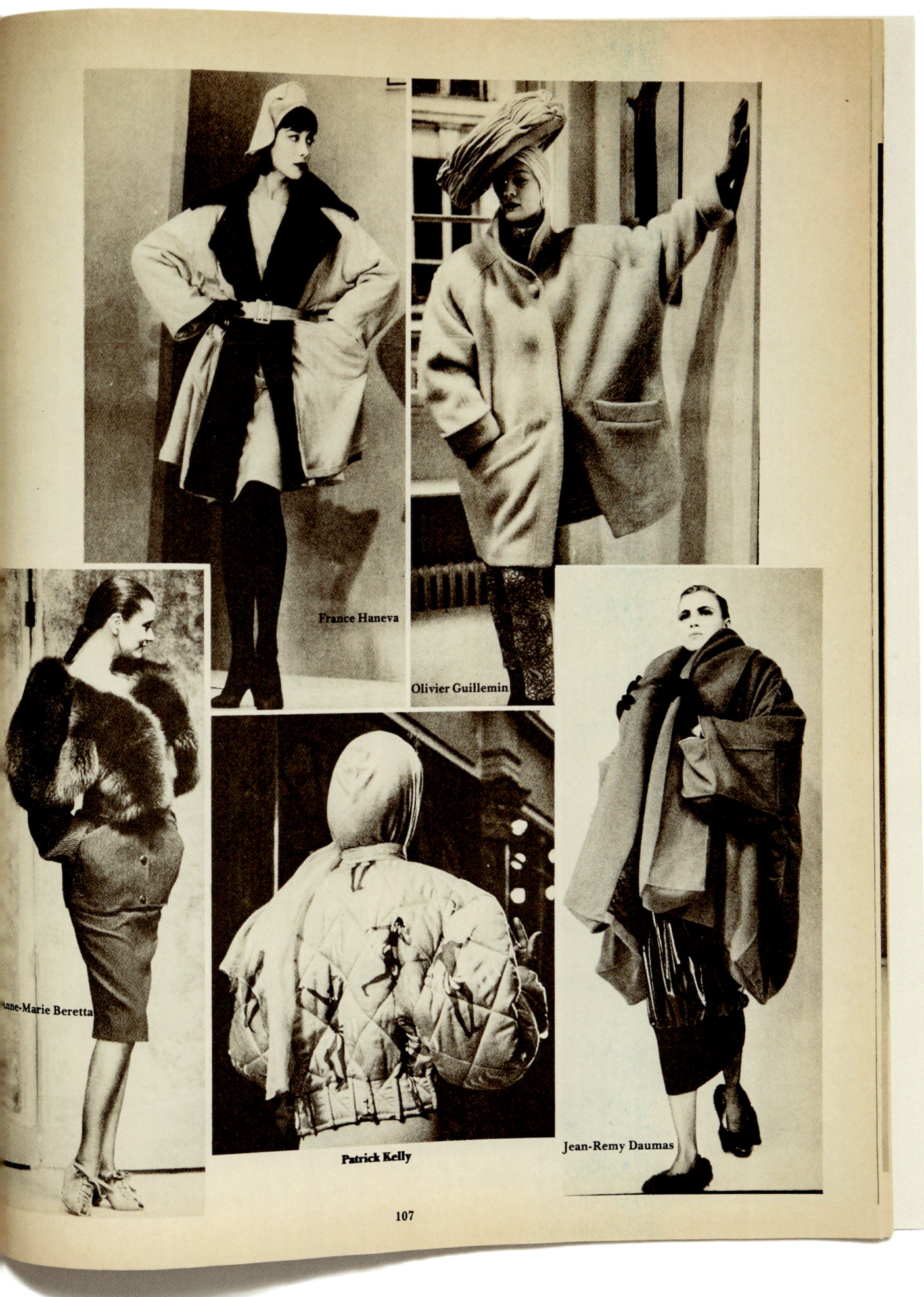

France Haneva

Olivier Guillemin

Anne-Marie Beretta

Patrick Kelly

Jean-Remy Daumas

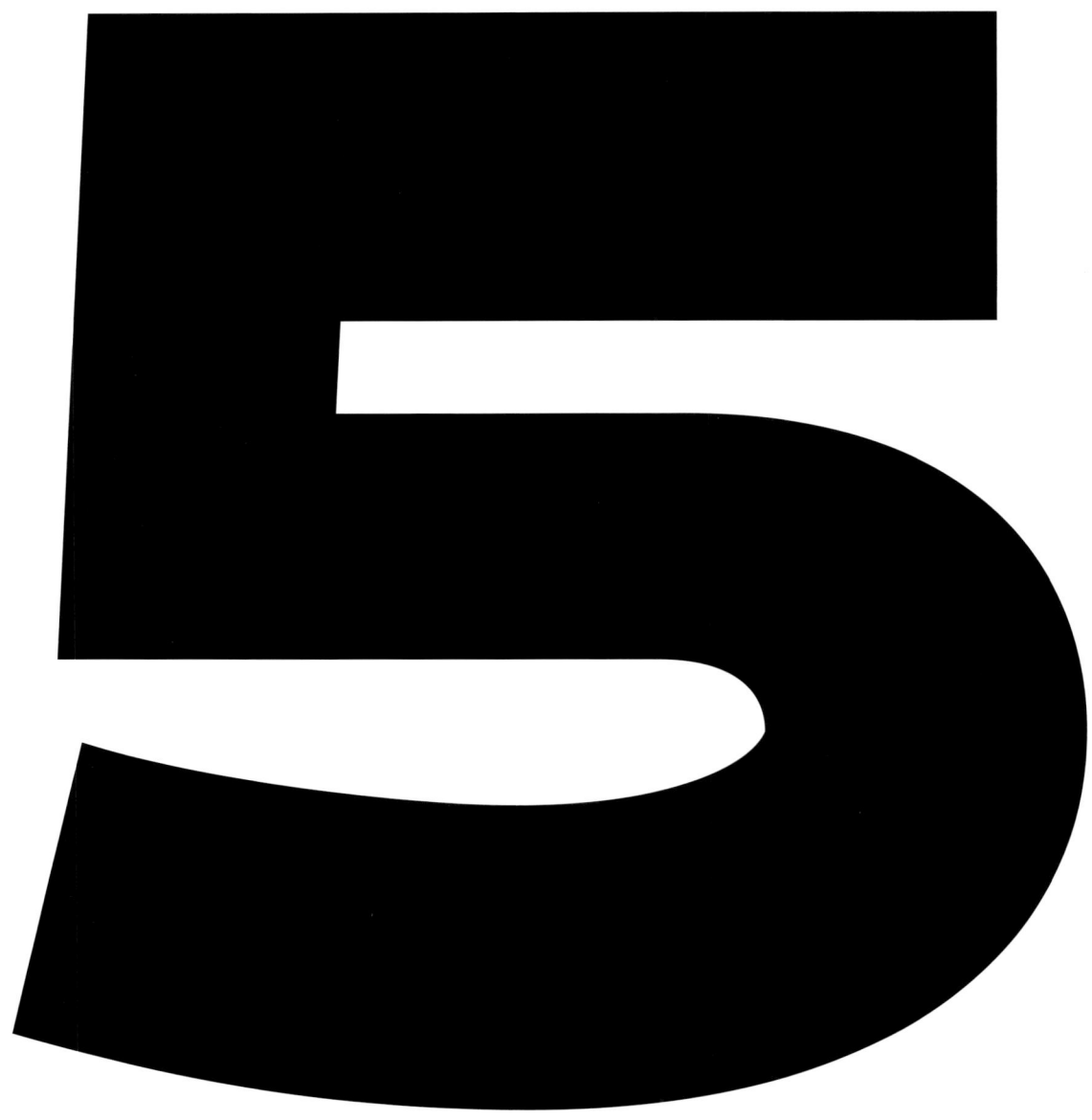

Corinne Day,
Kate Moss, "Under-exposure,"
British *Vogue*, June 1993

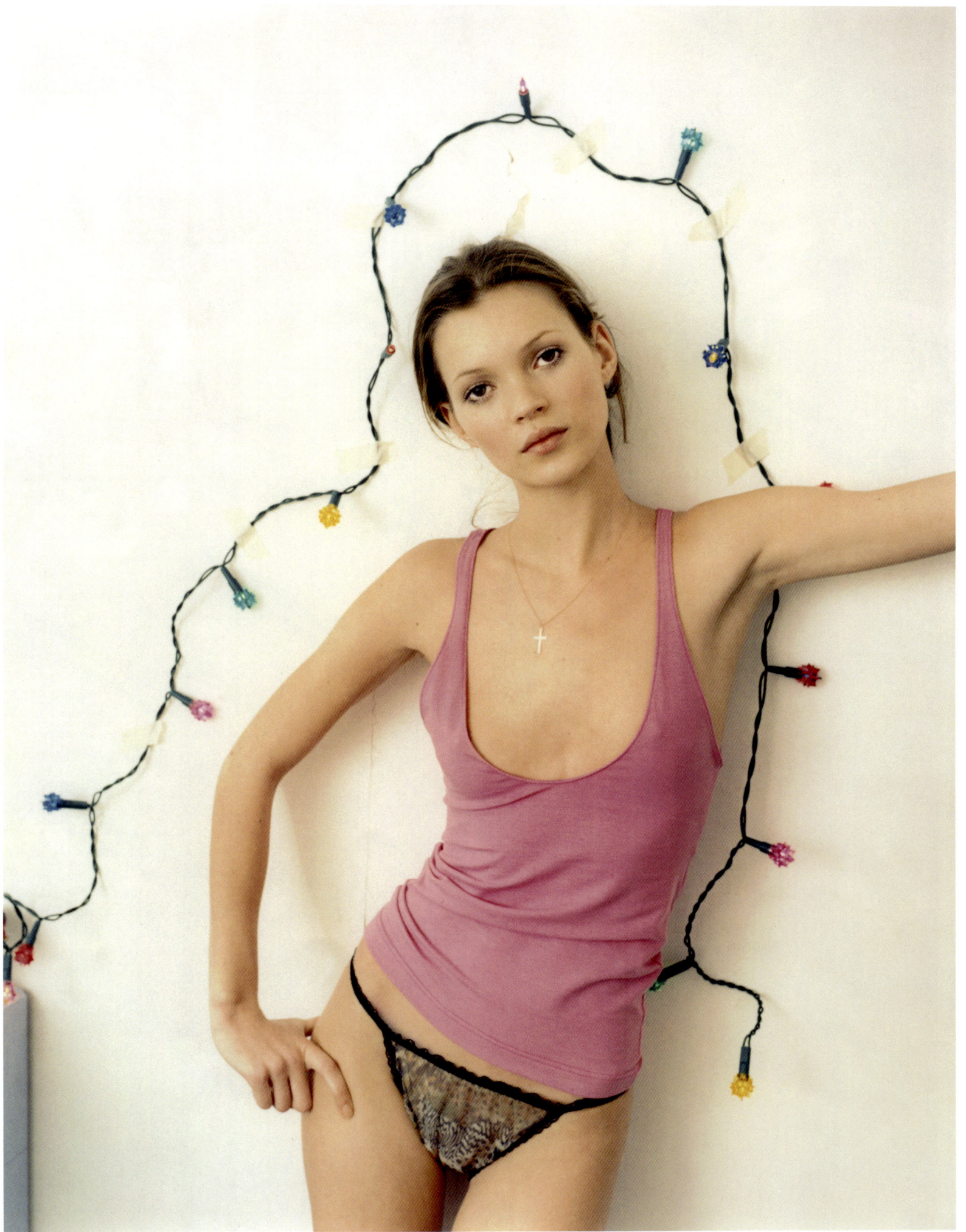

CORINNE DAY

Born in London, 1962;
died in Denham,
England, 2010

Corinne Day was a pioneer of the "grunge" aesthetic
that dominated fashion photography throughout
the 1990s. After leaving school at sixteen, Day spent
the next decade traveling and doing odd jobs,
including modeling. It was during this period that
she learned to use a camera, taking photographs
of friends and acquaintances. On her return
to London in 1989, Day showed some of her
photographs to Phil Bicker, art director of *The Face*,
and was offered work with the magazine. Day
chose fifteen-year-old Kate Moss to model for an
early assignment, attracted by her "unconventional"
looks—Moss was only five-foot-seven, with
crooked teeth and the body of a skinny adolescent.

Shortly afterward, Day met stylist Melanie
Ward, who shared her interest in secondhand
clothing and became a frequent collaborator. Shot
in her signature lo-fi, documentary style,
Day's photographs often featured her friends
and acquaintances posing makeup-free in
dingy surroundings, casually styled in their own
clothing. They stood in sharp contrast to the
work of contemporaries such as Peter Lindbergh
(p. 192) and Ellen von Unwerth (p. 190), whose
images of supermodels in haute couture graced
the pages of commercial fashion magazines.
As Day remarked, "I never thought about the
commercial aspect of fashion photography.
I wasn't recording anything more than the way
we were living."

Her gritty aesthetic was perfectly suited
to independent magazines, but "Under-exposure,"
shot in 1993 for British *Vogue*, provoked a strong
backlash from the more conservative, mainstream
fashion press. The images of a waifish Moss,
posing in cheap lingerie in the flat that she shared
with photographer Mario Sorrenti, were accused
of glamorizing anorexia and drug abuse. As
Day recalled, "It was said at the time that the shock
these photographs caused was like that of a cider-
obliterated punk wandering into a coming-out ball."
Within a year, however, Moss was on her way to
becoming one of the most iconic supermodels of
her generation.

Corinne Day,
Kate, 1990; printed in 2006

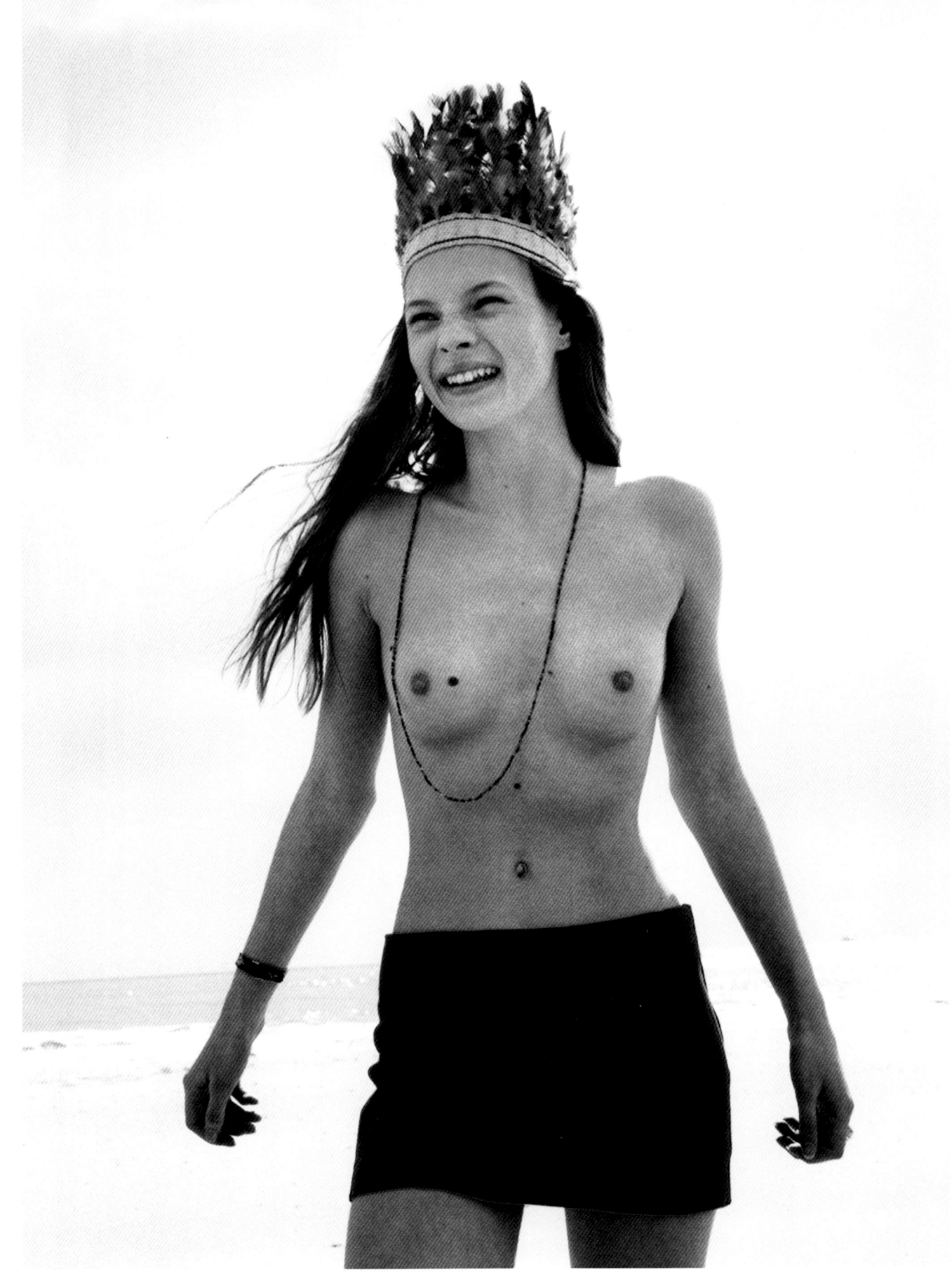

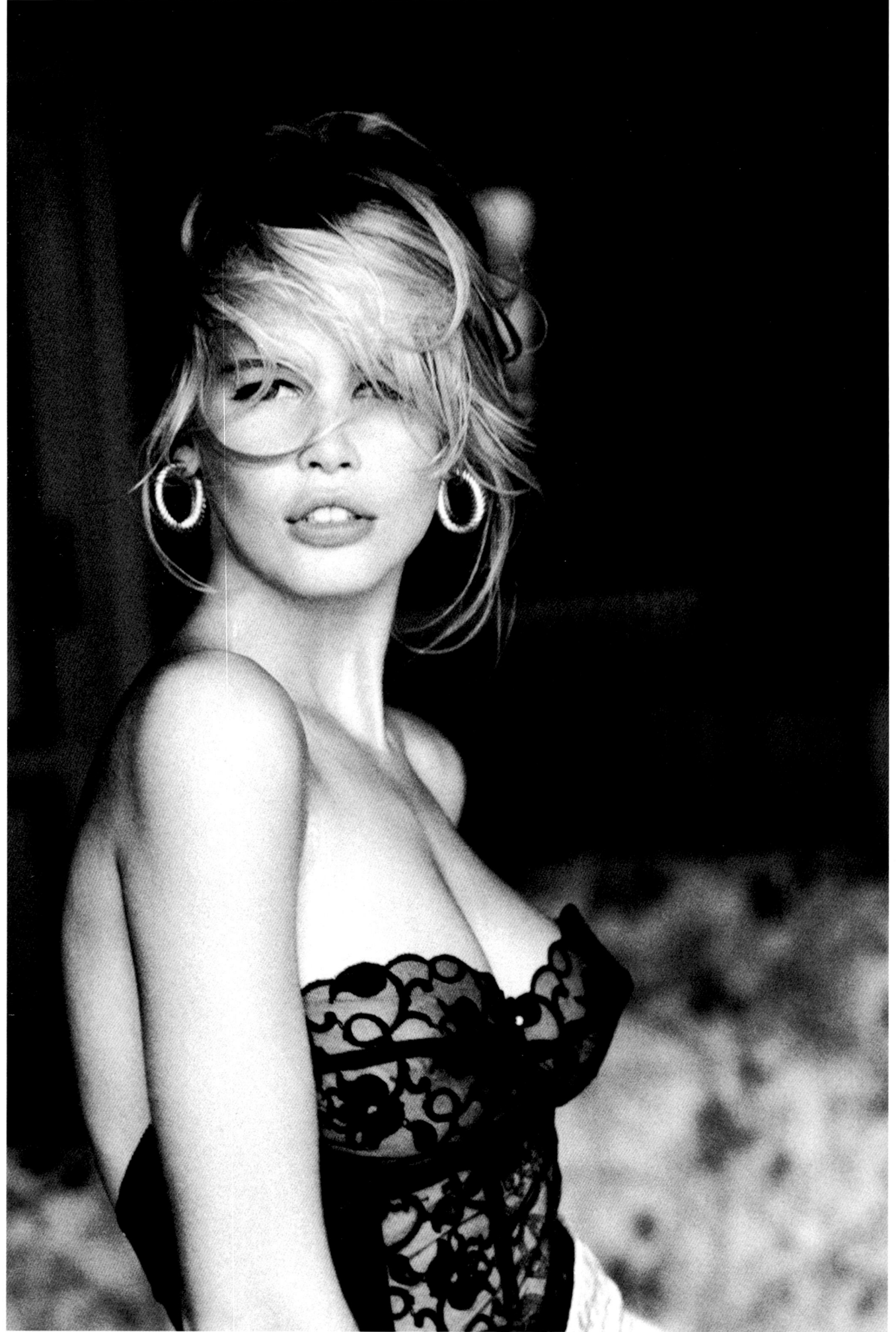

Born in Frankfurt, 1954

ELLEN VON UNWERTH

Ellen von Unwerth spent her early years in an orphanage, then moved back and forth between various foster families before leaving for Munich at age sixteen. It was here that she was discovered by a photographer with the German magazine *Bravo* and went on to become a model, working with photographers such as Helmut Newton (p. 134) and Michael Roberts.

Bored during an assignment in Kenya in 1986, Unwerth took out a camera that her boyfriend had given her and started snapping pictures. The resulting photographs were published by the French fashion magazine *Jill*, and Unwerth suddenly found herself on the other side of the camera. Within a few months she had landed an advertising campaign for British designer Katharine Hamnett, but her big break was the Guess campaigns she shot in 1989. Unwerth first worked with Claudia Schiffer when she was asked to photograph the then-unknown seventeen-year-old for *Elle*. Struck by Schiffer's resemblance to a young Brigitte Bardot, Unwerth cast her in the campaign that would make the names of both model and photographer.

Emerging during the early years of the supermodel era, Unwerth's photographs embraced an image of body-confident vitality that resembled the work of contemporaries such as Bruce Weber (p. 168) and Peter Lindbergh (p. 192), while her use of nudity and female eroticism has invited comparisons with the work of Helmut Newton (p. 134). However, the undertones of misogyny and violence that mark Newton's work are seldom evident in Unwerth's pictures, and she insists that her playful, spontaneous approach to female sexuality is different from that of a male photographer: "I understand the female body better, and I know from my own modeling days how you feel both constrained and free when you're in front of a camera."

Ellen von Unwerth,
Claudia Schiffer, Italy, 1989

191

PETER LINDBERGH

Born in Lissa, Germany, 1944

Fashion's so-called "supermodel era" is often said to have begun with Peter Lindbergh's 1988 photograph of a group of then-unknown models dressed in white shirts and posing in a group on a beach. "Those were the easy times," he recalled, "the years of the supermodels. . . . They were the photo. They just stood in front of my camera and I just pressed the button. That was that." Styled by Grace Coddington, "Wild at Heart" featured a roll call of famous faces: Cindy Crawford, Tatjana Patitz, Helena Christensen, Linda Evangelista, Claudia Schiffer, Naomi Campbell, Karen Mulder, and Stephanie Seymour.

Lindbergh had been uninspired by the fashion photography of the late 1970s and early '80s. "I wanted to move away from the rather formal, quite perfectly styled woman who was very artificial," he said. "I was more concerned about a more outspoken, adventurous woman in control of her life. . . . The supermodels represented this change." His crisp black-and-white images, with their simple styling and low-key makeup, represented a dramatic volte-face in an age that had become obsessed with the more contrived beauty of work by photographers such as Guy Bourdin (p. 144) and Chris von Wangenheim (p. 138). Aligned early on with some of the world's top designers, including Karl Lagerfeld, Jean Paul Gaultier, John Galliano, Gianni Versace, and Rei Kawakubo, Lindbergh rose to prominence as one of the highly paid "blue-chip" photographers who were called upon to reshape the images of major fashion brands.

The supermodel era lasted for about a decade. When it ended, Lindbergh, like many others, was eager to free himself from the narrow iconography of a period obsessed with a handful of iconic faces. Lindbergh's more recent work marks a return to his original motive for making pictures: his fascination with avant-garde and Hollywood cinema and the permeable line between illusion and reality. Many of his newer images have the spontaneous feel of a backstage or street photograph, often containing visible props, lights, and crew.

Peter Lindbergh,
Cindy Crawford, Tatjana Patitz, Helena Christensen,
Linda Evangelista, Claudia Schiffer, Naomi Campbell,
Karen Mulder and Stephanie Seymour, Brooklyn, 1991

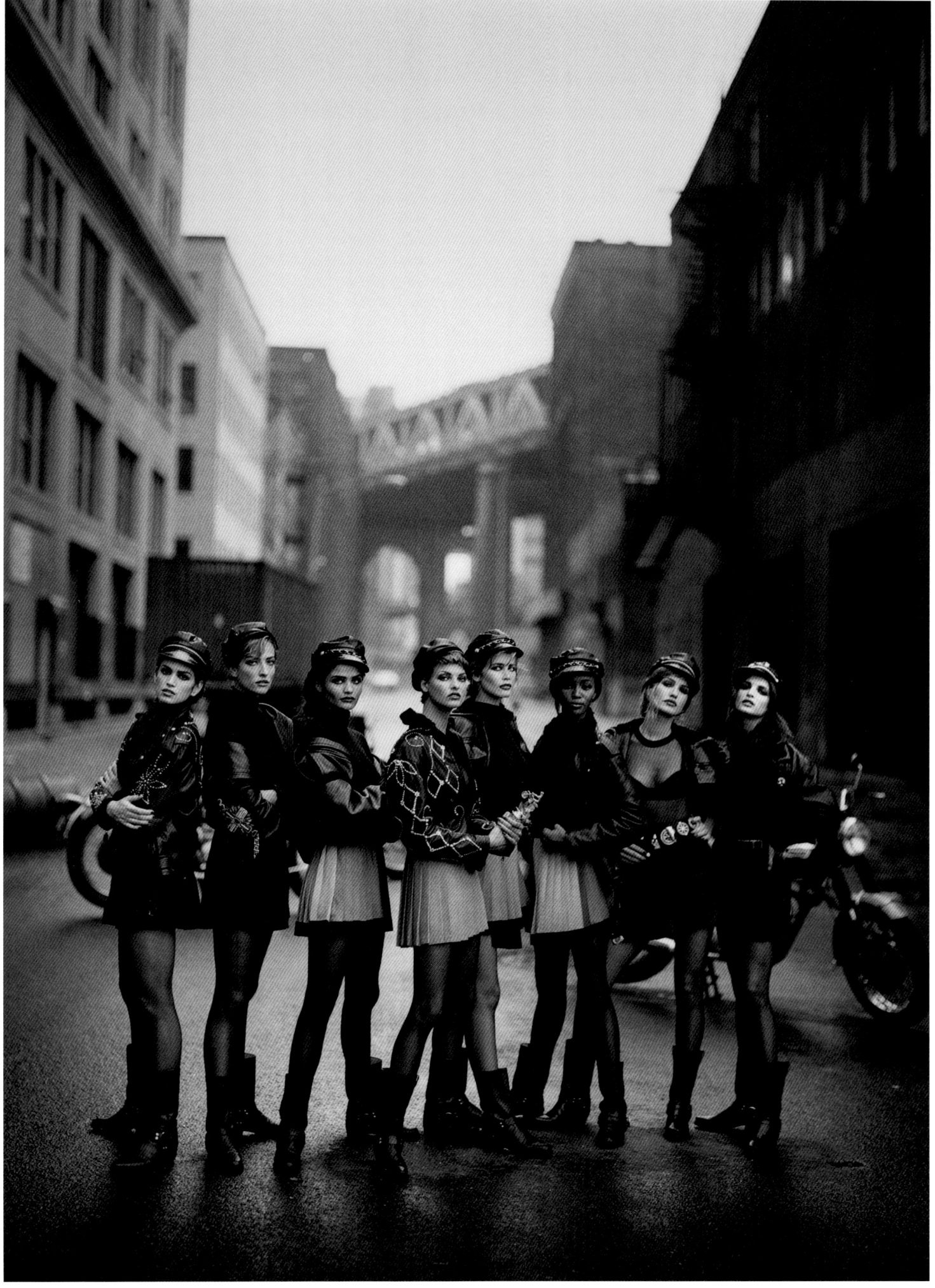

Born in London, 1964

Nigel Shafran began taking photographs at age sixteen and decided very quickly that he wanted to become a photographer. After assisting various advertising and fashion photographers in London, Shafran moved to New York in the mid-1980s, at age nineteen. Two days later, he was assisting Deborah Turbeville (p. 128) on a shoot for *Vogue Italia*. "She was very kind and generous to me," Shafran recalled. "She really helped me—she took me under her wing."

Shafran remained in New York for two-and-a-half years, doing various assisting jobs, before returning to London. His first photographs were published in *The Face* in 1989; "Teenage Precinct Shoppers" appeared in *i-D* in 1991. Although Shafran's work is often linked to that of contemporaries such as Corinne Day (p. 188), he has remained, by choice, on the periphery of the fashion world, preferring to focus on his personal work. Stylist Melanie Ward collaborated with Shafran in the production of "Teenage Precinct Shoppers," but there was no actual styling involved. All of the models were street-cast and photographed on location in their own clothes. "These weren't hip kids—these were kids walking around outside a shopping precinct in Ilford. . . . [They] were allowed to come forward, to show themselves," said Shafran. "To me, they look like busts in a way. It was to give them a bit of pride." Loosely sharing the aesthetic—if not the intention—of the straight-up, these photographs, though they appeared in a style magazine, are closer in spirit to street portraiture.

Shafran continues to shoot fashion occasionally, doing editorial work for magazines such as British *Vogue*, *Love*, and *Re-Edition*, as well as advertising for clients, including Loewe and Smythson.

NIGEL SHAFRAN

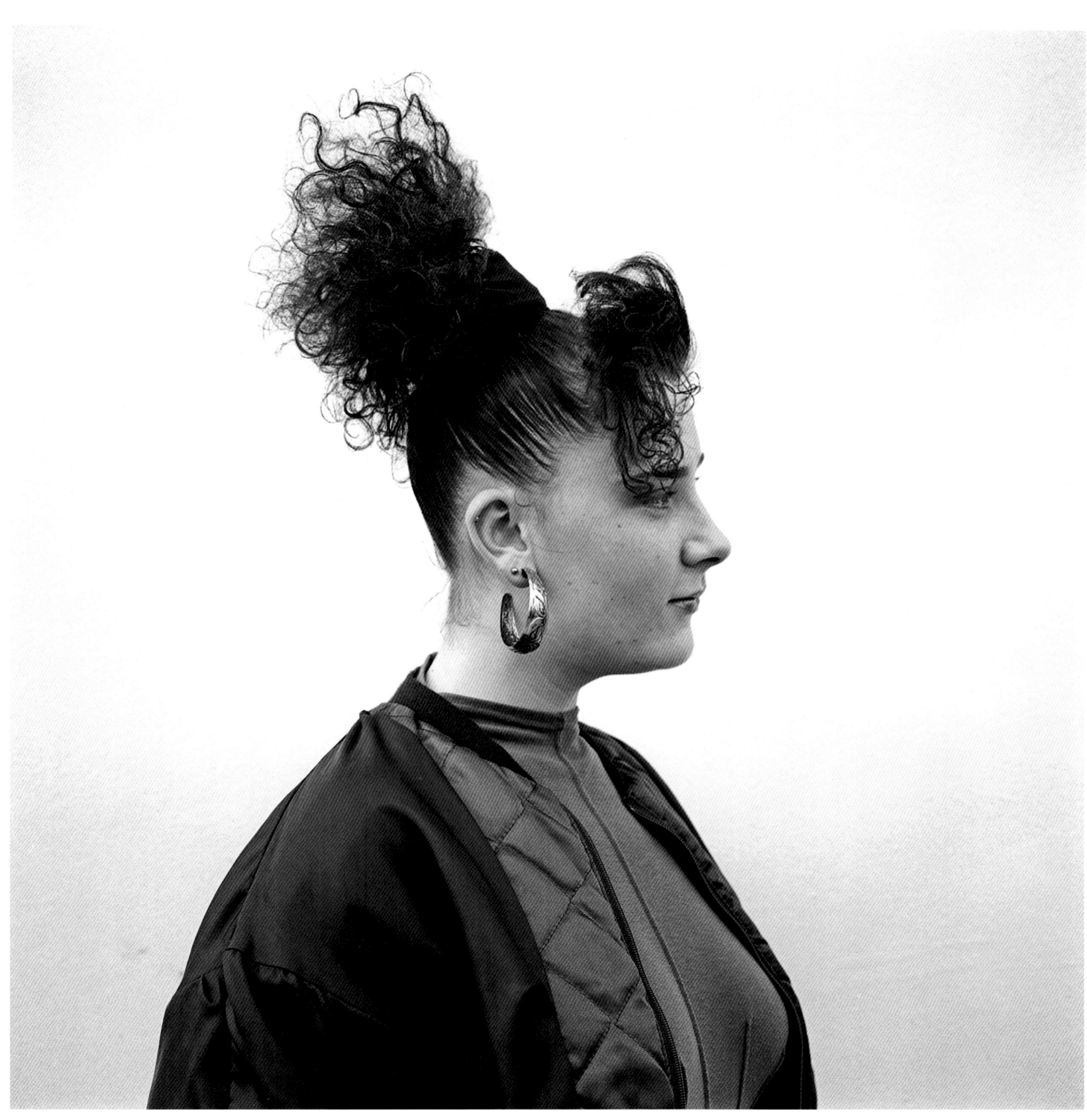

Nigel Shafran,
Nicola, Unemployed Seventeen-Year-Old from Ilford, Ilford
Shopping Precinct, London, 1990; with Melanie Ward

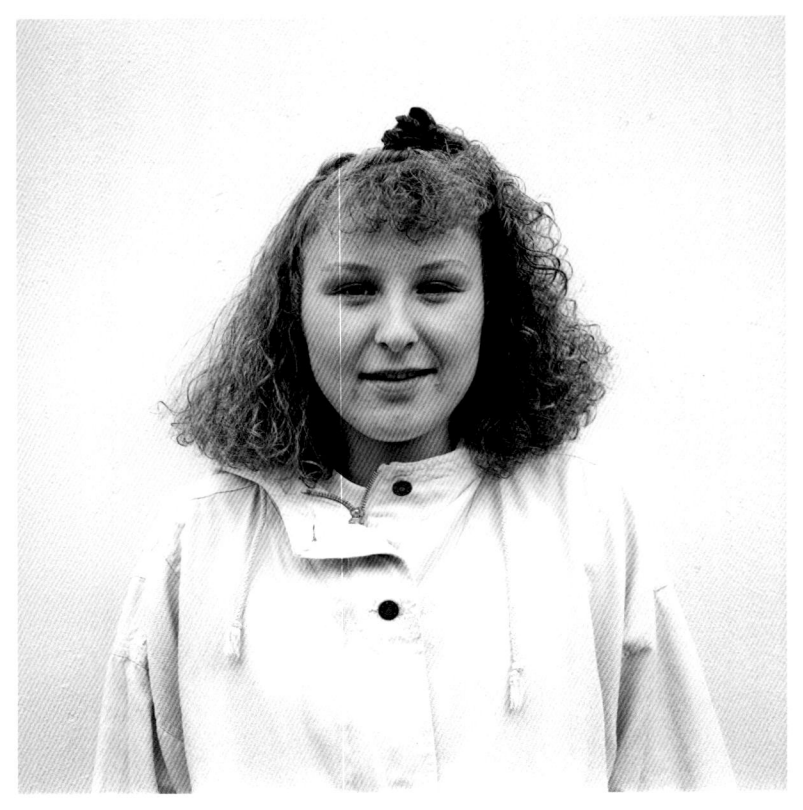
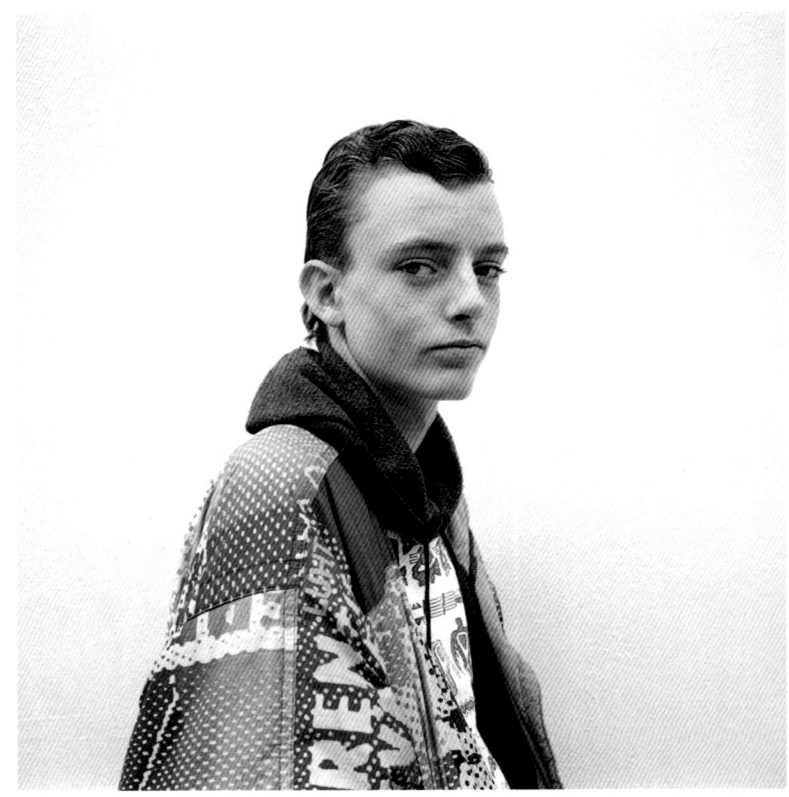
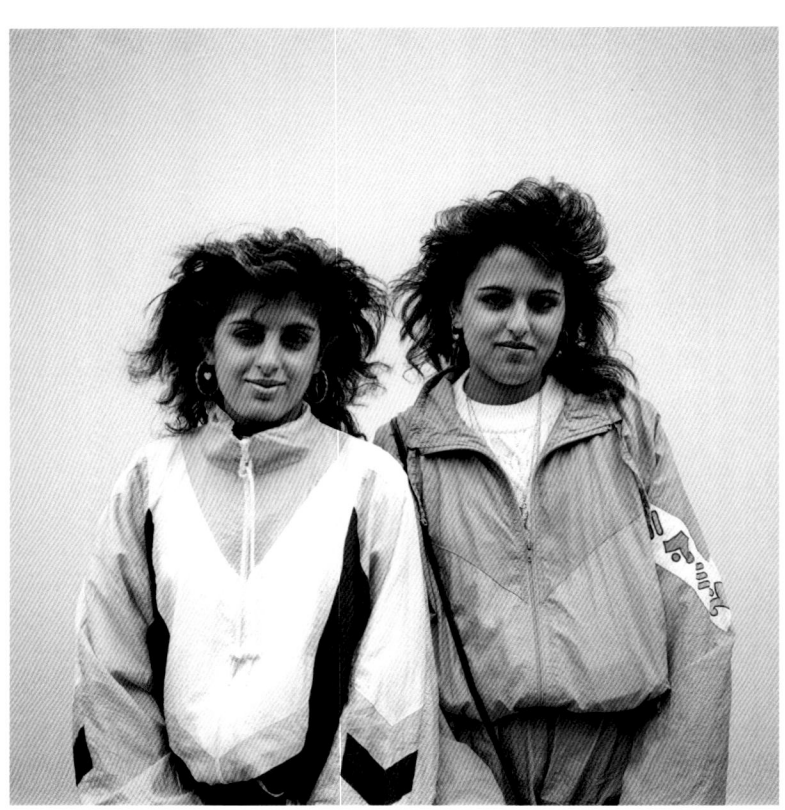
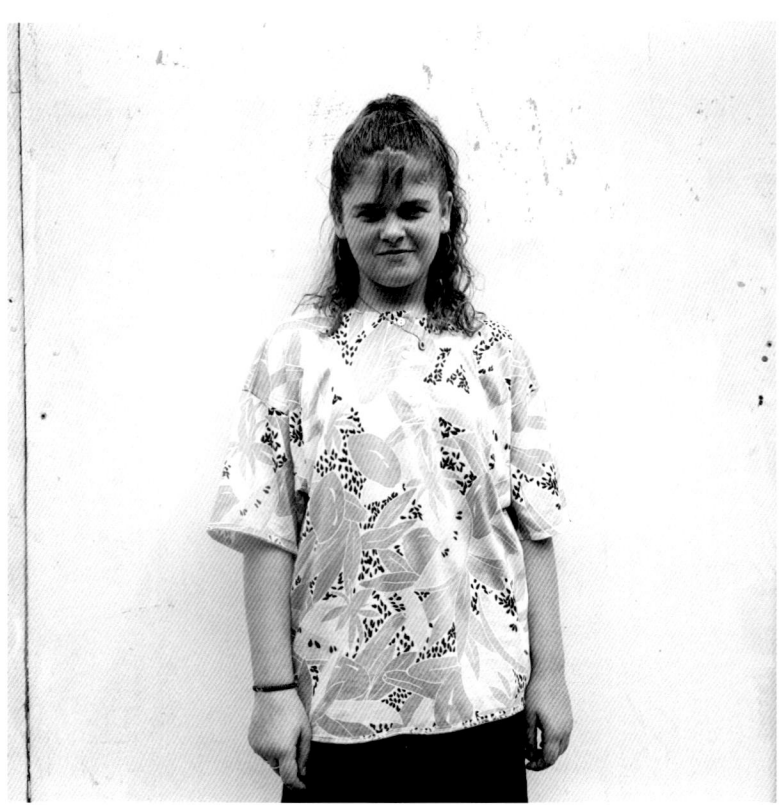

Nigel Shafran,
clockwise from top left: *Anonymous Shopper*; *Graham, Sixteen Years Old, from Beckton, Shopping for a Skateboard for His Birthday*; *Anonymous Shopper*; *Tina, Seventeen Years Old and Reena, Twenty-One Years Old, from Manor Park*; Ilford Shopping Precinct, London, 1990; with Melanie Ward

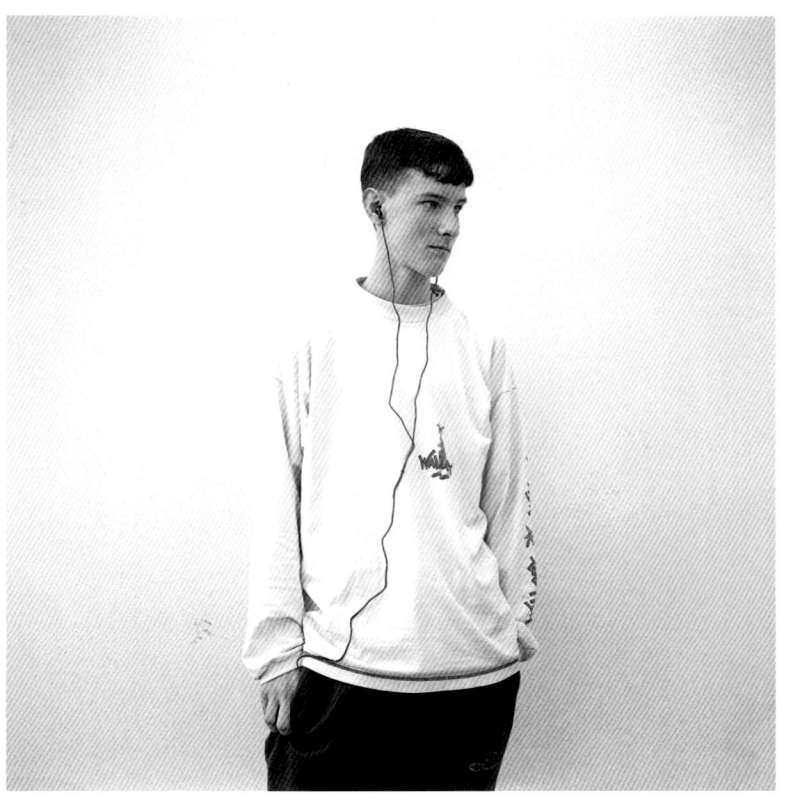
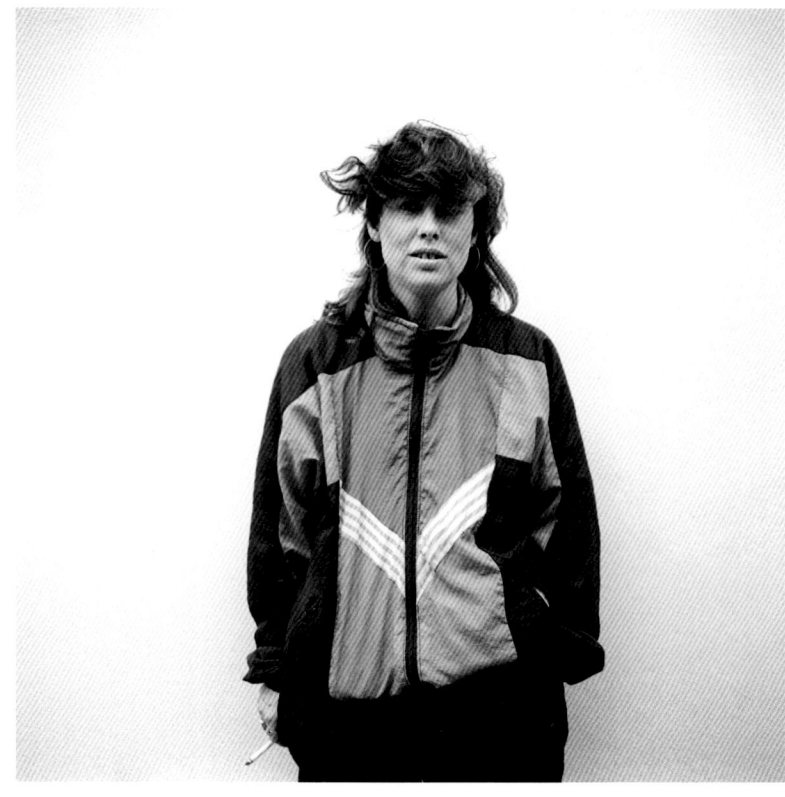
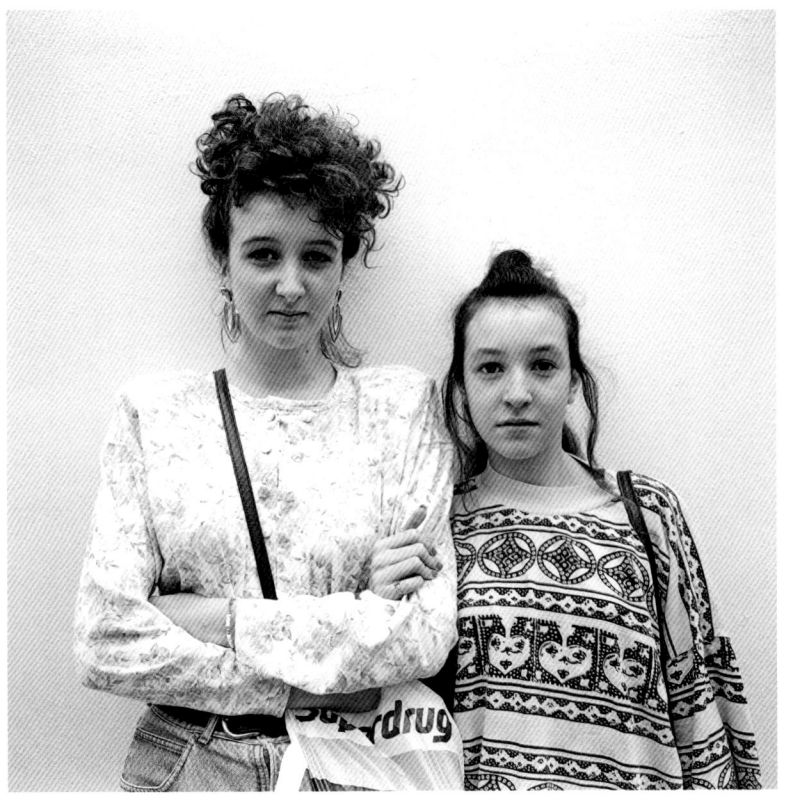
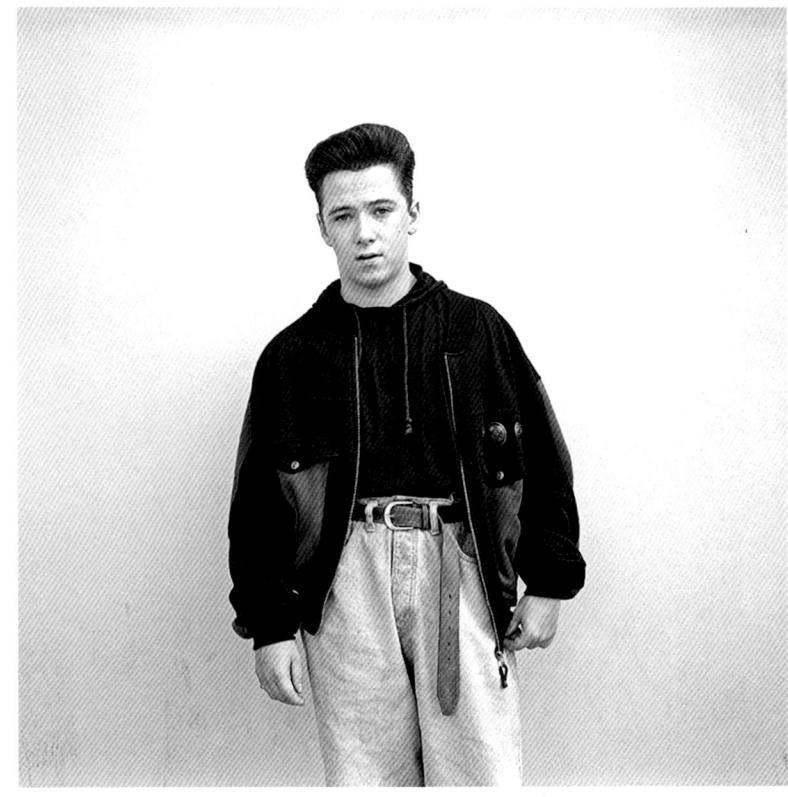

Nigel Shafran,
clockwise from top left: *Terry, Thirteen Years Old, from Loughton*; *Anonymous Shopper*;
Anonymous Shopper; *Melanie and Davina Hall*; Ilford Shopping Precinct, London,
1990; with Melanie Ward

JASON EVANS

Born in Holyhead,
Wales, 1968

It was not fashion or clothing, but rather the possibilities of fashion photography as a platform for exploring alternative political realities, that first attracted Jason Evans. "I was interested in what fashion photography says about us, in terms of gender, ethnicity, aspiration, opportunity," he has said. "Fashion photography, at best, is a really great place to dream, and fantasize, and project. . . . I wasn't especially excited about showing clothes, but I was very excited about constructing worlds."

Evans studied art in Sheffield, England, in the late 1980s. As a student, he was drawn to the magazine as a form of cultural communication —an alternative to the commercial incentives of the gallery system and the art world—and, in 1989, when he was in his final year of university, he applied for an internship with Nick Knight (p. 218) at *i-D*. This initial sojourn with *i-D* went on to last four years. At first, Evans worked primarily as a stylist, under the pseudonym of Travis, but his creative involvement with the magazine would eventually encompass photography, street-casting, clothing and record-cover design, and occasional modeling. This eclectic approach to creative work has driven Evans for most of his career, which has grown to include portraiture, sculpture, and video, as well as writing and curating.

Published in *i-D* in 1991, "Strictly" combined cultural perceptions of black youth and white suburbia with the nineteenth-century notion of the dandy. It was also driven by more serious questions about embedded social and racial prejudice. As Evans recalled, "I was interested in the sociopolitical implication of making a fashion editorial that only featured black faces." Styled by Simon Foxton and street-cast by Edward Enninful—Foxton's assistant at the time—"Strictly" was motivated, in part, by a sense of outrage at the racial bias that still predominated in the fashion industry.

Since leaving *i-D*, Evans has chosen to work outside the commercial fashion industry. "I've never shot a fashion advertising campaign," he said. "But that wasn't the point—the point was to infiltrate editorial culture and add a different message."

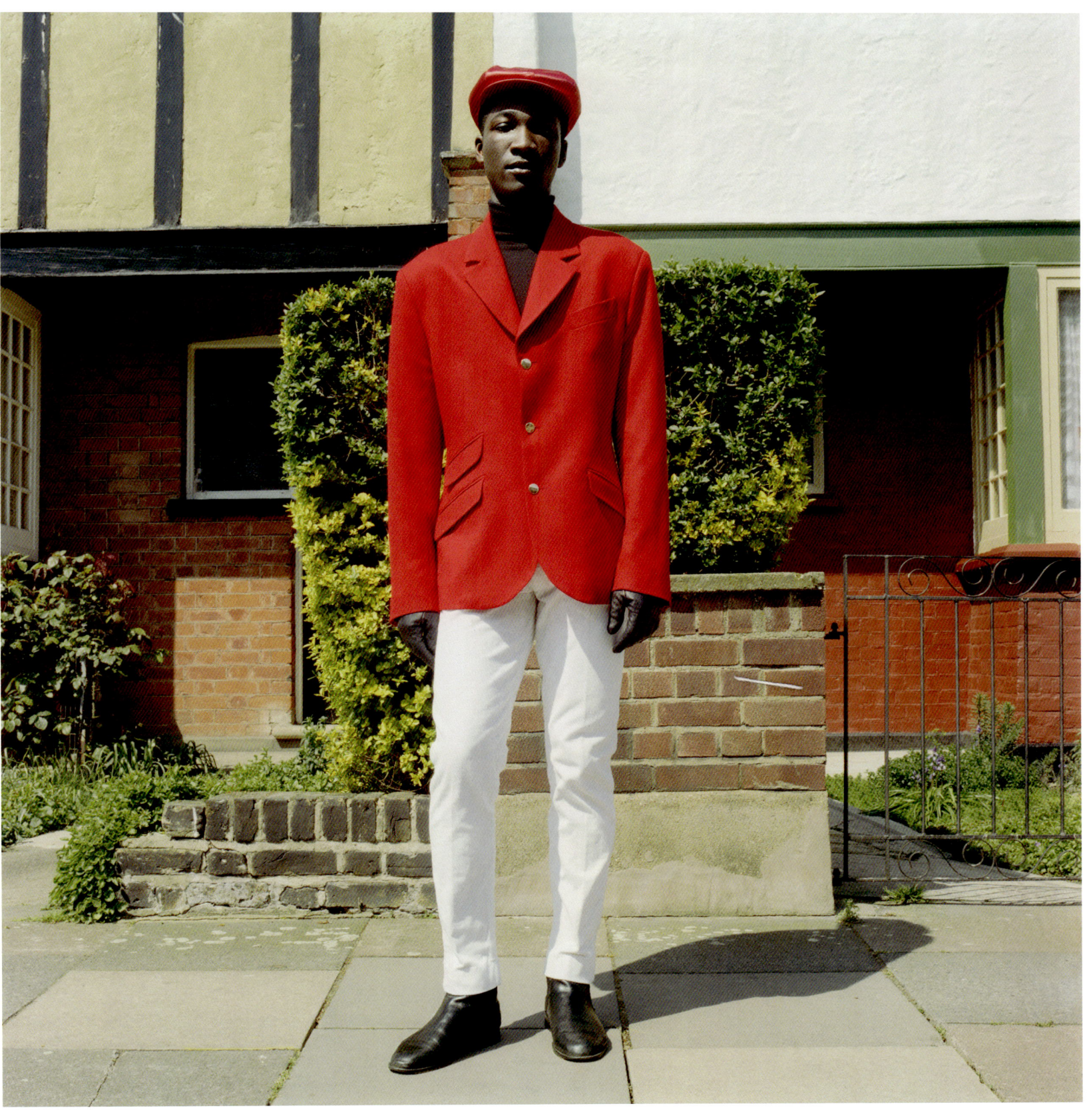

Jason Evans,
Untitled, from the series Strictly, 1991

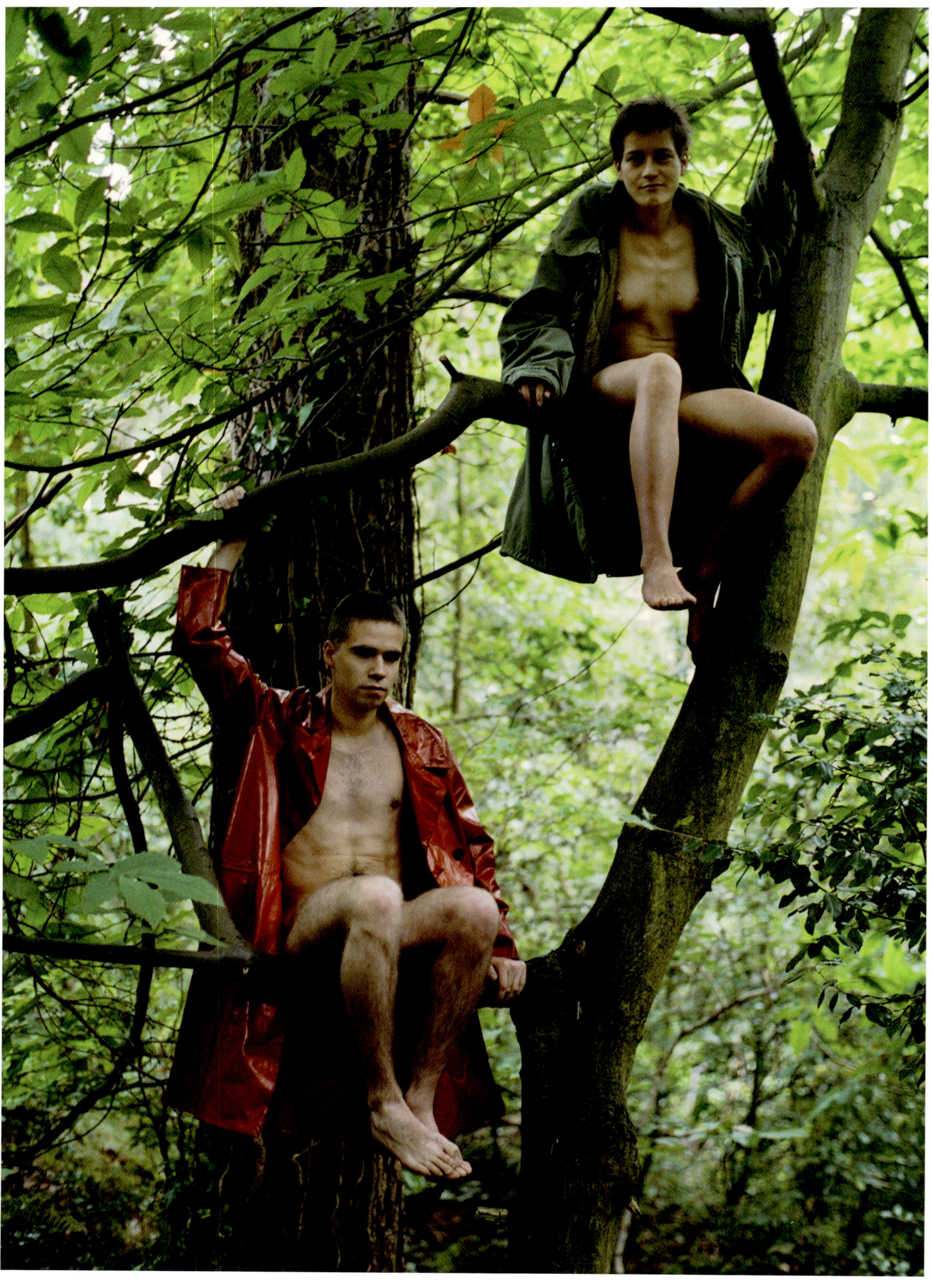

WOLFGANG TILLMANS

Born in Remscheid,
Germany, 1968

Wolfgang Tillmans is frequently named—alongside contemporaries such as Corinne Day (p. 188) and Juergen Teller (p. 208)—as one of the photographers who transformed the representation of fashion in the 1990s. However, like Jason Evans (p. 198), he has consistently refused to take on advertising commissions. Despite this, his casual-style images of alternative lifestyles, sexual politics, and club culture have proved to be memorable, even iconic, records of the street fashion and DIY style of the era.

Tillmans was also part of a growing number of young photographers using fashion photography as a vehicle for critical commentary. Although social critique—particularly of women's roles—had been implicit in work by photographers such as Richard Avedon (p. 94) since the early 1960s, the emergence of the alternative fashion press in the 1980s and '90s fostered a broader and more outspoken approach. When his work first appeared in *i-D* in 1989, Tillmans was insistent on its role as social commentary rather than corporate promotion. "The endless industry thirst for labels, trends, and fashions turns every style into another benign marketing plot," he said. "In a way, I try to channel attention to the multilayeredness of personality and identity."

"Like Brother Like Sister" first appeared as an editorial in *i-D* in 1992, in a themed issue on sexuality. Tillmans's photographs—which featured frontal nudity and some controversial physical contact between models Lutz Huelle and Alex Bircken—posed questions about beauty, sexual freedom, and gender identity. Individual images from the spread have had an extended afterlife as part of Tillmans's art practice, appearing on gallery walls either in their original form as magazine pages, or as larger single images.

Wolfgang Tillmans,
Lutz & Alex sitting in the trees, 1992

MARIO SORRENTI

Born in Naples,
1971

Like many of the photographers associated with the grunge scene, Mario Sorrenti had no formal training in photography. As a teenager growing up in New York, Sorrenti carried his camera with him everywhere, shooting black-and-white pictures of friends and pasting the photographs into diaries. His first introduction to fashion photography was as a model, sitting for the likes of Bruce Weber (p. 168), Steven Meisel (p. 242), Paolo Roversi (p. 180), and Richard Avedon (p. 94). Shortly after moving to London in 1991, Sorrenti was contacted by Phil Bicker of *The Face*, who asked to see his pictures. A spread in *The Face* with stylist Camilla Nickerson followed shortly after, and within six months, Sorrenti was offered a contract with *Harper's Bazaar*.

Sorrenti's famous Calvin Klein campaign—modeled by then-girlfriend Kate Moss—appeared in 1993, when Sorrenti was twenty-one. Shot without a crew—Klein hired a house in the Caribbean for the pair, who were sent there alone for five days—the resulting photographs have a raw, sensual energy that made some fashion editors uncomfortable. One image, of nineteen-year-old Moss lying naked on a sofa, elicited whispers about child pornography in the industry, and was banned in the United Kingdom.

The grunge phenomenon went commercial with unsettling speed, propelling Sorrenti—along with many of his peers—to the top of the profession and drawing often unwelcome attention from the press. The casual drug use that was so much a part of the grunge scene—and which is often erroneously said to have claimed the life of Sorrenti's younger brother Davide, also a fashion photographer—created a storm of media controversy that saw many of the grunge photographers, such as Sorrenti and Corinne Day (p. 188), accused of promoting "heroin chic." By 1994, Sorrenti had begun to experiment with color photography, creating rich, painterly images that moved away from the grunge aesthetic toward a more individual approach.

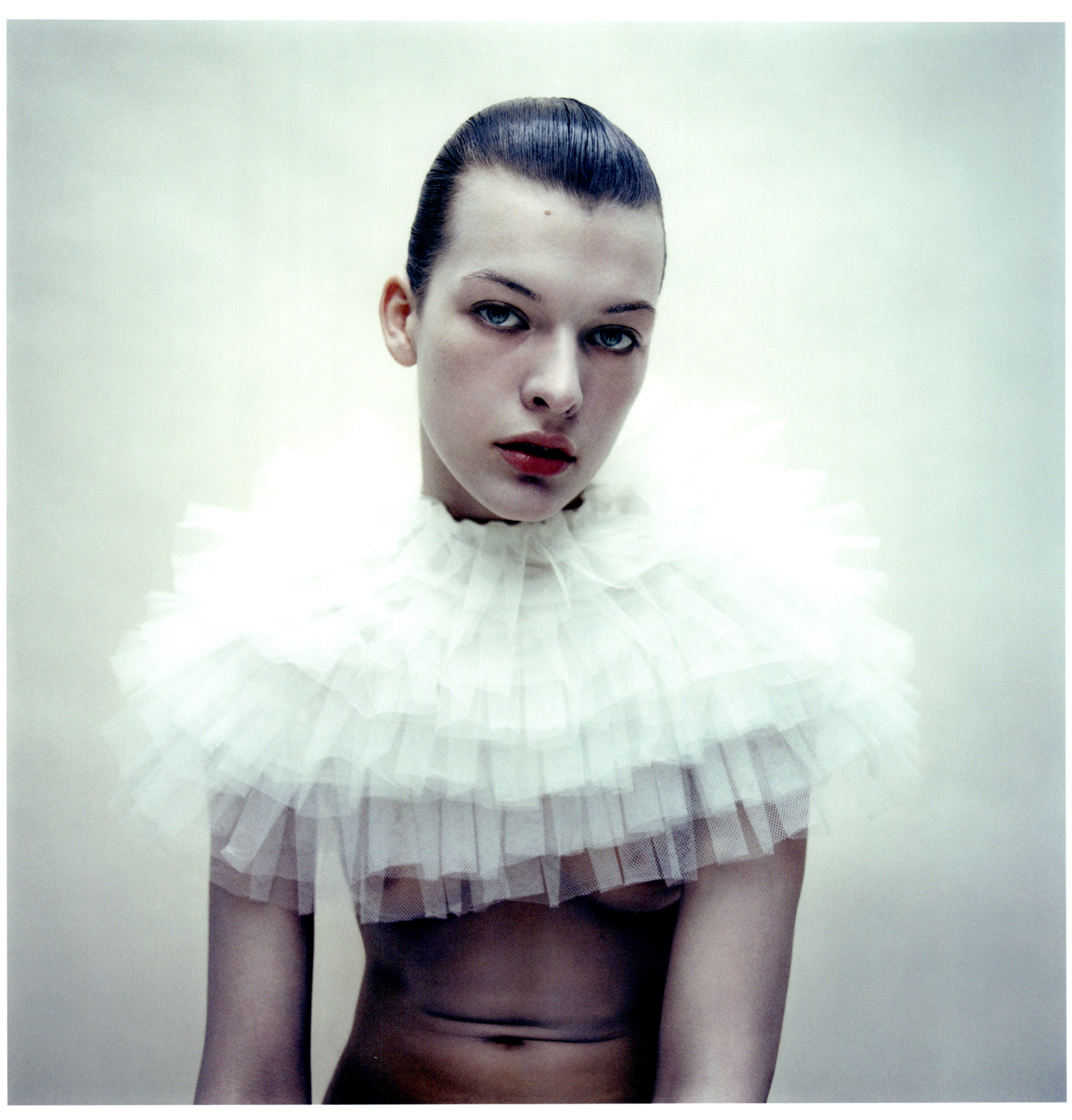

Mario Sorrenti,
Milla Jovovich with Ruffle, i-D, Febuary 1996

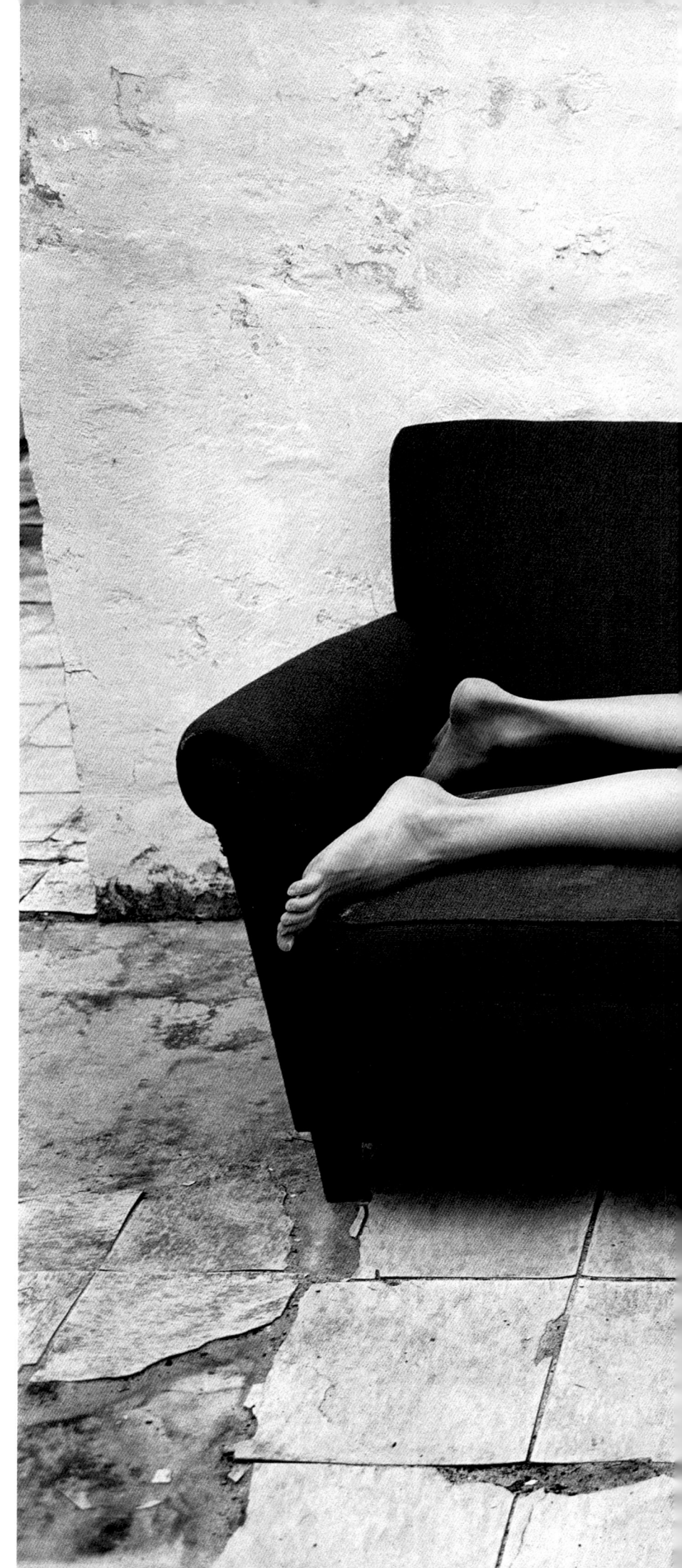

Mario Sorrenti,
Kate on Couch, 1993; for Calvin Klein Obsession
Campaign, Jost Van Dyke, British Virgin Islands

204

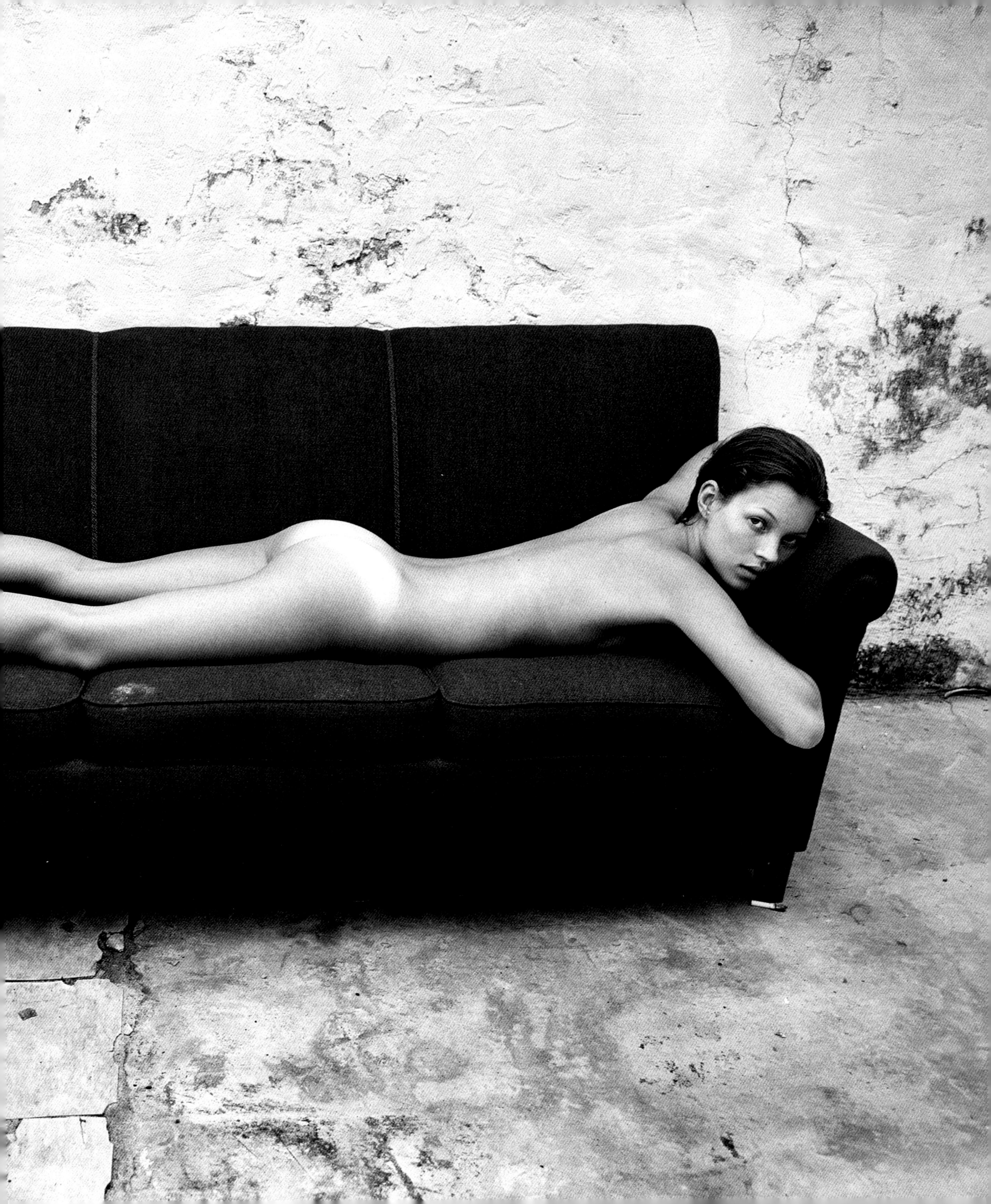

David Sims once remarked that his work is "almost entirely autobiographical." Growing up in northern England during the Thatcher years— a period of social and economic unrest and widespread unemployment—music and dress were among the few means of self-expression available to young people. The bourgeois lifestyles represented in the work of fashion photographers such as Bruce Weber (p. 168) and Patrick Demarchelier (p. 178) had little meaning for Sims and his contemporaries; instead, he recalled being attracted to the personal style of musicians such as David Bowie and Iggy Pop, and his early fashion work shares the raw, irreverent attitude of his rock-and-roll idols. Although the grunge era has often been described as antifashion, for Sims, it was more about a change in the tone of fashion photography, from glitzy self-indulgence to some-thing more melancholic. "I never really thought of myself as antifashion, because I didn't really have a grip on what fashion was," he later said.

Sims left school at the age of seventeen and moved to London at nineteen, where he assisted fashion photographer Robert Erdmann. Like many of his contemporaries, Sims got his start at *The Face* in the late 1980s. Soon, the grunge phenomenon was on the radar of major fashion brands—Perry Ellis and Anna Sui both incorporated the look into their collections in the early 1990s—and it wasn't long before mainstream fashion magazines followed suit. Sims was picked up quickly by Fabien Baron at *Harper's Bazaar* and, in 1993, was invited to shoot his first major ad campaign, for Calvin Klein. Sims's 1994 campaign for Helmut Lang married the dark, understated sexuality of Lang's designs with grunge's irreverent, "unstyled" aesthetic, as well as a predilection for "imperfect," street-cast models.

Born in Sheffield, England, 1966

DAVID SIMS

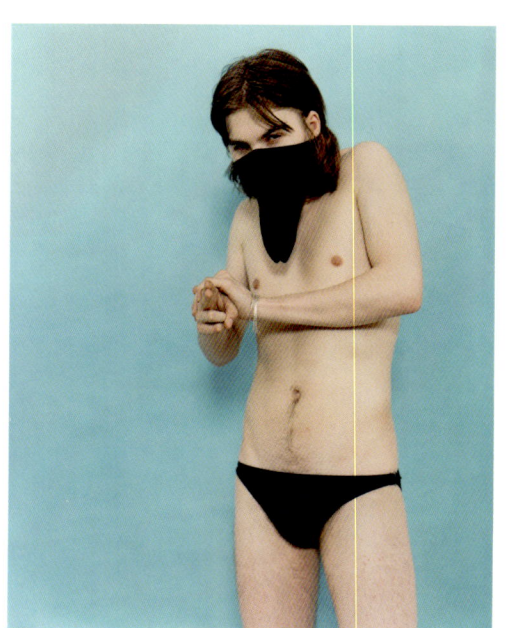

David Sims, *Tom the Robber for Helmut Lang*, 1992 Right: David Sims, *Isolated Heroes No. 14: Bart*, July 1999

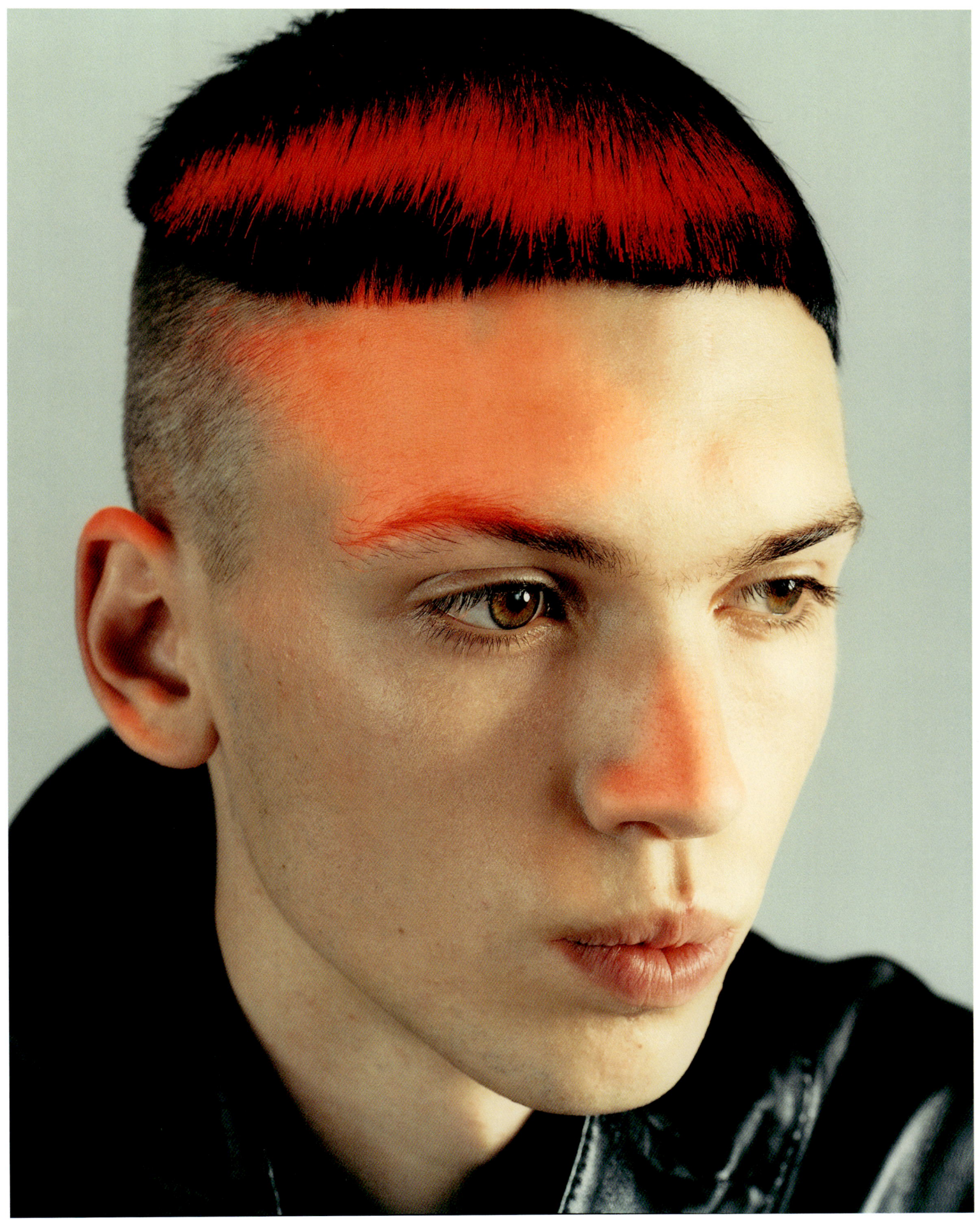

207

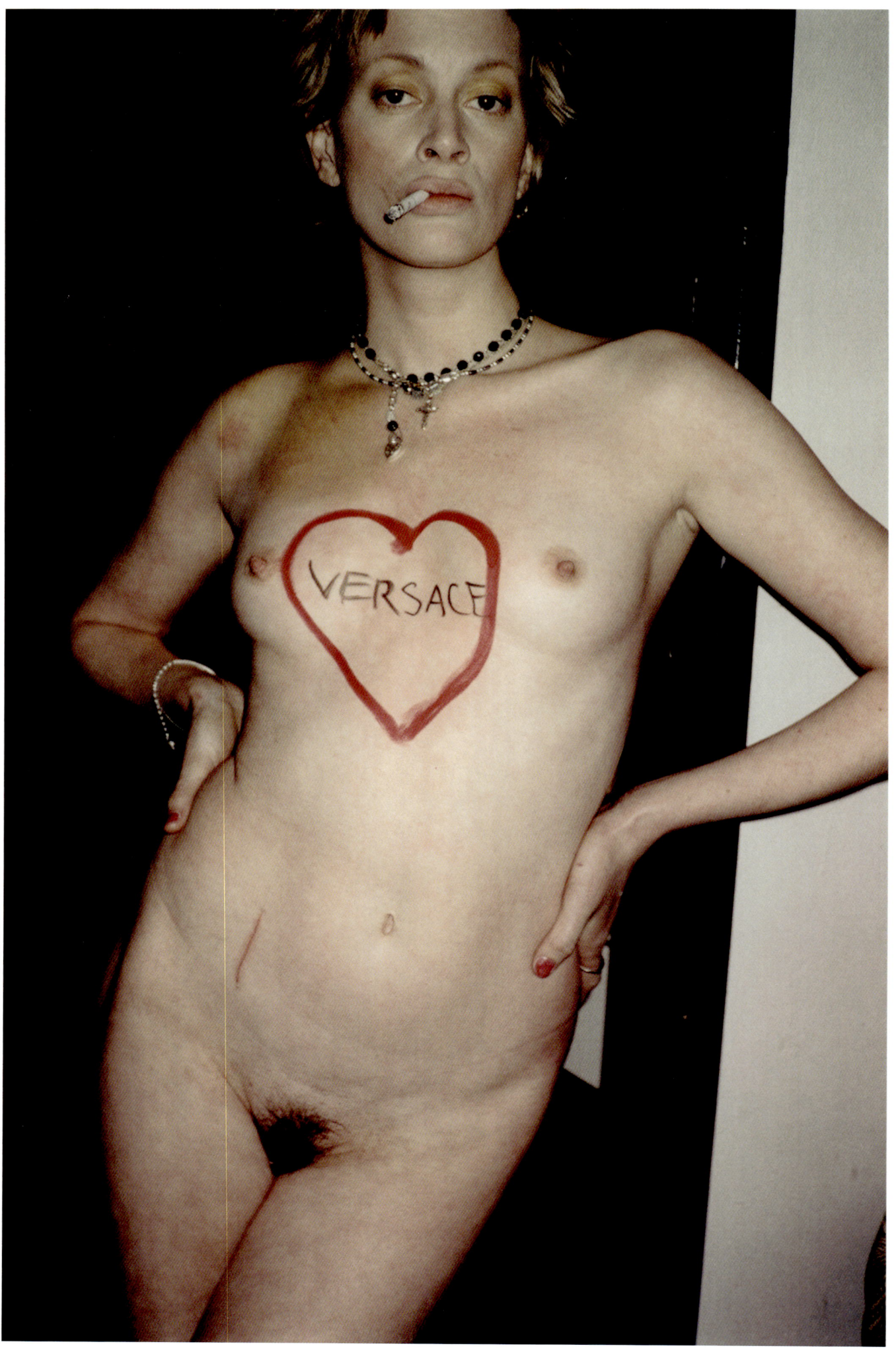

JUERGEN TELLER

Born in Erlangen,
Germany, 1964

Juergen Teller is often called one of the iconic photographers of the grunge movement. His "snapshot" aesthetic—with its hard flash and apparently casual composition—is instantly identifiable and has been widely imitated. Although he has maintained close links with major fashion labels since early in his career, Teller deliberately seeks out the awkward and unconventional in his subjects, and has never been afraid of picturing them—and often, himself—in a satirical and sometimes unflattering light.

Teller discovered photography at the age of eighteen, while he was completing an apprenticeship as a maker of violin bows. He went on to study at the Bayerische Staatslehranstalt für Photographie (Bavarian State Institute of Photography) in Munich before coming to London in 1986 and "stumbling" into fashion photography while looking for a job as an assistant. He found an early champion in Nick Knight (p. 218), and was soon working for *i-D* and *The Face*.

Driven by an intense curiosity about his own limits as a photographer, Teller has never considered fashion his only calling. His commercial and artistic careers are deeply entwined, and much of his work for advertising clients (such as Helmut Lang, with whom he worked from 1993 to 2003, and Marc Jacobs, from 1998 to 2013) has involved a significant degree of creative freedom. Other projects, such as his collaborations with Charlotte Rampling, Cindy Sherman, and Vivienne Westwood, deliberately blur the boundaries between art and fashion photography.

Teller's notorious Versace pictures were done in collaboration with model Kristen McMenamy, who scrawled the logo across her chest after being canceled for a Versace campaign. As Teller recalled, "I'd been asked by *Süddeutsche Zeitung* to do a shoot on the theme of fashion and morality. I wasn't out to shock, I just wanted to make a point—that there is another side to Kristen McMenamy, that this is what she actually looks like when she comes to the studio." Teller's images proclaimed the death of glamour in fashion photography, and they shocked the fashion world. McMenamy, however, was entirely at ease with the way that she appeared in Teller's photographs. "I think I look great," she remarked in an interview with Nick Knight.

Juergen Teller,
Kristen McMenamy 3, London, 1996
Following pages: Juergen Teller,
Lara Stone Lying on the Bed, Kiev, Ukraine, 2007

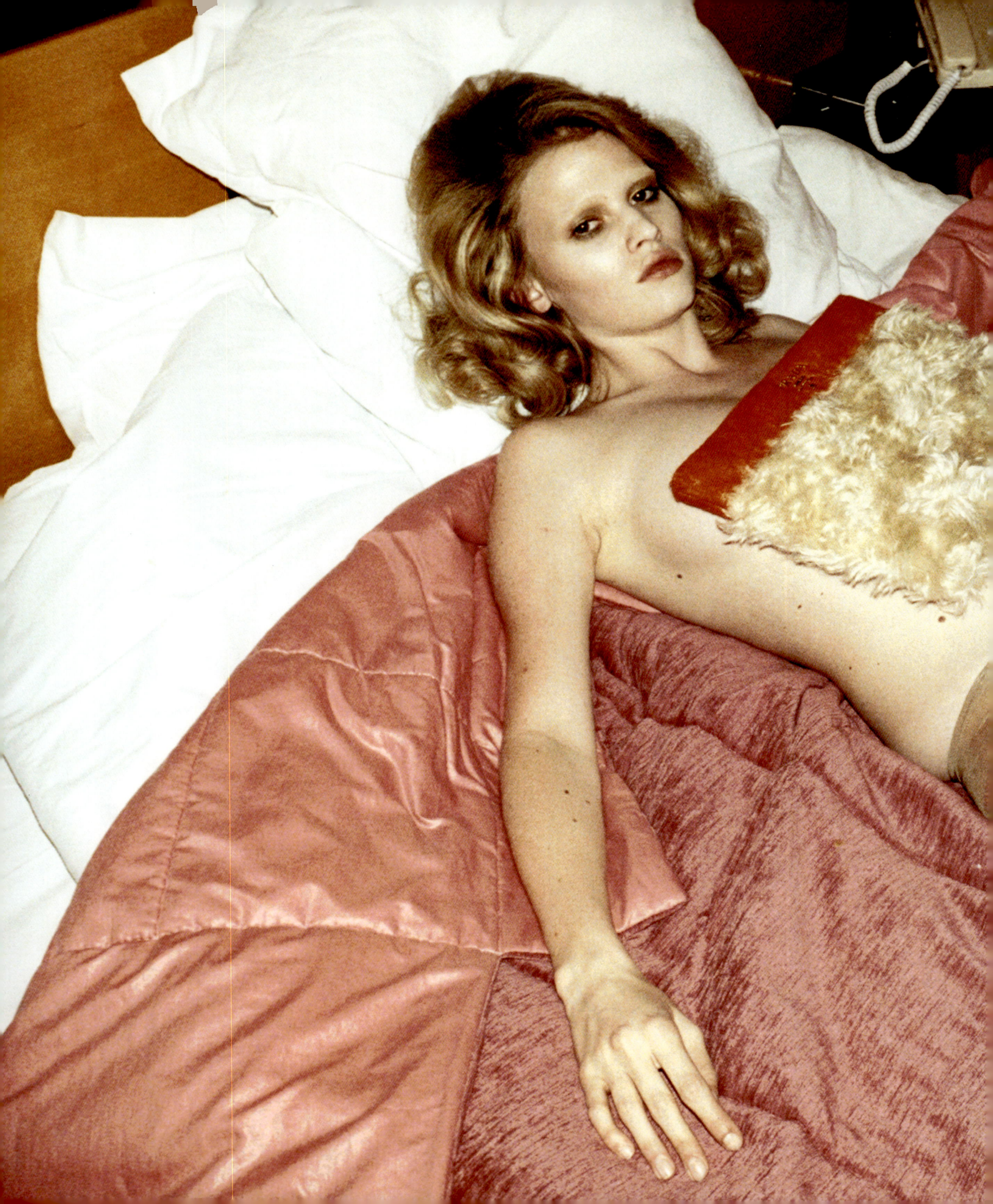

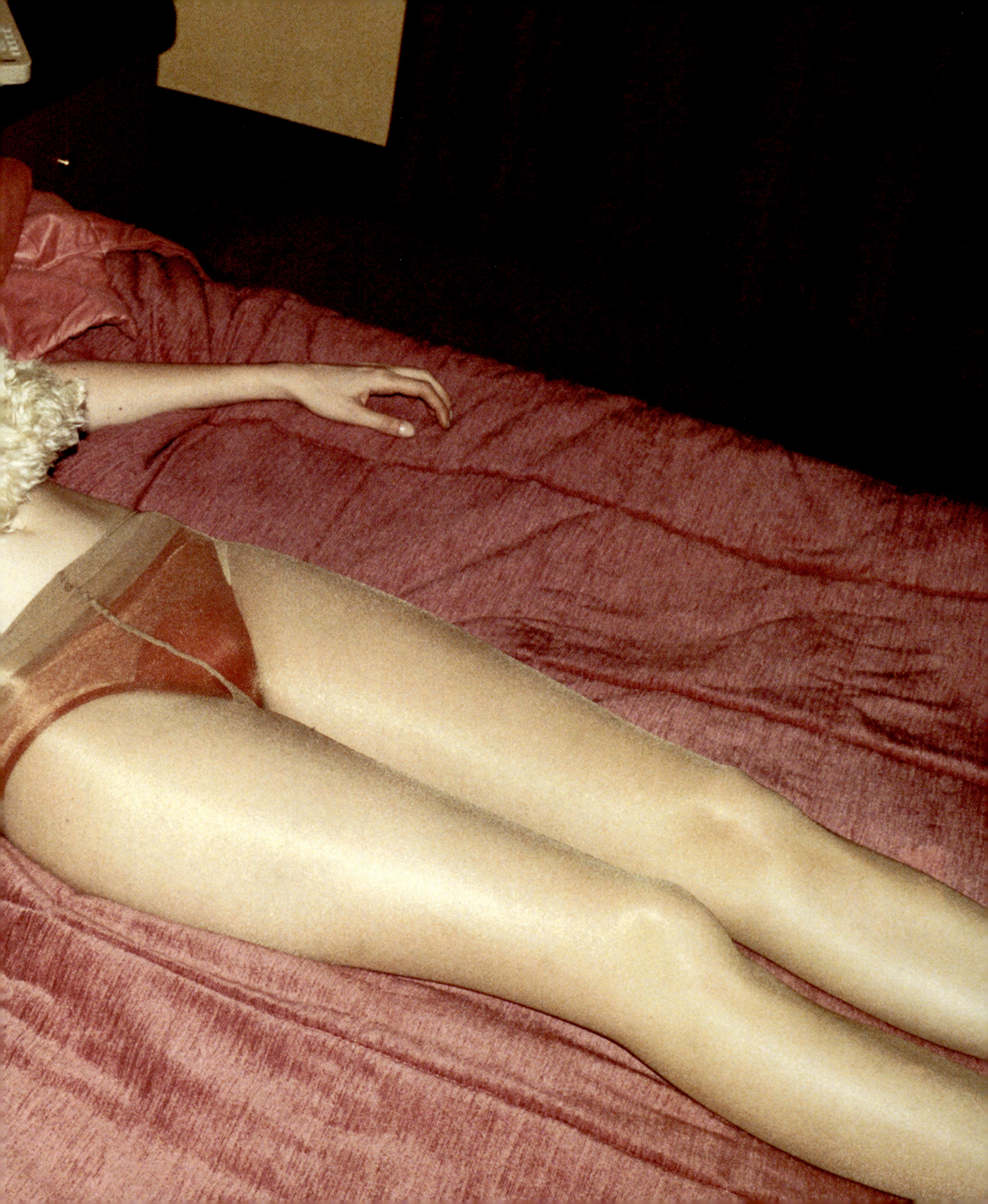

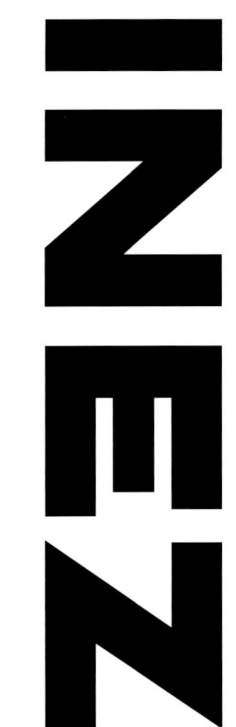 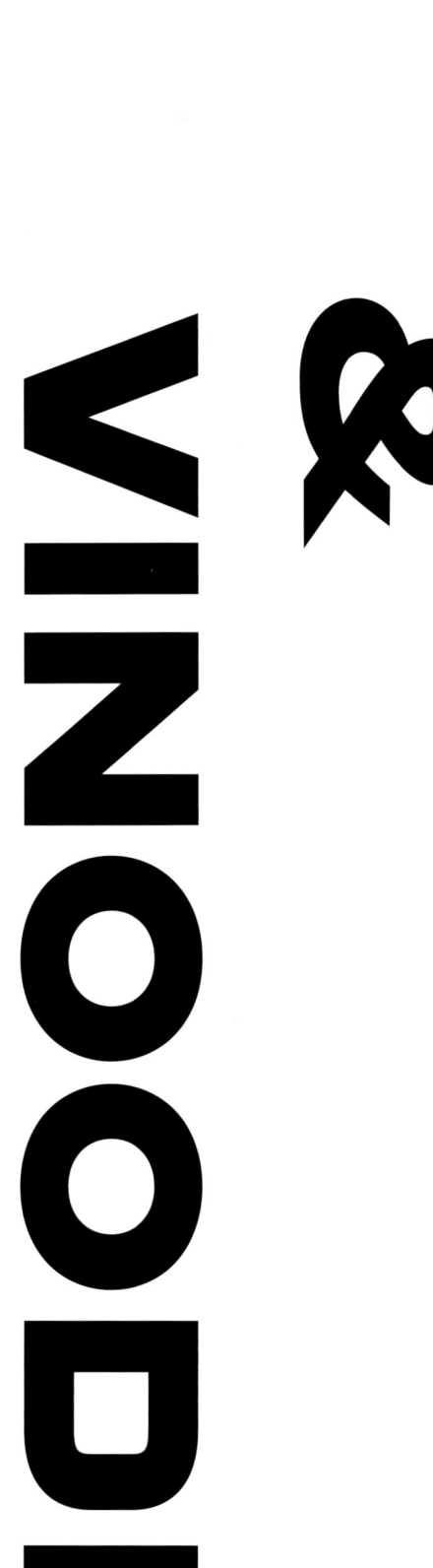

INEZ & VINOODH

Inez van Lamsweerde:
born in Amsterdam,
1963

Vinoodh Matadin:
born in Amsterdam,
1961

Inez van Lamsweerde and Vinoodh Matadin both got an early start in fashion: Van Lamsweerde's mother was a fashion journalist, Matadin's father a tailor. The pair met in the mid-1980s as students at the Akademie Vogue in Amsterdam, and began working together in 1986. Their early collaborative works used digital postproduction techniques, not to perfect the body and erase its flaws, but as a means of critiquing notions of sexuality and female beauty—a stance that would be reflected later on in their fashion photography.

Newly launched Dutch lifestyle magazine *Blvd* was one of the first to feature their work, publishing the editorial "For Your Pleasure" in 1993. Digitally superimposing highly saturated, 1970s-themed photographs of models against stock backgrounds, the series was an audacious rejection of lo-fi grunge aesthetics, replacing austere documentary-style images with lavish postproduction and high irony. The republication of "For Your Pleasure" in *The Face* in 1994 marked the duo's entry into the international photography scene. It was also an early indicator of things to come: as the millennium approached, more and more fashion photographers would come to regard digital postproduction as an essential part of their practices.

212

Inez & Vinoodh,
Maggie's Box—Yohji Yamamoto Campaign, 1998

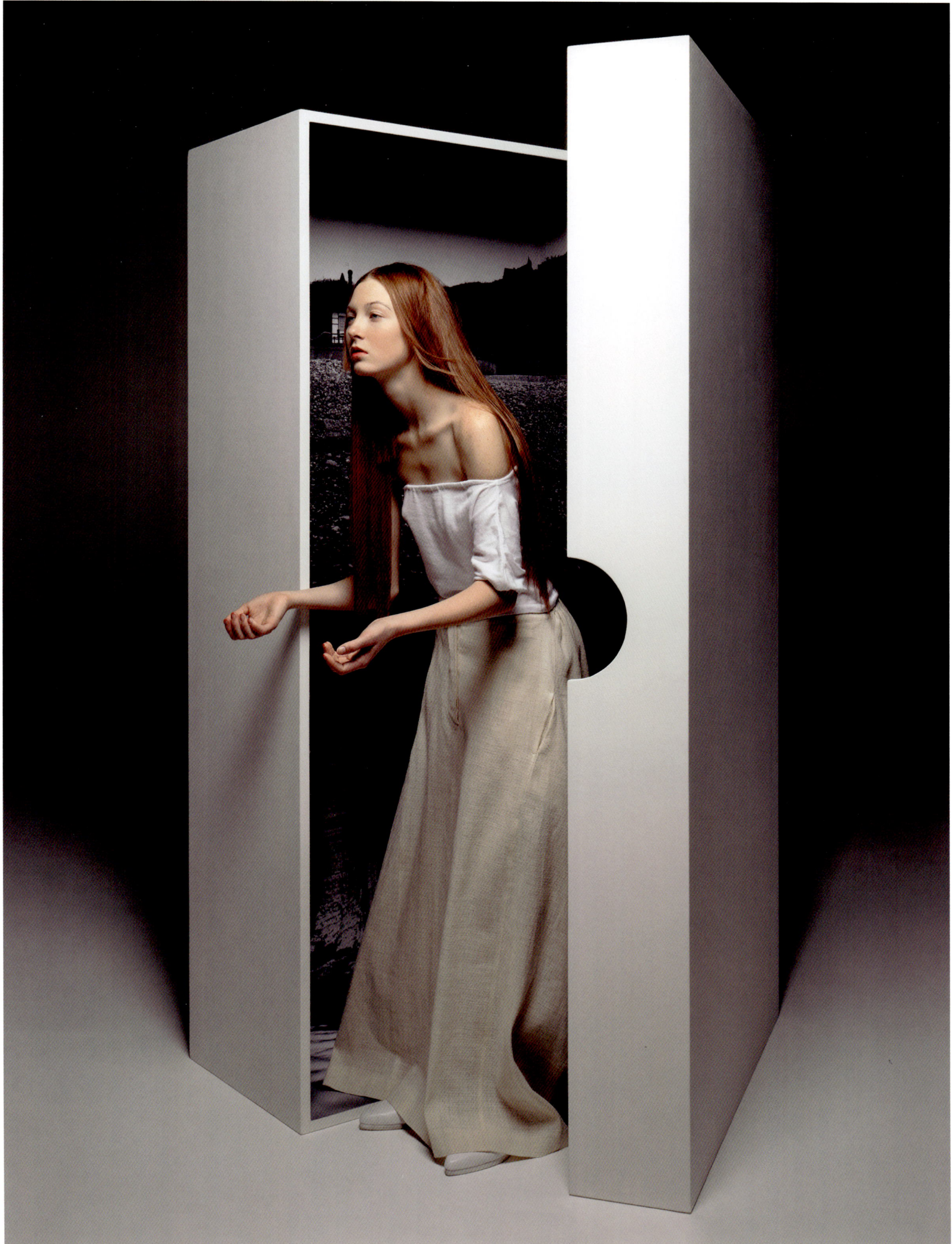

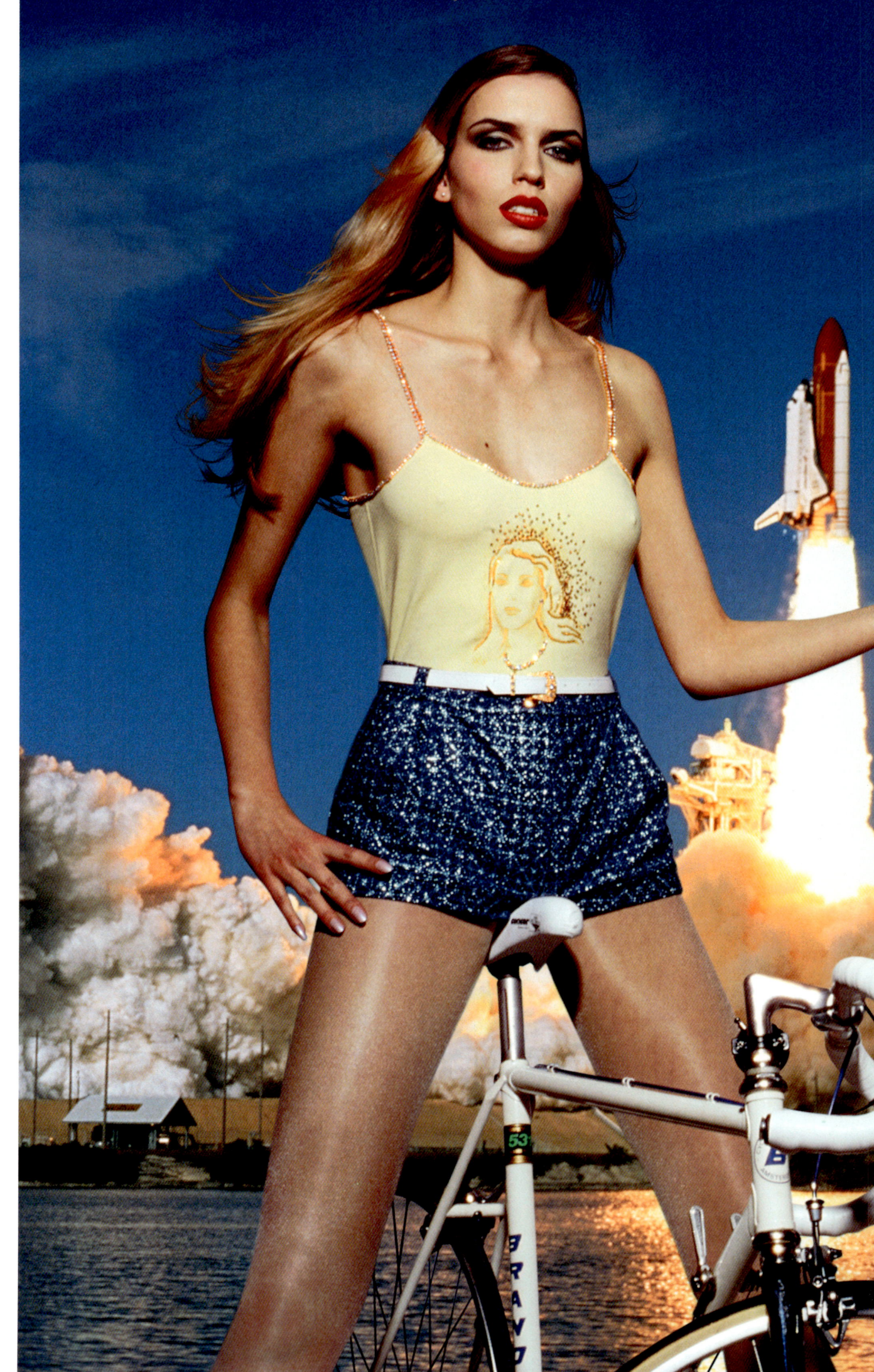

Inez & Vinoodh,
*Well Basically Basuco Is Coke
Mixed with Kerosene . . . ,*
The Face, 1994

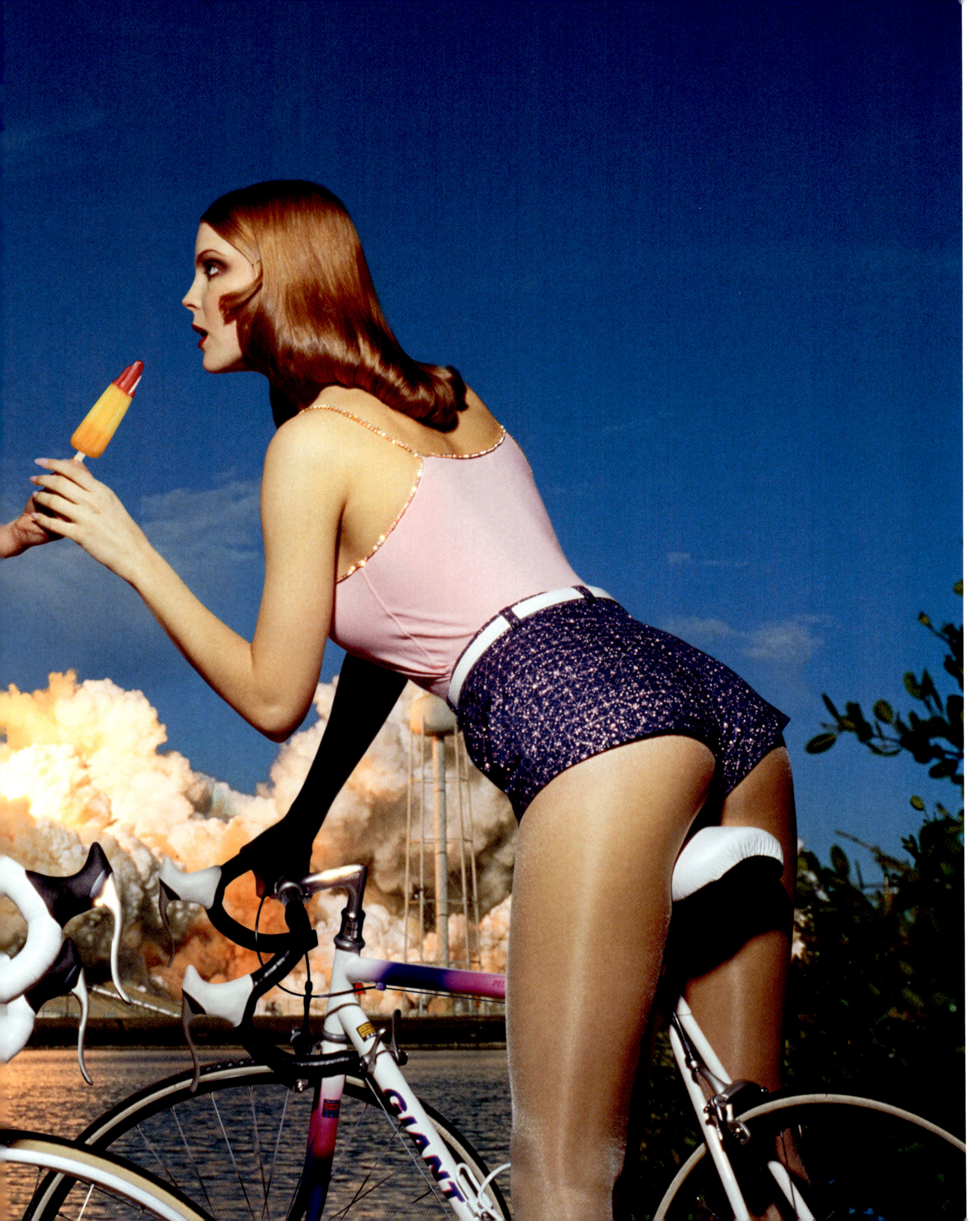

Born in Manchester,
England, 1964

CRAIG MCDEAN

Like many of his generation, Craig McDean
was championed by Nick Knight (p. 218). After
working as Knight's assistant at *i-D*, McDean
began freelancing in 1991, shooting first for *i-D*
and *The Face*, and later for French *Glamour*
and *Harpers & Queen*.

Described as a "documentary photographer
who shoots fashion," McDean was initially part
of a London-based group of photographers associated with the grunge movement. His first major
advertising commission, however, represented
an important departure from the grunge aesthetic:
approached by art director Marc Ascoli in 1995 to
shoot for Jil Sander, McDean's third campaign
for the brand—for Spring 1996—was a turning
point. It was very simple both visually and
conceptually, with the stripped-down set used as
a platform for exploring the idea of flawed beauty.
McDean was one of the first photographers to
appreciate model Guinevere van Seenus's unique
features, and the campaign was her first major
modeling gig. "Craig really helped me find things
about myself that I didn't understand were
beautiful," Van Seenus remarked. "The strange
expressions, the crooked smile I have, the kooky
looks." Shot on an 8-by-10 camera, the campaign's
simple design and undersaturated color palette
marked the beginning of a more grown-up
approach: a new, post-grunge minimalism.

McDean has gone on to become one of the
industry's most prominent photographers, working
for magazines, including *Love*, *W*, and *AnOther*;
his advertising portfolio includes clients such as
Calvin Klein, Chloé, and Alexander McQueen.

Craig McDean,
Guinevere van Seenus for Jil Sander,
Spring 1996

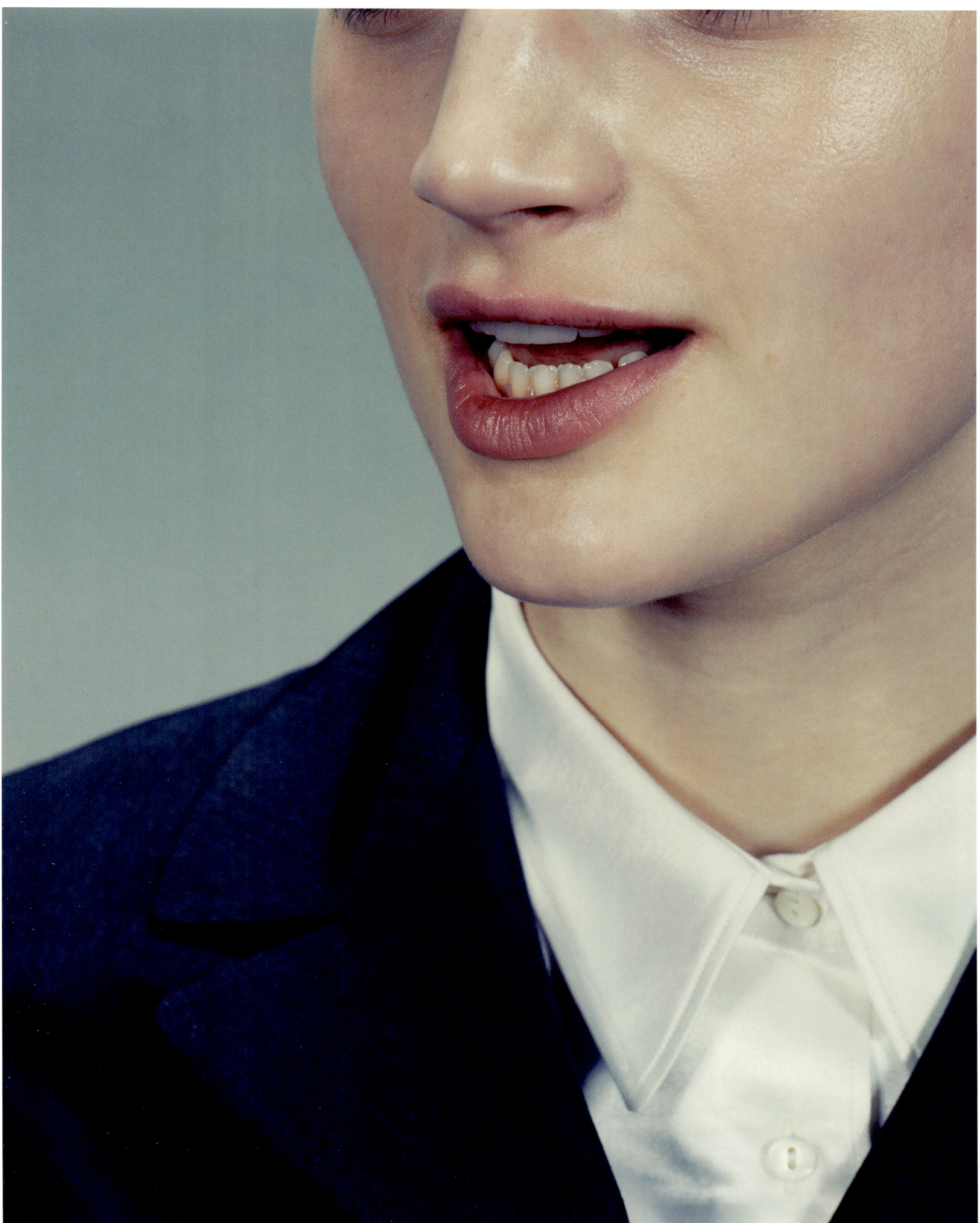

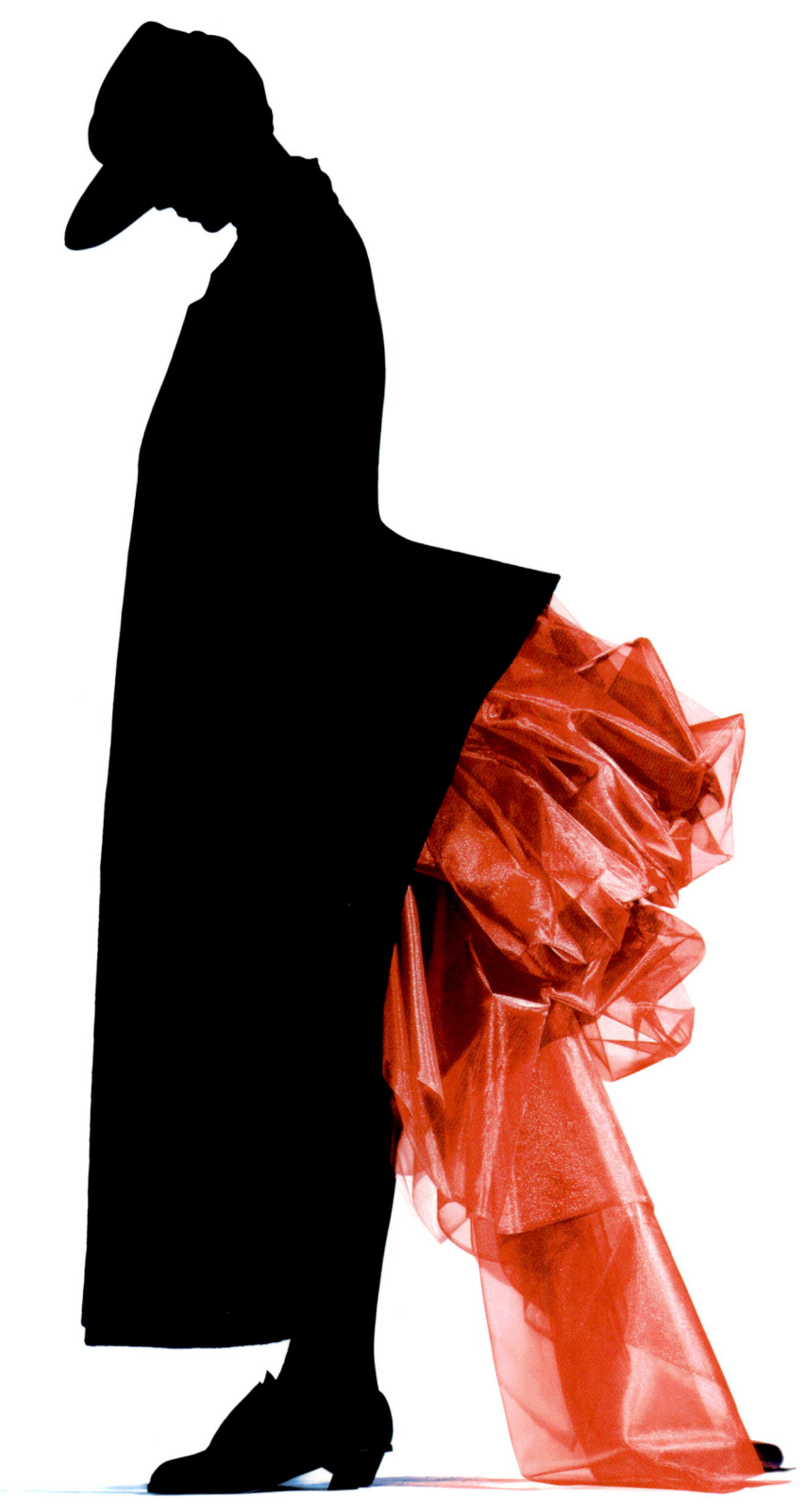

NICK KNIGHT

Born in London, 1958

Nick Knight's career has spanned more than thirty years of consistent innovation, but he is perhaps best known as the individual responsible for bringing the fashion world into the digital age. Knight originally planned to be a doctor, studying biology for a brief period before enrolling in a photography course. He began his career at *i-D* in 1982, after he approached editor Terry Jones for advice on publishing the photographs that would go on to become his first book, *Skinhead*. For the next few years, Knight worked regularly for *i-D*, along with other alternative titles such as *BLITZ* and *The Face*. It was also during this period that he met stylist Simon Foxton, who went on to become one of his most important creative collaborators.

The assignment that brought him to the attention of the fashion world was a 1985 editorial shoot for the fifth anniversary issue of *i-D*: a series of one hundred portraits of London's young creative personalities. The portraits came to the attention of art director Marc Ascoli, who invited Knight to photograph the 1986 Yohji Yamamoto campaign—widely regarded at the time as an important commission for emerging talents. Yamamoto's radical designs were based on line and form, and on an idea of femininity as an intellectual, rather than sexual quality; this appealed to Knight, who disliked the overt sexuality of much 1980s fashion photography. Inspired by the graphic character of Yamamoto's clothes, the image of model Sarah Wingate—silhouetted entirely in black, apart from the brilliant scarlet of her bustle—was the only color image in the catalogue, its high contrast produced by cross-processing color slide film using negative developer.

Knight was also an early adopter of video and digital photography, experimenting with 3-D scanning and HD cameras—but his most significant innovation came in 2000, with the launch of SHOWstudio, a digital fashion platform. SHOWstudio started as a creative platform for fashion-based content that wasn't getting shown in the mainstream fashion press; at the time of its launch, this included fashion film, which Knight felt was a better way of representing garments than static images. Knight has gone on to use SHOWStudio to explore live fashion broadcasting, interactive video, and e-commerce.

Knight's own fashion photography makes use of everything from high-end motion capture to relatively lo-fi technologies such as smartphones—he even shot a campaign for Diesel on his phone—and Instagram. "I've always felt that I've come at the end of photography, the end of its existence as a predominant image-making medium," Knight has reflected. "So I've never felt anything other than a sort of love for the future and a love of what's happening next."

Nick Knight,
Red Bustle for Yohji Yamamoto, Paris, 1986

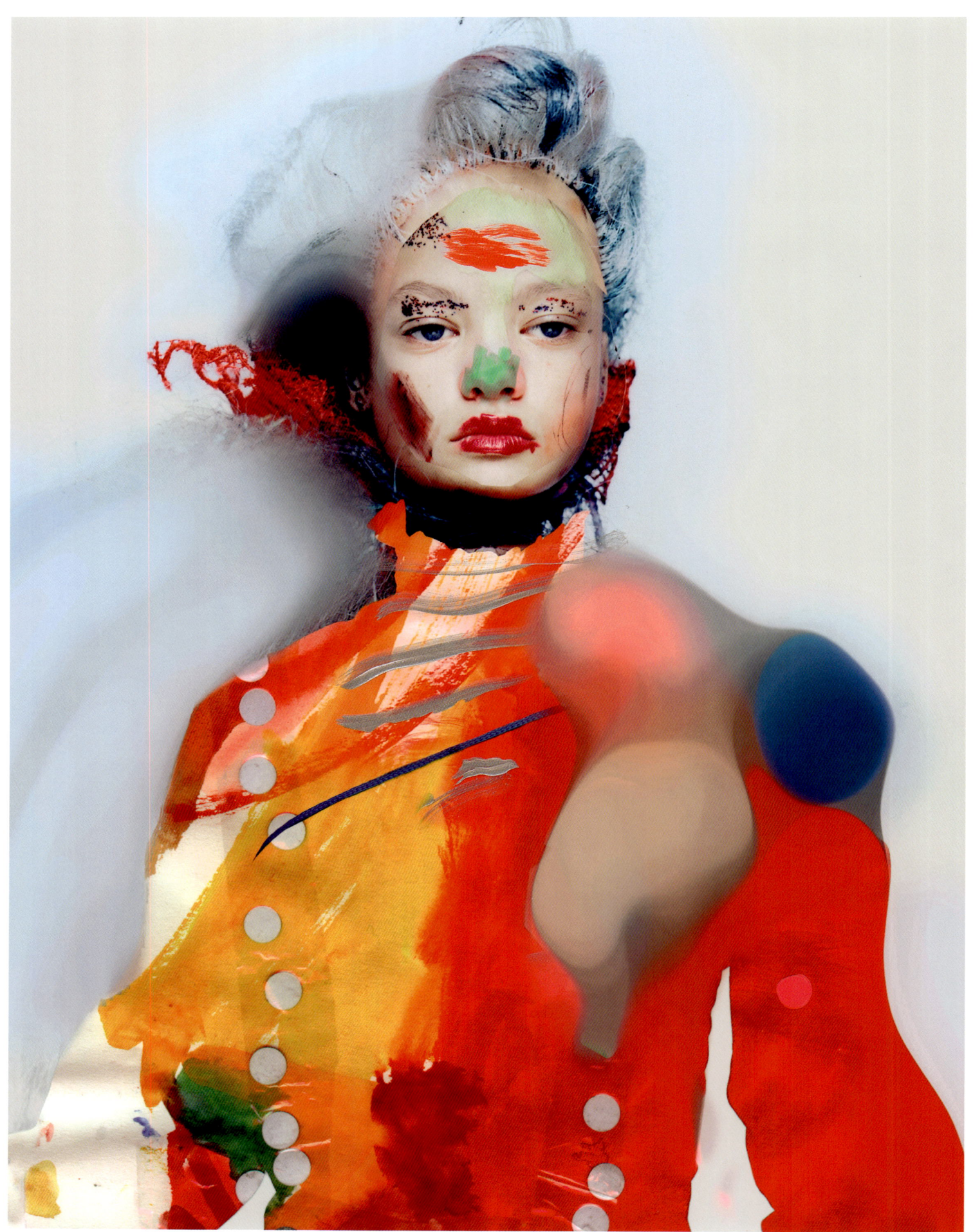

Nick Knight,
Micky Hicks Dolls 1, London, 2000

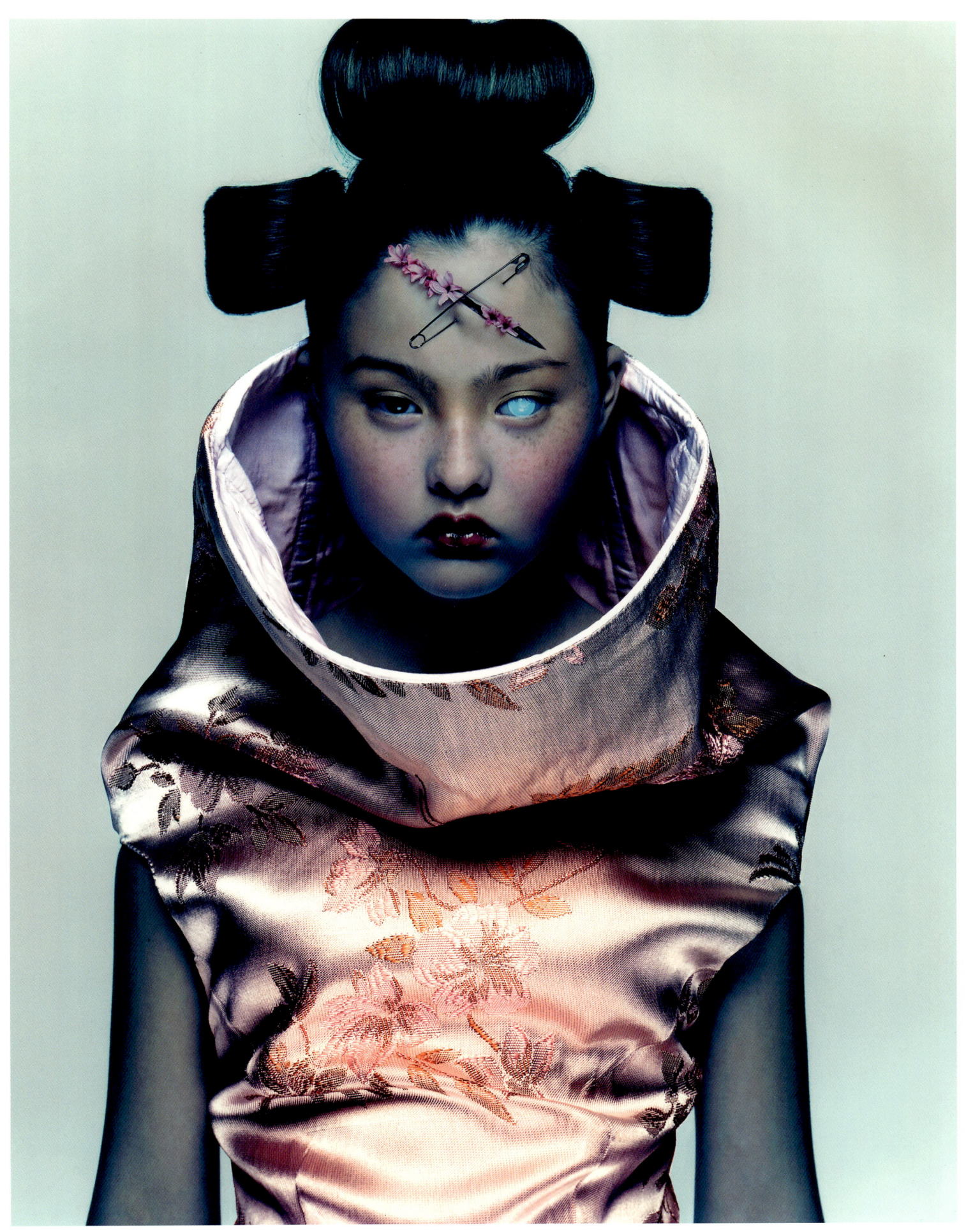

Nick Knight,
Devon Aoki for Alexander McQueen, London, 1997

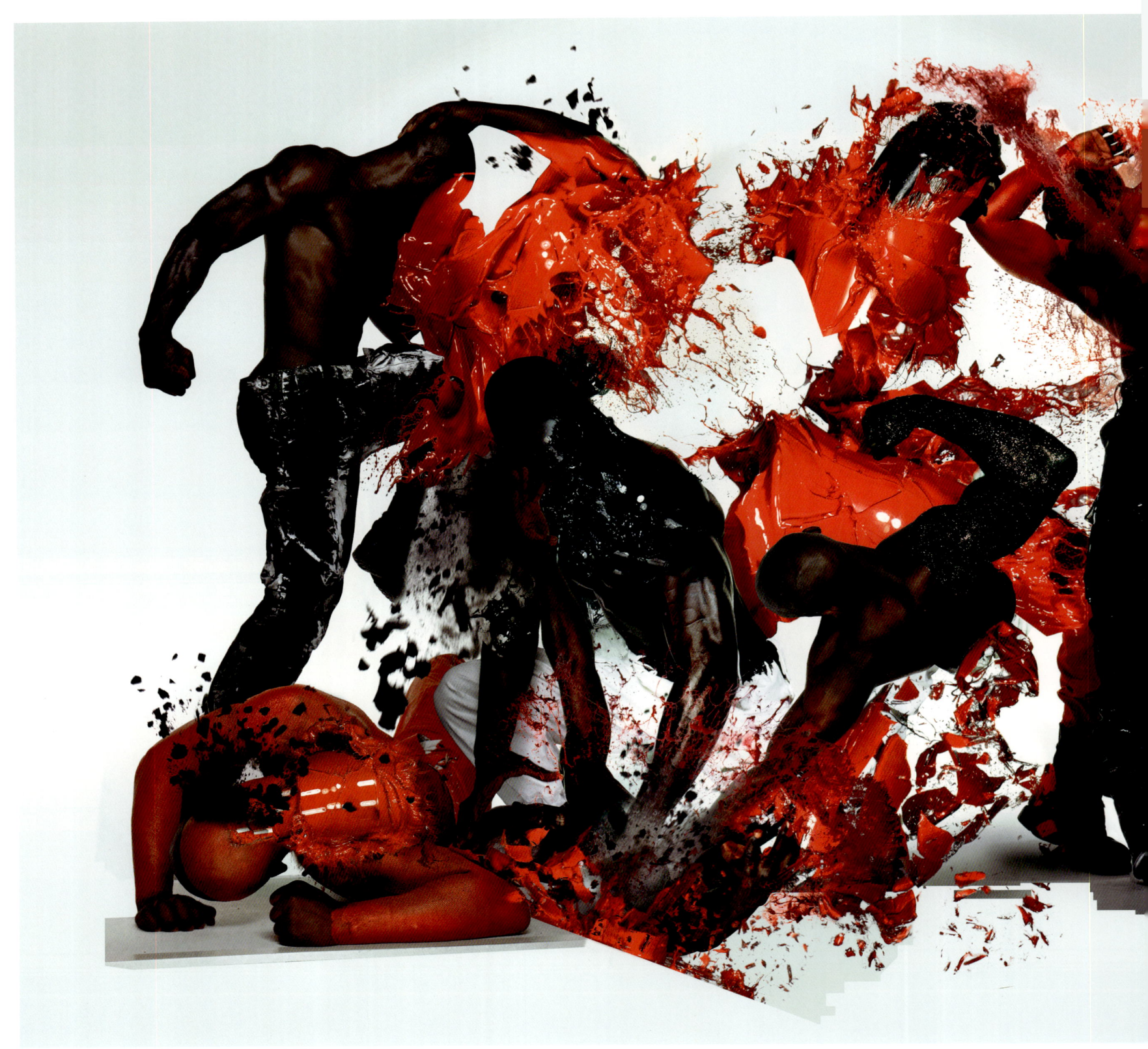

Nick Knight,
War, London, 1997

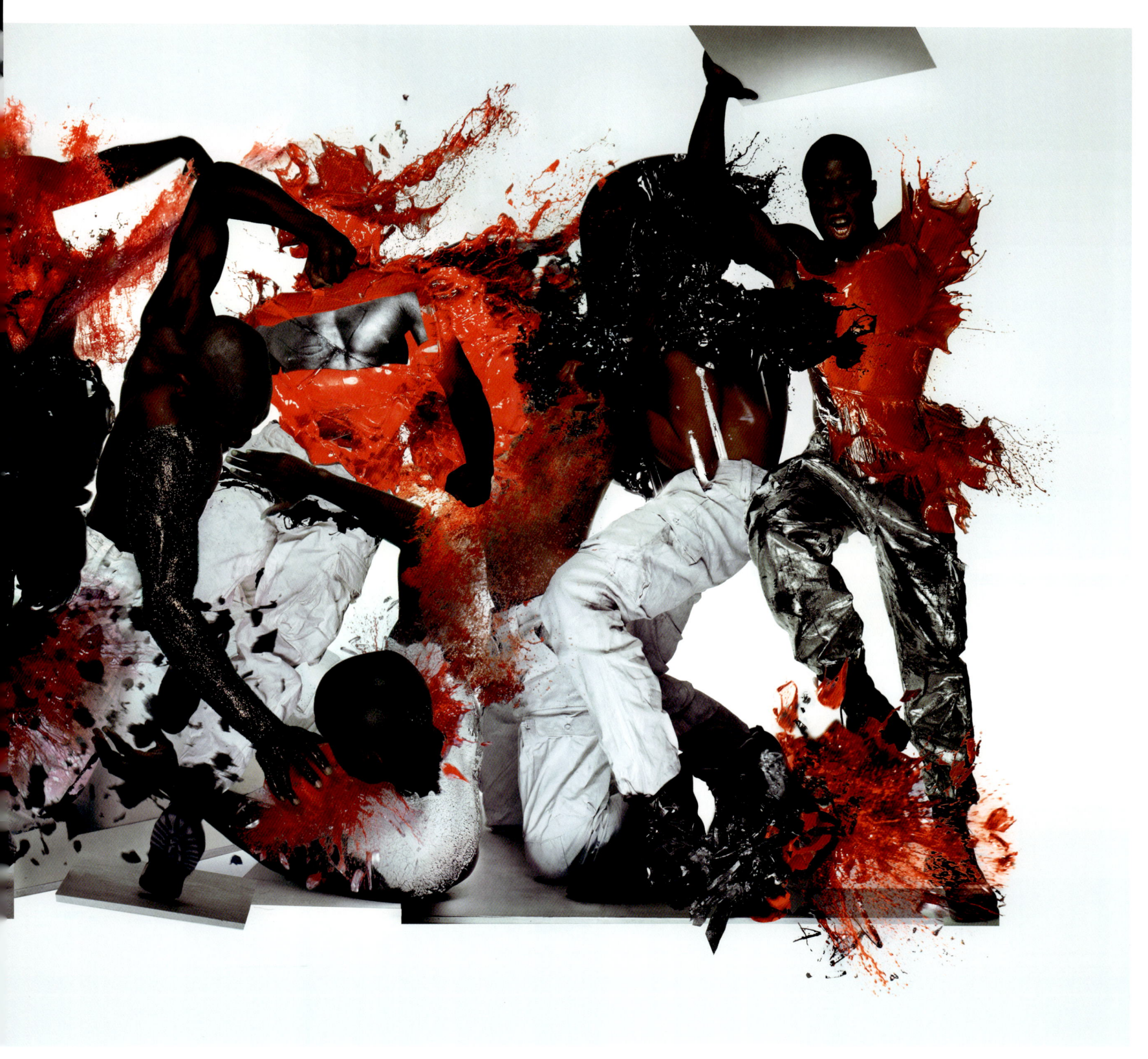

ELAINE CONSTAN-TINE

Born in Bury, England,
1965

Elaine Constantine began her photography career taking pictures of London's club scene, and her early documentary-inspired fashion work brought the energy of the dance floor to the depiction of clothing. As she said in 2000, "I think I am at the point of obsession in trying to articulate in photography my own dance-floor experience." Constantine worked as an assistant to Nick Knight (p. 218) and took her first photographs for *The Face* in 1993. She parted ways with the grunge aesthetic early on: rather than scruffy interiors and moody, indifferent models, Constantine's photographs featured rosy-cheeked exuberance and bright, saturated colors. Her fashion photographs of the 1990s and 2000s captured the energy of English rave culture, while making subtle reference to earlier periods. "Sarf Coastin'," which appeared in *The Face* in December 1997, includes a cheeky nod to Ronald Traeger's iconic image of Twiggy on a bicycle, shot for *Vogue* thirty years earlier.

Constantine has always preferred working with unusual, lesser-known models. "The famous models don't inspire me—it's too predictable and boring seeing these faces everywhere," she has said. Her 1999 editorial for American *Vogue*, featuring gap-toothed models Georgina Cooper and Lauren Hutton, brought her international attention.

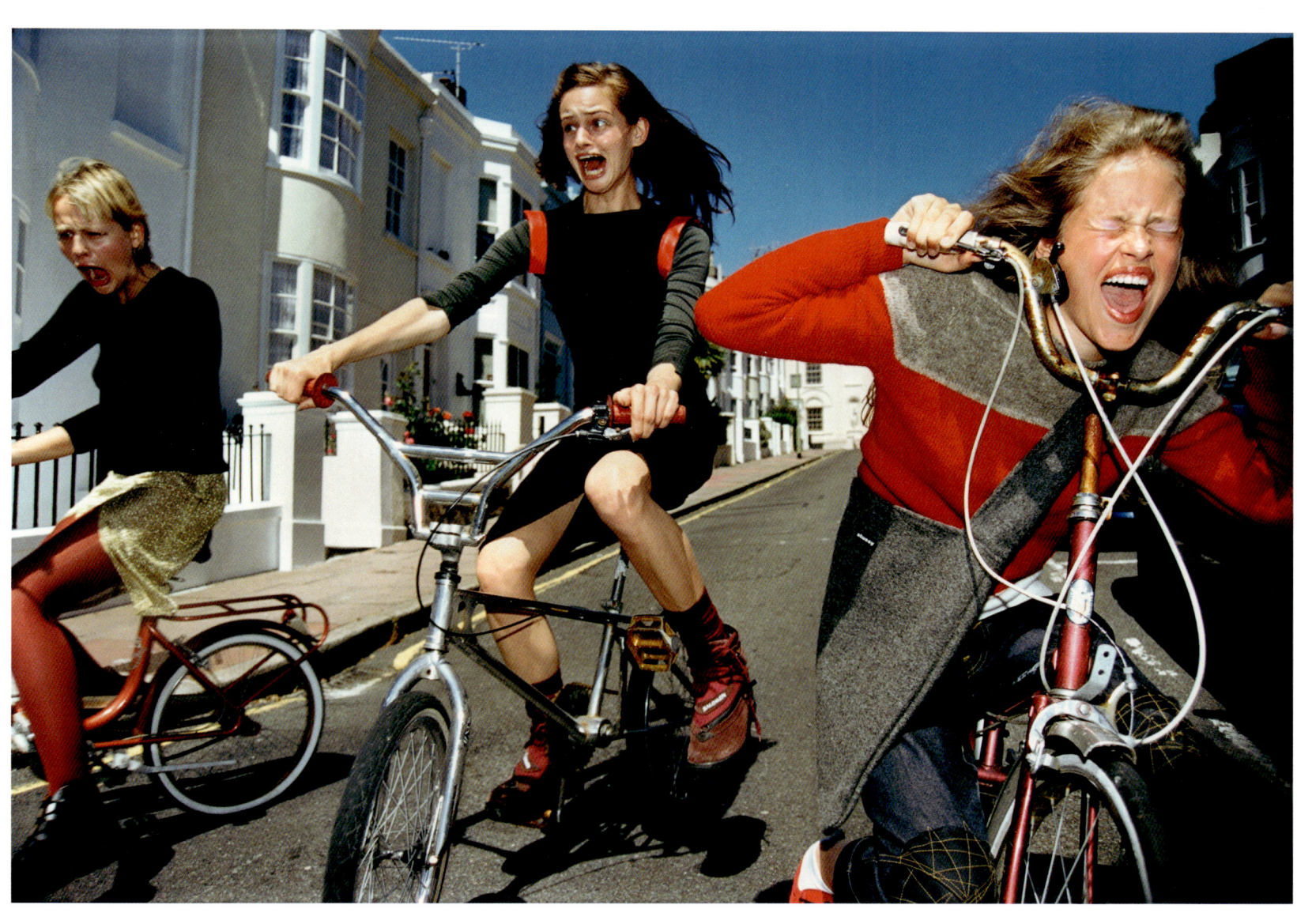

Elaine Constantine,
Girls on Bikes, "Sarf Coastin'," *The Face*, 1997
Following pages: Elaine Constantine,
"Sarf Coastin'," *The Face*, 1997

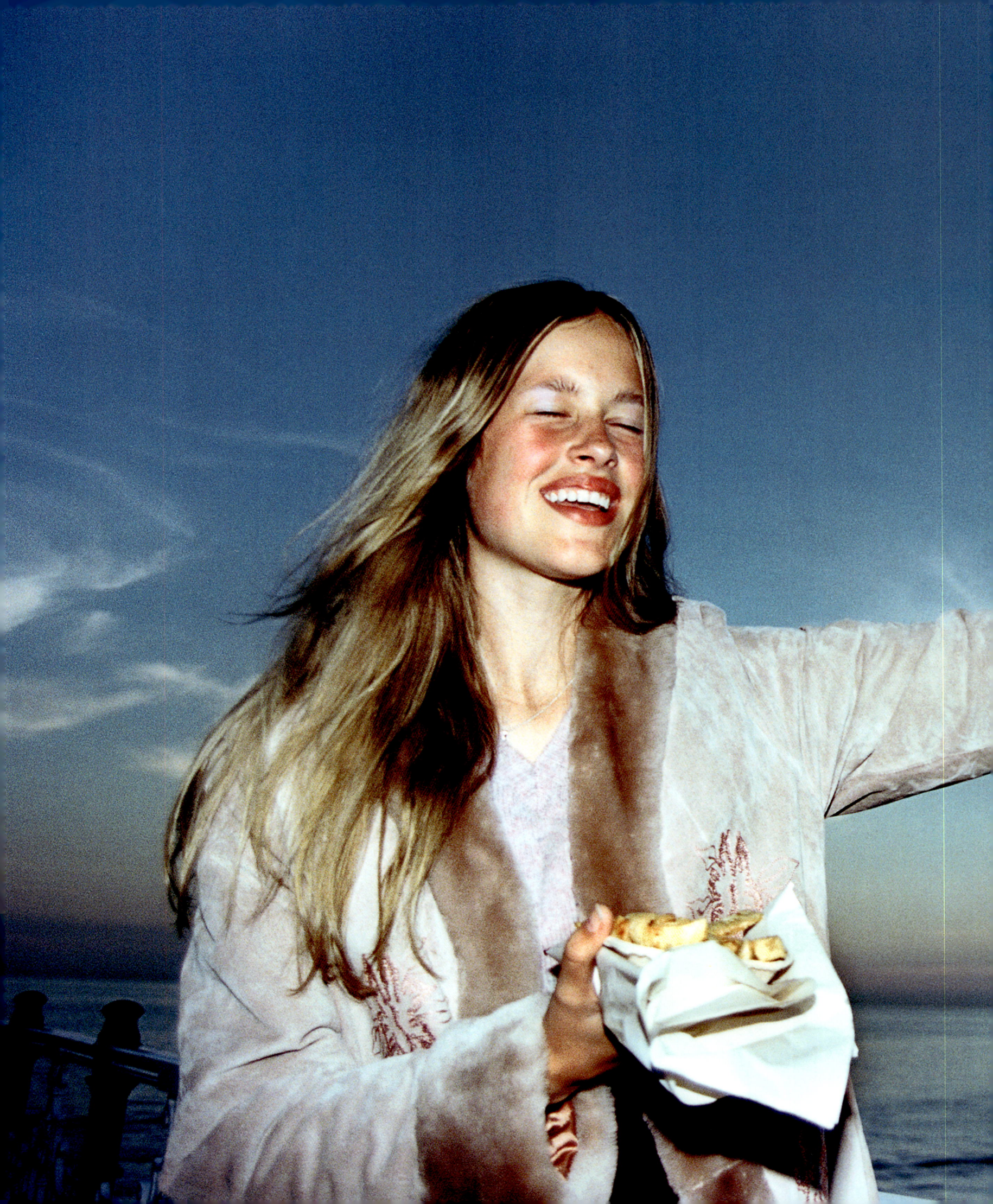

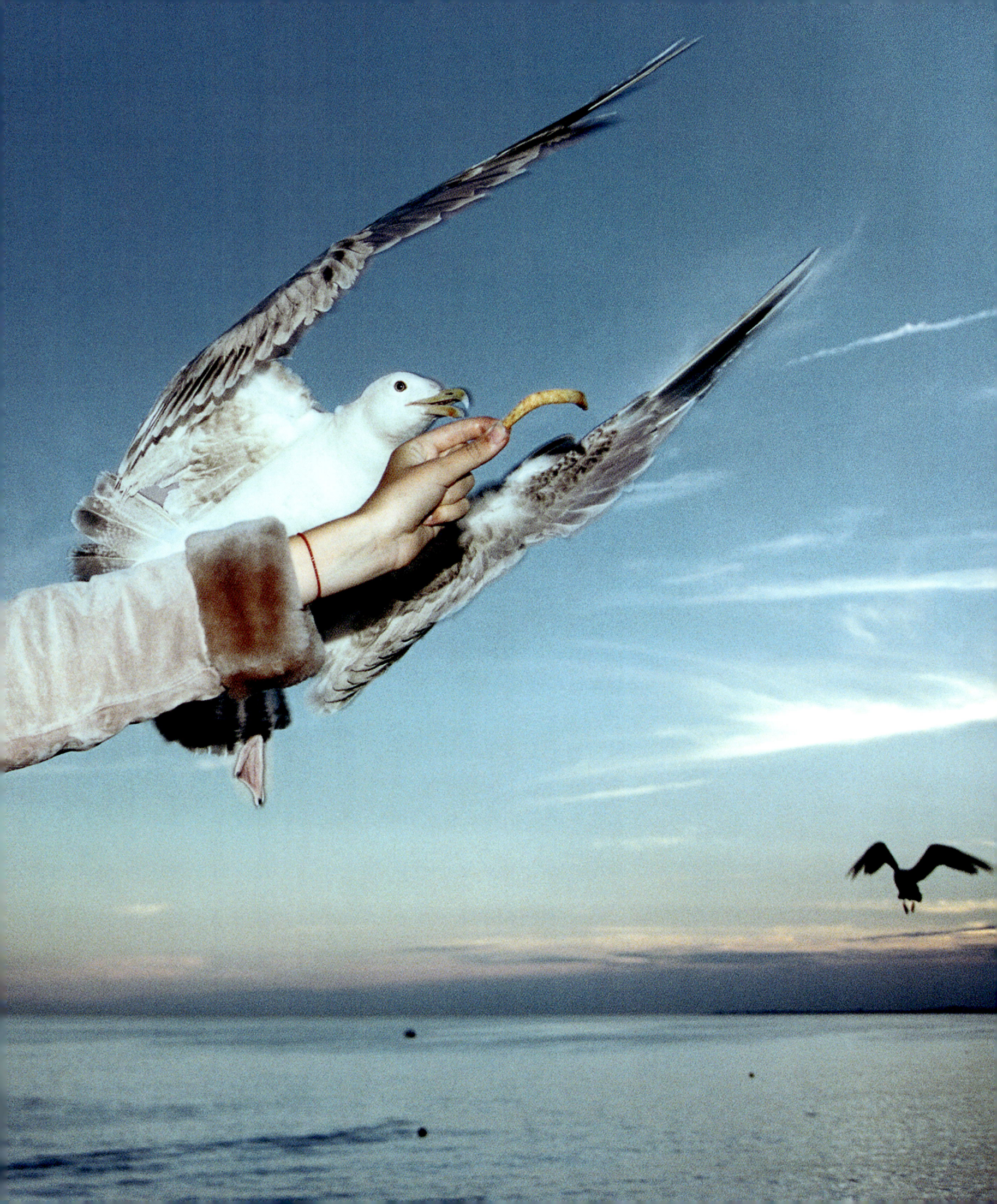

Anuschka Blommers
and Niels Schumm
both born in the
Netherlands, 1969

BLOMMERS & SCHUMM

Anuschka Blommers and Niels Schumm met as students at the Gerrit Rietveld Academie in Amsterdam, and have been working together since their graduation in 1997. Their work is representative of a shift in the way that photographers use fashion as a platform for wider issues: whereas fashion photographers of the 1980s and '90s introduced social and cultural critique into their work, some of the most exciting talents to have emerged around the new millennium have extended this critique into a practice that exists on the boundary between fashion and art, questioning the norms and conventions of both.

For their first commission, "Class of 1998," for independent fashion magazine *Self Service*, Blommers and Schumm photographed young, aspiring models on their first assignment. The offbeat, retro styling and confrontational framing emphasized the girls' awkwardness and insecurity; as Blommers remarked, "It was a totally bizarre experience. You can see that these girls were totally incapable of becoming models." Although Blommers and Schumm now produce work for both the alternative and mainstream fashion press—with clients including *Vogue*, *Dazed & Confused*, *The Gentlewoman*, *Baron*, *Purple*, *Self Service*, and *AnOther Magazine*—their interest is not in fashion per se, but rather the broader conceptual questions that surround vulnerability and everyday beauty. "Fashion is simply something that we use," Blommers has said. "It is not something we want to communicate."

Blommers & Schumm,
Sara, "Class of 1998," *Self Service*, 1998;
styling by Suzanne Koller

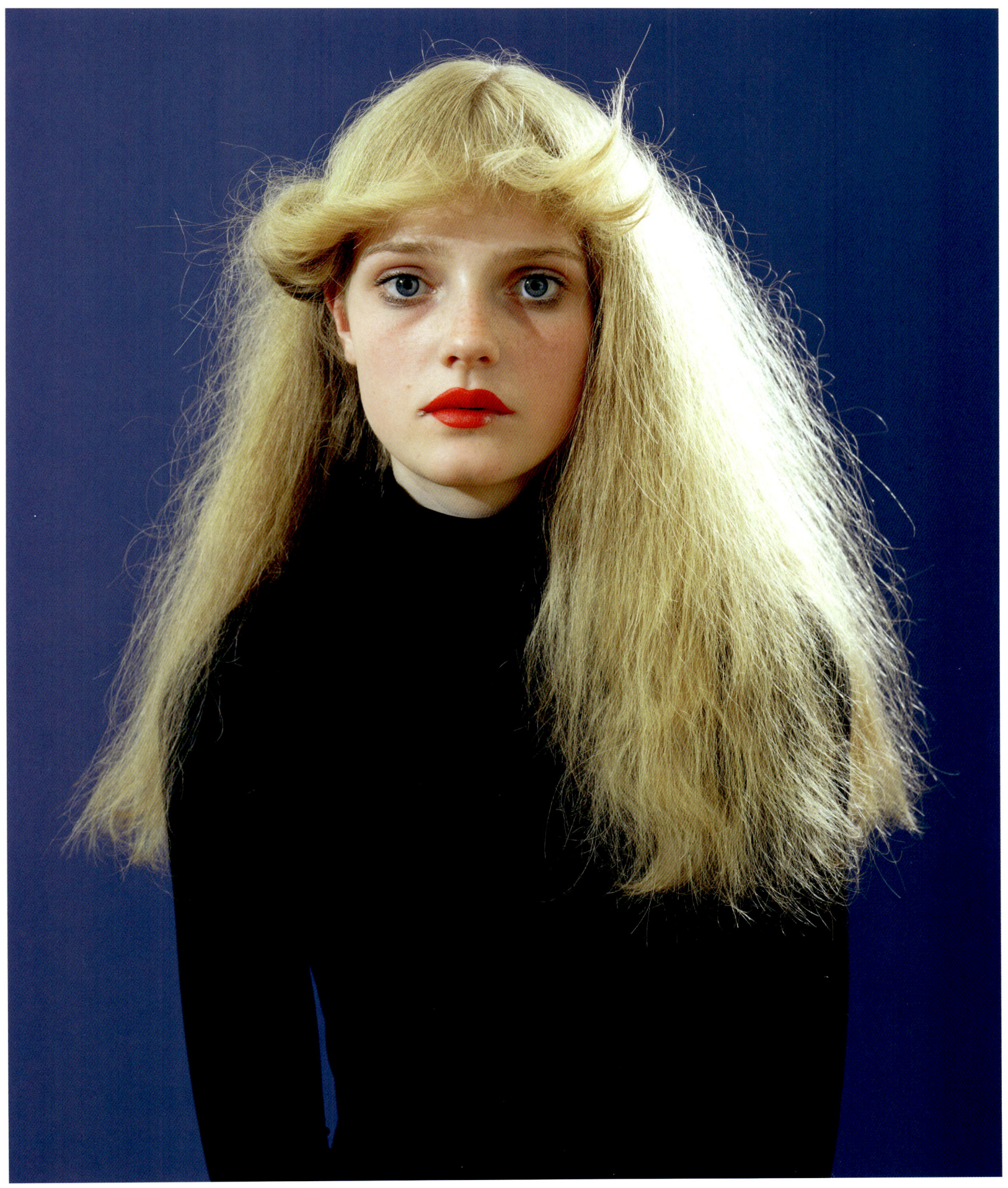

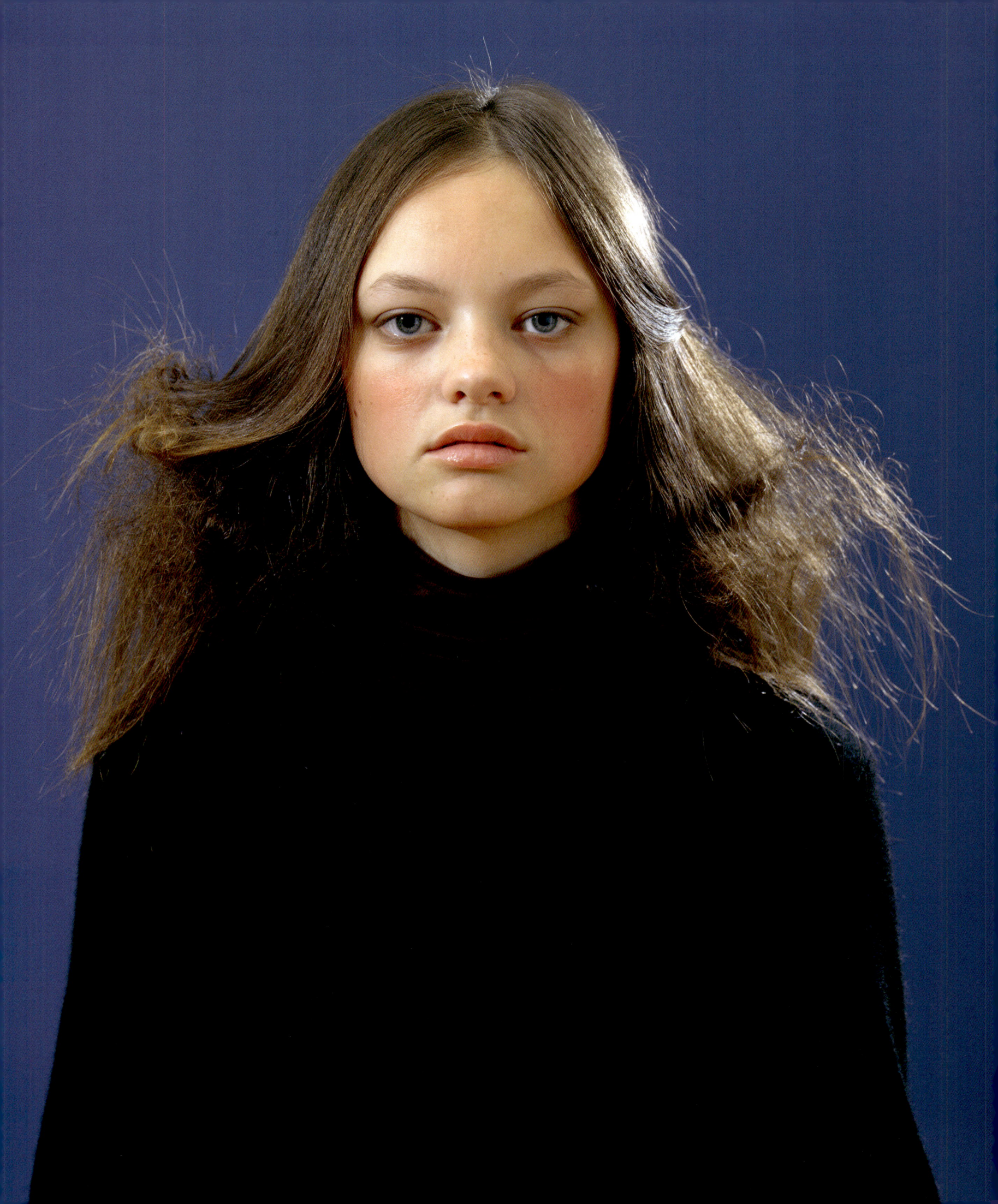

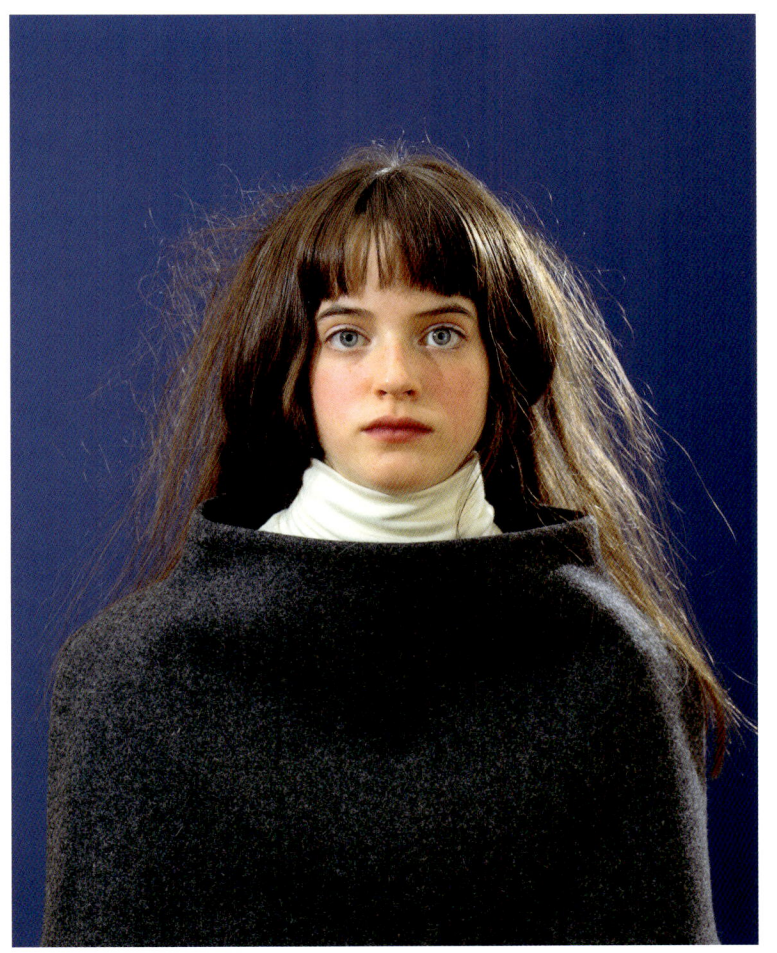
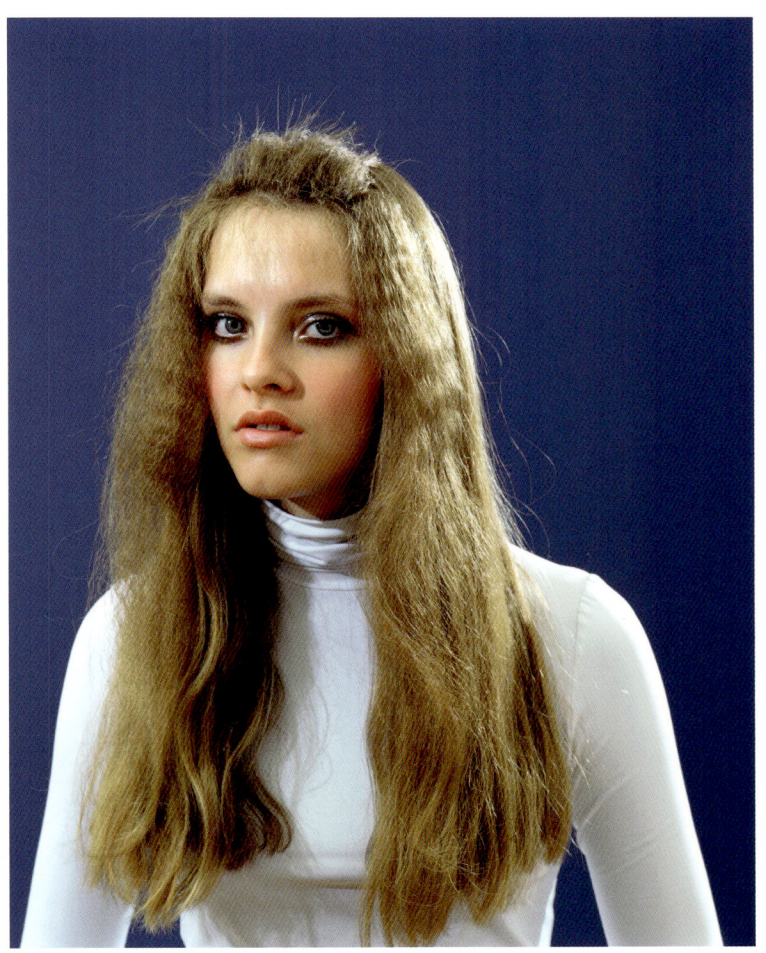
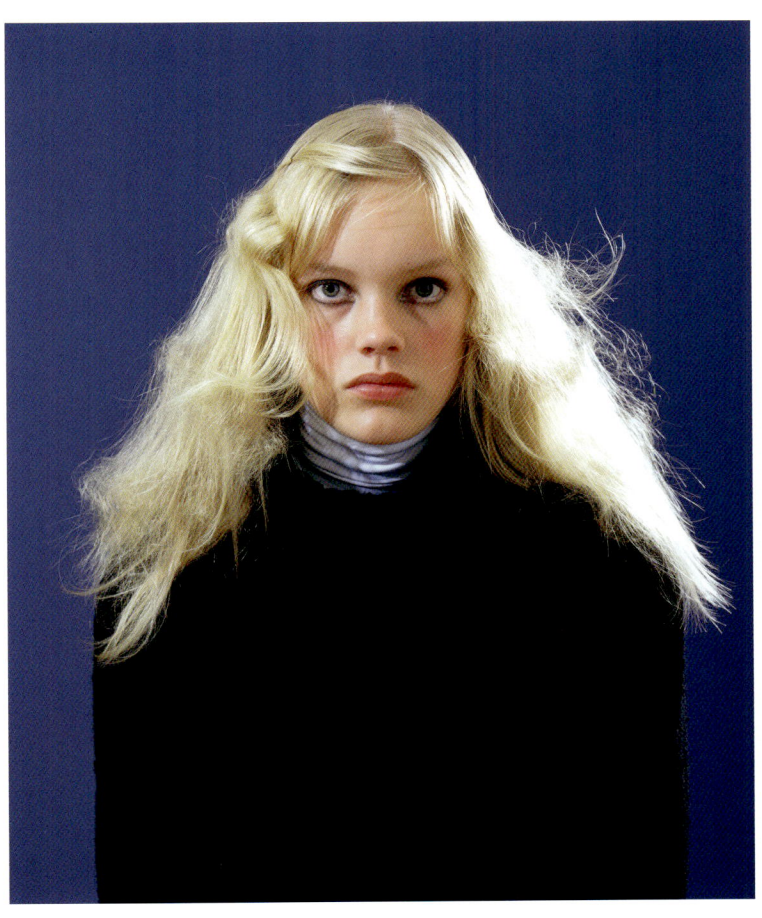
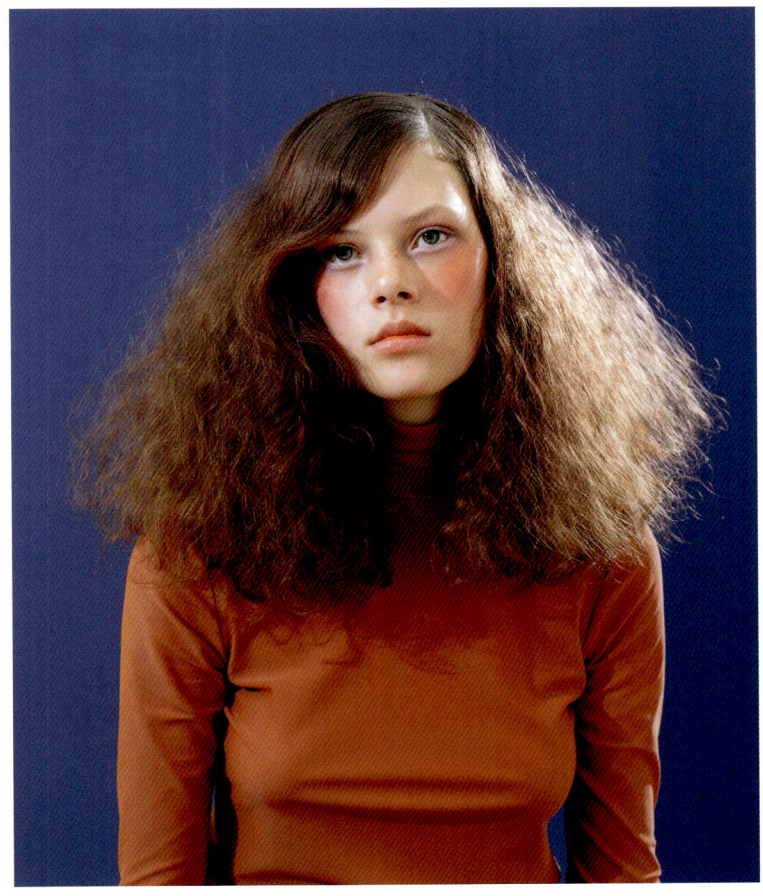

Blommers & Schumm, clockwise from left: *Michelle*; *Ciara*;
Laura; *Ruth*; *Sara*; "Class of 1998," *Self Service*, 1998;
styling by Suzanne Koller

MARK BORTH-WICK

Born in London,
1966

Before turning to photography in 1986, Mark Borthwick ran a small nightclub in Paris and worked as a professional makeup artist. His career in fashion photography was unplanned, evolving spontaneously out of a cluster of other creative interests and contacts in the fashion industry. Borthwick's approach to fashion has always been tongue-in-cheek: "Fashion to me just seemed so unfashionable and attached to material codes that didn't exist for me. . . . I wasn't inspired by it, so to make it interesting I would flip it and work my own way," he said. "I saw the humor behind fashion . . . I wanted to have fun, and create work that was fun even in a fashion context."

All of Borthwick's work is shot on slide film, with light leaks, experimentation, and happenstance playing important roles in the look of his images. While his irreverent approach has made him attractive to niche magazines such as *AnOther Magazine*, *Interview*, *Purple*, *Self Service*, and *i-D*, it has meant that his relationship with the more mainstream fashion press has been an ambivalent one. He chooses his commercial clients carefully —they have included Adidas, Nike, Comme des Garçons, Martin Margiela, Balenciaga, and Yohji Yamamoto—and works collaboratively with the brand, usually over an extended period. His iconic images of actress Chloë Sevigny modeling pieces from Martin Margiela's Size 74 collection combine the designer's critique of fashion with Borthwick's own unorthodox take on the relationship between clothing and the body. "Fashion was just a question," Borthwick has said. "I never wanted it to be an answer."

Mark Borthwick,
Chloë Sevigny, Size 74, Purple Magazine, 2000

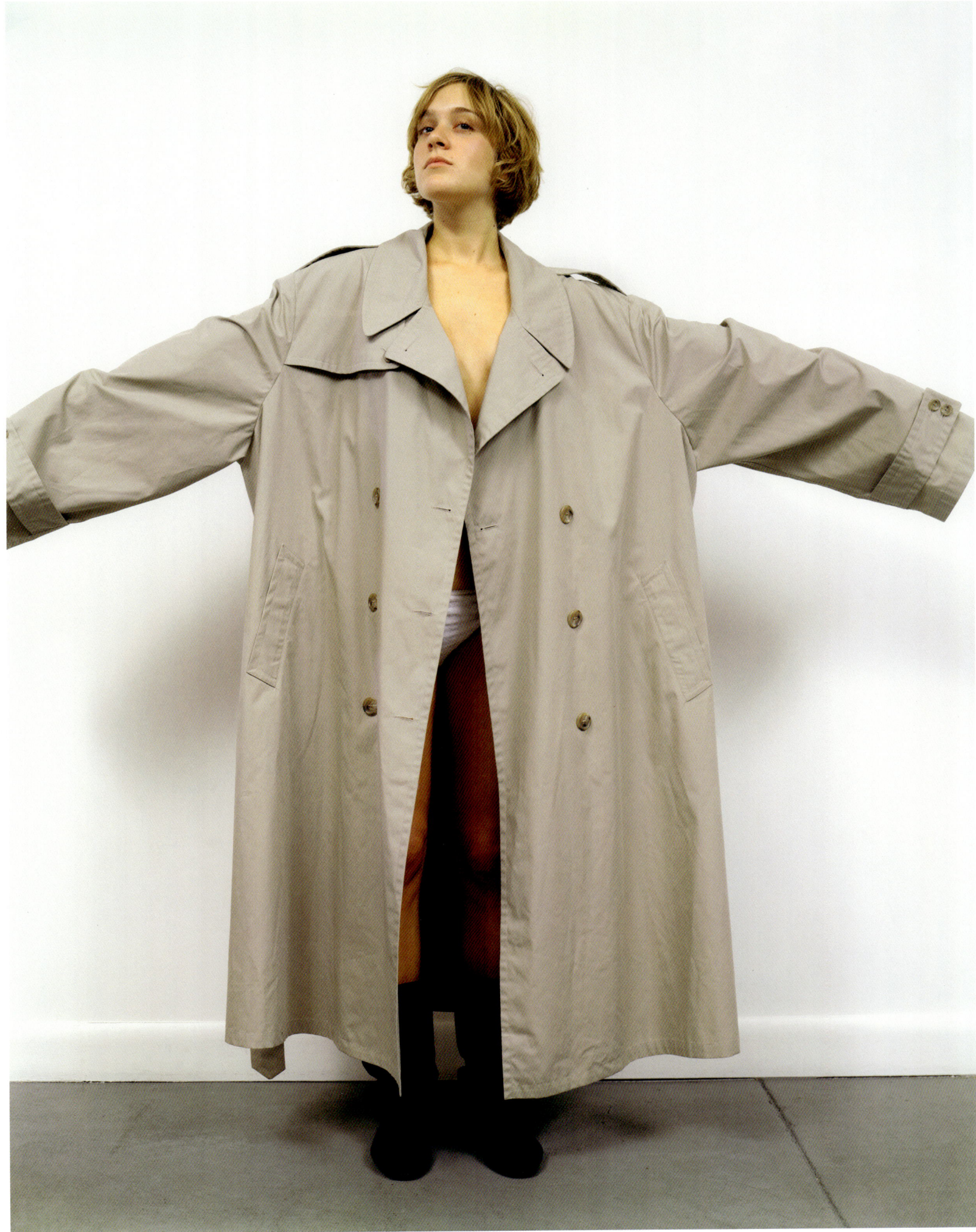

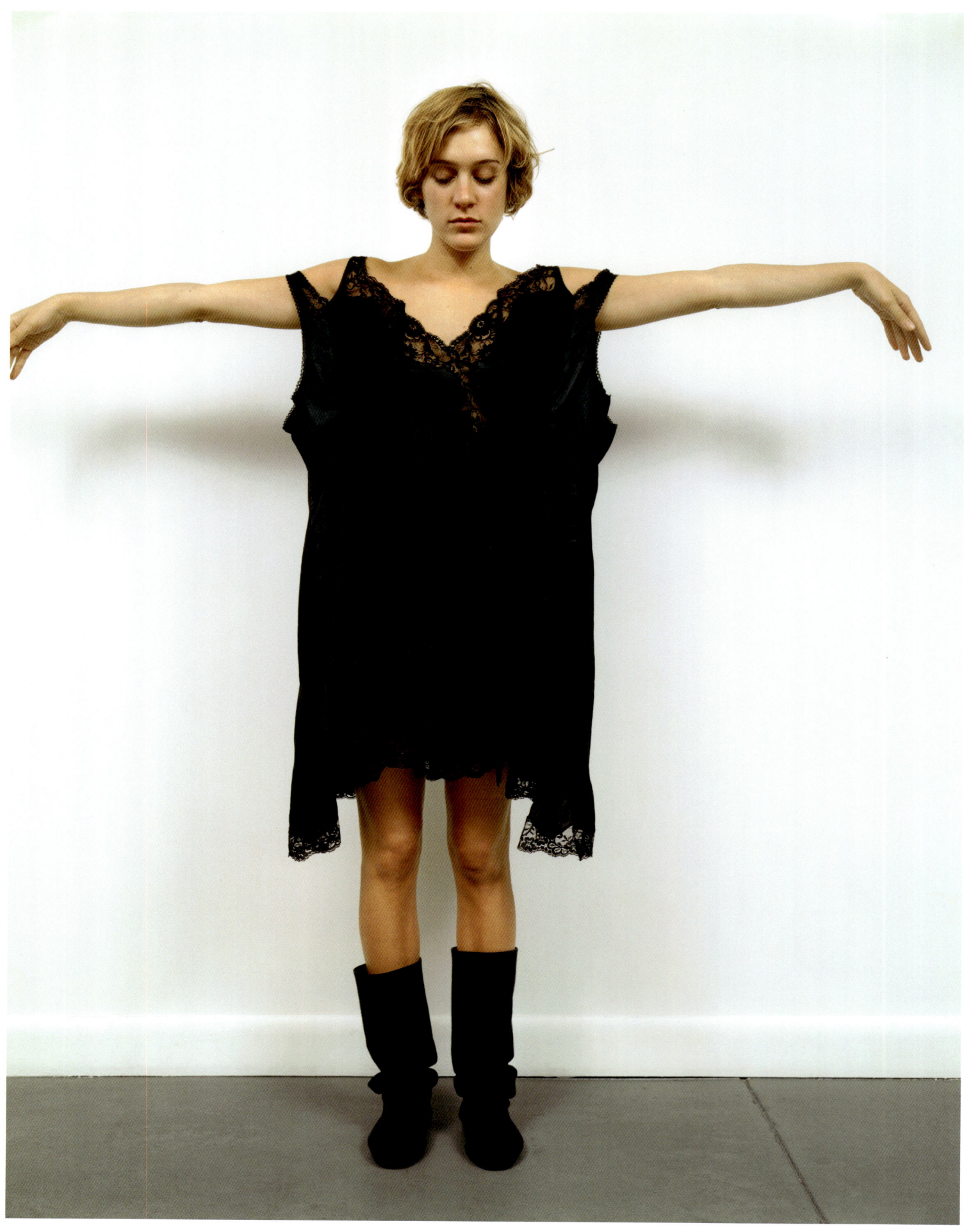

Above and right: Mark Borthwick,
Chloë Sevigny, Size 74, Purple Magazine, 2000

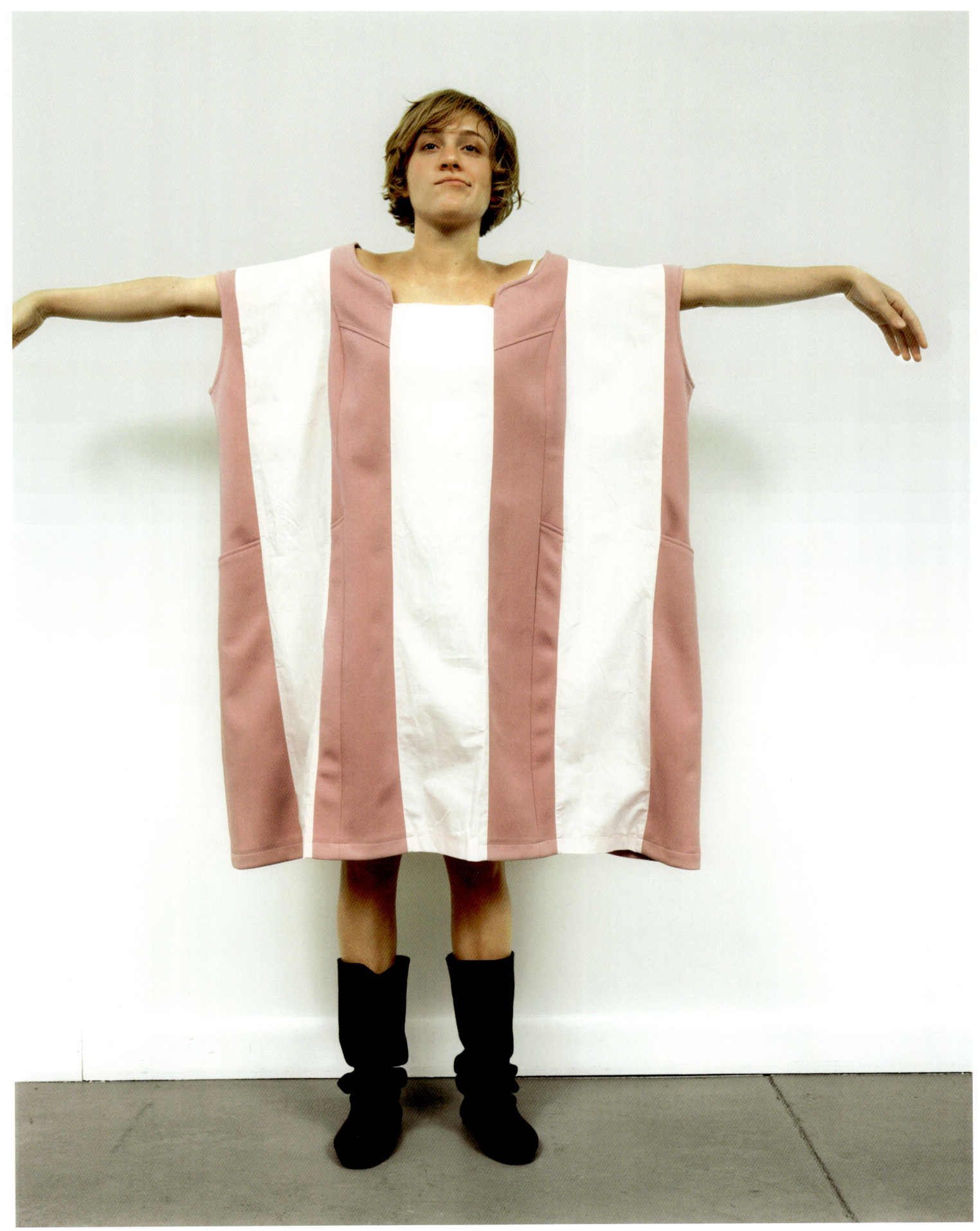

MARIO TESTINO

Born in Lima,
Peru, 1954

Mario Testino is known for his chameleonlike versatility: he works in a number of different idioms, tailoring his visual approach to suit the client, location, and shifting tides of the fashion world, yet always working in an aesthetic language uniquely his own. "Fashion photography is all about adaptation," he has quipped. "A photographer must be able to change as quickly as the times and the fashions themselves."

One of several constants in Testino's fashion work is the sexual energy in his pictures. If Tom Ford's 1995 Autumn/Winter collection for Gucci marked a reversal of the declining fortunes of the fashion house, Testino's supercharged photographs sealed the deal: styled by Carine Roitfeld, his campaigns for the brand from 1995 onward were audacious and unabashedly seductive. Perhaps the most iconic—and certainly the most controversial—of these was the Spring/Summer 2003 image featuring the Gucci logo shaved into a model's pubic hair. The creative team of Ford, Testino, and Roitfeld swung Gucci's fortunes, transforming it into a highly profitable global brand. Since 1997—when he photographed Diana, Princess of Wales, for *Vanity Fair*—Testino has expanded his portfolio with personal projects, such as his Towel series, exhibitions, and publications, alongside commercial work for clients, including Gucci, Burberry, Chanel, and Versace.

On blurring the lines between art and fashion, private and commissioned work, Testino is philosophical: "A lot of my shoots have the purpose of selling a product, and I find it interesting to develop a strategy for that. The art comes often by making this strategy appear instinctive."

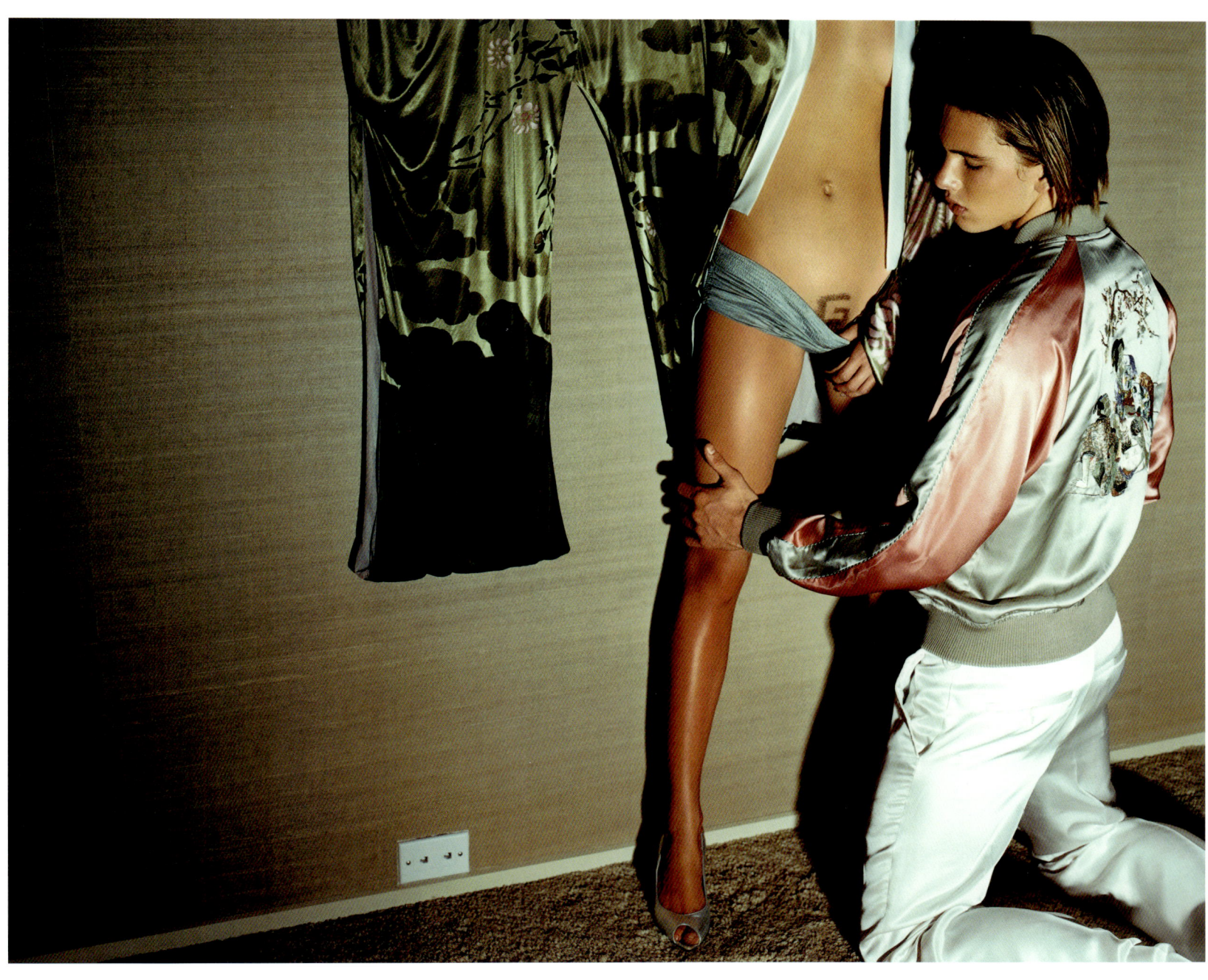

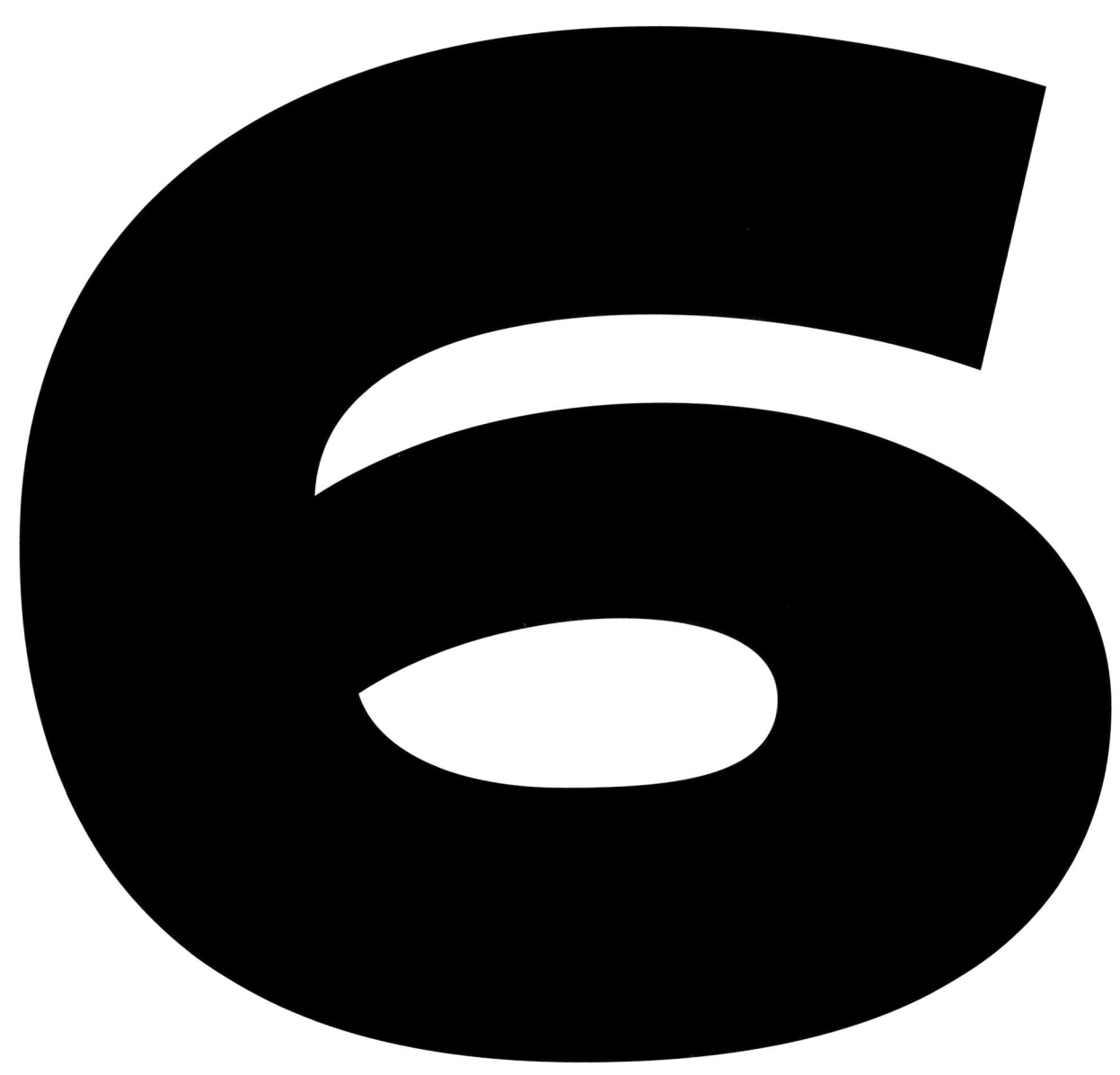

Francis Giacobetti,
Issey Miyake, 1998

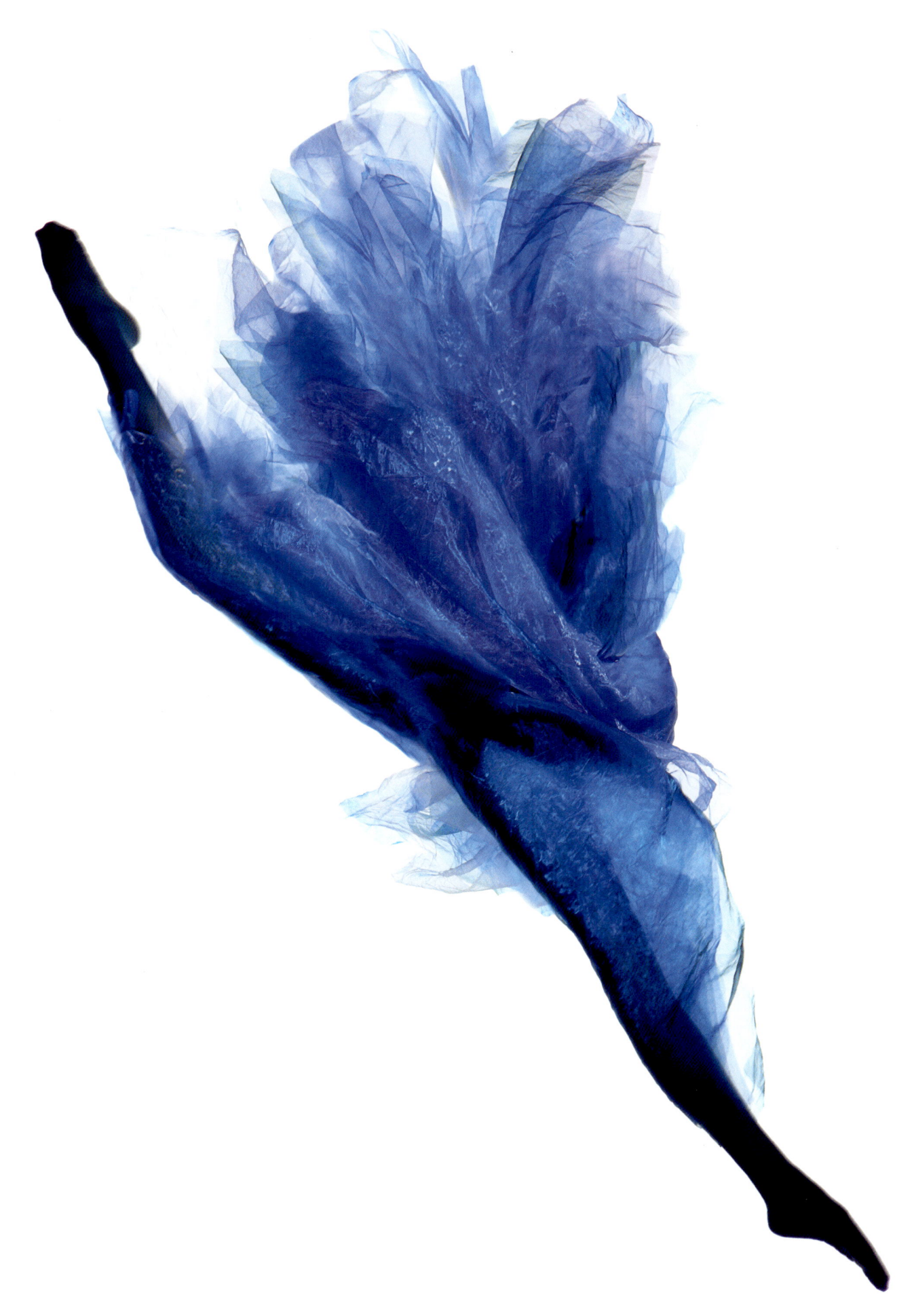

FRANCIS GIACOBETTI

Born in Marseille,
France, 1939

"I am no fashion photographer," claims Francis Giacobetti. Nevertheless, he has worked regularly for French and Italian *Vogue* since the 1960s and is responsible for one of the most inventive fashion campaigns of the new millennium, for Issey Miyake's Pleats Please.

Giacobetti's family moved to Paris in 1944, and he was given a Leica camera as a teenager. His first entry into the world of professional photography came as an assistant at *Paris Match* during the golden era of the picture press, and young Giacobetti was soon working as a photojournalist. His real calling was fashion and beauty, however, and he made the decision early on to specialize in color photography.

Giacobetti was also a talented photographer of nudes and a pioneer of the new eroticism that was beginning to make its way into fashion photography at the time. In 1963, he joined *Lui* magazine—a French version of *Playboy*—and is often cited as the grandfather of men's magazine photography. In the late 1970s he was asked to direct the soft-core porn film *Emmanuelle 2*— "a terrible experience," he said later. After that, he resumed his photography of the human body along more conceptual lines.

Giacobetti was first commissioned to shoot the Pleats Please campaigns between 1998 and 2001, returning to the brand in 2012. Originally created for the choreographer William Forsythe, Miyake's designs explore pleated fabric as a kind of "liquid architecture," transforming the outline of both the garment and the wearer's body as they move. Using dancers as models, Giacobetti's images bring out the functionality of the garments —the lightness of the fabric and its ability to stretch and resume its shape—alongside the dramatic, sculptural transformations that they undergo when in motion.

Francis Giacobetti,
Issey Miyake, 2016

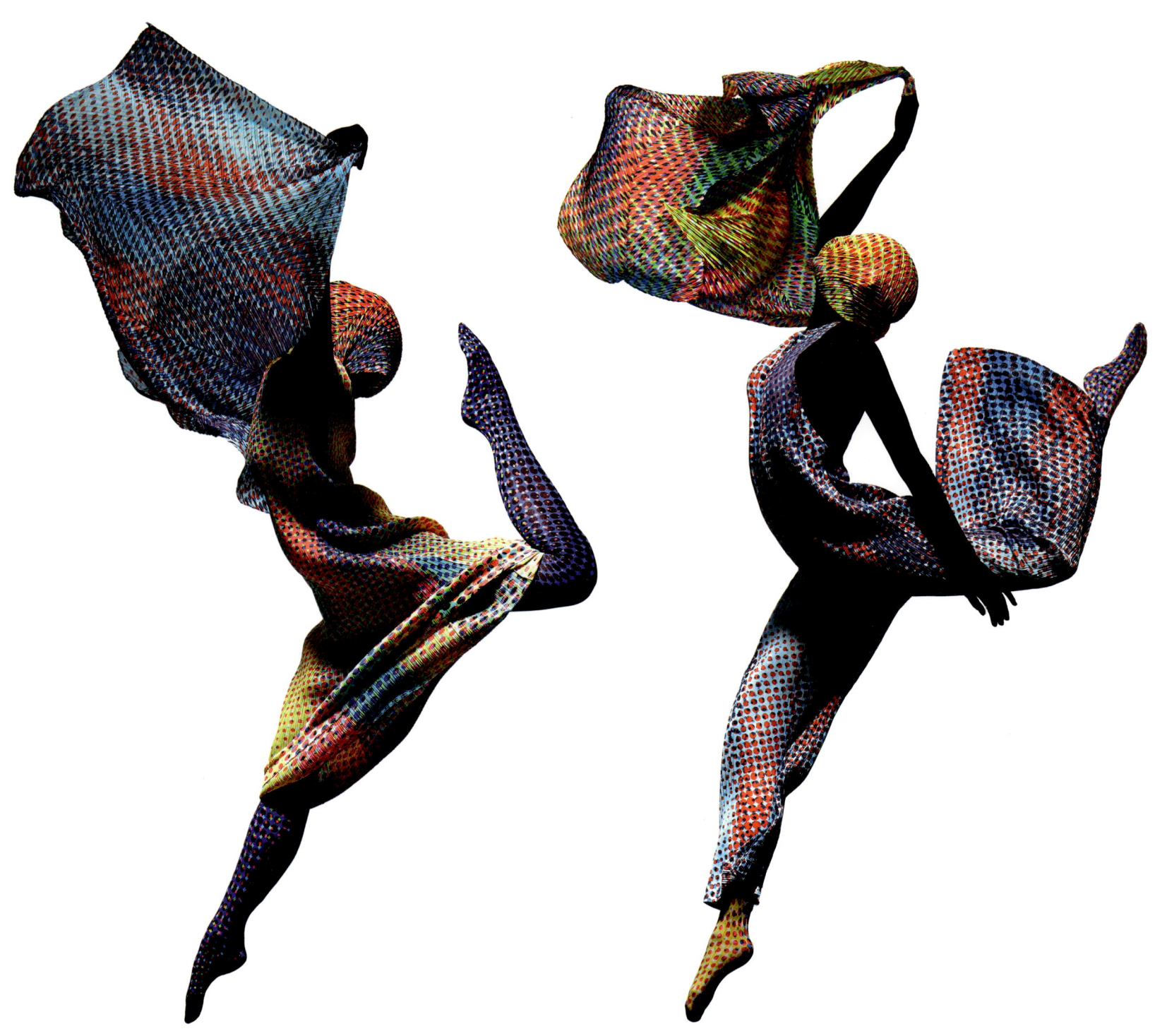

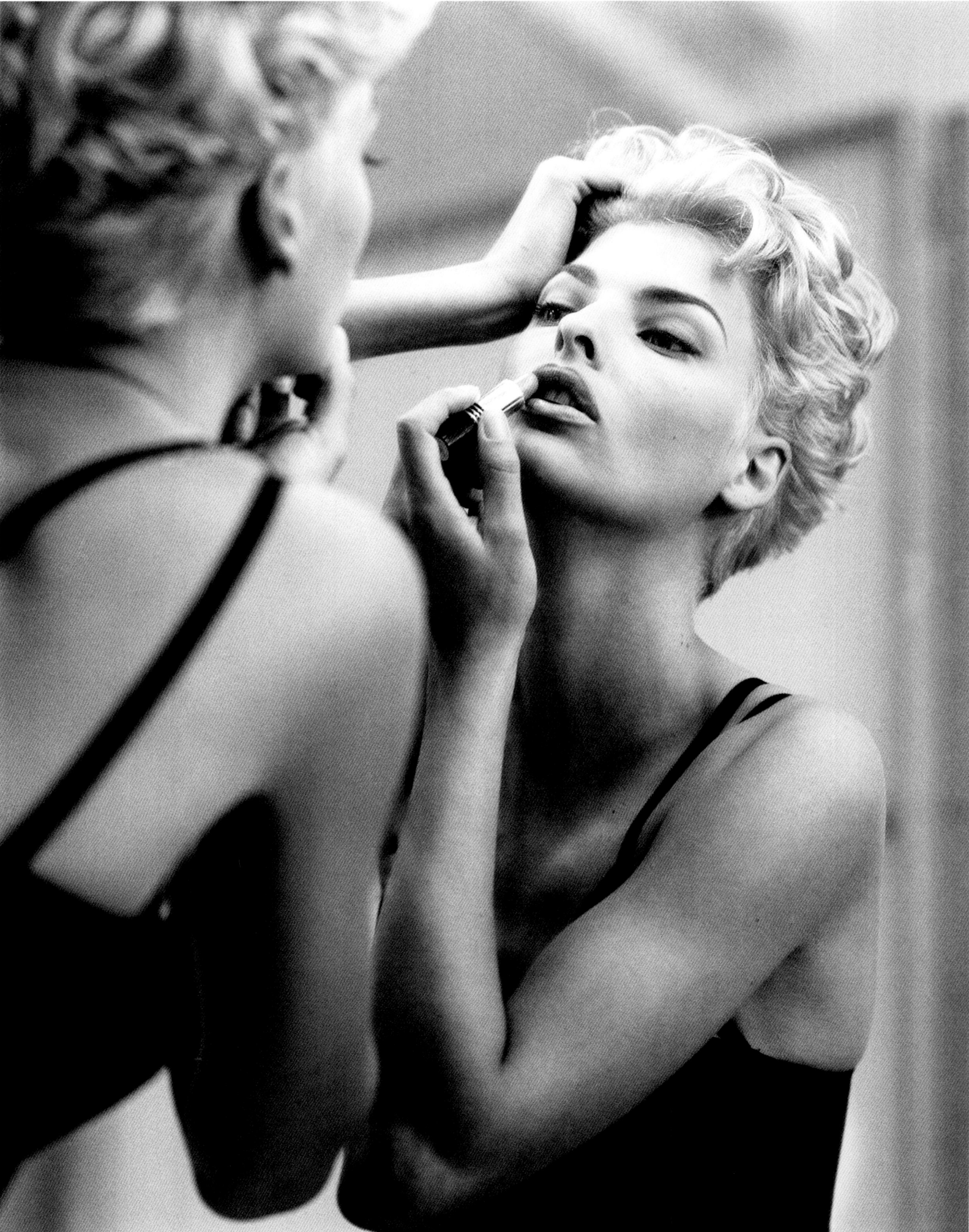

Born in New York City

STEVEN MEISEL

Possibly no other photographer has been as influential in shaping the idea and image of the supermodel as Steven Meisel. In the late 1980s, Meisel's career was taking off around the same time that an elite group of models—with Naomi Campbell, Christy Turlington, and Linda Evangelista at its center—began to dominate the fashion scene. His alignment with the supers was both professional and personal: "I was photographing the girls that I loved. I liked glamour and these girls were very glamorous. . . . We would go on vacation, go to dinner, hang out, and talk on the phone. We were friends; it was my beginning as it was theirs."

Meisel's obsession with fashion began in childhood; as a boy, he had collected model cards and took snapshots of models in the street with a compact camera. His first job was as a fashion illustrator for *Women's Wear Daily*. A familiar figure on New York's club scene, Meisel began taking photographs as a teenager in the late 1970s, and was soon testing aspiring models and shooting for *WWD*. His natural talents as an image-maker and stylist were apparent from early on; as editor and publisher Annie Flanders recalled, "He showed a very special, individual flair. He had an eye for fashion and fantasy, and he used his camera to transform everything into that fantasy." By the mid-1980s, Meisel was getting steady work from Italian and American *Vogue*, but his love of controversy and his tendency to push boundaries meant that many of his pictures were never run.

His reprieve came in the form of editor Franca Sozzani, who took over the editorship of *Vogue Italia* in 1988 and gave Meisel the creative freedom that he craved. Known in the industry for his willingness to tackle controversial topics —plastic surgery, rehab, and the 2010 Deepwater Horizon oil spill have all featured in recent work—Meisel draws extensively on his own encyclopedic knowledge of fashion photography, which has seen him alternately criticized and celebrated for his ability to appropriate and transform his sources.

Steven Meisel, *Linda Evangelista, New York*, 1991
Following pages: Steven Meisel, *Julia Stegner and Elise Crombez, New York*, 2005

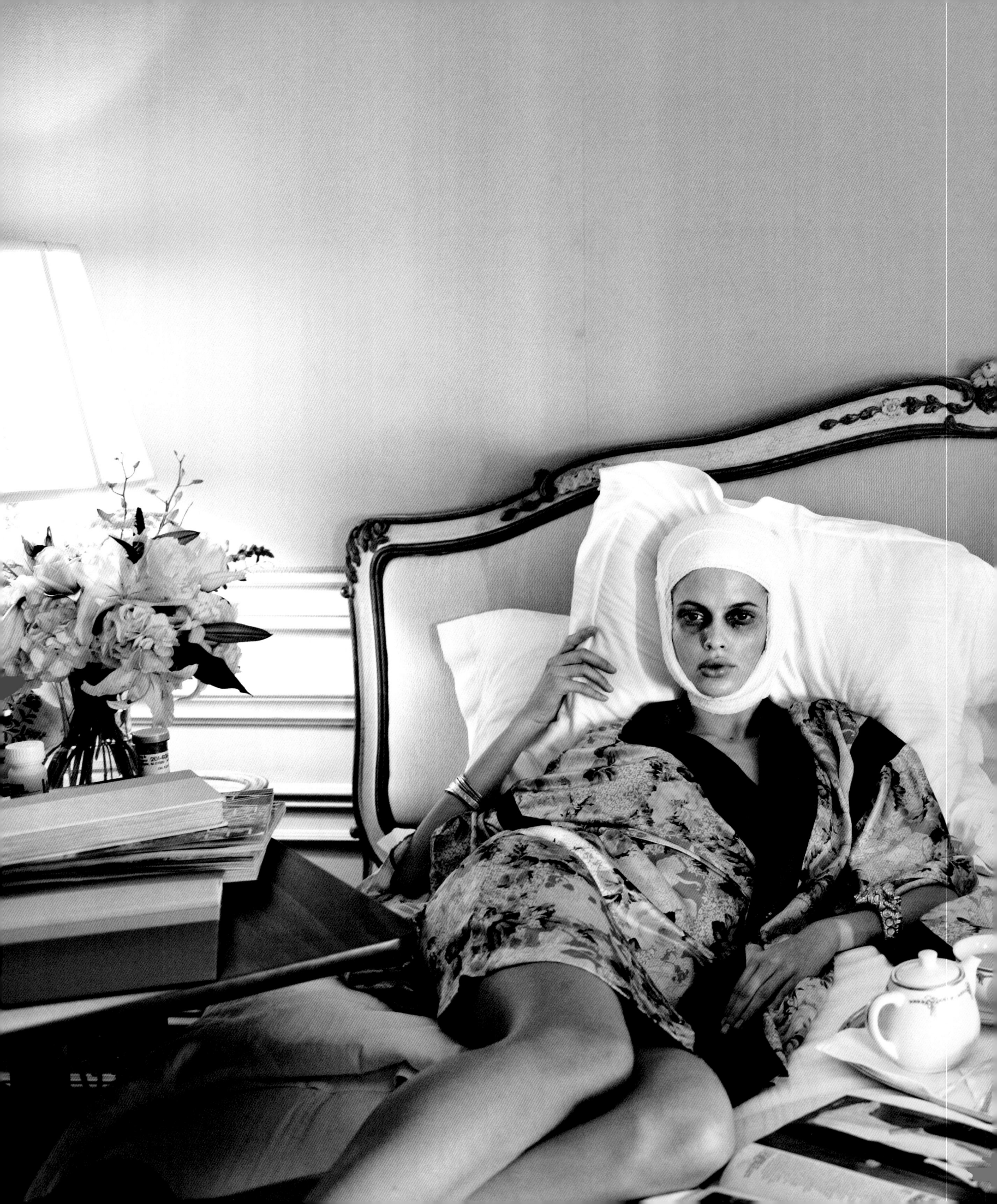

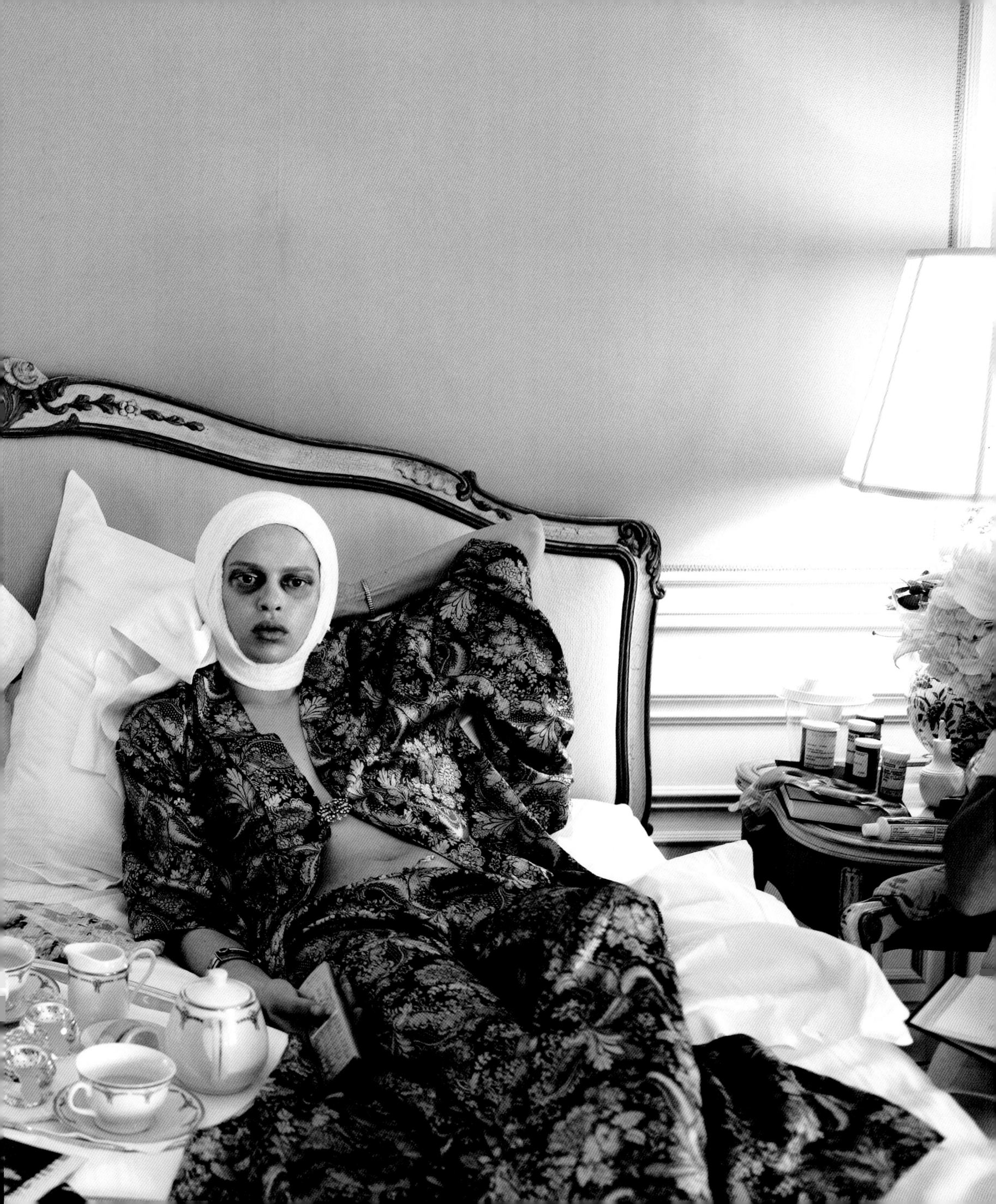

TIM WALKER

Tim Walker originally aspired to be a filmmaker—an ambition that shows clearly in his photographs, with their lavish sets, larger-than-life characters, and fairy-tale narratives. As a young man, Walker spent a summer as an intern at *Vogue*'s archives in London, organizing their collection of Cecil Beaton negatives and gaining a thorough grounding in the history of fashion photography. "What *Vogue* did made sense to me," Walker said later, "because it dealt with fantasy and the magical. As I studied its archive, I started to really understand photography." He went on to study photography at Exeter College of Art and Design in the UK; after graduation, he worked briefly as a photographer's assistant in London before moving to New York to assist Richard Avedon (p. 94).

In 1995, Walker shot his first editorial for *Vogue*; since then, he has gone on to work for the British, Italian, and American editions of the magazine, as well as other major fashion glossies such as *i-D*, *Love*, and *W*. Beaton's influence—his theatricality and the quintessential "Englishness" of his work—continues to resonate in Walker's photographs, which paint a romantic picture of the English landscape and a decidedly eccentric portrait of a genteel English lifestyle. In 2012, he paid homage to Beaton with a series of photographs produced in collaboration with *Vogue* fashion editor Grace Coddington. One of the images featured evening dresses constructed entirely out of paper by set designer Rhea Thierstein—a monochrome fantasy that Walker described as "a love letter to Beaton with paper."

Tim Walker, *Lily Cole and Spiral Staircase,
Wadhwan, Gujarat, India*, 2005
Following pages: Tim Walker, *Eight Models
in Paper Dresses After Cecil Beaton, London*, 2014

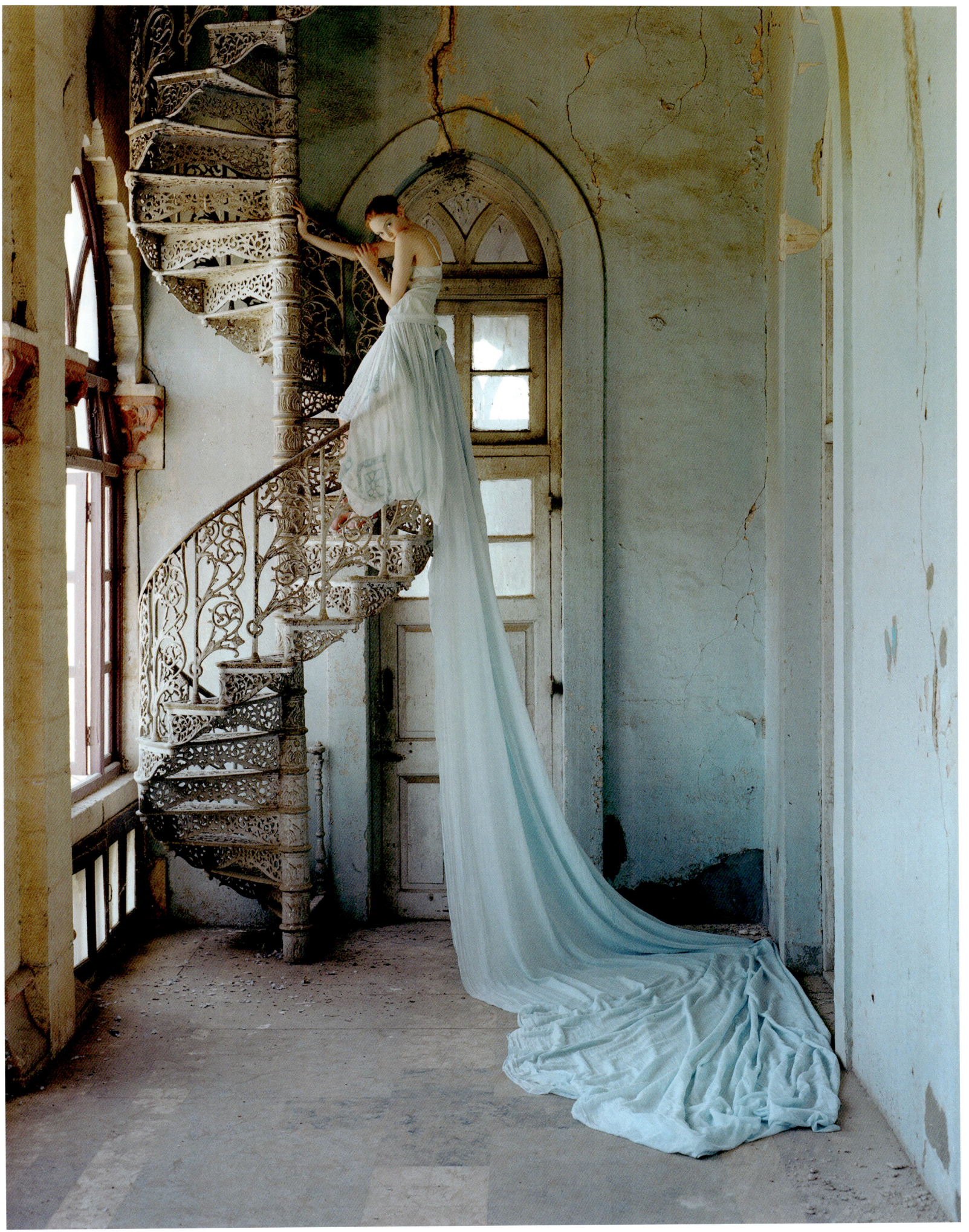

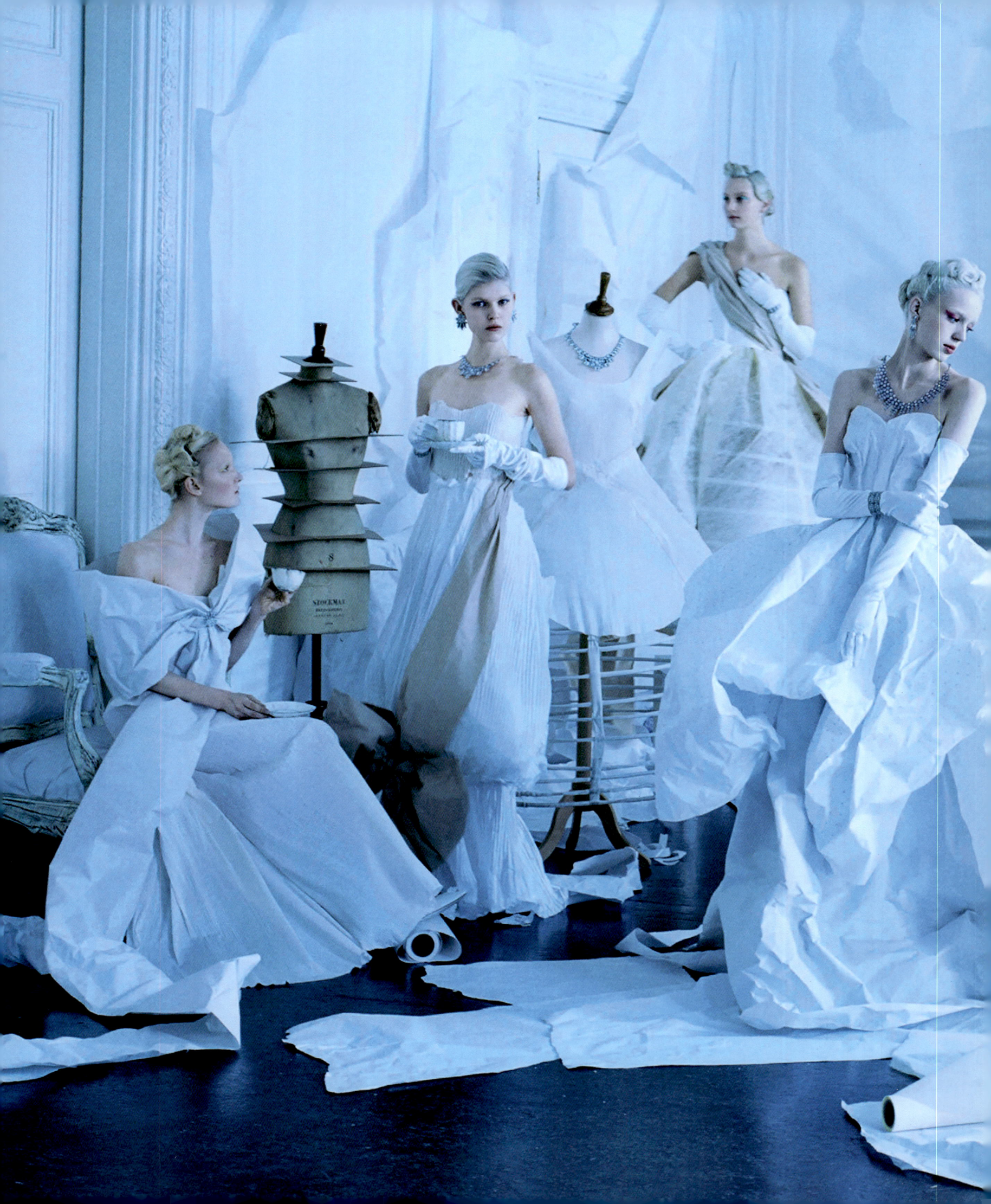

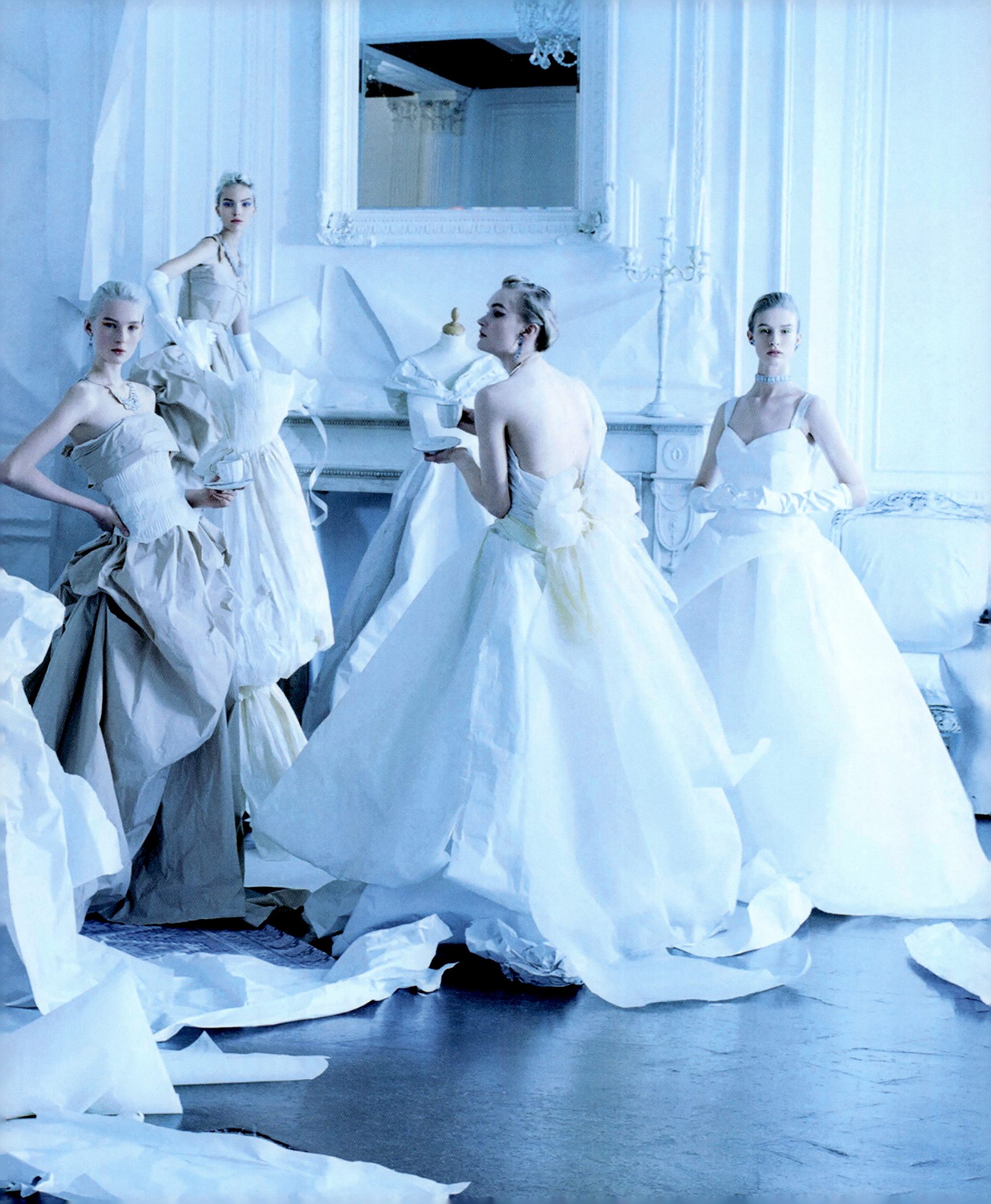

MILES ALDRIDGE

Born in London,
1964

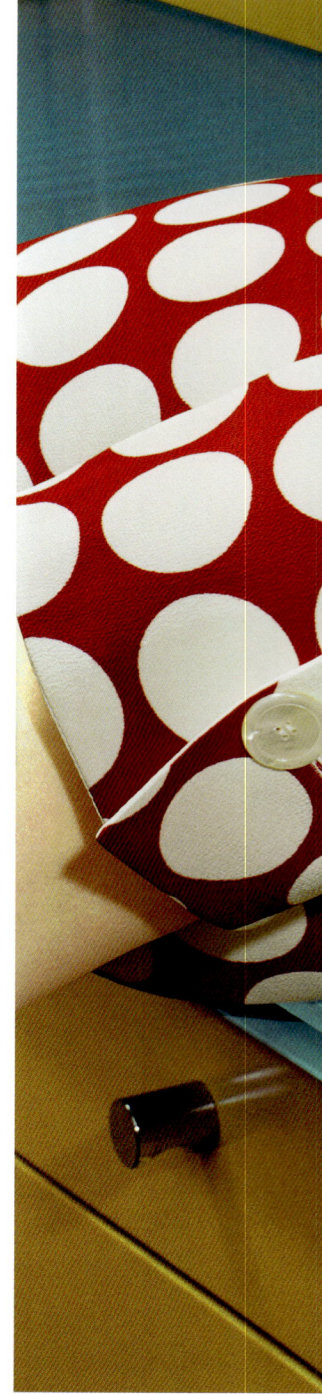

The son of renowned art director and illustrator Alan Aldridge, Miles Aldridge studied illustration at Central Saint Martins and began his career in 1993, at the height of fashion photography's grunge era. His early work bore little resemblance to the aesthetic he's best known for today: he recalled seeing, in a magazine store in New York, "three white background covers, all by me. . . . I kind of loathed it and wondered where I'd got lost. . . . I was much more interested in darker and stranger things, and the books I grew up with were books on Hieronymus Bosch and Bruegel. The complete opposite of what I was producing . . . I felt really uncomfortable about that." Aldridge decided to adopt a different creative vision, introducing narrative, vivid color, and elaborate sets into his work.

Before taking up photography, Aldridge directed music videos, and a director's sensibility continues to shape his imagery. His supersaturated color palette is inspired by 1950s Kodachrome and Technicolor processes, and the weird, dreamlike narratives in his photographs are heavily influenced by the films of directors such as Federico Fellini, David Lynch, Alfred Hitchcock, and Pedro Almodóvar. The world that he creates is filled with dark parodies of female stereotypes: Stepford wives smashing up their kitchens; robotic, power-dressed glamazons; vapid starlets; and Madonnas crying pearly tears.

Drawings are vital to Aldridge's creative process: concepts are sketched out in advance, along with detailed color schemes. He makes no distinction between his editorial work—much of it done for *Vogue Italia*—and his personal work, and he believes that fashion photographers should stretch themselves conceptually and aesthetically. "The job of the fashion photographer," he has remarked, "is to subtly make comment on the world he lives in."

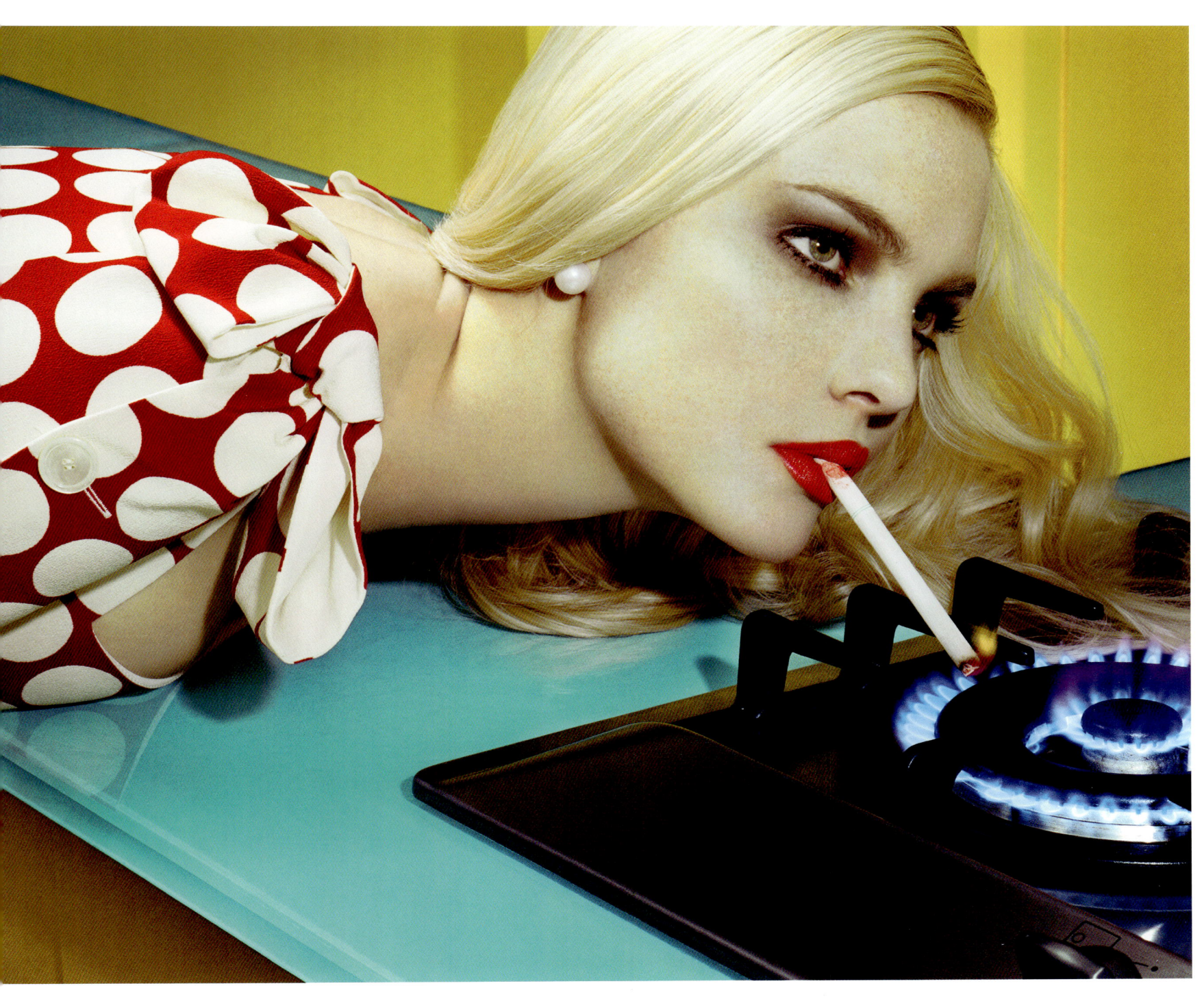

Miles Aldridge,
Home Works #3, 2008

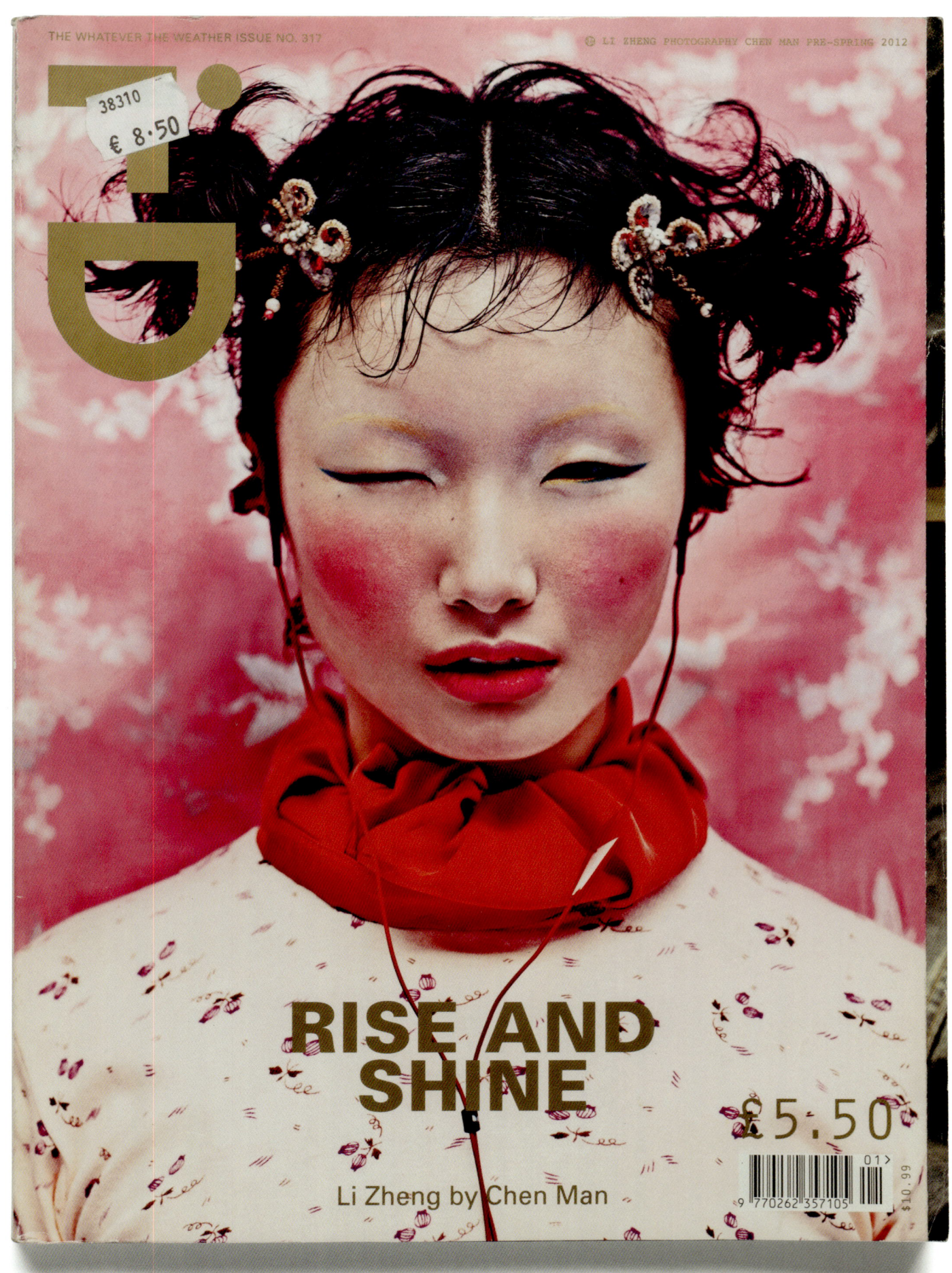

RISE AND SHINE

£5.50

Li Zheng by Chen Man

Born in Beijing,
1980

CHEN MAN

Sometimes known as "China's Mario Testino," Chen Man's career has grown alongside China's entry onto the global fashion scene. Her early work, for the Chinese magazine *Vision*, was done while she was still a student at the Central Academy of Fine Arts in Beijing. Chen's skillful use of bold colors and digital postproduction have been hallmarks of her practice since early on. Drawing on both Western and Chinese cultural influences, her work incorporates a subtle critique of Chinese ideals of beauty, culture, and consumption. "We're a generation that witnessed reform, a generation that's now witnessing the material dream coming true," she has pointed out. "What influences me most is this reality. I want to create a visual elaboration of traditional Chinese culture from this perspective."

Though she shares the critical sensibility of many of her contemporaries in Europe and North America, Chen's work presents this critique from a cultural perspective that has, until quite recently, remained underrepresented in fashion photography. Known for seeking out unconventional models (one of her favorites, Lu Yan, has been called China's ugliest model), she street-cast Tibetan teenagers for her 2012 series of covers for *i-D*'s "Whatever the Weather" issue.

Chen Man,
i-D cover, "Whatever the Weather" issue,
February 2012

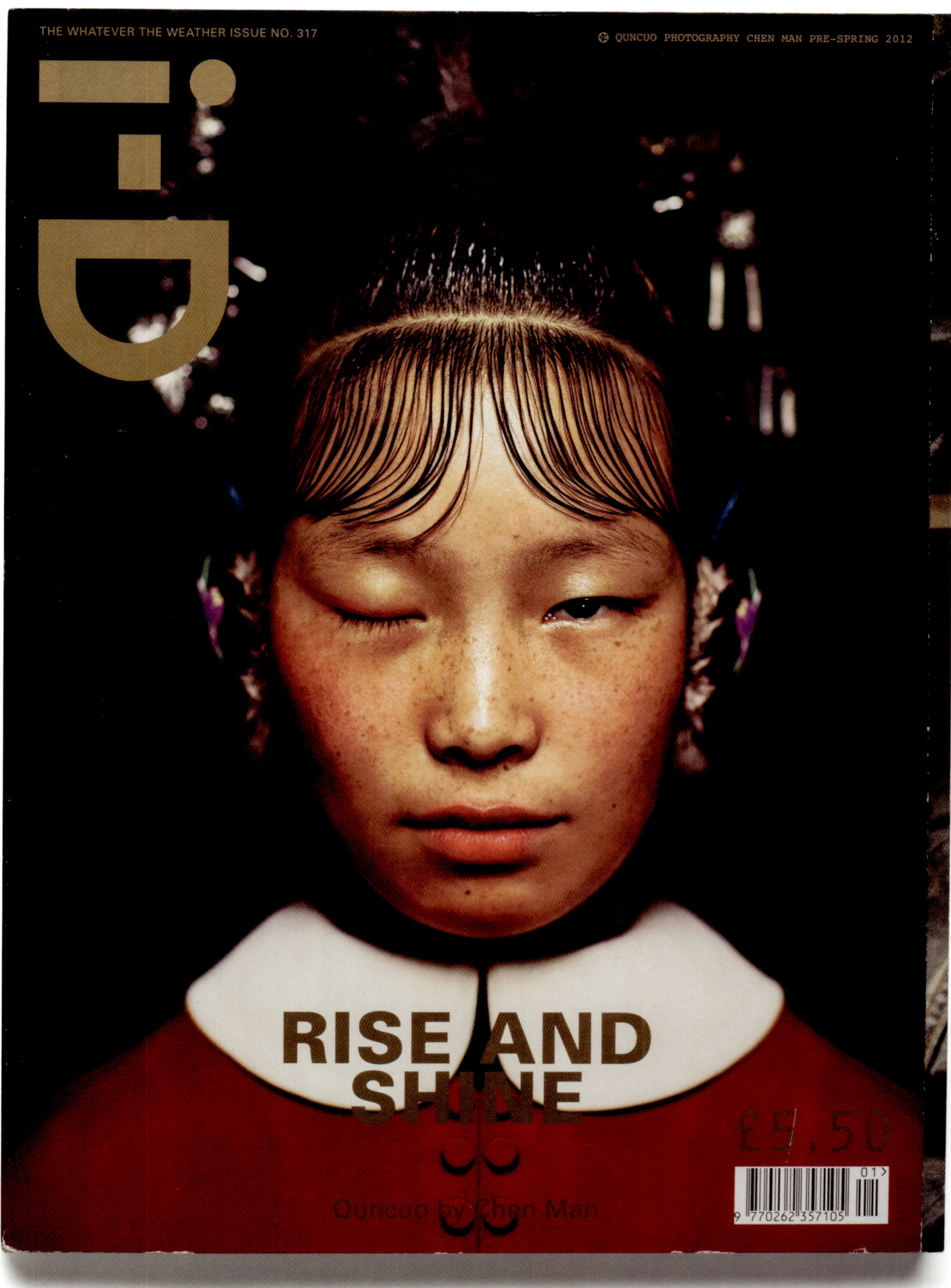

RISE AND SHINE

£5.50

Quncuo by Chen Man

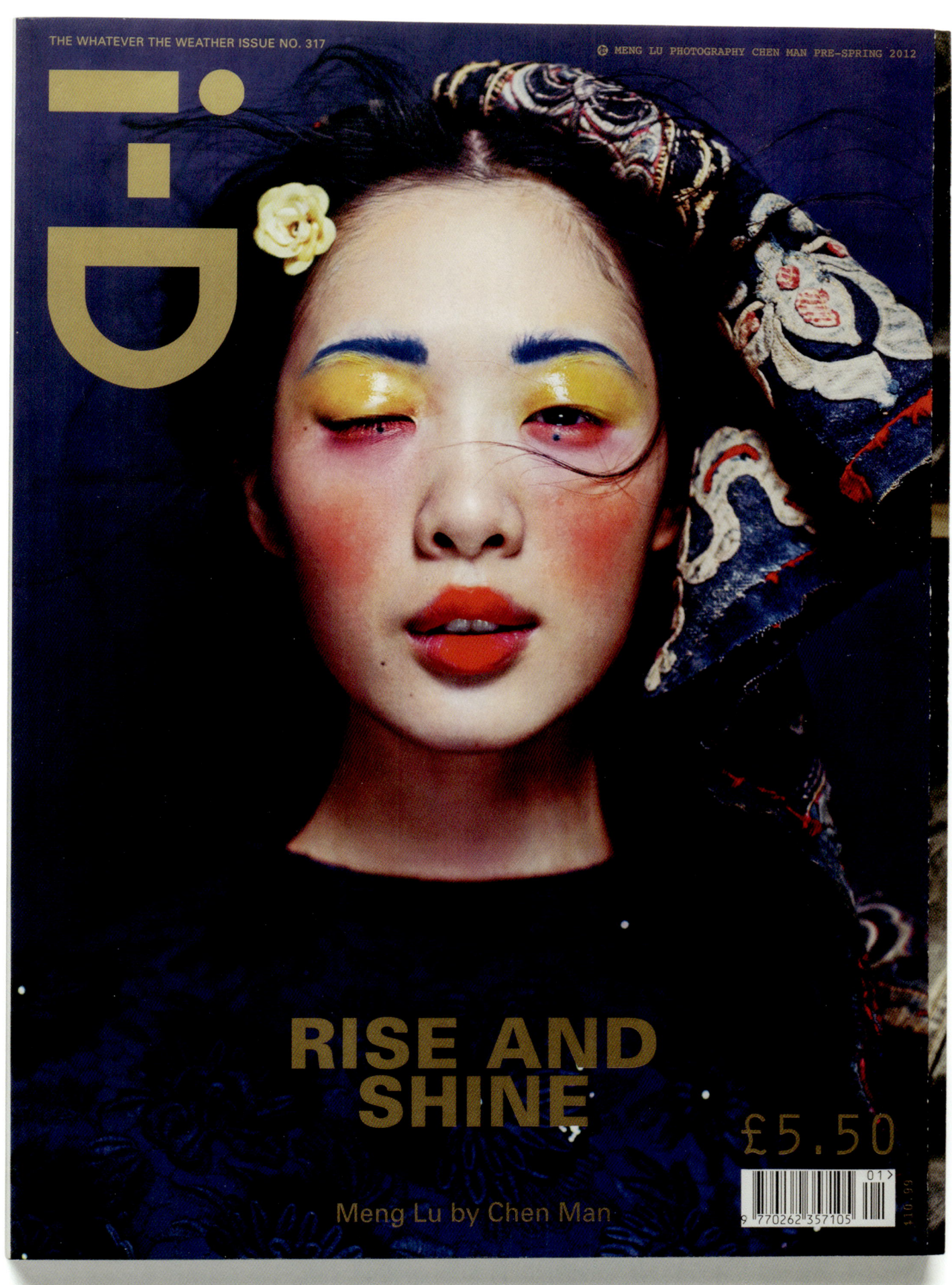

THE WHATEVER THE WEATHER ISSUE NO. 317

MENG LU PHOTOGRAPHY CHEN MAN PRE–SPRING 2012

i-D

RISE AND SHINE

£5.50

Meng Lu by Chen Man

Left and above: Chen Man,
i-D covers, "Whatever the Weather" issue,
February 2012

Born in Amsterdam,
1972

Viviane Sassen's characteristic visual language of strong light and shadow, bright, saturated color, and extreme, angular poses has been widely emulated within photographic art, as well as in fashion photography. One of a handful of image-makers who redefined fashion photography in the early 2000s, Sassen broke with the increasingly restrictive rules and parameters that had come to dominate fashion advertising from the mid-1990s onward.

Following a brief career as a model, Sassen began a photography degree in Utrecht, the Netherlands, in 1992; by the late '90s, she was publishing her fashion work in independent magazines such as *Sec*, *Blvd*, *Purple Fashion*, and *Self Service*. Sassen's work, which bridges the boundary between fashion and art photography, challenges conventional notions of glamour, beauty, and narrative, drawing on the aesthetics of abstract painting and collage to create ambiguous and often unsettling compositions. She makes extensive use of reflection, cropping, and doubling to blur the outlines of the human form, treating the body as a formal or sculptural element within her images.

VIVIANE SASSEN

Viviane Sassen,
In Bloom (1), Dazed & Confused, 2011

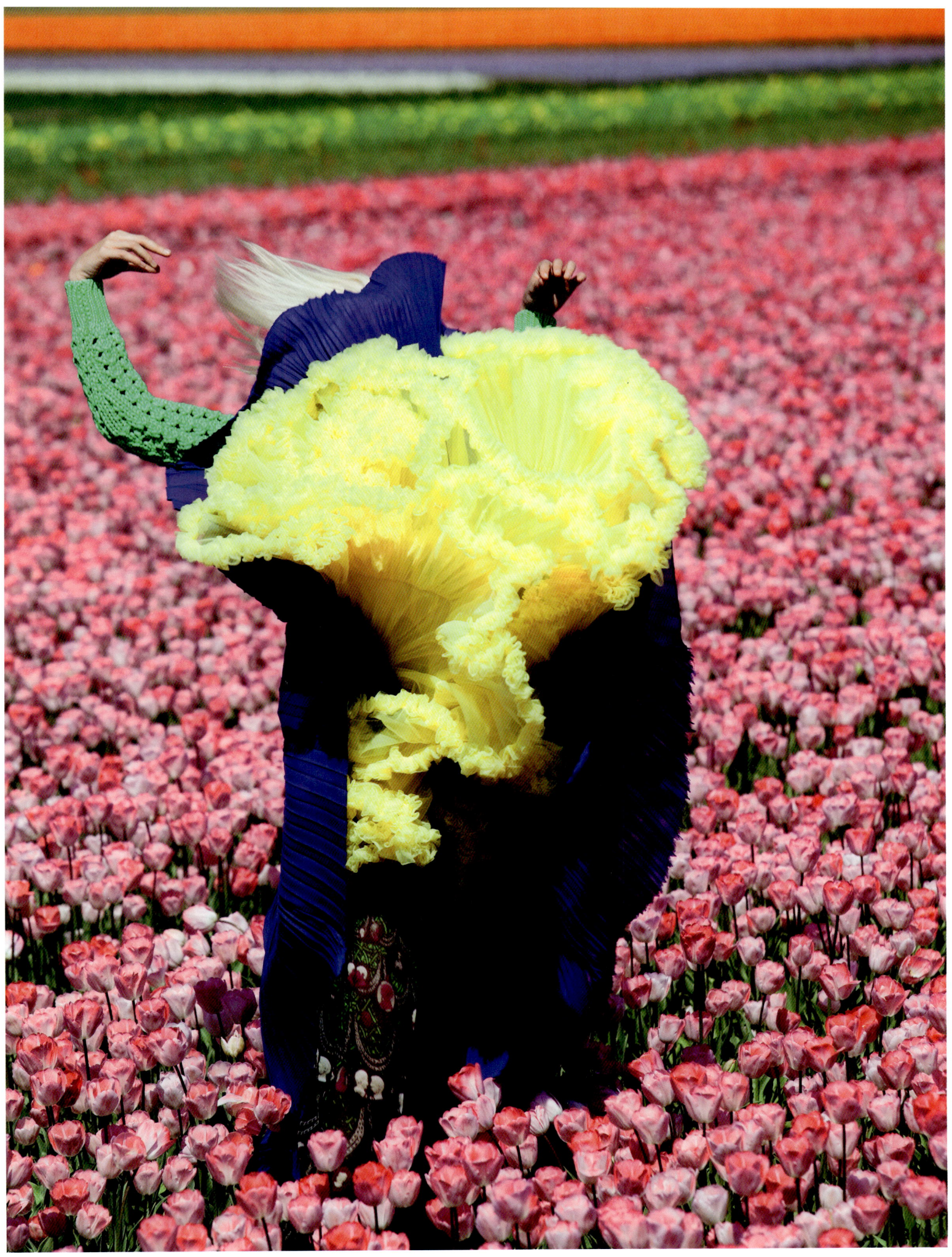

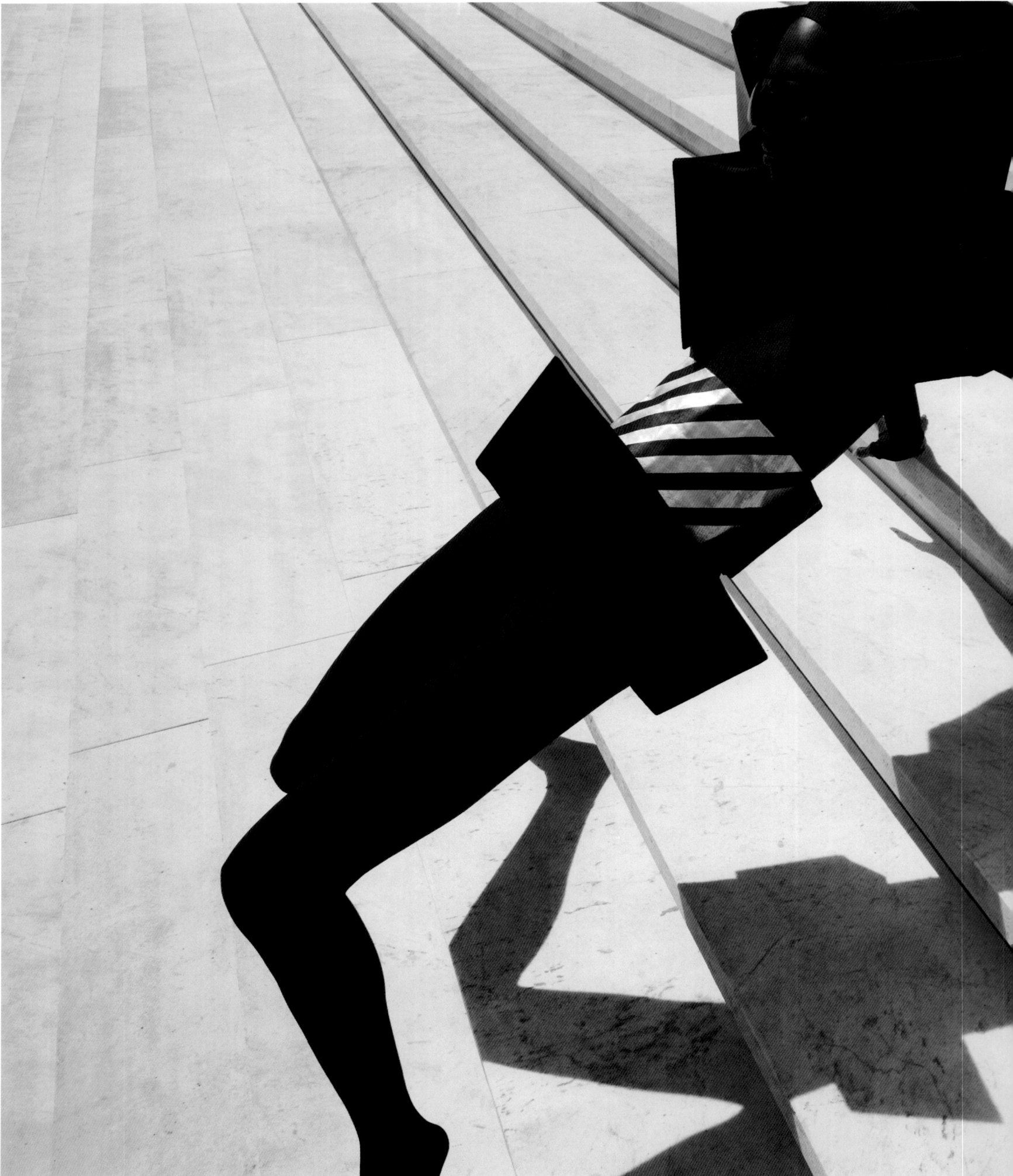

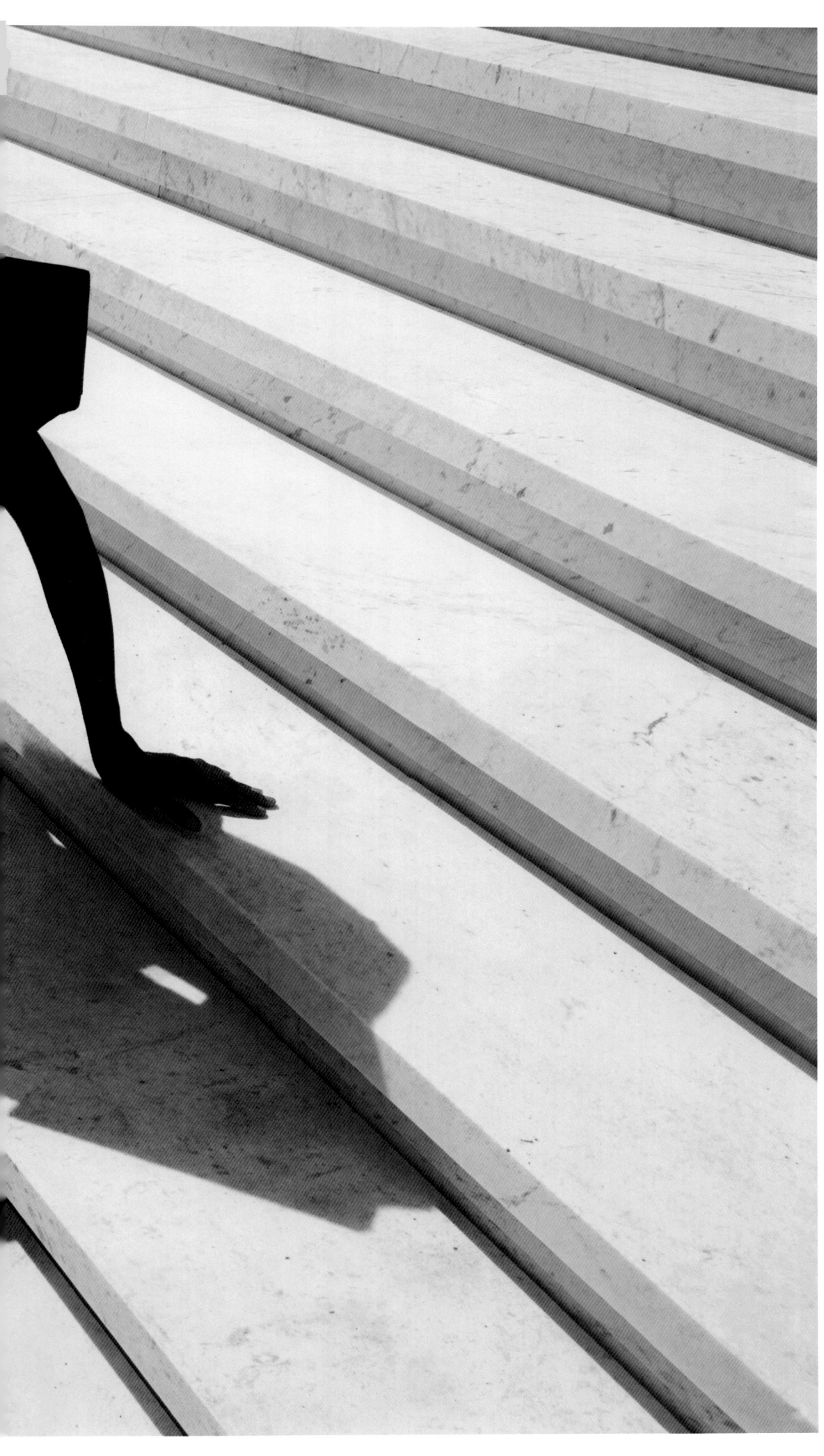

Viviane Sassen,
De La Mar Theatre, 2010

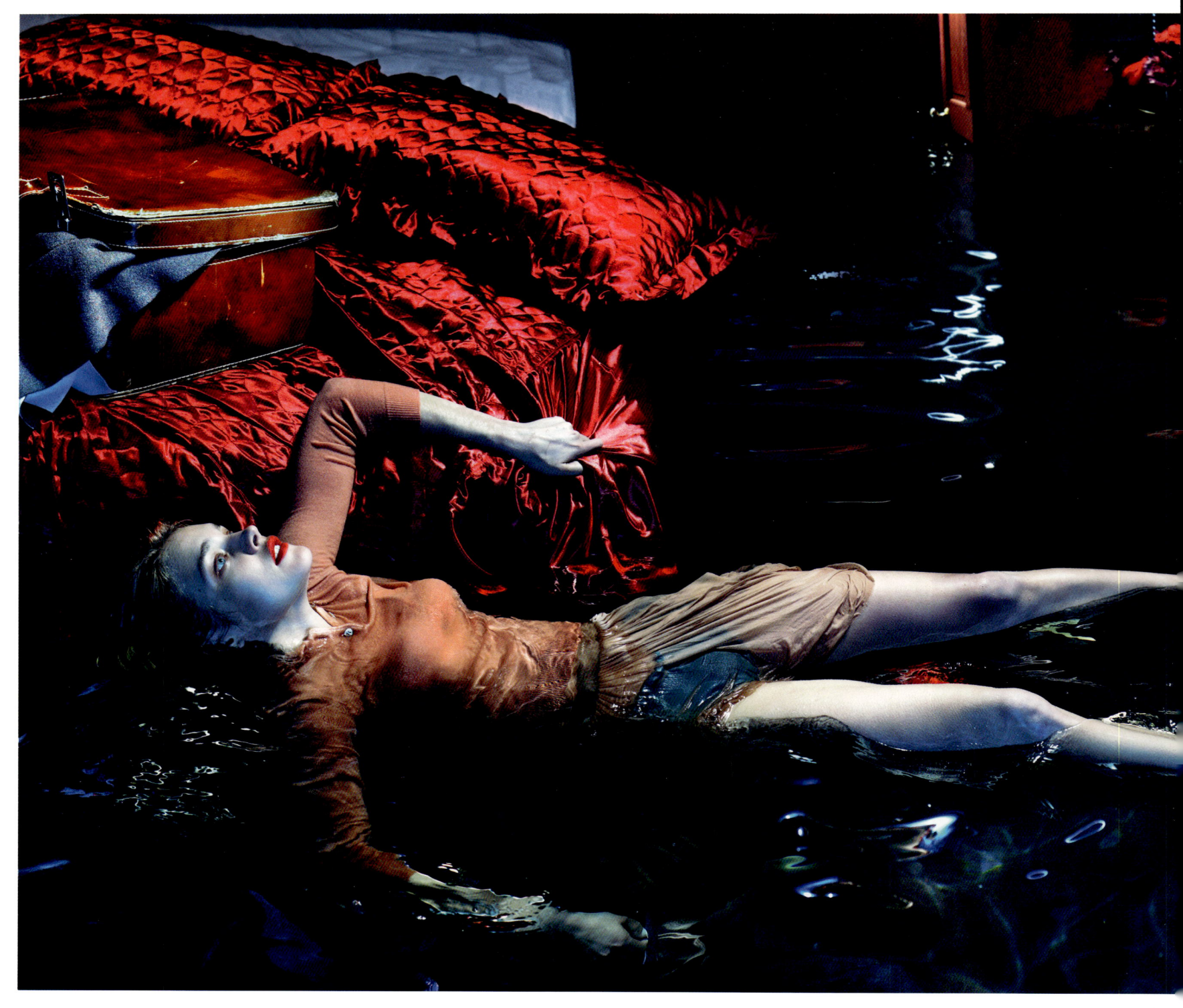

Mert & Marcus,
Bedroom, London, 2012

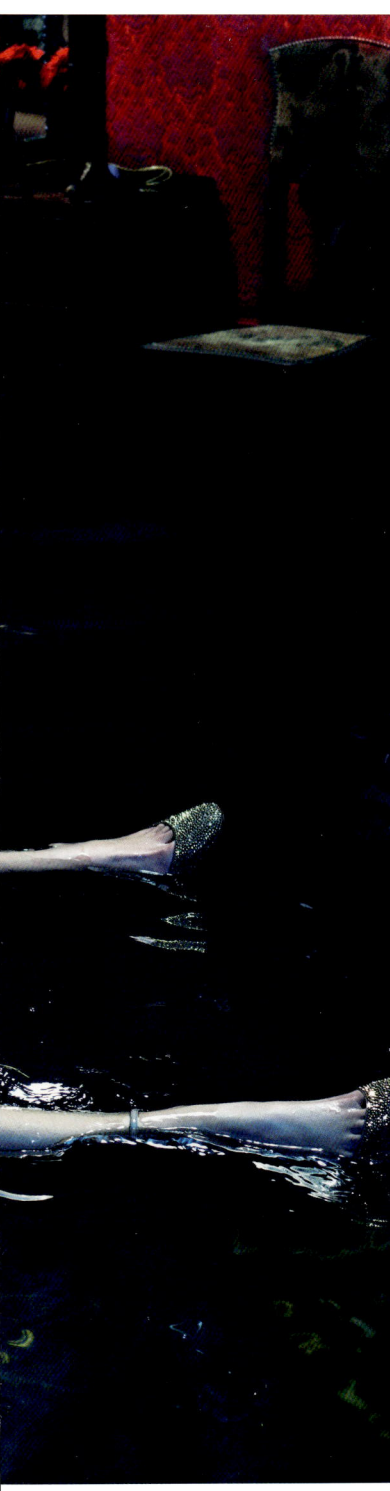

By the time fashion photography began to wholeheartedly embrace digital technology around the turn of the millennium, Mert and Marcus had already been experimenting with retouching for a number of years. Although they work in a variety of styles, the duo are best known for hyperreal, highly polished work that embraces the creative possibilities offered by digital postproduction: deliberately artificial, fantasy-inspired images in saturated colors.

The pair began their artistic collaboration after meeting at a party in 1993. At the time, Marcus Piggott was a photographer's assistant, while Mert Alas was modeling and doing occasional work with Alexander McQueen. They didn't start out with fashion in mind: "We used to take pictures—a lot of nudes," recalled Alas. "We'd be talking in the middle of the night; we'd imagine scenarios and phone up friends." Working out of a rented loft in London's East End, the pair did all their own styling, set design, hair, and makeup for their early photographs. Before digital postproduction became widely available, Alas and Piggott retouched their photographs by hand, often spending many hours on a single image, or abandoning an entire day's work because it wasn't perfect.

Mert and Marcus—as they are now known professionally—developed their aesthetic shooting for *Dazed & Confused* and *i-D*, but their first major commission was for *Visionaire* magazine in 1998. Since then, they've shot editorials for major publications, including *Numéro*, *Arena Homme+*, *Vogue*, *W*, and *Love*, as well as advertising campaigns for clients, including Miu Miu, Versace, Kenzo, Louis Vuitton, and Gucci. Although Mert and Marcus travel with a team of technicians, retouchers, and assistants, they enjoy working spontaneously. As Piggott has remarked, "We have the same kind of aesthetic and it's very fluid between us, so we both know when we've got the picture that we're looking for."

Mert Alas:
born in Turkey, 1971

Marcus Piggott:
born in Wales, 1971

MERT & MARCUS

Born in New York City,
1963

COLLIER SCHORR

For Collier Schorr, fashion photography is a natural extension of an art practice in which she has explored issues around gender, identity, and desire since the 1980s. Schorr, whose father was a photographer and editor at a car magazine, grew up surrounded by cameras and photographs. After studying photojournalism at New York's School of Visual Arts, she began producing her own work.

Schorr has used fashion imagery in her art since the 1980s—an early project consisted of Guess and Calvin Klein tear sheets, overlaid with text—but found her artistic voice with a project that began in the small town of Schwäbisch Gmünd in southern Germany in the early 1990s. Invited by a friend to spend a weekend there, Schorr began photographing the people and the surrounding landscape—then returned every year for the next twenty years. "Gender, religion, nationality are all in flux in my work," she has remarked. "The avenues to desire are skewed. I wanted to make work that spoke to as many people's desires as possible: maternal desire, fraternal desire, desire for romance, for youth . . ."

More recent projects, such as her 2005 artist's book *Jens F.*, use photography, painting, and collage to explore the fluidity of gender identity and the intimacy of the relationship between artist and model. Fashion photography has allowed Schorr to address female subjectivity in a way that her artwork has not: "I felt like there was a real problem with how women had been packaged and sold back to women. I didn't have a sense of how to solve that problem, so I completely avoided dealing with women as a subject in my work." One of her first major fashion assignments was 2009's "Clean Living" for *i-D*, with Freja Beha Erichsen; as Schorr later remarked, "Those were the first pictures I took of a beautiful woman where I felt like it was OK to look at her."

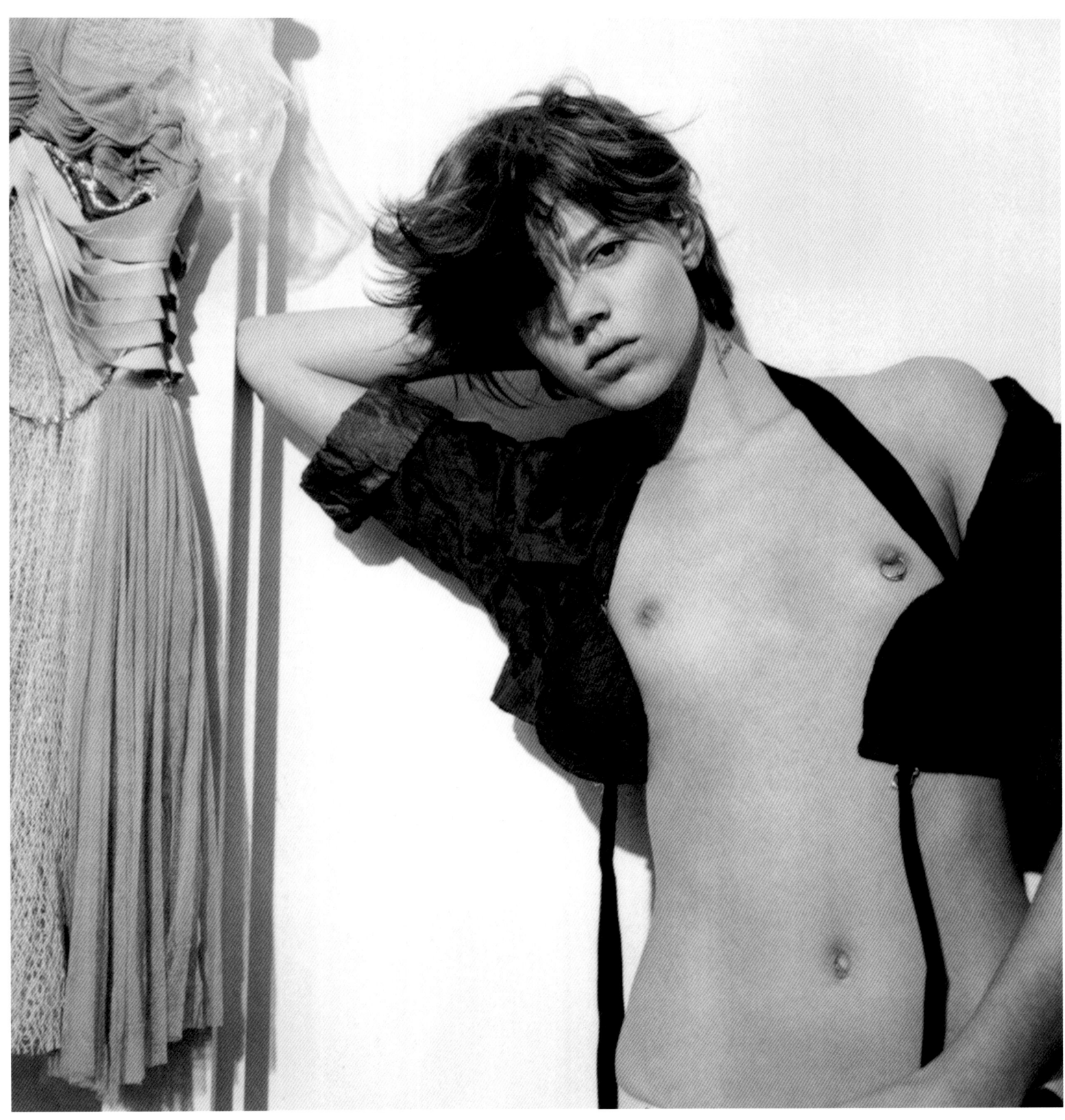

SCHELTENS & ABBENES

Maurice Scheltens:
born in Apeldoorn,
the Netherlands, 1972

Liesbeth Abbenes:
born in Asten,
the Netherlands, 1970

Amsterdam-based creative couple Maurice Scheltens and Liesbeth Abbenes have been working together since 2005, formalizing their collaboration in 2009 to become Scheltens and Abbenes. Scheltens, a trained technical photographer, and Abbenes, who studied mixed-media art, transform clothing and fashion products into striking, often abstract, still-life compositions. The pair rarely shoot with models or on location, preferring to build their images slowly, working on their own in their studio. As Scheltens has explained, "We're obsessed by still lifes because they're completely controllable. A still image can be manipulated and fine-tuned with an enormous precision."

Their work that first drew the attention of the fashion world was a series of product shots for Swedish retailer COS. However, the "White Shirt" editorial, shot for *Fantastic Man* in 2007—Scheltens and Abbenes's first to feature garments rather than accessories—represented an important turning point. "We had shown that we were able to create interesting still lifes using clothing," said Scheltens. "And by focusing on a seam or a collar, we had depicted fashion in a very pragmatic way." Despite the fact that brand names are rarely visible in their work, Scheltens and Abbenes have shot commissions for major fashion labels, including Hermès, Viktor & Rolf, Kenzo, Balenciaga, Louis Vuitton, Nike, and Yves Saint Laurent. Like many of their contemporaries, the pair are equally at home in the worlds of art and fashion: in 2012, they won an Infinity Award from the International Center of Photography for Applied/Fashion/Advertising Photography, a few months before opening their first solo gallery exhibition.

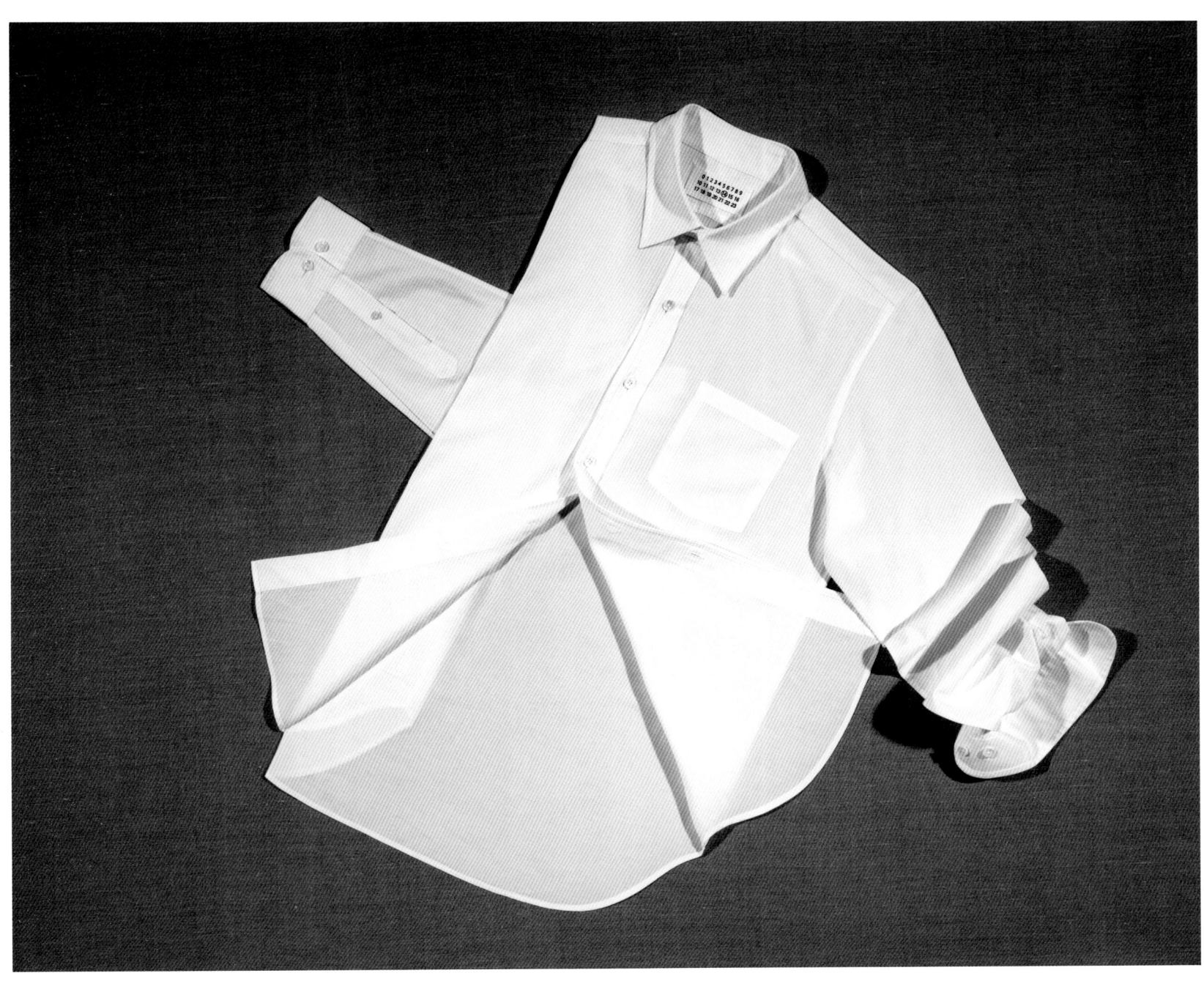

Scheltens & Abbenes,
White Shirts, Margiela, Fantastic Man, 2007

SUGGESTED READING

Ansel, Ruth, and Robin Muir. *Tim Walker: Story Teller*. London: Thames & Hudson, 2012.

Apraxine, Pierre. *La Comtesse de Castiglione par elle-même*. Paris: Éditions de la Réunion des musées nationaux, 2000.

Aubenas, Sylvie. *Elegance: The Séeberger Brothers and the Birth of Fashion Photography, 1909–1939*. San Francisco: Chronicle Books, 2007.

Bassman, Lillian. *Lillian Bassman Lingerie*. New York: Abrams, 2012.

Bassman, Lillian, and Paul Himmel. *Lillian Bassman & Paul Himmel: The First Retrospective*. Edited by Ingo Taubhorn and Brigitte Woischnik. Heidelberg, Germany: Kehrer Verlag, 2013.

Beaton, Cecil, and Gail Buckland. *The Magic Image: The Genius of Photography*. London: Pavilion Books, 1975.

Booth, Pat. *Master Photographers: The World's Great Photographers on Their Art and Technique*. London: Macmillan, 1983.

Bouqueret, Christian. *Jean Moral: l'Oeil Capteur*. Paris: Éditions Marval, 1999.

Bourdin, Guy. *Guy Bourdin: A Message for You*. Göttingen, Germany: Steidl, 2013.

Bright, Susan. *Face of Fashion*. London: National Portrait Gallery; New York: Aperture, 2007.

Brown, Susanna. *Horst: Photographer of Style*. London: V&A Publishing, 2014.

Cotton, Charlotte. *Imperfect Beauty: The Making of Contemporary Fashion Photographs*. London: V&A Publishing, 2000.

Cotton, Charlotte, and Nanda Van Den Berg. *Viviane Sassen: In and Out of Fashion*. New York: Prestel, 2012.

Dars, Celestine. *A Fashion Parade: The Séeberger Collection*. London: Blond & Briggs, 1979.

de Beaupre, Marion, Stephane Baumet, and Ulf Poschardt, eds. *Archaeology of Elegance, 1980–2000: 20 Years of Fashion Photography*. New York: Rizzoli, 2002.

de Cock, Liliane, and Reginald McGhee, eds. *James Van Der Zee*. New York: Morgan & Morgan, 1973.

Derrick, Robin, and Robin Muir. *Unseen Vogue: The Secret History of Fashion Photography*. New York: Little, Brown, 2004.

Ehrenkranz, Anne. *A Singular Elegance: The Photographs of Baron Adolph de Meyer*. San Francisco: Chronicle Books; New York: International Center of Photography, 1994.

Elgort, Arthur. *Arthur Elgort: The Big Picture*. Foreword by Grace Coddington. Göttingen, Germany: Steidl, 2014.

Esten, John, ed. *Man Ray: Bazaar Years*. New York: Rizzoli, 1988.

Evans, Jason, ed. *W'happen*. London: Shoreditch Biennale, 1998.

Ewing, William A. *Blumenfeld: A Fetish for Beauty*. London: Thames & Hudson, 1996.

Ewing, William A., and Todd Brandow. *Edward Steichen: In High Fashion—The Condé Nast Years, 1923–1937*. London: Thames & Hudson, 2008.

Faber, Monika. *Madame d'Ora, Wien, Paris—Vienna and Paris, 1907–1957: The Photography of Dora Kallmus*. Poughkeepsie, New York: Vassar College Art Gallery, 1987.

Frissell, Toni. *Toni Frissell, Photographs 1933–1967*. London: André Deutsch Ltd., 1994.

Garner, Philippe. *Cecil Beaton*. London: Collins, 1985.

———. *John Cowan: Through the Light Barrier*. Munich: Schirmer/Mosel, 1999.

Garner, Philippe, and David Alan Mellor. *The Essential Cecil Beaton: Photographs 1920–1970*. Munich: Schirmer/Mosel, 2012.

Goldberg, Vicki, and Nan Richardson. *Louise Dahl-Wolfe: A Retrospective*. New York: Abrams, 2000.

Gross, Michael. *Model: The Ugly Business of Beautiful Women*. New York: William Morrow & Co., 1995.

———. *Focus: The Secret, Sexy, Sometimes Sordid World of Fashion Photographers*. New York: Atria Books, 2016.

Gundlach, F. C., ed. *Martin Munkácsi*. London: Thames & Hudson, 2005.

Hall-Duncan, Nancy. *The History of Fashion Photography*. New York: Alpine Book Co., 1979.

Harrison, Martin. *Appearances: Fashion Photography Since 1945*. London: Jonathan Cape, 1992.

———. *David Bailey*. London: Collins, 1984.

———. *Patrick Demarchelier: Exposing Elegance*. New York: Tony Shafrazi Editions, 1997.

Haworth-Booth, Mark. *Camille Silvy: Photographer of Modern Life*. Los Angeles: J. Paul Getty Museum, 2010.

Henry Clarke: Photographe de la Mode. Paris: Somogy Éditions d'Art, 2002.

Hiett, Steve. *Steve Hiett: Beyond Blonde*. Edited by Patrick Remy. New York: Prestel, 2015.

Hiro. *Hiro: Photographs*. Edited by Richard Avedon. With Mark Holborn. New York: Bulfinch Press, 1999.

Horvat, Frank. *Please Don't Smile*. Ostfildern, Germany: Hatje Cantz, 2015.

Jones, Terry, ed. *Smile i-D: Fashion and Style: The Best from 20 Years of i-D*. Cologne: Taschen, 2001.

Kismaric, Susan, and Eva Respini. *Fashioning Fiction in Photography Since 1990*. New York: Museum of Modern Art, 2004.

Klein, William. *In and Out of Fashion*. London: Jonathan Cape, 1994.

Knight, Nick. *Nick Knight*. New York: Harper Design, 2009.

Leddick, David. *George Platt Lynes, 1907–1955*. Cologne: Taschen, 2000.

Lehmann, Ulrich, and Jessica Morgan, eds. *Chic Clicks: Creativity and Commerce in Contemporary Fashion Photography*. Berlin: Hatje Cantz, 2002.

Livingston, Kathryn E. *Fashion Photography: Patrick Demarchelier*. Boston, Toronto, and London: Bulfinch Press, 1989.

Loriot, Thierry-Maxime. *Peter Lindbergh: A Different Vision on Fashion Photography*. Cologne: Taschen, 2016.

Lovatt-Smith, Lisa. *Fashion: Images de Mode*. 6 vols. Göttingen, Germany: Steidl, 1997–2002.

Martineau, Paul. *Herb Ritts: LA Style*. Los Angeles: J. Paul Getty Museum, 2012.

Mendes, Valerie. *John French: Fashion Photographer*. London: Victoria and Albert Museum, 1984.

Moon, Sarah. *Sarah Moon 12345*. London: Thames & Hudson, 2008.

Morgan, Jamie, and Mitzi Lorenz. *Buffalo: The Style and Fashion of Ray Petri*. Brooklyn: powerHouse Books, 2000.

Muir, Robin. *Clifford Coffin: Photographs from Vogue 1945–1955*. Munich: Schirmer/Mosel, 1997.

———. *Norman Parkinson: Portraits in Fashion*. London: National Portrait Gallery, 2004.

Nickerson, Camilla, and Neville Wakefield, eds. *Fashion: Photography of the Nineties*. Zürich: Scalo, 1996.

Padilha, Roger, and Mauricio Padilha. *Gloss: The Work of Chris von Wangenheim*. New York: Rizzoli, 2015.

Parkinson, Norman. *Lifework*. London: Weidenfeld and Nicolson, 1983.

Parks, Gordon. *Gordon Parks: Collected Works*. 5 vols. Göttingen, Germany: Steidl, 2012.

———. *Voices in the Mirror*. New York: Doubleday, 1990.

Sieff, Jeanloup. *Jeanloup Sieff: 40 Years of Photography*. Cologne: Taschen, 1996.

Siemens, Jochen. *Bibliothek der Fotografie (Spezial Fotografie) Portfolio No. 28 (Stern): Ellen von Unwerth—Ellen's Girls*. Hamburg: Stern, 2001.

Sischy, Ingrid. *Ellen von Unwerth: Fräulein*. Cologne: Taschen, 2009.

Squiers, Carol, and Vince Aletti, eds. *Avedon Fashion: 1944–2000*. New York: Abrams, 2009.

Teunissen, José, and Jhim Lamoree. *Everything But Clothes: Fashion, Photography, Magazines*. Tielt, Belgium: Lannoo Publishers, 2015.

Tillmans, Wolfgang. *Wolfgang Tillmans*. With essays by Julie Ault et al. New Haven, Conn., and London: Yale University Press, 2006.

Turbeville, Deborah. *Deborah Turbeville: The Fashion Pictures*. New York: Rizzoli, 2011.

van Lamsweerde, Inez, Vinoodh Matadin, and Glenn O'Brien. *Pretty Much Everything: Inez van Lamsweerde and Vinoodh Matadin*. Cologne: Taschen, 2013.

Webb, Iain R. *As Seen in BLITZ—Fashioning '80s Style*. Woodbridge, England: ACC Editions, 2013.

Westerbeck, Colin, ed. *Irving Penn: A Career in Photography*. Chicago: Art Institute of Chicago, 1997.

Williams, Val, ed. *Look at Me: Fashion and Photography in Britain 1960–1997*. London: British Council Visual Arts Publications, 1998.

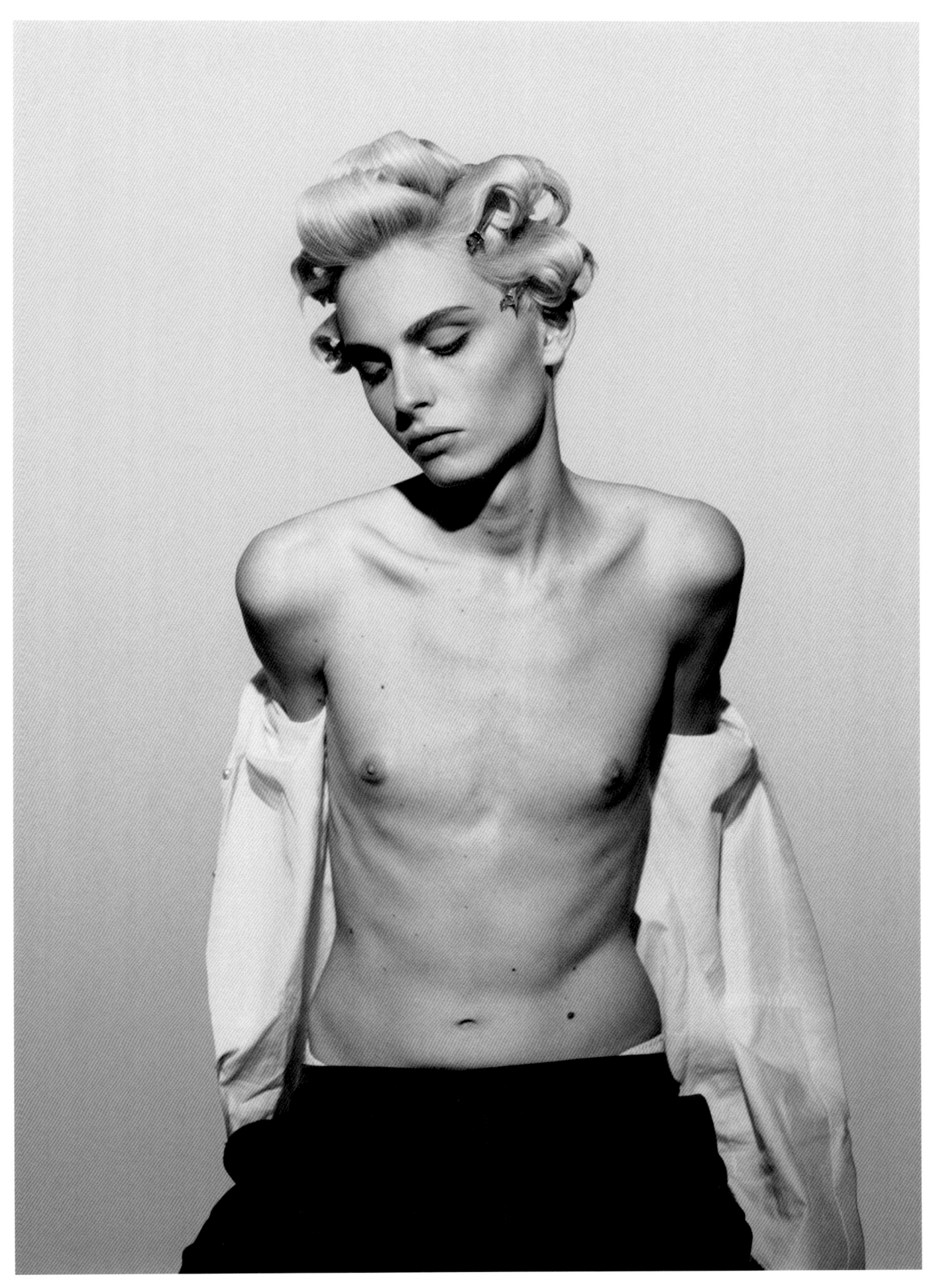

Collier Schorr,
Andrej Pejic, Dossier 7, April 2011

ACKNOWLEDGMENTS

This book couldn't have come together without the efforts of a lot of very talented people. At the top of the list is my editor at Aperture, Denise Wolff, for her vision and encouragement, and for reining in my weird hat fetish. Sally Knapp and Charlotte Chudy provided invaluable editorial assistance along the way. A shout out is due to Madeline Coleman and Susan Ciccotti for their eagle-eyed review of the text; to Nicole Moulaison, Nelson Chan, and Alta Image for their stellar production work; to Justine Bannwart for her detailed work on the layout; and to Dave Freeman at the University of Westminster for technical assistance and a very handy copy stand. Thanks also to Sonya Dyakova, for bringing the project to life with her inspired design.

For ideas and inspiration in the early stages—Itai Doron, Rebecca Arnold, Robin Muir, and Paul Hartnett. I'm indebted to all the photographers who have agreed to participate, and Ray Stevenson, Nigel Shafran, Coreen Simpson, and Jason Evans have all been especially accommodating. For assistance in the research phase, James Thickins at the University of Westminster, Lluis Tembleque Teres at the Courtauld Institute, and James Hyman and Alexia Marmara at the Hyman Archive. To David Campany, for friendship and wonderful conversations about photography, always.

Two people deserve a very special mention: Philippe Garner and Vince Aletti. Your expertise, your patience, and your incredible generosity have been an inspiration and a guide from start to finish. I owe you both a great deal.

—Eugénie Shinkle

Aperture wishes to thank:
Brian Anderson, VLM Studio; Sean Corcoran, the Museum of the City of New York; Anne Christensen; Pierre-Louis Denis and Tiffanie Pascal, William Klein studio; Margit Erb, the Saul Leiter Foundation; Natalie Evans, Isabel Hewitt, and Christine Teo, Thames & Hudson; Tom Gitterman; Erin Harris, the Richard Avedon Foundation; R. J. Horst; Isabella Howard, Howard Greenberg Gallery; Allison Ingram, Condé Nast Collection; Cassandra Johnson, Steven Kasher Gallery; Megan Jordan, Miles Aldridge Studio; Nathaniel Kilcer, Little Bear Inc.; Aris Kourkoumelis, Norman Parkinson Archive; Sal Lopes; Maconochie Photography; Chris Rawson, David Zwirner Gallery; Barbara Rix-Sieff and Aude Raimbault; Marco Santucci and Jen O'Farrel, Industry Art; Alexandra Shah, David Sims Photography; Paul Sinclair, Deborah Turbeville Foundation; Dean Snyder, Print & Contact; Etheleen Staley, Staley Wise Gallery; Michael Van Horne, Art + Commerce; Vincent Wilkie, Lehmann Maupin Gallery; and Leon Wong, Trunk Archive.

Thank you to Vince Aletti for graciously lending materials from his magnificent archive, and to Philippe Garner for generously providing images and information from photography's earliest days. Thanks to Inez and Vinoodh for the stunning cover image, and to Richard Marot for photographing the periodicals. Finally, special thanks to the artists who contributed to the book; to Sonya Dyakova, for her exquisite design; and to Eugénie Shinkle, for her tireless research and brilliant recounting of fashion photography's story.

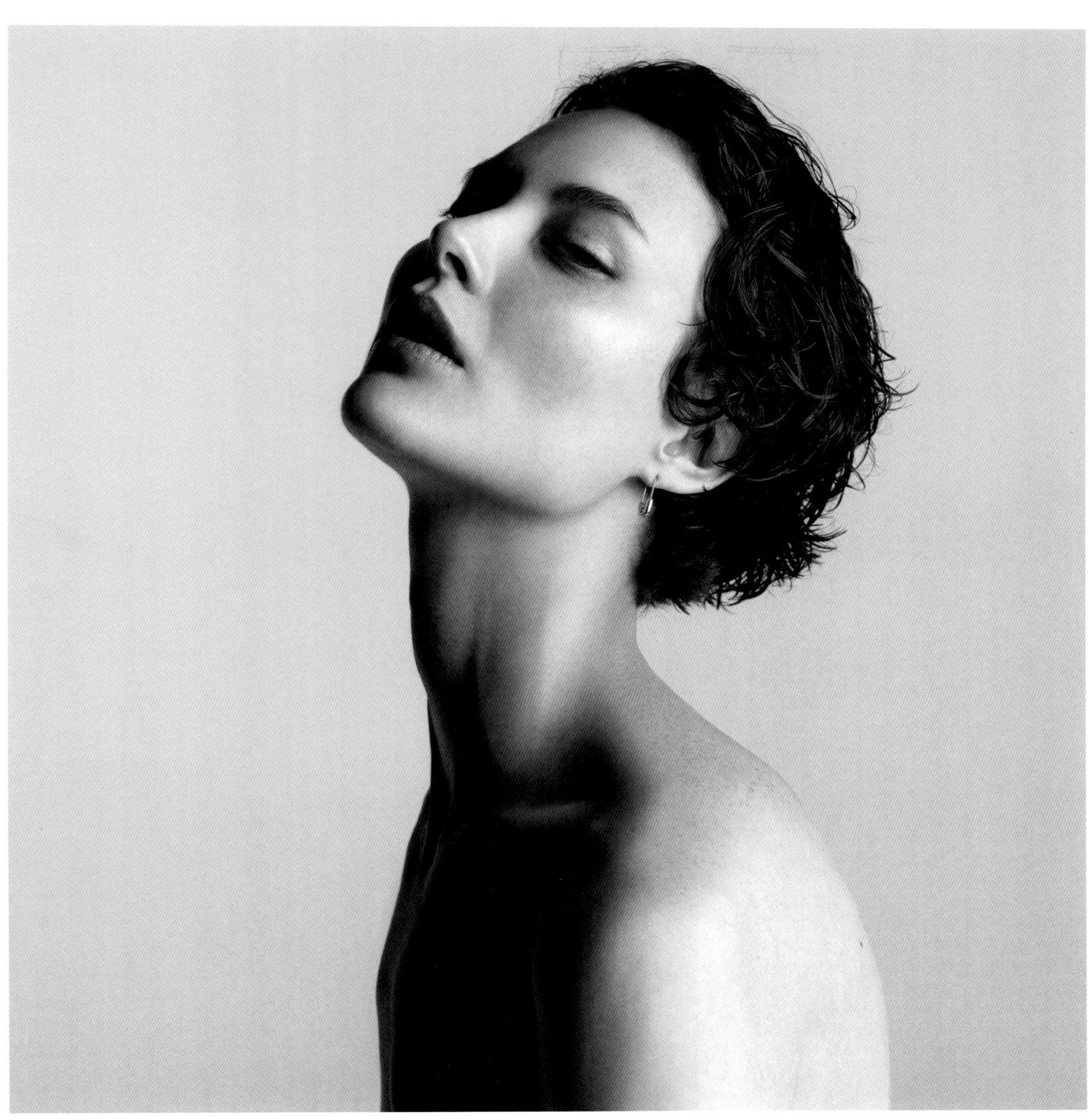

Inez & Vinoodh,
Shalom Harlow, V Magazine, 2007

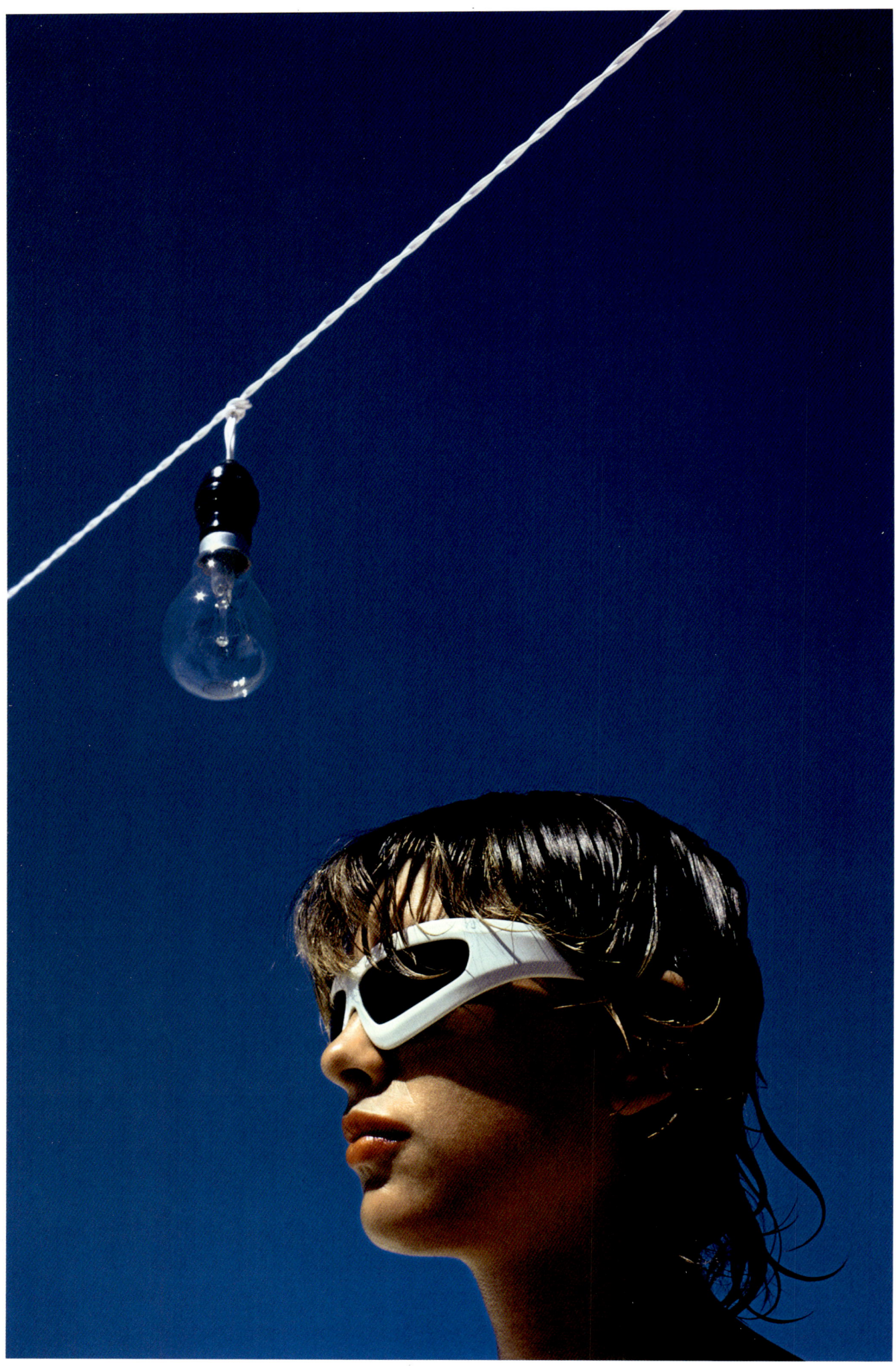

Steve Hiett,
Olga, La Baule, 1998

Fashion Photography: The Story in 180 Pictures
by Eugénie Shinkle

Front cover: Inez & Vinoodh,
Shalom Harlow, V Magazine, 2007
Back cover: George Hoyningen-Huene,
Swimwear, Paris, 1929; Horst P. Horst with models

Editor: Denise Wolff
Designer: Atelier Dyakova
Production Director: Nicole Moulaison
Production Manager: Nelson Chan
Associate Editor: Sally Knapp
Copy Editor: Madeline Coleman
Senior Text Editor: Susan Ciccotti
Work Scholars: David Arkin, Charlotte Chudy,
Lucas Vasilko, and Jasphy Zheng

Additional staff of the Aperture book program
includes: Chris Boot, *Executive Director;* Lesley
A. Martin, *Creative Director;* Amelia Lang, *Executive
Managing Editor;* Kellie McLaughlin, *Director of
Sales and Marketing;* Richard Gregg, *Sales Director,
Books;* Samantha Marlow, *Associate Editor;* Taia
Kwinter, *Associate Managing Editor*

First edition, 2017
Printed in China
10 9 8 7 6 5 4 3 2 1

Library of Congress Control Number: 2017942136
ISBN 978-1-59711-363-2

To order Aperture books, contact:
+1 212.946.7154
orders@aperture.org

For information about Aperture trade distribution
worldwide, visit: aperture.org/distribution

aperture

Aperture Foundation
547 West 27th Street, 4th Floor
New York, N.Y. 10001
aperture.org

Aperture, a not-for-profit foundation, connects
the photo community and its audiences with
the most inspiring work, the sharpest ideas, and
with each other—in print, in person, and online.